Identity Theft

JOHN R. VACCA

Prentice Hall PTR
Upper Saddle River, NJ 07458
www.phptr.com

ISBN 0-13-008275-9

90000

9 780130 082755

29.95

Library of Congress Cataloging-in-Publication Data

A CIP catalog record for this book can be obtained from the Library of Congress.

Editorial/Production Supervision: *MetroVoice Publishing Services*
Executive Editor: *Mary Franz*
Editorial Assistant: *Noreen Regina*
Marketing Manager: *Dan De Pasquale*
Manufacturing Manager: *Alexis Heydt-Long*
Manufacturing Buyer: *Maura Zaldivar*
Cover Design: *Talar Boorujy*
Cover Design Direction: *Jerry Votta*
Art Director: *Gail Cocker-Bogusz*
Series Design: *Meg VanArsdale*

PH PTR

© 2003 Pearson Education, Inc.
Publishing as Prentice Hall PTR
Upper Saddle River, New Jersey 07458

Prentice Hall books are widely used by corporations and government agencies for training, marketing, and resale. For information regarding corporate and government bulk discounts please contact: Corporate and Government Sales (800) 382-3419 or corpsales@pearsontechgroup.com

Printed in the United States of America

10 9 8 7 6 5 4 3 2 1

ISBN 0-13-008275-9

Pearson Education Ltd.
Pearson Education Australia PTY Ltd.
Pearson Education Singapore, Pte. Ltd.
Pearson Education North Asia Ltd.
Pearson Education Canada, Ltd.
Pearson Educación de Mexico, S.A. de C.V.
Pearson Education—Japan
Pearson Education Malaysia, Pte. Ltd.

*In memory of my father, Lt. Col. John V. Vacca
(U.S. Army), who taught me responsibility.*

CONTENTS

Contents

──

Header Contents

Contents

FOREWORD

This book is not only timely, it is essential. The incidence of identity theft is soaring out of control. It can cost individuals thousands of dollars to recover from the damage that can be caused when their identities are stolen. However, individuals are not the only ones at risk. Small and large businesses alike can have their identities hijacked and suffer staggering results.

Street criminals, burglars, pickpockets, Web site operators, and email scammers are making fortunes by stealing identities. They sell these stolen identities like stolen cell phones and hot jewelry. The profitability of identity theft is so high that organized criminal gangs are getting involved and building specialized organizations to take advantage of this lucrative opportunity.

Terrorists also steal identities. They use stolen documents to help move their forces around the world. They also use stolen credit cards to finance their operations. Terrorists even use stolen identities to rent cars, buy guns, and launch attacks.

John Vacca provides an in-depth analysis of identity theft issues, processes, and prevention methods. This book is an essential read for individuals, business managers, and law enforcement professionals around the world.

—Michael Erbschloe
Vice President of Research
Computer Economics
Carlsbad, CA

INTRODUCTION

Identity theft is the fastest growing crime in America. Based on credit bureau statistics, the Privacy Rights Clearinghouse estimates that between 700,000 and 900,000 Americans were victims of identity theft in 2001. According to a study of identity theft crimes performed by the Federal Trade Commission (FTC), the majority of cases relate to credit card fraud.

Usually, the first notice that consumers get that someone has fraudulently assumed their identity is either a call from a collection agency demanding payment on an overdue credit account that they never opened or when their own monthly billing statements do not arrive in the mail because the address on their account had been changed by an identity thief. Most victims never learn how the identity thieves accessed their personal information, although according to the FTC's study of reported cases, 48% resulted from a stolen wallet or purse.

The 1990s spawned this new variety of crooks whose stock in trade is the personal information available in your everyday transactions. Almost every transaction you make requires you to share some kind of personal information: getting money from your bank, charging to your credit card, making a long-distance phone call, or even getting your mail. An identity thief co-opts some piece of your personal information and appropriates it without your knowledge to commit fraud or theft. It can be as simple as a waiter or a clerk stealing your credit card number.

ID Fraud

You might think your good name is invaluable, but on the street it sells for about $25—like the fake Michigan driver's license that bore Jane Sprayberry's name, but another woman's photo. With it, the impersonator walked into an American Express office, claimed she'd lost her credit card, and asked for a replacement. The helpful customer representative handed one over, and the thief's shopping spree began. The binge included stops at a jewelry shop, two appliance stores, and Saks Fifth Avenue. The impersonator even bought Versace underwear, according to Sprayberry, who is more of the T.J. Maxx type.

It was déjà vu for Sprayberry: Her husband, Mark Sutton, had been the target of the same crime just one week before—but in addition to a retail blow-out, the crook also drained his checking account. In all, Sprayberry and Sutton estimate that their impersonators stole $90,000 in merchandise and cash.

Does this sound like something that's happened to a friend or family member—or to you? It's no surprise. Identity fraud is the fastest growing white-collar crime in the country. The Identity Theft Resource Center in San Diego, California, estimates that more than 900,000 Americans had their personal information used illegally in 2001.

Sprayberry and Sutton were not casualties of a solitary street tough who lifted their wallets and ran up their credit card balances. Stolen wallets do still lead to identity theft, but old-fashioned pickpocketing is only a fragment of today's identity fraud scene. Sprayberry and Sutton were among hundreds of victims of what investigators say was a large crime ring centered in Detroit—one that is typical of well-oiled criminal machines that operate in major cities throughout the country. These rings are behind the nationwide explosion of identity fraud. Their leaders have expertly honed the skills needed to steal identities en masse and use them in every conceivable way to steal money from financial institutions and retailers, tainting the financial lives of millions of consumers in the process.

Tip

For Sutton and Sprayberry, mopping up the damage took about six months.

In still another case, a young man (let's call him Roger) tells the story about the time one of his coworkers at a drug store (call him Stephen) asked Roger for permission to have a piece of merchandise delivered to Roger's home. Stephen explained to Roger that he was buying a present for his wife and didn't want her to see it before he could wrap it and give it to her. Roger gladly agreed. A week later, Stephen asked again and Roger began to smell a rat. Realizing that he could be implicated by the use of his address if there was something illegal going on, Roger confronted Stephen, who admitted he had stolen some credit card numbers from customers at the drug store. Roger immediately reported the facts to the store's management, thereby saving himself from being accused of the crime (after all, the merchandise was being delivered to his address).

Tip

For the protection of the people in this book, real names are not used.

An all-too-common example is when an identity thief steals a wallet or purse and uses the victim's personal information to open a credit card account in that name. A clever thief might be able to rapidly obtain thousands of dollars of credit in the victim's name. Many luxury or exclusive chain stores are willing to quickly open credit accounts with the proper identification. Identity thieves can then have a buy now, pay never shopping spree, racking up thousands of dollars in bills at their victim's expense. Even before the victim knows what's going on, a quick-acting thief can make hundreds of dollars in charges.

Now, consider the case of Babygear.com (based on a real case), which was targeted as a source of credit card numbers by an unknown identity thief in Eastern Europe. In December 2000, Ellen of Gilbert, Arizona, got a telephone call from an employee of The Boeing Co. in Seattle telling her the credit card she had used to buy a Boeing leather jacket had been declined. The employee asked if she wanted to use another card to make the purchase. Ellen told them she didn't try to buy a jacket, and she asked them what the shipping address was. They told her Yugoslavia.

Ellen wasn't surprised by the call because she had already canceled the card after being alerted by an employee of online auction site eBay that someone had tried to use her card to make almost $700 in purchases and have them shipped to Yugoslavia. Ellen was one of 240 customers of online baby products retailer Babygear.com whose credit card data was apparently stolen from the site in September 2000 and traced to a hacker in Yugoslavia. Babygear.com has since filed for bankruptcy protection.

The former Babygear.com CEO indicated he was unaware of any widespread security breaches at the site, which was shut down in early December 2000. Meanwhile, other Babygear customers recounted what happened after their credit card data was snatched.

In still another case, Diane of River Falls, Wisconsin, was lucky, because she found out her credit card information had been stolen before any charges were made to her card. Around Thanksgiving 2000, she got a call from someone at a computer company in Florida asking if she was charging computer equipment to send to Yugoslavia. Thus warned, she was able to cancel her card before any charges were made to it. However, unlike Ellen, who indicated she still uses her new card to make online purchases, Diane said she's had it with buying on the Internet. She hasn't used her new card online since then.

In the case of Irene of Coeburn, Virginia, it was debit card data that was stolen from the Babygear.com site. She didn't notice any charges until January 2001, but then she noticed that someone had taken out $700 cash on January 2, 2001, and put it back in again on the same day. On January 3, 2001, there were two charges for $300 and $400 from an online payment service. Irene indicated that although she was lucky that her bank reimbursed her for the money taken out of her account, the entire episode was a nightmare. As a result of someone draining her account unbeknownst to her, the checks she had been writing bounced.

Silvia of San Ramon, California, found out that she was a victim of credit card fraud while making a small purchase at a drugstore. She found out during January 2001 that something was wrong when she was at the drugstore with her two young children and was told her credit card was declined for a $14 purchase. Silvia didn't realize what had happened until she got a call from an employee of Gap.com who said the jeans she ordered were returned because the shipping address was incorrect.

Teresa of Redwood City, California, indicated someone charged a total of $700 to her card before she discovered there was a problem. The only time she used her card online was at Babygear.com, and there is no way she'll use it online again.

Quick Tips From the Trenches

As you can see from the preceding examples, identity theft is epidemic, with an estimated more than 1,700 people losing their identity everyday in the United States alone. Obviously everyone is at risk.

With the preceding in mind, you already know the standard advice for minimizing the odds that your identity will be stolen: Don't keep your Social Security card in your wallet and give out your number as seldom as possible. Shred financial documents. Use a mail slot or locked mailbox. However, investigators and prosecutors who see firsthand how identity thieves ply their trade have some less conventional ideas for protecting yourself. In many cases, these are precautions they themselves have taken.

You should tell your credit card issuers to stop sending you unsolicited convenience checks, which are a favorite of credit fraudsters, because the account holder isn't likely to spot the charge for at least 30 days. Often these checks are stolen from residential mailboxes. In one New York case involving stolen mail, a fraud ring wrote $850,000 worth of convenience checks.

You should also switch to using gas-company credit cards, rather than an all-purpose Visa or MasterCard, at the pump. The reason? Gas-station attendants and other employees have access to customers' names and account numbers, even if the card is only swiped at the pump. A gas-only card has far less appeal to an identity thief. A gas station attendant can get paid $25 for each good credit card number he or she gets. It's the same with restaurant workers, but there's no restaurant-only alternative to Visa and MasterCard.

Such precautions may reduce the odds of you becoming an identity-theft victim, but there's no magic bullet. Just by having a job and health insurance, applying for credit, or making routine transactions, you inherently put your personal information at risk. There's no way to protect yourself, other than having bad credit.

Who This Book Is For

This book can be used by domestic and international system administrators, government computer security officials, network administrators, senior managers, engineers, sales engineers, marketing staff, Web developers, military top brass, network designers, and technicians. With regard to identity theft, the book is primarily targeted at those in government and law enforcement who require the fundamental skills to develop and implement security schemes designed to protect their organizations' information from attacks, including managers, network and systems administrators, technical staff, and support personnel. This also includes those involved in securing Web sites, including Web developers; Webmasters; and systems, network, and security administrators.

This book is also valuable for systems analysts, design engineers, programmers, technical managers, and all data processing, telecommunications, and office automation professionals involved in designing, configuring, or implementing ID theft prevention and protection techniques. In short, the book is targeted toward all types of people and organizations around the globe who have responsibility for managing and maintaining the Web site service continuity of organizational systems including line and project managers, team members, consultants, software and security engineers, and other information technology (IT) professionals who manage Web site cost justification, investments, and standards. Others who might find it useful are scientists, engineers, educators, top-level executives, IT and department managers, technical staff, and the more than 1 billion Internet, intranet, and extranet users around the world.

What's So Special About This Book?

Identity Theft shows experienced (intermediate to advanced) security and law enforcement professionals how to protect corporations, Web sites, and individuals and detect ID theft, and report the findings that will lead to the incarceration of the perpetrators. This book also provides the fundamental knowledge you need to analyze risks to your system and implement a workable security and antifraud policy that protects your information assets from potential intrusion, damage, or theft. Through extensive hands-on examples (field and trial experiments) and case studies, you will gain the knowledge and skills required to master the deployment of ID theft countermeasures to thwart potential attacks.

Throughout the book, extensive hands-on examples provide individuals with practical experience in ID theft detection, analysis, and reporting, as well as countermeasures and future directions. In addition to future ID theft detection, prevention, and protection solutions in personal, commercial organizations and governments, the book addresses, but is not limited to, the following key features:

- You will learn how to detect and analyze your exposure to security threats and protect your organization's systems and data; manage risks emanating from inside the organization and from the Internet and extranets; protect network users from hostile applications and viruses; reduce your susceptibility to an attack by deploying firewalls, data encryption, decryption, and other ID theft countermeasures; and identify the security risks that need to be addressed in security and antifraud policies.

- Chapters on how to gain practical experience in analyzing the security risks and ID theft countermeasures that need to be addressed in your organization also include maintaining strong authentication and authenticity, preventing eavesdropping, retaining integrity of information, evaluating the strength of user passwords, selecting a firewall topology, and evaluating computer and hacker ethics.

This book leaves little doubt that the new and emerging field of ID theft detection, prevention, and protection techniques is about to evolve. This new area of knowledge is now being researched, organized, and taught. This book will certainly benefit organizations and governments, as well as their antifraud and security professionals.

The book is organized into five parts and includes appendices as well as an extensive glossary of fraud and ID theft terms and acronyms. It provides a step-by-step approach to everything you need to know about preventing and protecting ID theft, as well as information about many topics relevant to the planning, design, and implementation of them. The book gives an in-depth overview of the latest ID fraud and theft countermeasures. It discusses what background work needs to be done, such as developing an anti-ID-fraud plan, and shows how to develop anti-ID-theft plans for individuals, organizations, and educational institutions. More important, this book shows how to install an anti-ID-fraud system, along with the detection techniques used to test the system. The book concludes with a discussion about future anti-ID-theft planning and development solutions and technologies.

Part I: Identity Theft Fundamentals

This part of the book covers the process of guarding against and recovering from identity theft and sets the stage for the rest of the book. Next, it discusses in specific detail how to minimize your risk of identity theft. Remember, you ultimately cannot prevent identity theft from happening, but you can reduce the odds. Finally, this part helps you begin the process of detecting, reporting, and recovering from identity theft.

Part II: Identity Theft Protection on the Internet

Part II begins by giving you an overview of how the issues related to identity theft require a multifaceted response that involves e-businesses, consumer education, and public policy. Only through this level of cooperation and action will the issues and victims of identity theft be addressed. Businesses (or any entity on the Net) must prevent the illicit use of an identity and protect private information. Other types of e-business, like service bureaus and marketing companies, need to take steps to ensure that private information is correctly stored and unavailable for abuse. Additionally, e-businesses involved with the issuance of online credit or online revolving credit need to take steps that verify information and use technology to reduce the ability for a stolen identity to be used to create a new account. Consumers can't expect that some big brother will watch out for their privacy or verify that information is not used without their authorization. Furthermore, consumers need to know where to report identity theft issues, what action e-businesses can take, and to what extent business will protect their privacy. Governments need to provide mechanisms for consumers to report crimes to the appropriate law enforcement agencies, provide training and education to law enforcement, and capture statistical information about the use and abuse of stolen identities and make this information available to both public and private-sector groups.

Next, Part II shows Internet service providers (ISPs) how to prevent identity theft by looking at types of identity theft prevention techniques and technologies. In spite of the ease of committing this crime, there are steps ISPs can take to reduce customers' exposure to the consequences. This part also shows you how to protect the identity information of customers. Finally, Part II discusses ISP testing and performance of identity theft protection techniques.

Part III: Identity Theft Protection for Corporations

Part III begins by showing you how companies can protect their customers and employees from identity theft. The nature of identity theft fraud is changing, not so much in the types of offenses being committed, but rather in the means by which those offenses are being perpetrated. Traditional fraud offenses are increasingly being facilitated by and perpetrated using the new electronic technology. Electronic systems have increased the opportunity for fraud by providing increased access to opportunities and also increasing the ease, speed, and anonymity of criminal activity. This provides challenges to law enforcement and business in terms of prevention, detection, and investigation. Solutions to the problems of identity theft protection lie in increased awareness of the changing risks, especially the increased risk of external attacks through connection to external electronic systems; in prevention, including the widespread use of effective electronic security and identity verification systems; and in international cooperation in regulation, information sharing, and enforcement. These measures should be supported by accountability, transparency, and effective risk management strategies in both the public and private sectors. Many of the most effective solutions need to be built into business systems and organizational practice.

This part also discusses guidelines for protecting the identity and confidentiality of personal information when working outside the corporate office. Finally, it examines the management of ongoing identity theft prevention and protection techniques.

Part IV: Identity Theft Future Solutions and Technologies

Part IV opens with a discussion of the use of enhancing security and privacy in biometrics-based authentication systems, biometrics at work, voice identity and electronic addressing, fingerprint scanning, facial scanning, and DNA scanning. Biometrics-based authentication to prevent ID theft has many usability advantages over traditional systems such as passwords. Specifically, users can never lose their biometrics, and the biometric signal is difficult to steal or forge. This part also shows that the intrinsic bit strength of a biometric signal can be quite good, especially for fingerprints, when compared to conventional passwords. Yet, any system, including a biometric system, is vulnerable when attacked by determined hackers. This part highlights eight points of vulnerability in a generic biometric system and discusses possible attacks. Several recommendations are made to alleviate some of these security threats. Replay attacks are addressed using data-hiding techniques to secretly embed a telltale mark directly in the compressed fingerprint image. A challenge/response method is proposed to check the liveliness of the signal acquired from an intelligent sensor. This part also touches on the often-neglected problems of privacy and revocation of biometrics. It is somewhat ironic that the greatest strength of biometrics—that they do not change over time—is at the same time its greatest liability. Once a set of biometric data has been compromised, it is compromised forever. To address this issue, I propose applying repeatable noninvertible distortions to the biometric signal. Cancellation simply requires the specification of a new distortion transform. Privacy is enhanced because different distortions can be used for different services and the true biometrics are never stored or revealed to the authentication server. In addition, such intentionally distorted biometrics cannot be used for searching legacy databases and thus alleviate some privacy violation concerns.

In this part, I hope that throughout this process you, the reader, have thought about your own personal information and how important it is that no company misuse it. After all, we are all individuals with some level of concern about our own information. At the same time that you might be the developer of one application, you are the customer of other applications. Just as you want to provide good customer service, you also want to receive good customer service. In the information economy, customer service is taking on a new look—privacy. As an example of what can go wrong, when caller identification applications were first introduced, many companies assumed that responding to customers by name when they called would be seen as good customer service. They soon found that people often did not take kindly to that approach. "How do you know my name?" expressed in angry tones, was frequently heard. We all value our privacy in a general sense and we are becoming more sensitive about the protection of our personal information. This part also presents examples of applications that require user authentication and transaction authorization with a very high level of security. More and more, Web applications with similar security requirements will emerge as the volume of financial transactions conducted via the Internet increases steadily. The pure Java architecture presented in this part allows such applications to be secured in an elegant and flexible way, using smart cards to provide a higher level of security. A prototype for performing biometric authentications inside a smart card is also presented. Three biometric techniques are studied to analyze their viability: speaker recognition, hand geometry, and iris identification. The results show the possibility of integrating biometrics as a card holder verification method, therefore improving user authentication in smart-card-based applications. Better results can be obtained building a new smart card mask, instead of using an open operating system card, such as the Java-Cards used in the prototypes developed. If this last option is not possible, results with the RISC-based JavaCard are good enough for a commercial product. Further efforts will be applied to integrate other biometric techniques in the prototypes developed, such as fingerprint or facial recognition.

Email encryption is a powerful tool in helping to protect an individual's privacy. In this part, I map out the basic concepts. You should put this new knowledge into practice and actively investigate use of email encryption software. Because I provide only a brief overview of the topic, you should follow the links previously cited to gain an even better understanding of email encryption. It is always useful to start with a list of your requirements that can be used to assess any potential products. If possible, test some products yourself. Soon, using encryption software will become second nature. If you don't protect your privacy with tools like email encryption, you may well lose it. That could result in anything from a minor annoyance, to a gut-wrenching feeling of violation, to the loss of significant amounts of money. Guard your privacy and identity well; the tools are out there for you to do so.

Next, Part IV discusses how, in an era of networked information technologies, personal information has acquired intrinsic commercial value, whether collected directly or indirectly, to serve a variety of commercial purposes. However, an open networked system such as the Internet remains at present an uncertain environment, particularly for the conduct of commercial transactions. Such transactions in the "real" world are enveloped in a framework of laws, customs, and practices that create the necessary trust and confidence to ensure wide public participation. In the unstructured framework of the virtual world, however, the traditional ways of conducting business are not always appropriate or adequate. To a much greater extent, the virtual world, a creation of technology, will be dependent on technology for many of its solutions. The challenge is to transport the basic principles that exist in the physical world through laws, customs, and practices into the virtual world—in effect, to create a parallel process. This is the case to be made for privacy and the principles that protect our personal information in the world of e-commerce. Specifically, fair information practices provide a framework by which to assess technology-based solutions and to serve as a benchmark in creating those solutions. The combined efforts of technology experts, cryptographers, lawyers, policymakers, privacy advocates, and ultimately the public will be needed to create acceptable solutions to the privacy dilemmas arising out of a networked world. Given the broad public apprehension about using the Internet to conduct commercial transactions and consumers' concerns over the prospect of losing their privacy, it is incumbent on all of us who wish to make electronic commerce a viable form of transacting business to inform the public about these issues. It is particularly important that the public understand the different options being considered and the choices available to them. Throughout the 21st century, all indications suggest that privacy will continue to resonate as a significant public issue. The challenge will be to develop and advance information technologies, supported by appropriate legal and policy frameworks, that can minimize the public's apprehensions about technology, and, in the process, enhance personal privacy.

The need to protect and manage personal information has been likened to the management of natural resources. Personal information is a resource, exploited commercially, but valued as an element of human dignity and enjoyment of one's private life. It is therefore to be protected and managed, not unlike the protection and management of other resources. As with early efforts to protect the environment in the absence of legislation, privacy protection currently relies on ancient common law principles that continue to adapt to new technological challenges to personal integrity, happiness, and freedom. These principles have now found legislative expression in various statutes relating to environmental protection. Information, however, has some unique qualities in need of special regulatory and judicial attention. Looking ahead, consumers will not only want goods and services, but assurances that the information they provide to a business is, from a privacy perspective, protected. To deal with this need, a shared responsibility for the management of personal information will be essential, involving government, the business community, and consumers. Only through shared responsibility, sustained by the business community through a culture of privacy, and strengthened by the voice of consumers, can personal information become a protected, managed, and valued resource. This part gives all three parties (consumers, businesses, and government) incentives for action toward protecting personal information in the marketplace. The tension between technology and privacy can be minimized if privacy safeguards are made a key consideration up front, rather than an afterthought. Although current data-mining practices are somewhat beyond the up-front stage, there is still time to ease this tension before applications become commonplace. One short-term approach might be for businesses to provide consumers with choices in the form of multiple selection opt-outs. The final chapter of this book provides a summary of identity theft, conclusions, and recommendations.

Part V: Appendices

Five appendices provide direction to additional resources available about IDtheft. Appendix A is a listing of Federal ID theft laws. Appendix B is a listing of state ID theft laws. Appendix C contains a listing of reports, testimony, and comments relating to ID theft. Appendix D consists of a listing of ID theft cases and scams. Appendix E contains an ID theft affidavit and corresponding information. Appendix F is a glossary of ID fraud and theft terms and acronyms.

Conventions

This book has several conventions to help you find important facts, notes, cautions, and warnings, as follows:

Sidebars. I use sidebars to highlight related information, give an example, discuss an item in greater detail, or help you make sense of the swirl of terms, acronyms, and abbreviations so abundant to this subject. The sidebars are meant to supplement each chapter's topic. If you're in a hurry for a cover-to-cover read, skip the sidebars. If you're quickly flipping through the book looking for juicy information, read only the sidebars.

Tips. A tip highlights a special point of interest.

Cautions. A caution tells you to watch your step to avoid any ID theft-related problems (privacy, fraud, security, etc.).

ACKNOWLEDGMENTS

There are many people whose efforts on this book have contributed to its successful completion. I owe each a debt of gratitude and want to take this opportunity to offer my sincere thanks.

A very special thanks to my editor Mary Franz, whose continued interest and support made this book possible, and editorial assistant Noreen Regina, who provided staunch support and encouragement when it was most needed. Special thanks to my technical reviewers, Jorj Bauer and Warwick Ford, who ensured the technical accuracy of the book and whose expertise in Identity Theft and security technology was indispensable. Thanks to my production editor, Anne Garcia; project manager, Scott Suckling; and, copyeditor, Laura Specht-Patchkofsky whose fine editorial work has been invaluable. Thanks also to my marketing manager, whose efforts on this book have been greatly appreciated. And, a special thanks to Michael Erbcshloe who wrote the foreword for this book. Finally, thanks to all of the other people at Prentice Hall whose many talents and skills are essential to a finished book.

Thanks to my wife, Bee Vacca, for her love, her help, and her understanding of my long work hours.

I wish to thank the organizations and individuals who granted me permission to use the research material and information necessary for the completion of this book.

Finally, a very special thanks to my publisher, Jeff Pepper, whose initial interest and support made this book possible, and for his guidance and encouragement over and above the business of being a publisher.

Identity Theft Fundamentals

Chapter 1

IDENTITY THEFT DEFINED

The telephone rings. It's the repo man. He's coming for your car—that nice one you just bought and have been using to cruise around Miami. The problem is that you didn't buy a cruiser. You haven't bought any cars, and you live in Philadelphia.

The phone rings again. This time it's the mortgage company. It's about that nice house you just bought in Seattle. They want to know why you are late on your payment. You're beginning to get a sinking feeling.

The next call is from your credit card company. It occurs to you that you have not seen a bill in a while. Your card is maxed, you are two months late, and they are courteously telling you that they are canceling your card because your statements have been returned to them with a stamp from the U.S. Post Office stating that there is no such address.

The next time the phone rings, you just can't bring yourself to pick up. From the answering machine, you can hear Uncle Jim's voice—the uncle you are in business with. He is screaming! His father and your father go back—oh well, you know the story. He wants to know why you are declaring bankruptcy on him.

Sinking into your chair, you get the final call. If the first four weren't enough, the last is the best. From the answering machine (remember, you're no longer answering the phone) you hear a nasty voice you do not recognize. The person introduces himself—as you—and then laughs. This stranger

3

knows about your new car, your new house, your credit cards, and your bank-ruptcy. This stranger has stolen your identity and has called to taunt you.

This story is based on a notorious true case. The thief claimed he could pose as the victim for as long as he wanted because, at that time, identity theft was not a crime. Ultimately, the thief made a mistake: He made a false state-ment to procure a firearm and got caught, receiving a brief sentence. The vic-tim, in the meantime, spent four years and a few buckets of money to restore his credit and reputation. This is one of the cases that prompted Congress in 1998 to pass the Identity Theft and Assumption Deterrence Act.

 Tip

The Identity Theft and Assumption Deterrence Act of 1998, which became effective October 30, 1998, makes identity theft a federal crime with penalties up to 15 years imprisonment and a maximum fine of $250,000. It establishes that the person whose identity was stolen is a true victim. Previously, only the credit grantors who suffered monetary losses were considered victims. This leg-islation enables the Secret Service, the Federal Bureau of Investigation, and other law enforcement agencies to combat this crime. It allows for the identity theft victim to seek restitution if there is a conviction. It also establishes the Federal Trade Commission as a central agency to act as a clearinghouse for complaints (against credit reporting agencies and credit grantors), referrals, and resources for assistance for victims of identity theft. This statute may serve as a model for your state to enact similar legislation. It should also provide you leverage to influence law enforcement to investigate your case.

With the preceding in mind, the aim of this introductory chapter is to help you begin the process of guarding against and recovering from identity theft. It also sets the stage for the rest of the book (see the Introduction that pre-cedes this chapter for a road map of what is included in this book). So, what really is identity theft?

What Is Identity Theft?

Quite simply, identity theft is the appropriation of an individual's personal information to impersonate that person in a legal sense. Stealing someone's identity enables the thief to make a frightening number of financial and per-sonal transactions in someone else's name, leaving the victim responsible for what might turn out to be mind-boggling turmoil in his or her life.

Identity theft is not new. It has been around for a long time. There was a time when an individual could flee his or her life, town, and mistakes, and go somewhere far away, pretending to be someone else—and no one knew any better. The ramifications of stealing someone's identity then did not have the far-reaching implications that they do today for the person whose identity is stolen. Those were the days before credit reporting and high-tech methods of tracking and sharing information were commonplace.

Identity theft can still be done by such low-tech means as previously described—knowing someone else's basic identifying information and initiating personal transactions in that person's name. Today, however, identities can also be stolen using highly technical and sophisticated means of obtaining the personal data of a stranger. However it is done, whether the identity thief uses high-tech or low-tech means of getting a victim's personal information, an individual can become someone else very easily. The difference today is what an identity thief does as someone else reflects very quickly on the victim's reputation. An individual's life can be devastated by the loss of his or her good name and the financial or personal mess that results.

Identity theft is always personal—after all, it is one's own identity that is stolen! Someone literally assumes your identity and leaves a damaging trail of credit card abuse and exposed personal information all over the Internet (to your creditors and possibly worse). Thieves could be roommates, relatives, friends, estranged spouses, or household workers— all with ready access to their victims' personal papers.

In the case described at the beginning of this chapter, the thief's motivation seemed to have been a deliberate attack on that individual. It could be that the perpetrator had a grudge against the victim and was out for revenge. Although this type of attack accounts for a small percentage of the identity theft crimes reported, the personal nature of it is terrifying.

It's an Opportunity Too Good to Pass Up

The thief may be an opportunist—one who sees his chance and takes it. The thief's motive is to gain goods and services at someone else's expense. For example, in one case, the identity thief blames the U.S. Securities and Exchange Commission (SEC). According to Thomas Seitz, a 24-year-old computer buff from Old Bridge, New Jersey, if the agency hadn't posted names and Social Security numbers on its Web site for the entire world to see, he would not have applied for car loans in 14 of those individuals' names. He would also not be sitting in a Jacksonville, Florida courtroom awaiting sentencing for bank fraud. It was a crime of opportunity.

☞ **Tip**

For the protection of the people in this book, real names are not used.

Seitz's weapon was the publicly available computer at the Old Bridge Public Library. Surfing around the Internet one day, he stumbled across a database of disclosure forms that public companies and their officials file with the SEC. It was too tempting. Seitz assumed one of the names and applied for a car loan online through Nations Bank (now Bank of America). It was rejected, along with his subsequent 11 applications under different aliases. However, on his next try, Seitz scored a $15,000 check. He tried to buy a car at a local Buick dealer but backed out, in part because he lacked car insurance. Still, he forged ahead.

He assumed his 14th identity, that of a 58-year-old former official of EFI Electronics in Salt Lake City. Within days, Seitz had a $44,000 loan check from Nations Bank that he could present to a car dealership. He got a free online quote for car insurance with his new identity, and, through an online chat room, a couple of stolen MasterCard numbers to pay for the policy.

Now all Seitz needed was evidence that he was the 58-year-old former official. As luck would have it, the Internet has at least 400 Web sites that offer counterfeit driver's licenses, law enforcement credentials, passports, Social Security cards, and military IDs. All a user has to do is log in and type *fake ID* and click Search. Seitz soon had a fake birth certificate and a W-2 in his new identity's name.

At a local Honda dealership, Seitz opted for a loaded black Prelude. He had to dicker a little. In fact, thanks to his new identity's good credit history, Seitz was able to negotiate even better financing than what he got from Nations Bank. He knew he did something illegal, but he always came out of a situation better than he anticipated.

Not this time, however. When the dealer tried to register the car, the state caught on to the bogus driver's license. Seitz had no defense. At the same time, Nations Bank and the FBI were piecing together the scam. You don't have to be a genius to do what he did.

Living Large on Your Good Name

Recently, Marvin Young, Jr. of Oakland, California, received a letter from Sears, Roebuck & Co., denying his credit application. The only trouble was that Young had not applied for a Sears credit card. Alarmed, Young obtained a copy of his credit report and found that more than 30 new credit cards had been issued in his name in the previous 90 days. He almost had a heart attack because he hadn't requested any of those accounts.

Marvin Young had a pretty good idea of who did open those accounts, however. In 1990, a former roommate had obtained Young's Social Security number and birth date and subsequently opened a checking account, a business, and at least one credit account in Young's name.

Although Young had placed a warning on his credit report years earlier, it apparently had expired. Now he is busy supplying such stores as Bloomingdale's and J.C. Penney with notarized affidavits to prove he is not responsible for the thousands of dollars in bills charged by the impostor.

What's most infuriating is that Young, like all identity theft victims, has to notify every single credit issuer of the fraud, a common lament of identity theft victims. Although victims might not be liable for the credit bills an identity thief runs up, they still are compelled to spend time, effort, and money to clear up the mess. They spend hours and hours filing expensive legal affidavits, writing letters, and making telephone calls to clear their names. Young's one mistake (neglecting to keep the warning at the credit bureau from expiring) could take him years to untangle.

The sad part is that it is almost impossible to stop a determined identity thief. Who is going to apprehend him? Occasionally law enforcement agencies, including the Secret Service, bust up identity theft crime rings that involve many victims and millions of dollars. However, they don't chase down single crooks that commit victimless crimes.

Then Again, It's a Living

Identity thieves may be professionals. They could be individual hackers out to get what they can or highly sophisticated crime rings that make a business out of fraud.

Remember the recent case of the busboy in New York who allegedly masterminded a huge ring of identity thieves? When Abraham Abdallah's father spoke to television reporters recently, he denied that his son was capable of the crime with which he was charged: the largest identity theft in the history of the Internet, breaching the private finances of 217 of the Forbes 400 wealthiest people in America. If Abdallah was in the process of stealing millions of dollars, his father reasoned, why would he always be asking him to borrow $10? If Abdallah was the criminal mastermind behind an elaborate scam to rip off the likes of Warren E. Buffett, Ross Perot, and Oprah Winfrey, what in the world was he doing still working as a busboy at a restaurant in Brooklyn?

7

Using a few Web-enabled cell phones and a public library computer, the busboy is said to have guessed the passwords of his favorite tycoons, input personal information that conveniently appeared in *Forbes* magazine, swiped Social Security numbers, and accessed brokerage accounts—all between shifts sorting silverware. Soon he was forging bank stationery, deploying multiple messengers to escape detection, and running around with a credit card in Steven Spielberg's name.

Investigators first grew suspicious after he used a Yahoo! address to request a transfer of $10 million belonging to the software magnate Thomas Siebel into an offshore account. On February 23, 2001, after pursuing the case for six months, police arrested him, with one of the detectives jumping into the sunroof of his getaway car. It turned out that Abdallah had four prior arrests and had served time for passing counterfeit checks.

How Identity Theft Is Done

In the course of a normal day, you might write a check at the grocery store, charge tickets to a ball game, rent a car, mail your tax returns, call home on your cell phone, order new checks, or apply for a credit card. You might do any of a hundred little things each of us does every day that involve someone knowing who you are. Chances are you don't give these everyday transactions a second thought, but an identity thief does. In fact, those who make a profession of stealing identities give it a great deal of thought, indeed.

Despite your best efforts to manage the flow of your personal information or to keep it to yourself, skilled identity thieves use a variety of methods (low-tech and high-tech) to gain access to your data. The following are some of the ways imposters can acquire and use your personal information and take over your identity:

- They steal wallets and purses containing identification, credit cards, and bank cards.

- They steal mail, including bank and credit card statements, preapproved credit offers, telephone calling cards, and tax information.

- They complete a "change of address form" to divert mail to another location.

- They rummage through trash, both of individuals and of businesses, for personal data in a practice known as "dumpster diving."

- They fraudulently obtain credit reports by posing as a landlord, employer, or someone else who might have a legitimate need for (and a legal right to) the information.
- They get business or personnel records at work.
- They find personal information in peoples homes.
- They use personal information people share on the Internet.
- They buy personal information from "inside" sources. For example, an identity thief might pay a store employee for information about someone that appears on an application for goods, services, or credit.
- They call credit card issuers and, pretending to be their victims, ask to change the mailing address on a credit card account. The imposter then runs up charges on that account. Because the bills are being sent to the new address, it might take some time before the victim realizes there's a problem.
- They open a new credit card account, using someone else's name, date of birth, and Social Security number. When they use the credit card and don't pay the bills, the delinquent account is reported on the victim's credit report.
- They establish phone or wireless service in someone else's name.
- They open a bank account in someone else's name and write bad checks on that account.
- They file for bankruptcy under someone else's name to avoid paying debts they've incurred or to avoid eviction.
- They counterfeit checks or debit cards, and drain bank accounts.
- They buy cars by taking out auto loans in someone else's name.

How Your Personal Information Can Be Used Against You

Once the thief has basic information about you, there are a number of ways it can be used. If the thief has seen your credit card, he or she knows who issued it. It is then a simple matter to call the financial institution and request a change of mailing address. Now, the thief can run up charges on your account. You don't realize what's happening for a while because you haven't gotten a bill. By the time you wonder what has happened to your bill and call the credit card company, it is too late.

An identity thief who has enough information about you can open a new credit card account in your name. With your personal data for approval, the thief has at least a month (maybe more, depending on the policy of the lender) before the account is closed for lack of payment. The balance on "your" new account by that time could be devastating—not to mention that the late payments have been reported to the credit bureau.

Next, there are the counterfeit phone services that the identity thief can open in your name with the right information. Huge long-distance and service bills can be charged to you because the identity thief is getting the bill—not you. Of course, the identity thief isn't paying the bill, so you are left with a monstrous bill and your delinquency is reported to the credit bureau.

If an identity thief is able to steal your checkbook or obtain new checks on your account through some illegal method, he or she could bleed your bank account dry before you know what's happened. In other words, an identity thief can hurt you by opening a bank account in your name, possibly with a cash advance from your bogus credit card, and then write bad checks against that account as often as possible before the bank reports *the* felonious conduct.

An identity thief with access to your personal data can take out loans in your name: house loans, car loans, boat loans, and so on. If the thief is good enough, he or she gets the goods and you get the bill!

The ultimate dirty deed an identity thief can do is to file for bankruptcy under your name. This would prevent the thief from having to pay debts incurred in your name. If they've been living in a home or apartment as you, they might file for bankruptcy to avoid eviction. Never forget the thief who has a personal agenda to cause you harm—what could be better than bankruptcy?

These are just some of the ways that the theft of your identity can wreak havoc in your life, and thinking about them should be enough to scare the daylights out of you. It definitely is enough to make a person start thinking about how to protect himself or herself (see Chapter 2, "Minimizing Your Risk of Identity Theft," for some of the ways you can protect yourself).

Once the thieves have some of your personal information, they can start applying for credit cards in your name—giving an address that is often different from yours. Sloppy credit-granting procedures give thieves plenty of opportunities. Many credit companies are not checking records. They are more interested in capturing new applicants than in verifying their authenticity.

Identity thieves might buy a car or rent an apartment in your name. Some might even commit crimes in your name. For example, in one case, the impostor was a major drug dealer using the identity of a high-ranking corporate executive. When traveling overseas, the executive has to carry an official letter that explains he is not the drug dealer. Still, police recently broke into the man's bedroom with guns drawn. Although this is an extreme case, many identity theft victims have been denied student loans, mortgages, credit accounts, and even jobs. Some have wrongly had their telephone service disconnected and their driver's licenses suspended, or been harassed by collection agencies.

Where can you get immediate help if your identity has been stolen? Let's take a look.

Where There's Help

The FTC collects complaints about identity theft from consumers who have been victimized. Although the FTC does not have the authority to bring criminal cases, it can help victims of identity theft by providing information to assist them in resolving the financial and other problems that can result from this crime. The FTC also refers victim complaints to other appropriate government agencies and private organizations for further action.

If you've been a victim of identity theft, file a complaint with the FTC by contacting the FTC's Identity Theft Hotline by telephone toll-free at 1-877-IDTHEFT (438-4338); by TDD at 202-326-2502; by mail at Identity Theft Clearinghouse, Federal Trade Commission, 600 Pennsylvania Avenue, NW, Washington, DC 20580; or online at *www.consumer.gov/idtheft*.

Other agencies and organizations also are working to combat identity theft. If specific institutions and companies are not being responsive to your questions and complaints, you can also contact the government agencies with jurisdiction over those companies. They are listed in Chapter 3, "Detecting, Reporting, and Recovering From Identity Theft." For additional detailed information, see the Appendices.

Getting Serious About Identity Theft

Victims of identity theft are finally getting some respect—or at least some long-deserved recognition. In 1998, when Congress made identity theft a federal crime, it directed the FTC to establish a clearinghouse for identity theft complaints and assistance. That came on the heels of a General Accounting Office report documenting how widespread identity theft is becoming. The Secret Service, for example, says victims and institutions in its identity fraud investigations lost $1.78 billion in 2000, up from $745 million in 1997.

As previously discussed, identity theft occurs when someone uses your personal information, such as your name, Social Security number, and date of birth, to establish a parallel identity. That allows them to pretend to be you to open bank accounts and apply for loans, for example. The impostors don't pay the bills. Although victims are not liable for charges made on fraudulent accounts, it can be a nightmare to get credit reports cleaned up.

Even with the new clearinghouse, however, the burden remains on victims to straighten out the credit mess the impostor has made. The clearinghouse's Web site (*www.consumer.gov/idtheft*) and the counselors who staff the FTC's toll-free hotline (877-438-4338) can provide advice on what steps to take, such as getting fraud alerts placed on credit reports. Many victims don't know where to begin.

Limited Resources

The FTC maintains a database of complaints, referring them to law enforcement agencies at the state and federal levels. Consumers don't have to call the FTC, the Secret Service, and the FBI. The FTC thinks that identity theft is a significant, growing problem so it is expected that there will be a significant increase in the number of federal prosecutions.

Federal Enforcement typically focuses on large-scale scams however. That leaves many cases in the hands of local police. Most police departments don't have the resources to investigate many cases, as suspects are often unknown and located in other jurisdictions. All policemen can do in most instances is file a police report, but, that still helps.

 Tip

A sure sign that a phenomenon has reached critical mass is when marketers swoop in. Recently, Travelers Property Casualty Corp. rolled out its Identity Fraud Expense Coverage, which reimburses victims for expenses they incur, such as loan reapplication fees and lost wages.

An Age of Betrayal

Finally, of all the stories of fraud scandalous enough to merit airtime, the tale of the busboy is perhaps the most bizarre, but it is only the latest in the evolution of new and improved forms of deception and betrayal. Thanks to recent cautionary tales, it's easy to wonder if everyone is out to get us. Treachery just isn't what it used to be in the good old days of gentlemen's duels. From an FBI counterintelligence expert to a Brooklyn busboy, cutting-edge duplicity fuels the rising public suspicion that no one is to be trusted. It's a simple lesson, urged by media outlets that can agree on little else: Trust no one.

Even emotional exhibitionists can have their trust breached. On the reality shows *Temptation Island* and *Change of Heart*, infidelity reached new and alarming heights, as TV cameras captured the lowest points of romantic relationships. With the Webcam craze, ardent self-documenters have found themselves breaking up with their lovers in real time online. Science has entered the sphere of treachery, too, with the first divorce case in history to use DNA evidence as proof of marital betrayal. Suddenly, in a court of law, nagging suspicions are transformed into definitive facts. Genetic testing has also revealed infidelity in custody cases; in 29% of paternity tests conducted in 2000, the man being tested turned out not to be the father.

Unfortunately, when the busboy wanted credit reports, the people and computers who gave them out weren't quite as paranoid as the rest of us. They happily accepted the busboy as George Soros, David Geffen, and Martha Stewart.

He avoided impersonating the richest person on the list, maybe thinking Bill Gates would have airtight security. Not quite. Recently, it came out that VeriSign, Inc., a provider of digital signatures, had been duped into issuing false electronic certificates in Microsoft's name. Yes, even Microsoft's signature has been forged.

With private citizens using cyberanonymizers and purchasing paper shredders, in a way, the busboy's best move was to remain a busboy. After all, if you are in the process of rerouting millions of dollars to the Cayman Islands, being a busboy is an even more impressive cover than working as head of counterintelligence while being a double agent. Double agents are supposed to balance multiple identities, whereas busboys are supposed to balance cups on plates. They are supposed to be noble bringers of ice water. They throw out crumpled checks with credit card numbers all the time. Don't they? Hmm. What if the suspected thief is not the ringleader, but is just working for someone with an even more compelling cover? Then again, if the busboy is guilty, one can only imagine what the head waiter might be up to.

Chapter 2

MINIMIZING YOUR RISK
OF IDENTITY THEFT

A s the number of victims of credit card theft mounts, it's unlikely that the hackers will ever be caught. Unless it's a high-profile case, such as the New York man arrested recently for stealing the identities of movie and TV celebrities (see the case in Chapter 1, "Identity Theft Defined"), it's unlikely that law enforcement can or will do anything. It's even more difficult when the hackers are in foreign countries where political and legal systems are in flux, such as Yugoslavia.

The better the relationship between countries, the better the exchange of information. However, unless there are very high-profile cases (and the theft of credit card data is not very high-profile in many cases) nothing really happens. Cases have been pushed aside because they were just too time consuming and very frustrating.

Lately, there have been a lot of Eastern European hackers. What should the United States do? There's no simple answer. It's apparent that if the hacker were in the United States, he or she could be tracked down and prosecuted. However, there's no cooperative effort between law enforcement in Yugoslavia and the United States to try and track down the hackers. If it were a large transaction from a large bank, it would be different, but someone stealing a person's credit card information is not enough to attract attention.

No agency really keeps detailed statistics on identity theft, but law enforcement agencies agree the problem is growing, with thousands of new cases being reported each month. MasterCard reported that credit card losses from

15

identity theft in 2001 were four times greater than in 1997; Visa doesn't keep such statistics. The Federal Reserve Board reported to Congress in March 2000 that, overall, identity theft losses to the U.S. financial system were comparatively small, although many instances of identity theft go unreported.

Guarding Against Identity Theft to Minimize Your Risk

It is impossible for you to entirely prevent the distribution of your personal identification and credit information. It is impossible to exercise control over all of the possible uses (or misuses) of that information. Nonetheless, you can reduce the risk of becoming a victim by managing your personal information wisely, cautiously, and with an awareness of the potential ramifications of not doing so. You can't completely eliminate the possibility of identity theft, but you can guard against it by taking some basic security precautions, shown in Table 2.1, and making them habits.

Table 2.1. Basic ID Theft Security Precautions Checklist

ID Theft Security Precautions Checklist
Date: _____

Identity thieves can ruin your good name to commit fraud. The following are steps to guard against it and minimize your risk (check all tasks completed):

❑ Before revealing personal identifying information, find out how it will be used and if it will be shared with others. Ask if you have a choice about the use of your information: Can you choose to have it kept confidential?

❑ Pay attention to your billing cycles. Follow up with creditors if bills do not arrive on time.

❑ Give your Social Security number only when absolutely necessary. Ask to use other types of identifiers when possible.

❑ Minimize the identification information and the number of cards you carry to what you actually need. If your ID or credit cards are lost or stolen, notify the creditors by phone immediately, and call the credit bureaus to ask that a fraud alert (see sidebar, "ID Fraud") be placed in your file.

Table 2.1. Basic ID Theft Security Precautions Checklist (Continued)

❑ Order a copy of your credit report from the three credit reporting agencies every year. Make sure it's accurate and includes only those activities you've authorized.

❑ Keep items with personal information in a safe place; tear them up when you don't need them anymore. Make sure charge receipts, copies of credit applications, insurance forms, bank checks and statements, expired charge cards, and credit offers you get in the mail are disposed of appropriately.

There are three major areas of exposure of your personal information: personal documents, personal data on the Internet, and personal data in corporations where you may be an employee or customer. There are also three entities that have responsibility to provide security for your personal data: the ISPs, the corporations, and yourself. The areas of exposure roughly parallel the entity that has responsibility for control of that exposure. You are personally responsible for the security of your personal documents. ISPs are responsible for providing protection of personal data that we put on the Internet. Businesses and corporations are responsible for protecting your personal data whether you are their employees or their customers. This chapter focuses on the area over which you have control (your personal documents), and helps you take the precautions needed to avoid becoming a victim of identity theft.

Basic Security Precautions

When you think about it, there is a lot of personal information that you need to protect. Chapter 1 showed how most individuals leave information trails like Hansel and Gretel left bread crumbs, and they do. You trail information here and you scatter it there, usually quite inadvertently. However, once you realize that your personal information can be turned against you, the necessity of protecting that information becomes patently obvious. You realize that it behooves you to protect your personal information on a wide variety of fronts. How do you start? What do you do?

Before answering those questions, let's test your identity quotient. Table 2.2 consists of a quiz to assess how vulnerable you are [1].

Table 2.2. Identity Theft Vulnerability Quiz

Are You at Risk for Identity Theft?—Test Your Identity Quotient
Score: _____

You might not be able to prevent identity theft, but you can take steps to make yourself less vulnerable. Here's a quiz to see how vulnerable you are. Each one of these statements represents a possible avenue for an ID theft. If you agree with any of them, add the points to your score.

❑ You receive several offers of preapproved credit every week. (5 points)

❑ Add 5 more points if you do not shred them before putting them in the trash.

❑ You carry your Social Security card in your wallet. (10 points)

❑ You do not have a post office box or a locked, secured mailbox. (5 points)

❑ You drop off your outgoing mail at an open, unlocked box or basket. (10 points).

❑ You carry your military ID in your wallet at all times. (10 points)

❑ You do not shred or tear banking and credit information when you throw it in the trash. (10 points)

❑ You provide your Social Security number whenever asked. (10 points)

❑ Add 5 points if you provide it orally without checking to see who might be listening.

❑ You are required to use your Social Security number as an employee or student ID number. (5 points)

❑ Your Social Security number is printed on an employee badge that you wear. (10 points)

❑ Your Social Security number or driver's license number is printed on your personal checks. (20 points)

❑ You are listed in a Who's Who guide. (5 points)

❑ You carry your insurance card in your wallet and it contains your Social Security number or your spouse's Social Security Number. (20 points)

❑ You have not ordered a copy of your credit report for at least two years. (10 points)

❑ You do not believe that people would root around in your trash looking for credit or financial information. (10 points)

What Your Score Means:

100+ points: More than 600,000 people (estimated) will become victims of ID theft this year. You are at high risk. You should purchase a paper shredder, become more security-aware in document handling, and start to question why people need your personal data.

50–100 points: Your odds of being victimized are about average, higher if you have good credit.

0–50 points: Congratulations. You have a high security IQ. Keep up the good work and don't let your guard down now.

Now, let's delve into some of the areas in which your personal information is most vulnerable and the basic security precautions that you should take to help ensure your privacy. These simple precautions can be a major factor in protecting yourself from identity theft. You make it easy for someone to take advantage of you when you leave your wallet on the table in the restaurant or allow someone to stand close to you when you are inputting your telephone calling card number into a pay phone. It is the equivalent to leaving the keys in your car for an opportunistic car thief! However, it is equally easy to develop habits (basic security precautions) that will safeguard you from the identity thieves.

Protect Your Purse or Wallet

How fat is your wallet and how many unnecessary cards are in it? What happens when that wallet is pinched? The identity thief goes for these items, not for the cash a wallet might contain (although that might be a bonus if you carry large amounts), but for the information the wallet contains about you: driver's license, Social Security card, credit cards, debit cards, checkbooks, insurance cards, and emergency information.

Minimize the identification information and the number of cards you carry to what you'll actually need on any given outing. Do not routinely carry such things as your Social Security card, your birth certificate, your passport, or more than one credit card. When you must carry some (or all) of these, take special precautions to reduce the risk of loss or theft. Keep the items with personal information that you do not carry with you in a secure place. By no means should you carry a cheat sheet of all of your passwords with you.

Protect Your Trash

Whether it is bagged and left at the curb or tossed into a dumpster, your garbage can be a target of any thief who wants it badly enough. Your trash is potentially a gold mine of personal information. It could provide the same type of information that your mailbox would, and it isn't a federal offense to steal it.

It is nearly impossible to protect your trash from a determined identity thief, so the best way to prevent theft of your personal information is to tear or shred the information before disposing of it. Consider shredding such items as charge receipts, copies of credit applications, insurance forms, physician statements, bank checks and statements that you are discarding, expired charge cards, and credit offers you get in the mail. Also consider shredding the following documents: unused preapproved credit card solicitations, convenience checks, cancelled checks, deposit slips, paycheck or earning statements, utility bills, and investment reports.

Protect Your Information at Home

Your home is a huge reservoir of personal information, and an enterprising thief can break in at a convenient time when no one is home and get whatever information he or she is after. Be cautious about where you leave personal information in your home, because the information there is also vulnerable if you have employees, roommates, outside help, or service people in your home, or if others have temporary, unrestricted access to your home.

Consider a professionally installed, monitored home security system to prevent a determined identity thief from breaking in to access your information. Be wary of the unusual visitor, perhaps a door-to-door salesperson who seems too chatty, maybe about you or about your neighbors. You could be unwittingly arming an identity thief!

Protect Your Information at Work

Find out who has access to your personal information at work. Also, verify with your employer that the records are kept in a secure location.

Protect Your Telephone Listing

Consider not listing your residence telephone number in the telephone book, or consider listing just your name and residence telephone number. If you decide to list your name and telephone number, consider not listing your professional qualification or affiliation (e.g., Dr., Atty., or Ph.D.).

Protect Your Applications

When you fill out a loan or credit application, be sure that the business considers the safety of that information by storing the forms in locked files and protecting their premises with a monitored security system. These applications often contain all of the information someone needs to assume your credit identity.

Hand Out Personal Information Only on a Need-to-Know Basis

You might need to give out your Social Security number to apply for a credit card, but does your local video store really need it? If you have to give up information, find out how it will be used and with whom it will be shared. Many states, for instance, no longer require you to use your Social Security number on your driver's license. The fact is that you have most of the control over this personal information. Also, you must learn to depend on yourself for protection and minimize your risk by performing the following tasks:

- Before you reveal any personally identifying information, find out how it will be used and whether it will be shared with others. Ask if you have a choice about the use of your information: Can you choose to have it kept confidential?

- Be cautious about filling out forms, answering questionnaires, or responding to surveys or sales calls that require a lot of information. Ask yourself if these people really need to know your Social Security number or mother's maiden name. Don't be afraid to withhold information if you think it's unnecessary.

- Do not give out personal information on the phone, through the mail, or over the Internet, unless you have initiated the contact or know with whom you are dealing. Identity thieves may pose as representatives of banks, ISPs, and even government agencies to get you to reveal your Social Security number, mother's maiden name, financial account numbers, and other identifying information. Legitimate organizations with which you do business have the information they need and will not call to ask you for it.

- Do not allow retailers to write down your credit card number, Social Security number, phone or bank account numbers, or address on your personal check, gift certificate, traveler's check, or money order.

Getting Purse-onal

Want to know a secret? A lost or stolen wallet or purse is a gold mine of information for the identity thief. As previously discussed, identity thieves can use information found in your wallet or purse—from credit cards, checks, your Social Security card, and even health insurance cards—to establish new accounts in your name. That could create an identity crisis that can take months to detect and even longer to unravel. If your wallet or purse is lost or stolen, the FTC suggests that you perform the tasks shown in Table 2.3.

Table 2.3.   FTC Lost or Stolen Purse or Wallet Checklist

Federal Trade Commission
Lost or Stolen Purse or Wallet Checklist
Date: _____

You should ensure that you have completed the following (check all tasks completed):

❏ File a report with the police immediately. Get a copy in case your bank, credit card company, or insurance company needs proof of the crime.

❏ Cancel each credit and charge card. Get new cards with new account numbers. Call the fraud departments of the major credit reporting agencies: Ask them to put a fraud alert on your account and add a victim's statement to your file requesting that creditors contact you before opening new accounts in your name.

❏ Ask the credit bureaus for copies of your credit reports. Review your reports carefully to make sure no additional fraudulent accounts have been opened in your name or unauthorized changes made to your existing accounts. In a few months, order new copies of your reports to verify your corrections and changes and to make sure no new fraudulent activity has occurred.

❏ Report the loss to your bank if your wallet or purse contained bank account information, including account numbers, ATM cards, or checks. Cancel checking and savings accounts and open new ones. Stop payments on outstanding checks.

❏ Get a new ATM card, account number, and personal identification number (PIN) or password.

❏ Report your missing driver's license to the Department of Motor Vehicles. If your state uses your Social Security number as your driver's license number, ask to substitute another number.

❏ Change the locks on your home and car if your keys were taken. Don't give an identity thief access to even more personal property and information.

Identifying Documents

There are many personal documents that include information about your identity. These documents are used to separate you from someone else. For example, your birth certificate (and your first personal document) is your introduction to the world. It provides information to your society that you now exist. It has identifying information on it to link you to your parents and to your specific time and date of birth, so that you are a unique being. Throughout your life, you accumulate other documents that identify you and distinguish your behavior and your transactions from those of other individuals. These forms of personal identification are used in a number of ways, and it is important to guard this information zealously because once someone else has enough of it, they can use it just like you do. Let's talk about some of the types of information you need to manage and protect to minimize your risk of identity theft.

Social Security Numbers

Your Social Security number is a critical item of personal information. It is used to get jobs, to get loans, and so on. Your Social Security number is the main key to your credit safety. Anyone with your Social Security number can easily create a credit nightmare that will take years to resolve. The following are some precautions you can take to protect the misuse of your Social Security number:

- Do not routinely carry your Social Security card. Store it when it is not needed in a secure place. When you must carry it, take special precautions to reduce the risk of loss or theft.

- Guard against overuse of your Social Security number. Release it only when necessary—for example, on tax forms and employment records, or for banking, stock, and property transactions.

- Do not have your Social Security number printed on your checks. Do not allow a merchant to write your Social Security number on your check.

- If a business requests your Social Security number for identification purposes, ask to use an alternate number. Some businesses have systems to identify their customers that do not use Social Security numbers. If the business does not have such an alternate system, ask to use an alternate identifier that you will remember (e.g., a combination of the letters of your last name and numbers). You can lawfully refuse to give a private business your Social Security number, but the business then can refuse to provide you service.

- Avoid having your Social Security number used for IDs at work. Request a different number if possible.

- If a government agency asks for your Social Security number, a Privacy Act notice should accompany the request. This notice explains whether your Social Security number is required or merely requested, what use will be made of your Social Security number, and what will happen if you refuse to provide it.

- Never give out your Social Security number over the phone unless it is to someone with whom you have a trusted relationship, and even only if you initiate the call. Also, consider the vulnerability of your phone connection. Are you on wireless? Cordless? These are not secure connections and anyone could be listening.

- Request a copy of your Social Security Personal Earnings and Benefit Estimate Statement at least every three years to make certain the information in the file is correct. Verify that someone else is not using your Social Security number for employment. Contact the Social Security Administration at 800-772-1213 to learn how to order this free report.

- Avoid using your Social Security number as your drivers license number. Request that your Department of Motor Vehicles use an alternative number; most states will provide one.

- Ensure that those requesting your Social Security number are doing so for legitimate reasons, not merely bureaucratic reasons.

- Never place your Social Security number in any public record, unless it is absolutely required. An identity thief, as well as the public, can get these. Social Security numbers have actually been listed in deeds! These are public records, so smart identity thieves can steal them.

When It Is Okay to Give out Your Social Security Number

Your employer and financial institution will likely need your Social Security number for wage and tax reporting purposes. Other private businesses might ask you for your Social Security number to do a credit check, such as when you apply for a car loan. Sometimes, however, they simply want your Social Security number for general record keeping. You don't have to give a business your Social Security number just because they ask for it. If someone asks for it, ask the following questions:

- Why do you need my Social Security number?

- How will my Social Security number be used?

- What law requires me to give you my Social Security number?

- What will happen if I don't give you my Social Security number? [2]

Sometimes a business might not provide you with the service or benefit you're seeking if you don't provide your Social Security number. Getting answers to these questions will help you decide whether you want to share your information with the business. Remember, though, that the decision is yours.

Departments of Motor Vehicles

Take a look at your driver's license. All the personal information on it (and more) is on file with your state Department of Motor Vehicles (DMV). A state DMV can distribute your personal information for law enforcement, court proceedings, and insurance underwriting purposes, but cannot distribute it for direct marketing without your express consent. Contact your state DMV for more information.

 Tip

Did you know that 52% of this country's major insurance companies use the information that is on the credit bureau reports (underwriting purposes) to set your car insurance rates? What this means is that if you a have a flawless driving record, but have a poor credit rating, your insurance rates will be higher. This doesn't really seem fair. What does a poor credit rating have to do with higher auto insurance rates? Nothing, in my opinion! But this is why it is so important to have erroneous information removed from your credit report.

Banking Institutions

An identity thief could bribe bank employees or other people with sensitive data about you. In turn, they would turn over key information about you to the identity thief. The following precautionary steps should be taken to minimize your risk here:

- Ask your bank or credit union to add additional security protection to your account. Most will allow the use of a special code or password to carry out financial transactions, especially withdrawals.
- Do not preprint or write your driver's license number on your checks.
- When you order new checks, pick them up at the bank instead of having them mailed to your home.
- To frustrate identity thieves, ask the bank if extra password security protection can be added for withdrawals.

- Quickly reconcile bank and credit card statements to check for unauthorized charges by identity thieves and other crooks.

Credit Cards

Getting a credit card issued is quite a simple process, especially at department stores. You are typically required to show only two forms of identification—a picture ID such as a driver's license, and a second identification, like your Social Security card. A department store credit card is usually issued on the spot and can be used right away. Although getting a major credit card is a little more complicated because more personal information is necessary, usually companies do not verify personal attributes, such as your signature—even though that could make it harder for crooks.

Your credit card information is the way you borrow money from the lending institution that issued it. Whether this is in the form of a department store card (where the use of the card is for the sole purpose of making purchases in their store), or whether it is from a major financial institution (where we can make purchases in many places and even obtain a cash advance), credit cards can get you almost anything you want. In the wrong hands, these cards can be used to run up outrageous bills that you are then responsible for. The importance of protecting your credit card information goes without saying. Now, let's discuss some of the ways you can protect these valuable financial tools.

Credit Card Fraud

Credit fraud involves the theft of your credit card or account number to make unauthorized charges to your account. Although consumers are protected financially from this abuse, other creditors may take note of all this activity and decide to raise your interest rates or refuse to grant you a loan. As previously mentioned, ordering your credit report will help you catch new activity on accounts that you haven't been using, or might have closed (see sidebar, "Why a Free Credit Report Could Save You a Bundle of Time, Money, and Distress"). If you would like to get a free copy of your credit report, visit the following Web address: *www.freecreditreport.com/index.asp?sourceid=00199619314495337871.*

Why a Free Credit Report Could Save You a Bundle: Of Time, Money, and Distress

One way to obtain and monitor your credit worthiness is through organizations that work with the major reporting agencies. ConsumerInfo.com is one such agency that provides copies of reports and a credit check monitoring service right over the Internet.

A free credit report could prevent identity theft from destroying your credit. When someone uses your identification (Social Security number, driver's license, or bank account) to obtain cash or credit in your name, your credit can be seriously damaged. It might be impossible for you to obtain a job, get a loan, or rent an apartment.

The first sign of identity theft may be a phone call from a collection agency or rejection for a new credit card, all because you now have bad credit.

Problems

Inaccurate indications of unpaid bills, delinquent payments, bounced checks, or overdrawn bank accounts could be an indication of identity theft. You can see these indications on your credit report. You typically will not find out about such problems until a credit provider contacts you for payment or you are rejected when you apply for credit.

Inaccurate reports are also caused by data input mistakes. Keying the wrong Social Security number or mixing up similar names are common mistakes. The Public Research Interest Group estimates that 70% of credit reports contain some sort of erroneous information. Your best defense against errors is to examine your credit report at least once a year.

Credit Report Monitoring

You should periodically monitor your credit report. To find out how to obtain a copy of your credit report and its cost you can contact the major reporting agencies:

Equifax Credit Reporting Agency (*www.equifax.com/*)
P.O. Box 740241
Atlanta, GA 30374-0241
Telephone: 800-685-1111

Experian Credit Reporting Agency (formerly TRW) (*www.experian.com/*)
Experian National Consumer Assistance Center
P.O. Box 2104

Allen, TX 75013
Telephone: 888-EXPERIAN (397-3742)

Trans Union Credit Reporting Agency (*www.tuc.com/*)
P.O. Box 390
Springfield, PA 19064
Telephone: 800-888-4213

Although it's well over a $2 billion-a-year racket, most people don't lose any sleep over credit card fraud. If bogus charges show up on your bill, or if your card is lost or stolen, you simply call the credit card issuer and let them know. Getting things straightened out takes a little time, but usually it doesn't cost you anything. Visa, MasterCard, American Express eats the losses—not you, the customer.

Of course, everyone ultimately pays for credit card fraud—it's part of the reason for those sky-high interest rates. But, as long as you check your statements, you're not going to be personally hurt by a credit thief. Right? Wrong!

Two types of credit fraud can hit individuals very hard. The first is debit card theft, which directly impacts your bank account, and not the hefty coffers of Visa or MasterCard. The second and more serious type of fraud is outright identity theft. A swindler assumes your credit identity and embarks on a spree that can last for years or even decades.

Both credit-granting institutions and the credit bureaus need to improve verification systems to help prevent identity theft, but there's little chance of anything meaningful being done to make it harder for anyone to get credit. You have to look out for yourself, and do the following:

- Avoid signing a blank charge card slip. If forced to, use a low-limit credit card to thwart identity thieves.

- Avoid giving out your credit card number in public. Be careful in phone booths, because an identity thief might be eavesdropping! In fact, if you are giving out a credit card number (which is generally not advised), give out eight numbers then move the receiver away (or cover it with your hand) say four (4) more numbers (to confuse an identity thief listening to you) then remove your hand and put your mouth back on the phone speaker, and then continue completing the number. This should confuse the identity thief.

- Don't give credit card numbers over the phone, unless you absolutely have to. It's usually best that you initiate the call, and make sure the other party is not on a mobile phone. An identity thief could be listening. Faxing the number could be a useful alternative. If necessary, consider using a low-limit credit card. Identity hates that! In fact, it's a good idea to have at least one low-limit card for use for questionable transactions.

- Make a list of or photocopy all of your credit cards. For each card, include the account number, expiration date, credit limit, and telephone numbers of customer service and fraud departments. Keep this list in a safe place (not your wallet or purse), so that you can contact each creditor quickly if your cards are lost or stolen. Make a similar list of your bank accounts.

- Ask stores at which you are applying for credit how they safeguard credit applications. Ensure that they are treated as secure documents.

- Ask businesses how they store and dispose of credit card transaction slips and be sure that the business has proper safeguards in place to treat these documents securely.

- Sign your credit cards in permanent ink as soon as you obtain them.

- Carefully examine each monthly credit card statement to ensure that every charge accurately matches your credit card receipts.

- Do not sign a blank charge slip. Draw a line through all areas for recording charges above the total.

- Cancel your unused credit cards so that their account numbers will not appear on your credit report. If an identity thief obtains your credit report, the thief could use the account numbers to obtain credit in your name. To help avoid this problem, some credit reporting agencies truncate account numbers on credit reports.

Credit cards are also at risk on the Internet and in business. A discussion of this topic ensues in Part II, "Identity Theft Protection on the Internet," which deals with ISPs and Part III, "Identity Theft Protection for Corporations," which deals with corporations. However, there are areas in which you cannot personally protect your credit card information. Still, the precautions relating to monitoring your credit report apply. You still need to know if someone is impersonating you, regardless of how he or she obtained your personal information.

Credit Bureau Information

Any organization with which you have financial dealings can submit information about you to credit bureaus. This includes banks, utility companies, credit card companies, stores, courts from across the country, and home repair providers. Your credit report contains information such as your Social Security number, current and past addresses, and status of payments on your credit cards and utility bills. It might contain certain legal data such as employment information, court records, liens, and bankruptcy. Also included is a list of credit grantors who have received your credit report.

Thieves can get essential information (including the quality of prospective victims' credit) by illegally accessing the huge databases of the three credit reporting bureaus, which have thousands of computer terminals in places like car dealerships and real estate agencies. Here thieves can shop for victims at will.

A brave identity thief might pose as someone with a legal right to have access to your credit report. The imposter could pretend to be a potential employer, a credit clerk in a store, a landlord, or someone else who has a legitimate interest in your creditworthiness.

Who Gets Access? Practically anyone with a legitimate business need can obtain your credit report. This includes the following entities:

- Government agencies required to review credit for issuing licenses or benefit payments
- Landlords and prospective landlords
- Employers and prospective employers
- Insurance companies
- Banks and other lenders
- Collection agencies
- Companies that currently grant or could grant you credit [3]

Protect Your Credit. Review your credit report annually by ordering your report from each of the three major credit reporting agencies. Check each credit report carefully for accuracy and for indications of fraud, such as credit accounts that you did not open, applications for credit that you did not authorize, credit inquiries that you did not initiate, charges that you did not incur, and defaults and delinquencies that you did not cause. Check the identifying information in your credit report to be sure it is accurate (especially your name, address, and Social Security number).

Call or write the three major credit bureaus and ask them to place security alerts on your accounts so they will call you to verify all new accounts being opened:

- Equifax: 800-525-6285, P.O. Box 740341, Atlanta, GA 30374-0241
- Experian: 800-301-7195, P.O. Box 1017, Allen TX 75013
- Trans Union: 800-680-7289, P.O. Box 390, Springfield, PA 19064
- TrueCredit.com: For $29.95, you can order a "3-in-1" report that compares standardized information from all three agencies *www.transunion.com/*).

To opt out of receiving prescreened credit card offers, call 1-888-5-OPTOUT (1-888-567-8688). The three major credit bureaus use the same toll-free number to let consumers choose not to receive these offers.

Caution

All phone numbers and URLs contained in this book could change without notice.

The credit bureaus (previously listed) are legally permitted to charge you no more than $8.50 for a copy of your credit report. Nevertheless, the most important advice anyone can give for protecting your personal information is to lie, lie, and lie. There are lots of people asking lots of questions about you for numerous reasons. On many occasions, there is no reason you have to tell them the truth. One strategy is to provide the information they ask for, but let it all be misinformation.

If they want to know your date of birth, make one up. Randomly pick a salary. Say you have 40 children. Never give out your actual email address unless you like spam. When a devious person tries to create a personal profile of you, it will be so full of conflicting information that it will be useless.

Finally, add a fraud alert to your credit files that alerts the three major credit bureaus to inform creditors to call you for verification of any credit applications. Your letters should contain your name, address, Social Security number, and spouse's name. Fraud alerts normally remain active for seven years.

Protect Accounts With Passwords, But Use Caution

Protecting your accounts every way you can is a good idea. Many banks and credit cards now permit you to place passwords on accounts that must be provided before changes are made. Putting passwords on any account possible adds one level of security to protect these accounts from misuse. Here are a few basic precautions you should consider:

- Put carefully selected passwords on your credit card, bank, and phone accounts.
- When creating passwords and PINs, do not use any part of your Social Security number, birth date, middle name, wife's name, child's name, pet's name, mother's maiden name, address, consecutive numbers, or anything that a thief could easily deduce or discover.
- Memorize all your passwords and PINs; never write them in your wallet, purse, or Rolodex.

- Shield the keypad when punching in your PIN at an ATM or when placing a calling card call. Be aware of what is around you when approaching an ATM. Someone might be looking over your shoulder with binoculars or a telephoto lens on a video camera.

Your Mail

Your mailbox holds a wealth of information for the identity thief—not every day, but if your mailbox is unprotected so that a thief can access it periodically, there are sources of personal information there that would make a thief happy. In addition, an energetic thief can fill out a change of address form at the post office and get your mail sent to a new address where it is readily available to him or her. Mail theft is a growing concern throughout the country, and if you use a nonlocking mailbox to either send or receive mail, you are at risk.

Bill payment checks can be stolen, altered (usually chemically), and then cashed. The victim is unaware of the theft until either the bill payment is late or checks start bouncing on his or her account because the check was altered for a higher dollar amount. Often, the criminal uses a second victim's account number (obtained from a stolen bank statement) to negotiate the altered check, thus creating two victims with one crime. To magnify the problem, criminals can create additional checks using an inexpensive computer program that can be purchased at any office supply store.

Having boxes of checks delivered to a nonlocking mailbox opens the door for an even larger problem. Families' credit records have been destroyed in a very short period of time using a stolen box of checks. The victims eventually get their money back, but the cost and time of cleaning up the damaged credit can be devastating. It literally can take years to repair the damage. To make matters worse, the thief often shares the stolen checks with cohorts or trades the blank books of checks for drugs. Because of this, it is not unusual to see stolen checks circulated over a large geographical area.

A third area of concern is credit card checks. These come in the mail and most of us aren't even aware they're coming. Victims don't become aware that a crime has occurred until the credit card bill arrives. By then, the damage is done and the criminal is long gone.

Your mail, both incoming and outgoing, is a source of valuable information to an identity thief. It is important to protect it physically and to monitor the mail you receive carefully to spot items that should be there and are not. Here are some basic security precautions you can use to protect your mail:

- Guard your mail from theft. Deposit outgoing mail in post office collection boxes or at your local post office rather than leaving it in your home mailbox where anyone can access it. Checks in stolen bill payments can be altered and cashed by an imposter.

- Promptly remove mail from your mailbox after it has been delivered. If you're planning to be away from home and can't pick up your mail, call your local post office to request a vacation hold. The U.S. Postal Service will hold your mail at your local post office until you can pick it up.

- If your mail suddenly stops, check with the post office. Someone might have filed a change of address form.

- Obtain a post office box if you live in an area where it would be easy for someone to get into your mailbox without being noticed or install a lock on your mailbox at home to reduce the risk of mail theft.

- Pay attention to your billing cycles. Follow up with creditors if your bills (or your new or recently renewed credit cards) don't arrive on time. A missing credit card bill could mean an identity thief has taken over your credit card account and changed your billing address to cover his or her tracks. Or it could mean that the thief has filed a change of address request in your name with the post office. Identity thieves do this to divert their victims' mail to themselves. If you miss your bill, call the creditor to see if a change of address request has been filed in your name or if additional or replacement credit cards have been requested on your account. If either has happened, inform the creditor that you did not make the request and instruct the creditor not to honor it. If there has been no change with the credit card company, call the post office to see if a change of address request has been filed in your name. If this has happened, immediately notify the Postal Inspector (see the Postal Service listing under "United States Government" in the white pages of the telephone directory).

- Do not sign up for unfamiliar contests or sweepstakes that arrive in your mail. Information you provide could be sold and reproduced hundreds of times.

- Ask every company sending junk mail to stop using your name. Do not sign up for contests—your name will be resold multiple times! Stop credit bureaus from selling your header information—contact them.

- Consider using electronic bill pay and direct deposit.

Tip

If you are a victim of mailbox theft, alert your financial institution, local law enforcement, and post office. If you suspect a credit card bill was stolen, notify that company also.

33

Public Documents

Identity thieves can even photocopy your vital credit information legally at the local courthouse. If you've been divorced, the transcripts of your case, including the financial and credit account information you divulged as part of the proceedings, as well as your Social Security number, are part of the public record. Why would an identity thief go dumpster diving?

Marketing Lists

Finally, many businesses use marketing information to send mail and make telephone solicitations to consumers. Credit card issuers often compile lists of marketing information about cardholders based on their purchases. You should take the following precautionary steps to minimize your risk:

- The three major credit reporting agencies (previously listed) use information from credit reports to develop lists of consumers who meet criteria specified by potential creditors. You can request that your credit information not be used for these purposes. Doing this will limit the number of pre approved credit offers you receive.

- Consider having your name removed from marketing lists. Of the three major credit bureaus, only Experian offers consumers the opportunity to have their names removed from lists that are used for marketing and promotional purposes. To have your name removed from Experian's marketing lists, call 1-800-407-1088.

- The Direct Marketing Association (DMA) Mail, Email, and Telephone Preference Services allow consumers to opt out of direct mail marketing, email marketing, and telemarketing solicitations from many national companies. Because your name will not be on their lists, it also means that these companies can't rent or sell your name to other companies. You can request that your name be added to the DMA's Mail Preference Service and Telephone Preference Service name-removal lists. To remove your name from many national direct mail lists, write:
  - Direct Marketing Association
    P.O. Box 9008
    Farmingdale, NY 11735-9014

  or

  - Preference Service Manager
    Direct Marketing Association
    1120 Avenue of the Americas

New York, NY 10036-6700
Send via fax to: 212-790-1427

- To remove your email address from many national direct email lists, visit *www.e-mps.org*. To avoid unwanted phone calls from many national marketers, send your name, address, and telephone number to:

  - DMA Telephone Preference Service
  P.O. Box 9014
  Farmingdale, NY 11735-9014

  or

  - Preference Service Manager
  Direct Marketing Association
  1120 Avenue of the Americas
  New York, NY 10036-6700
  Send via fax to: 212-790-1427

- Stop credit bureaus from selling your name (header information). Call the toll-free telephone number used by all three credit bureaus and take advantage of their opt-out service. One number, 888-5OPTOUT, or 888-567-8688, reaches all three bureaus.

- Write to National Demographics and Lifestyles and ask to be deleted from its mailing list:

  - National Demographics & Lifestyles
  List Order Department
  1621 18th Street, Suite 300
  Denver, CO 80202
  Phone: 800-525-3533

End Notes

[1] Privacy Rights Clearinghouse/Utility Consumers' Action Network (UCAN), 3100 5th Ave., Suite B, San Diego, CA, 92103, 2001.

[2] Federal Trade Commission, 600 Pennsylvania Ave., NW, Washington, DC 20580, 2001.

[3] "Fact Sheet 6: How Private Is My Credit Report?" Privacy Rights Clearinghouse/Utility Consumers' Action Network (UCAN), 3100 5th Ave., Suite B, San Diego, CA 92103, 2002.

Chapter 3

DETECTING, REPORTING, AND RECOVERING FROM IDENTITY THEFT

H ave you become a victim of identity theft? You might be and still don't know it. What if you learn that there is another "you" out there living on your name? How do you detect it? Who do you tell or report it to? Once it has happened, and you have made the appropriate reports, how do you recover from such an invasion of your life? Let's talk first about how you can detect whether you have been or are being victimized by the illegal use of your identity.

Detecting Your Misappropriated Identity

Generally the way you find out that your personal information is being misused is through some horrible shock—like a credit card bill for $16,606 on a credit card you never had, or a policeman coming to arrest you for a crime you never committed! These are dead giveaways that you have been had. Of course, you have the option of keeping a close eye on your personal business to catch that phony credit card before the bill gets so out of hand.

Regularly Check Your Credit Report

Request a copy of your credit report at least once a year to be sure there are no fraudulent accounts showing up. For a period of time after the victimization you are entitled to get your credit reports at no cost to clean up the credit mess and monitor new inquiries. That varies depending on state laws and credit reporting agency policies. After that time, be sure to continue to monitor your reports at least every six months.

Identity theft is a repetitive crime. People who commit this crime are likely to do it again. Therefore, some people prefer to subscribe to a credit monitoring service and there are several currently available in the United States. Many victims choose to monitor their own credit reports. Costs for 10 years could be estimated like this: three reports every six months or six reports per year, times 10 years. That equals 60 reports multiplied by the cost per report.

Run a Background Check on Yourself

If you've been the victim of identity theft, it might be worth the cost to hire a professional investigator or agency to run a thorough check to see whether the crimes committed by the thief go beyond consumer fraud. The worst case scenario is an identity thief who commits a felony in your name and adds a criminal record to your nightmare.

Reporting ID Theft

Sometimes an identity thief can strike even if you've been very careful about keeping your personal information to yourself. If you suspect that your personal information has been hijacked and misappropriated to commit fraud or theft, take action immediately and keep a record of your conversations and correspondence. You might want to use the form shown in Figure 3.1. [1] Exactly which steps you should take to protect yourself depends on your circumstances and how your identity has been misused.

Credit Bureaus—Report Fraud

Bureau	Date Contacted	Contact Person	Comments
Equifax 1-800-525-6285			
Experian 1-888-397-3742			
Trans Union 1-800-680-7289			

Banks, Credit Card Issuers, and Other Creditors
(Contact each creditor promptly to protect your legal rights.)

Creditor	Address/Phone Number	Date Contacted	Contact Person	Comments

Law Enforcement Authorities—Report Identity Theft

Agency/Dept.	Phone Number	Date Contacted	Contact Person	Report #	Comments
Federal Trade Commission	1-877-IDTHEFT				
Local Police Department					

Figure 3.1 Use this form to record the steps you've taken to report the fraudulent use of your identity. Keep this list in a safe place for reference.

The Victim

If you become a victim of identity theft, it is important to act immediately to stop the thief's further use of your identity. Unfortunately, victims themselves are burdened with resolving the problem. It is important to act quickly and assertively to minimize the damage. In dealing with authorities and financial institutions, keep a log of all conversations, dates, names, and telephone numbers. Note the time spent and any expenses incurred. Confirm conversations in writing. Provide your police report number to expedite reporting the crime.

Send correspondence by certified mail (with a return receipt requested). Keep copies of all letters and documents. Sometimes identity theft victims are wrongfully accused of crimes committed by an imposter. If a civil judgment has been entered in your name for actions taken by an imposter, contact the court where the judgment was entered and report that you are a victim of identity theft. If you are wrongfully prosecuted of criminal charges, contact the state Department of Justice and the FBI and ask how to clear your name.

Therefore, with the preceding in mind, if you become an identity fraud victim, you should take the following three steps immediately, in addition to completing all of the tasks in Table 3.1:

1. Call the fraud departments of the three major credit bureaus to get copies of your credit report and to have fraud flags and statements added to your report indicating that all potential creditors should contact you to verify credit applications.
2. Contact all banks and other institutions where your name has been used fraudulently, sending a copy of a police report or other documentation to show that you are a fraud victim.
3. Report the identity theft to local law enforcement authorities, including the police, postal inspectors, and the Secret Service.

Your First Three Steps

First, contact the fraud departments of each of the three major credit bureaus. Tell them that you're an identity theft victim and request that a fraud alert be placed in your file, as well as a victim's statement asking that creditors call you before opening any new accounts or changing your existing accounts. This can help prevent an identity thief from opening additional accounts in your name.

At the same time, order copies of your credit reports from the credit bureaus. Credit bureaus must give you a free copy of your report if your report is inaccurate because of fraud and you request it in writing. Review your reports carefully to make sure no additional fraudulent accounts have been opened in your name or unauthorized changes made to your existing accounts. Also, check the section of your report that lists inquiries. Where inquiries appear from the companies that opened the fraudulent accounts, request that these inquiries be removed from your report. In a few months, order new copies of your reports to verify your corrections and changes and to make sure no new fraudulent activity has occurred.

Second, contact the creditors for any accounts that have been tampered with or opened fraudulently. Creditors can include credit card companies, phone companies and other utilities, and banks and other lenders. Ask to speak with someone in the security or fraud department at each creditor, and follow up with a letter. It's particularly important to notify credit card companies in writing because that's the consumer protection procedure the law spells out for resolving errors on credit card billing statements. Immediately close accounts that have been tampered with and open new ones with new PINs and passwords. Here again, avoid using easily available information like your mother's maiden name, your birth date, the last four digits of your Social Security number or your phone number, or a series of consecutive numbers.

Third, file a report with your local police or the police in the community where the identity theft took place. Get a copy of the police report in case the bank, credit card company, or others need proof of the crime. Even if the police can't catch the identity thief in your case, having a copy of the police report can help you when dealing with creditors.

Table 3.1. ID Theft Victim Checklist

What To Do If Your Identity Has Been Stolen
ID Theft Victims Checklist
Date: _____

If you are a victim of ID theft there are a number of other steps you can take. In other words, if you discover that an identity thief is off and running at your expense, you must act immediately. Here are some tips to follow if you should become a victim of identity theft. You should ensure that you have completed the following (check all tasks completed):

❑ Cancel all fraudulent credit cards.

❑ Contact any accounts that have been tampered with, close or block those accounts, and file a report in writing with their fraud department (frequently, the quicker you contact them, the less you will be liable for).

❑ Immediately notify your bank and every bank that issued a credit card to you.

Table 3.1. ID Theft Victim Checklist (Continued)

❑ Call the companies and make it clear that the cards were issued without your consent and that you did not make any purchases with them. Most credit card companies have procedures to erase the debt of credit card fraud victims.

❑ Keep meticulous dated records of your attempts to clean your record—letters, phone calls, and what was said. You'll need them. If multiple thefts were made, keep records in separate files for quick reference.

❑ At the first sight of fraud, begin a log of dates and time spent solving this problem; take notes of every phone conversation and keep copies of all documents you send out and receive.

❑ Make sure you get the names, titles, and phone numbers of everyone you talk to.

❑ Contact the fraud departments of the credit bureaus and ask that a fraud alert be placed in your file. This should (although it doesn't always) alert credit grantors to check a new application. Your letter should contain your address, Social Security number, and spouse's first name. Ask to include a statement about the fraud, in which you tell creditors to call you to verify all future applications.

❑ Ask that you be contacted before any new accounts are authorized.

❑ Request a copy of your credit report and tell the credit bureaus to remove the fraudulent information. The three major credit reporting companies are Equifax (*www.equifax.com*), Experian (*www.experian.com*) and Trans Union (*www.tuc.com*).

❑ Call And Write All Creditors On Your Credit Report.

❑ Alert all credit card companies and stores about your ordeal.

❑ Demand that the inaccurate information be immediately erased.

❑ Get replacement cards and new account numbers for all accounts—even those that have not been stolen.

❑ Report the fraud to your local law enforcement precinct.

❑ Notify your local police department and request a copy of the police report after you filled it out.

❑ Depending upon your circumstances, you may also want to contact the U.S. Postal Inspection Service and the U.S. Secret Service. Their telephone number can be found on the front page of your local phone book and/or in the white pages.

❑ Contact your local police and retain a copy of the crime report. It will be useful in dealing with creditors in the future. Many states have passed laws related to identity theft.

❑ Contact your local federal law enforcement agency for investigations under the ID Theft and Assumption Deterrence Act. Your local field office of the FBI can be found

Table 3.1. ID Theft Victim Checklist (Continued)

in the phone book or on the FBI Web site (*www.fbi.gov*). Your identity theft could likely have violated several other federal laws as well, such as Mail Fraud or Social Security Fraud.

❏ Contact the credit bureaus that hold your credit report. Ask them to log the theft and remove the bad accounts from your report, giving as much proof as possible. You may meet difficulties, but by law the bureau must correct any wrong information.

❏ Get a copy of the fraudulent contract or application. This is the key document that proves the person who signed it isn't you. Finding the company that issued it and the right person to talk to is not always easy. Try to get past the gatekeepers to someone in charge.

❏ Never agree to pay any portion of the debt just to get debt collectors off your back. The balance will stay on your record [3].

❏ Contact the FTC's ID Theft Hotline: 1-877-IDTheft (1-877-438-4338).

❏ What you do next will depend on the type of identity theft you experienced. If your address was changed, you need to contact the post office.

❏ If the crime involved investments, you should contact the Security Exchange Commission.

❏ If you've been a victim of identity theft, file a complaint with the FTC by contacting the FTC's Identity Theft Hotline by telephone: toll-free 1-877-IDTHEFT (438-4338); TDD: 202-326-2502; by mail: Identity Theft Clearinghouse, Federal Trade Commission, 600 Pennsylvania Avenue, NW, Washington, DC 20580; or online: *www.consumer.gov/idtheft*. The FTC has an ID Theft Form entitled "Chart your Course of Action" that you can use to make sure you take all appropriate steps (see Figure 3-1). If the crime has resulted in credit problems, you may need to explore your rights under the Fair Credit Reporting Act. The Truth in Lending Act limits your liability for unauthorized credit card charges to $50 per card in most cases (many companies now offer zero liability, marketing their cards as safe to use on the internet). The FTC collects complaints about identity theft from consumers who have been victimized. Although the FTC does not have the authority to bring criminal cases, the Commission can help victims of identity theft by providing information to assist them in resolving the financial and other problems that can result from this crime. The FTC also refers victim complaints to other appropriate government agencies and private organizations for further action.

❏ Contact the ID Theft Clearinghouse The clearinghouse was established by the Federal Trade Commission at the direction of Congress. This clearinghouse is for identity-theft complaints and assistance. But even with the new clearinghouse, the burden

Table 3.1. ID Theft Victim Checklist (Continued)

remains on victims to straighten out the credit mess the impostor has made. The clearinghouse's Web site (*www.consumer.gov/idtheft*) and the counselors who staff the FTC's toll-free hotline (877-438-4338) will provide advice on what steps to take, such as getting fraud alerts placed on credit reports. A lot of people don't have a clue.

❑ Other agencies and organizations also are working to combat identity theft. If specific institutions and companies are not being responsive to your questions and complaints, you also may want to contact the government agencies with jurisdiction over those companies.

❑ Trust Your Instincts. If something seems wrong, it probably is. Guard your wallet and purse when in crowded areas.

Recovering From Identity Theft

Resolving credit problems resulting from identity theft can be time-consuming and frustrating. The good news is that there are federal laws that establish procedures for correcting credit report errors and billing errors and for stopping debt collectors from contacting you about debts you don't owe.

In other words, your credit report contains information on where you work and live, the credit accounts that have been opened in your name, how you pay your bills, and whether you've been sued, arrested, or filed for bankruptcy. Checking your report on a regular basis can help you catch mistakes and fraud before they wreak havoc on your personal finances. See Chapter 2, "Minimizing Your Risk of Identity Theft," for detailed information on this topic.

Your Next Steps

Although there's no question that identity thieves can wreak havoc on your personal finances, there are some things you can do to take control of the situation.

Credit Reports

The Fair Credit Reporting Act (FCRA) establishes procedures for correcting mistakes on your credit record and requires that your record be made available only for certain legitimate business needs. Under the FCRA, both the credit bureau and the organization that provided the information to the credit bureau (the information provider), such as a bank or credit card company, are responsible for correcting inaccurate or incomplete information in your report. To protect your rights under the law, contact both the credit bureau and the information provider.

First, call the credit bureau and follow up in writing. Tell them what information you believe is inaccurate. Include copies (not originals) of documents that support your position. In addition to providing your complete name and address, your letter should clearly identify each item in your report that you dispute, give the facts, and explain why you dispute the information, and request deletion or correction. You might want to enclose a copy of your report with circles around the items in question. Your letter might look something like the sample in Figure 3.2. [1] Send your letter by certified mail, and

```
Date
Your Name
Your Address
Your City, State, Zip Code

Complaint Department
Name of Credit Bureau
Address
City, State, Zip Code

Dear Sir or Madam:

I am writing to dispute the following information in my file. The
items I dispute also are circled on the attached copy of the report I
received. (Identify item(s) disputed by name of source, such as cred-
itors or tax court, and identify type of item, such as credit account,
judgment, etc.)

This item is (inaccurate or incomplete) because (describe what is
inaccurate or incomplete and why). I am requesting that the item be
deleted (or request another specific change) to correct the informa-
tion.

Enclosed are copies of (use this sentence if applicable and describe
any enclosed documentation, such as payment records, court documents)
supporting my position. Please investigate this (these) matter(s) and
(delete or correct) the disputed item(s) as soon as possible.



Sincerely, Your Name

Enclosures: (List what you are enclosing.)
```

Figure 3.2 Credit bureau sample dispute letter.

45

request a return receipt so you can document what the credit bureau received and when. Keep copies of your dispute letter and enclosures.

Credit bureaus must investigate the items in question, usually within 30 days, unless they consider your dispute frivolous. They also must forward all relevant data you provide about the dispute to the information provider. After the information provider receives notice of a dispute from the credit bureau, it must investigate, review all relevant information provided by the credit bureau, and report the results to the credit bureau. If the information provider finds the disputed information to be inaccurate, it must notify any nationwide credit bureau that it reports to so that the credit bureaus can correct this information in your file.

Tip

Disputed information that cannot be verified must be deleted from your file. If your report contains erroneous information, the credit bureau must correct it. If an item is incomplete, the credit bureau must complete it. For example, if your file shows that you have been late making payments, but fails to show that you are no longer delinquent, the credit bureau must show that you're current. If your file shows an account that belongs to someone else, the credit bureau must delete it.

When the investigation is complete, the credit bureau must give you the written results and a free copy of your report if the dispute results in a change. If an item is changed or removed, the credit bureau cannot put the disputed information back in your file unless the information provider verifies its accuracy and completeness, and the credit bureau gives you a written notice that includes the name, address, and phone number of the information provider.

If you request it, the credit bureau must send notices of corrections to anyone who received your report in the past six months. Job applicants can have a corrected copy of their report sent to anyone who received a copy during the past two years for employment purposes. If an investigation does not resolve your dispute, ask the credit bureau to include your statement of the dispute in your file and in future reports.

Second, in addition to writing to the credit bureau, tell the creditor or other information provider in writing that you dispute an item. Again, include copies (not originals) of documents that support your position. Many information providers specify an address for disputes. If the information provider then reports the item to any credit bureau, it must include a notice of your dispute. In addition, if you are correct—that is, if the disputed information is not accurate—the information provider cannot use it again.

Credit Cards

As previously explained, the Truth in Lending Act limits your liability for unauthorized credit card charges in most cases to $50 per card. The Fair Credit Billing Act establishes procedures for resolving billing errors on your credit card accounts.

The Act's settlement procedures apply to disputes about billing errors, which includes fraudulent charges on your accounts. To take advantage of the law's consumer protections, you must write to the creditor at the address given for billing inquiries, not the address for sending your payments. Include your name, address, account number, and a description of the billing error, including the amount and date of the error. Your letter might look something like the sample shown in Figure 3.3. [1]

```
Date

Your Name
Your Address
Your City, State, Zip Code
Your Account Number

Name of Creditor
Billing Inquiries
Address
City, State, Zip Code

Dear Sir or Madam:

I am writing to dispute a billing error in the amount of $_____on my
account. The amount is inaccurate because (describe the problem). I
am requesting that the error be corrected, that any finance and other
charges related to the disputed amount be credited as well, and that
I receive an accurate statement.

Enclosed are copies of (use this sentence to describe any enclosed
information, such as sales slips, payment records) supporting my
position. Please investigate this matter and correct the billing
error as soon as possible.

Sincerely,


Your name
Enclosures: (List what you are enclosing.)
```

Figure 3.3 Credit card issuers sample dispute letter.

You should also send your letter so that it reaches the creditor within 60 days after the first bill containing the error was mailed to you. If the address on your account was changed by an identity thief and you never received the bill, your dispute letter still must reach the creditor within 60 days of when the creditor would have mailed the bill. This is why it's so important to keep track of your billing statements and immediately follow up when bills don't arrive on time.

Send your letter by certified mail and request a return receipt. This will be your proof of the date the creditor received the letter. Include copies (not originals) of sales slips or other documents that support your position and keep a copy of your dispute letter.

The creditor must acknowledge your complaint in writing within 30 days after receiving it, unless the problem has been resolved. The creditor must resolve the dispute within two billing cycles (but not more than 90 days) after receiving your letter.

Debt Collectors

The Fair Debt Collection Practices Act prohibits debt collectors from using unfair or deceptive practices to collect overdue bills that a creditor has forwarded for collection. You can stop a debt collector from contacting you by writing a letter to the collection agency telling them to stop. Once the debt collector receives your letter, the company cannot contact you again, with two exceptions: They can tell you there will be no further contact and they can tell you that the debt collector or the creditor intends to take some specific action.

A collector also may not contact you if, within 30 days after you receive the written notice, you send the collection agency a letter stating you do not owe the money. Although such a letter should stop the debt collector's calls, it will not necessarily get rid of the debt itself, which might still turn up on your credit report. In addition, a collector can renew collection activities if you are sent proof of the debt. Therefore, along with your letter stating you don't owe the money, include copies of documents that support your position. If you're a victim of identity theft, including a copy (not original) of the police report you filed might be particularly useful.

ATM Cards, Debit Cards, and Electronic Fund Transfers

The Electronic Fund Transfer Act provides consumer protections for transactions involving an ATM or debit card or other electronic means of debiting or crediting an account. It also limits your liability for unauthorized electronic fund transfers.

It's important to report lost or stolen ATM and debit cards immediately because the amount you can be held responsible for depends on how quickly you report the loss. For example:

- If you report your ATM card lost or stolen within two business days of discovering the loss or theft, your losses are limited to $50.
- If you report your ATM card lost or stolen after the two business days, but within 60 days after a statement showing an unauthorized electronic fund transfer, you can be liable for up to $500 of what a thief withdraws.
- If you wait more than 60 days, you could lose all the money that was taken from your account after the end of the 60 days and before you report your card missing. [1]

The best way to protect yourself in the event of an error or fraudulent transaction is to call the financial institution and follow up in writing (by certified letter, with a return receipt requested) so you can prove when the institution received your letter. Keep a copy of the letter you send for your records.

After notification about an error on your statement, the institution generally has 10 business days to investigate. The financial institution must tell you the results of its investigation within three business days after completing it and must correct an error within one business day after determining that the error has occurred. If the institution needs more time, it can take up to 45 days to complete the investigation—but only if the money in dispute is returned to your account and you are notified promptly of the credit. At the end of the investigation, if no error has been found, the institution can take the money back if it sends you a written explanation.

☞ **Tip**

As previously mentioned, Visa and MasterCard voluntarily have agreed to limit consumers' liability for unauthorized use of their debit cards in most instances to $50 per card, no matter how much time has elapsed since the discovery of the loss or theft of the card.

Stolen Mail

If an identity thief has stolen your mail to get new credit cards, bank and credit card statements, prescreened credit offers, or tax information, or if an identity thief has falsified change of address forms, that's a crime. Report it to your local postal inspector. Contact your local post office for the phone number for the nearest postal inspection service office or check the U.S. Postal Service Web site at *www.usps.gov/websites/depart/inspect.*

Caution

Web addresses are subject to change without notice!

Change of Address on Credit Card Accounts

If you discover that an identity thief has changed the billing address on an existing credit card account, close the account immediately. When you open a new account, ask that a password be used before any inquiries or changes can be made on the account. Avoid using easily available information like your mother's maiden name, your birth date, the last four digits of your Social Security number, or your phone number, or a series of consecutive numbers. Avoid using the same information and numbers when you create a PIN.

Bank Accounts

If you have reason to believe that an identity thief has tampered with your bank accounts, checks, or ATM card, close the accounts immediately. When you open new accounts, insist on password-only access to minimize the chance that an identity thief can violate the accounts.

Tip

A special word is in order about lost or stolen checks. Although no federal law limits your losses if someone steals your checks and forges your signature, state laws protect you. Most states hold the bank responsible for losses from a forged check. At the same time, however, most states require you to take reasonable care of your account. For example, you might be held responsible for the forgery if you fail to notify the bank in a timely manner that a check was lost or stolen. Contact your state banking or consumer protection agency for more information.

In addition, if your checks have been stolen or misused, stop payment. Also contact the major check verification companies to request that they notify retailers using their databases not to accept these checks, or ask your bank to notify the check verification service with which it does business:

- *National Check Fraud Service:* 1-843-571-2143
- *SCAN:* 1-800-262-7771
- *TeleCheck:* 1-800-710-9898 or 927-0188 or 366-2425

- *CrossCheck:* 1-707-586-0551
- *Equifax-Telecredit (or Check Systems):* 1-800-437-5120
- *International Check Services (or NPC):* 1-800-526-5380.
- *Check Rite:* 1-800-766-2748
- *Chex Systems:* 1-800-328-5121

Caution

Phone numbers can change without notice!

If your ATM card has been lost, stolen or otherwise compromised, cancel the card. You should do this as soon as you can and get another with a new PIN.

Investments

If you believe that an identity thief has tampered with your securities investments or a brokerage account, immediately report it to your broker or account manager. You should also report it to the SEC.

Phone Service

If an identity thief has established new phone service in your name, is making unauthorized calls that seem to come from (and are billed to) your cellular phone, or is using your calling card and PIN, contact your service provider immediately to cancel the account or calling card. Open new accounts and choose new PINs.

If you are having trouble getting fraudulent phone charges removed from your account, contact your state Public Utility Commission for local service providers or the Federal Communications Commission for long-distance service providers and cellular providers at *www.fcc.gov/ccb/enforce/complaints .html* or 1-888-CALL-FCC.

Employment

If you believe someone is using your Social Security number to apply for a job or to work, that's a crime. Report it to the Social Security Administrations Fraud Hotline at 1-800-269-0271. Also call them at 1-800-772-1213 to verify the accuracy of the earnings reported on your Social Security number, and to request a copy of your Social Security statement. Follow up on your calls in writing.

Should You Apply for a New Social Security Number?   Under certain circumstances, the Social Security Administration may issue you a new Social Security number (at your request) if, after trying to resolve the problems brought on by identity theft, you continue to experience problems. Consider this option carefully. A new number might not resolve your identity theft problems, and could actually create new problems. For example, a new Social Security number does not necessarily ensure a new credit record because credit bureaus might combine the credit records from your old Social Security number with those from your new one. Even when the old credit information is not associated with your new number, the absence of any credit history under your new Social Security number might make it more difficult for you to get credit. Finally, there's no guarantee that a new number wouldn't also be misused by an identity thief.

Driver's License

If you suspect that your name or Social Security number is being used by an identity thief to get a driver's license or a nondriver's ID card, contact your DMV. If your state uses your Social Security number as your driver's license number, ask to substitute another number.

Bankruptcy

If you believe someone has filed for bankruptcy using your name, write to the U.S. Trustee in the region where the bankruptcy was filed. A listing of the U.S. Trustee Program's regions can be found at *www.usdoj.gov/ust*, or look in the blue pages of your phone book under U.S. Government—Bankruptcy Administration.

Your letter should describe the situation and provide proof of your identity. The U.S. Trustee, if appropriate, will make a referral to criminal law enforcement authorities if you provide appropriate documentation to substantiate your claim. You also might want to file a complaint with the U.S. Attorney or the FBI in the city where the bankruptcy was filed.

Criminal Records and Arrests

In rare instances, an identity thief might create a criminal record under your name. For example, your imposter might give your name when being arrested. If this happens to you, you might need to hire an attorney to help resolve the problem. The procedures for clearing your name vary by jurisdiction.

When All Else Fails, Sue!

Finally, if the ID theft recovery procedures fail to resolve the problem, you should just sue! Call a lawyer. Credit issuers and reporting agencies are sometimes slow in responding to complaints from consumers. The threat of lawsuits can provide some incentive.

David Szwak barely had finished taking his bar exam back in 1997 when a law firm secretary presented him with a nightmare scenario. Creditors and bill collectors were mercilessly harassing her parents, trying to collect $230,000 in bills run up by a credit identity thief.

A used-car salesman had stolen the couple's credit report by gaining computer access to the credit reporting agencies through his car dealership. The crook picked this couple because he had the same last name. He also collected the credit reports of other folks with the same name.

The thief then obtained a post office box and began filling out credit card applications. Among his purchases was a mobile home, delivered to a trailer park lot. In attempting to locate the thief, the creditors came across the secretary's parents instead.

No Remedy to Clear a Name

The couple brought Szwak a box full of documents, including letters they had sent to lawmakers, credit reporting agencies, and creditors. They were trying to get this remedied and it wasn't working.

Szwak began writing his own letters to creditors on behalf of the couple, but he also was ignored. So he filed suit against the creditors and credit reporting agencies, 16 in all, in Jonesboro, Arkansas, federal court.

A very short time later, once the credit reporting agencies had a full understanding of what they had been doing, they settled the case for an enormous amount of money. Incidentally, the thief also was convicted of mail fraud and sentenced to two years of house arrest with electronic surveillance.

Once the news media reported the case, other identity theft victims, including small business owners, scientists, military officers, and even a CIA agent, began to contact Szwak, and a career was launched. He has handled hundreds of identity theft cases, typically involving tens of thousands, and sometimes hundreds of thousands, of dollars.

Attorneys have been able to bring a number of these cases to court and get the victims' credit straightened out. These are people who pay their bills and people who work, who are the targets of other people who don't pay their bills.

System Works Most of the Time

The Washington, DC-based Associated Credit Bureaus, a trade association of the three large credit reporting companies, has procedures to help consumers purge their credit reports of fraudulent information. The credit reporting industry issues 800 million credit reports a year on about 210 million Americans who have credit records. The system works the vast majority of the time, and the American public is enamored with the use of credit and access to credit right now.

There are a lot of parts to this process. It is unfair to lay the blame solely with the credit agencies. What about law enforcement, the creditors, and consumers? We all have to be part of the solution. Most of us are no fans of credit bureaus or the credit industry. Easy credit and the lax checking procedures of stores and credit card companies that make identity theft a relatively easy crime to commit should be denounced. These people are absolutely rabid to give out credit. There are trillions of dollars in consumer debt out there and it is out of control.

The credit reporting agencies are even worse. If you ever try to work out an error with the credit bureau, they will tell you that regardless of what the law is, they will take the side of the subscriber (the provider of credit, such as a store or car dealer, who subscribes to their service) 100% of the time.

If You Can't Resolve a Problem

If the preceding happens to you, you need to keep impeccable written records, including letters and telephone logs, of your communications with credit bureaus and creditors in your effort to clear up your credit report. If you are unable to resolve the situation satisfactorily, or if you are unable or unwilling to keep detailed records, you should contact a lawyer.

File a suit if your credit is not cleaned up. That will usually get the attention of both the creditors and the credit agencies. If you have a good case, the result will be the correction of your credit report and a monetary settlement.

Identity theft today can be considered financial terrorism. The victims are nice people who are legitimately damaged. They want to straighten out the mess and get on with their lives.

Endnotes

[1] Federal Trade Commission, 600 Pennsylvania Ave., NW, Washington, DC 20580, 2001.

Identity Theft Protection on the Internet

Chapter 4

IDENTITY THEFT ON THE INTERNET

This chapter is not for the faint of heart. Those who would rather ignore the dark side of the Internet might be well advised to stop reading, pack a bag, and disappear into the Australian outback. As previously explained, identity theft is a crime where one person masquerades under the identity of another. This does not involve just the stealing of a credit card number, theft of a check, or the fabrication of false documents. This is also not an act that is limited only to the age of technology, even though identity theft was not considered a crime in and of itself until 1998. Prior to that, the theft of an identity was considered to be a tool used in the commission of some other crime. However, improvements in computing and telecommunication technologies in the late 1990s fueled a resurgence of identity thefts, allowing criminals to hide more efficiently.

In the past, a criminal would have to appear at a bank or lending institution to apply for an account, increasing the risk of being captured. However with instant credit accounts on the Internet, the likelihood of a criminal being captured is greatly reduced and the immediate rewards for an identity thief increased as well. A smart crook working on the Internet might turn a tax-free gain of as much as $70,000 per week. Compare this to the bank robber who passes a note to a teller and, if he or she is lucky, walks off with $1,200. The media plays up the crime of bank robbery and the criminal is hunted, prosecuted as a menace to society, convicted, and put away for years. The identity thief, on the other hand, committed only fraud, a white-collar crime if and when he or she is captured. The fraudster will use his or her victim's funds to pay for defense, and might serve less than one year (if at all) in prison.

In January 2001, the U.S. Fair Trade Commission estimated approximately 32,000 identities were stolen via the Internet, a sobering statistic. With that in mind, this chapter covers the characteristics of Internet identity theft, common methods of prevention and detection, the role of privacy and security policies in the private sector, and public policy on this topic.

Although the cases and legal policy discussions presented in this chapter describe the situation in the United States, the subject and occurrence of Internet identity theft is a global issue. E-businesses, consumers, policymakers, and law enforcement agencies need to be aware of the threat and understand how to prevent, detect, and respond to this crime.

Understanding Internet Identity Theft

On the Internet, an ID thief remains hidden from detection as a virtual entity on a public network. In other words, the technology of the Internet allows the suspect to move quickly, opening new accounts, striking merchant sites with rapid attacks, creating new victims in the number of merchants and volume of transactions that can be posted, and then disappearing into another identity. In this part of the chapter, let's take a look at some of the common factors related to stealing and using identities on the Internet.

Identities Are Stolen to Commit Other Crimes

In all cases, the theft of an identity is done to commit some other form of crime. The criminal might commit fraud, sell the identities to others who commit fraud, generate new illegal forms of personal identity (like a birth certificate, driver's license, or even a passport), use the identity to acquire new access points to the Internet, and more.

The Victim Doesn't Know

When it is done over the Internet, the victim of an identity theft might not even know how or when their identity was stolen. Until the suspect trips over some systemic control (as in the case of a velocity check) or bill collectors locate and contact the victim, the crime remains concealed (see the sidebar, "Fatal Attraction Victim").

Fatal Attraction Victim

Sometimes (fortunately, not often) the results of such invasions of privacy can be fatal. In October 1999, Amy Boyer, a 20-year-old college senior in Nashua, New Hampshire, was killed by a stalker who had been obsessed with her since the 10th grade.

Liam Youens had tracked her to her workplace using an Internet service, which, for less than $150, gave him all the information he needed to find and kill her. "It's actually obsene [sic] what you can find out about a person on the internet," Youens wrote on his Web page just before the shooting.

Note: For more, see *www.amyboyer.org*.

Reacting to Amy's death, Representative Ed Markey and Senator Dianne Feinstein immediately drafted a law intended to restrict the trade in citizens' Social Security numbers and similar personal information. But, after lobbying by credit reporting agencies, direct marketing firms, banks, and other large corporations, the Amy Boyer Law was so distorted by amendments that it facilitated rather than prevented identity theft. Privacy advocates who formerly advocated the law scrambled madly to ensure that it was voted down.

Although the problem of identity theft transcends the Internet, ISPs can and should recognize the problem and help their users to protect themselves. Chapter 5, "Prevention Methods for Internet Site Operators," discusses some specific measures ISPs can take to help forestall identity theft.

Greed Drives Identity Theft

In any fraud, there can be many victims, but the fraudster plays to the greed of someone or some entity. This part of the chapter introduces types of associated crimes, like account takeover and account creation.

Account creation preys on the greed and willingness of the bank or merchant to issue an instant account. All too often, these entities understand the potential risk and will quickly write off losses when faced with a nonpaying customer. For example, in the case of Lt. Col. Jones (see the sidebar, "Internet Identity Theft Case of Lt. Col. Jones"), the lender even restored the identity and increased the credit line after apparently being notified by the suspect of a change of billing address. After three more months, the account was again closed and written off.

Internet Identity Theft Case of Lt. Col. Jones

In October 2001, a list of current and retired command officers in the U.S. armed services was posted on a public Web site. The posting was based on a publicly available document from the U.S. Congressional Record. For over the last 25 years, the U.S. military has used the Social Security number as the *serial* number for soldiers, sailors, and marines.

The clever criminal takes a copy of the list, goes to several other Web sites and applies for online credit, both at stores offering instant credit and those offering major brand instant revolving online accounts, like issuing an instant Visa account. One of the identities from the list is that of Retired Lt. Colonel James Jones, who still lives in Baltimore, Maryland.

At some point in time, the criminal had to arrange addresses to receive the stolen funds and goods. It's believed that he used addresses from private mailboxes located throughout the Northeastern United States. According to Lt. Col. Jones, the suspect ran up charges for products including numerous computer systems, consumer electronics, and video game equipment. The suspect also took cash advances on the accounts. All transactions were placed over the Internet.

After the suspect attempted to make another cash advance, the bank decided to try and contact Lt. Col. Jones. In this situation, the account had been opened with a bogus address and phone number. On discovery, the bank ran a credit report on the Social Security number and located another phone number for Jones, at which time they contacted him. Lt. Col. Jones ran a credit report on himself and discovered that the suspect had run up over $70,000 of charges using the stolen identity. Jones contacted law enforcement authorities in Baltimore, who subsequently contacted the U.S. Secret Service.

At this time, the suspect has not been located and continues to open new charge accounts online. During this period, numerous lenders have written off this bad debt, foregoing traditional collection agencies and sending negative reports to the credit bureaus. These actions have served to destroy the reputation and creditworthiness of Lt. Col. Jones and his wife. They have been denied credit, been told that they could only purchase a car with cash, and invested constant agonizing hours of work to clear their report.

Analysis of Case

The identifying information, specifically the Social Security number, was acquired by a criminal from a document published on the public Internet.

This document was a part of the U.S. Congressional record in the public domain. Beyond the fact that there is little reason for the complete Social Security number to be included in the record, this is a publicly available document.

Commercial Issues: General Business Practice Issues

There are a few issues of interest in this case:

1. Instant credit was approved for the presenter of the identity. Even though the credit line was small, it suggests that online verification of presented information might not be sufficiently strong to verify the identity presented. Some online verification of information beyond the presence of a Social Security number is needed.

2. Follow up credit verification needs to take into account physical address information as well as all credit bureau header information. If the information seems inconsistent with other data (especially if there are other active credit accounts where the address has not changed), this should raise suspicions.

3. Use of Internet predictive variables to assist in identification and credit scoring is important. If the same set of Internet environment values have opened other accounts using other names, this should highlight a potential problem.

4. Follow up with the applicant via telephone call and verify that the telephone number presented is consistent with addresses and Internet environment variables.

Note: As you know, there are different types of models and procedures to determine if the person using a credit card on the Internet is the same person that the card has been issued to, and whether an Internet order from an e-commerce site will be filled using that particular credit card. *Internet predictive variables* are built-in factors (in the e-commerce site) of an e-commerce order that can predict whether the credit card used in the order is valid. If the credit card does not meet certain predictive criteria, the order will be flagged for human review. In other words, if a credit order came into the U.S. Calvary e-commerce site from Turkmenistan (a former Soviet republic) for 100 AR-15 fully automatic weapons, red flags and alarms would go off all over the place. Based on the predictive built-in factors for that e-commerce site, you would be alerted that you should not fill that order because it would violate the State Department's munitions ban on the sale of firearms to a foreign nation. Furthermore, there would also be a 99.9% probability that the credit card number used to make the purchase was stolen and that the person making the order had assumed someone else's identity.

Commercial Issues: Issues Related to Privacy

No apparent business-to-consumer privacy issues are present in this case.

Commercial Issues: Issues Related to Security

No apparent security issues or breaches of security are apparent in this case.

Commercial Issues: Issues Related to Databases

Do database systems used to evaluate credit applications store sufficient information about Internet predictive variables and their historical use to help identify potential problems? If such a system and information for a system is not readily available, this sort of service can be sourced from an Internet fraud detection company. This type of information needs to be used at both the credit issuance and shopping transactions to detect a potential problem.

Commercial Issues: Issues Related to Use of Stolen Identity

The Web site where the identity was presented to issue the online credit account (in the case of Lt. Col. Jones, a revolving credit card account) should have performed a detailed analysis of the presented identity and scored the information presented along with prior transactional information, credit bureau information, specific geographic information, and Internet predictive variables. Had a system been employed that generated a risk score based on the information presented, data from static databases (like a credit bureau) and data about the Internet connection, the system may have detected (a) the address change, in that the new billing address did not match any preexisting information; (b) a potential mismatch of the address in a situation that the billing address in the credit bureau record was being used to post existing payments; (c) possible Internet velocity issues; and (d) identity changes related to the Internet environment data.

Public Policy Issues: Issues Related to Privacy

The republication of private information, even though that private information might exist in the public domain and be readily accessible, might be considered unethical. The entity that republished the congressional record was committing no crime as the content was in the public domain. The problem was that private information was republished in an efficient medium where hackers and legitimate browsers could acquire the data. Jones' Social Security number should have been masked from the document. The same privacy standards and practices required of U.S. businesses need to be extended to Government entities as well.

Public Policy Issues: Issues Related to Security

The protection of Social Security data, even though this is listed as a military serial number, must be implemented. This information should be masked, or can even be represented as a hashed value. A hashed value is the use of a computer algorithm to one-way encrypt (scramble) a data value so that the resulting value is unique, yet unrecoverable. In essence, this would have created a surrogate value for a Social Security number that could not be recognized by any credit issuing company.

Public Policy Issues: Issues Related to Response

It is unclear what response the involved government agencies will take to ensure this type of security breach will not occur in the future. [1]

For example, in the case of account takeover (not described in the preceding and upcoming cases, but a form of identity theft), the greed or desire of a merchant or another person to close a business transaction drives the fraud. This might include an e-business that is willing to risk fraud for the sake of increasing sales revenue, or an e-business that has a large backlog of products to sell and is offering bargain-basement pricing to move the goods.

Another form of greed is the lender's failure to run complete credit checks before issuing a new account. The instant credit accounts issued on the Internet are completed and set up in a few minutes. Given the speed with which *instant* credit is approved, it is clearly not possible that a complete review of a credit file could have taken place. One can only surmise the lender's intense desire to open new accounts contributes to this problem.

Authentic Bogus Addresses

In each account creation case, the billing address was a valid address and serviced by the U.S. Postal Service, it just wasn't the address of the suspect. In some cases, the address was a private mail service or mail forwarding address. Goods and services that had to be shipped were sent to the same address as listed in the billing address. The use of large, upscale hotel addresses is also common.

Types of Associated Internet Identity Theft Crimes

There are several types of crimes associated with Internet identity theft. These are some of the more common ones:

- New account creation
- Account takeover
- Fraudulent transactions

New Account Creation

New account creation involves stealing sufficient identifying information about an individual to open new credit accounts. The information needed to create new accounts can be gathered from a variety of sources including trash bins, legitimate files, or even public records (as in the case of Lt. Col. Jones).

Account Takeover

Account takeover involves assuming the identity from a single account and using the account to make purchases. The theft of the account information can be accomplished in many forms. In some cases, a criminal needing to increase his or her stock of cases might even use a prior stolen identity to help steal more. Some of the common tools and venues are covered in the following sections.

Social Engineering

The new term *link capture* describes the tool and method for using chat room information. In this case, the criminal makes a posting that includes a hot link to a site that is outside the domain of the chat room. This site is actually a Web page where the victim is asked to enter information on a form. The look and feel of the page might mimic the original chat room or a service screen exactly. However, in reality, the graphic content of the page will have been stolen from the site and reproduced to look the same.

Site Cloning

Site cloning is a variant of the chat room method where a merchant Web site will have been cloned and will mimic the completion of a e-commerce purchase transaction, including the response of an email receipt. The only problem is that the product will never arrive.

False Merchant Site

The false merchant site is another variant on the link capture. In this situation, the suspect is running a merchant site, usually an adult site, that accepts credit cards for access or even accepts credit cards as proof of age. In all of these cases, the consumer's actual account is never charged (at least not on this site). Once the identities are gathered, the suspect makes purchases on real merchant sites, or acquires cash advances on the accounts by possibly using the identities on an Internet casino site.

Hacking and Cracking

Hacking and cracking into a merchant database with the intent of stealing credit card accounts is another problem. This is probably the least common form of account takeover on the Internet, because it requires specific technical skills to perform from the outside. The theft of account data from inside an e-business is more likely and would have the same impact.

There are several other situations that can lead to account takeover, including trash bin diving, stealing account information from telephone services, and removal of credit card data from fax machines, to name a few.

Fraudulent Transactions

On the Internet, fraudulent transactions are the most common crime committed with stolen identities. Whether a credit card account has been taken over or a stolen identity was used to create a new credit account, these accounts are used to attack e-businesses.

In essence, a fraudulent transaction involves an individual filling out an order form as though they were someone else, the merchant accepting the order, and the shipment of goods or services that the suspect can receive. One key difference from a traditional in-store fraud is that the criminal can "hit" a lot of different merchants and do a lot of damage very fast in the virtual world of the Internet. The suspect doesn't have to drive between merchants, doesn't have to risk being identified by a sales clerk, doesn't have to be videotaped by surveillance cameras, and doesn't have to speak to a telephone operator to commit the crime.

Compared to robbing a liquor store, this form of fraud is nearly perfect. The chance of capture is small and the crime is considered a nonviolent, white-collar economic crime. Although fraud is a crime, the perception of it is significantly different than the image of some bad guy poking a gun in the nose of a store clerk. Needless to say, unless the loss is significant, one probably won't see identity crimes featured on the nightly news.

Role of Privacy And Security Policies

Privacy and security policies are important steps in protecting consumers from fraud. E-businesses should have both privacy and security policies to ensure that there are clear rules to which the company and its employees adhere and that consumers understand the operations of a company with which they choose to do business.

Developing a good privacy policy helps an e-business examine and analyze its own information practices. Many times, e-businesses find that in the process of writing and implementing a privacy policy, they might be able to change how the firm collects data, what data is collected, how data is stored or used, and where consumer choices can be introduced. By taking a comprehensive approach to writing a privacy policy, e-businesses are forced to examine their own practices and, in the process, might modify their current practices to be more consumer-friendly. The result is generally a raised awareness within an e-business about consumer privacy concerns, a greater sensitivity to consumer preferences about personal data, and greater attention to the security of personally identifiable data. For ISPs, there is the additional benefit of improved consumer perceptions as e-businesses work with their customers to identify their consumers' concerns and preferences about privacy.

For consumers, the benefit is a greater sense of trust and security when doing business online or providing personally identifiable information to Web sites. Individuals are far more likely to share information if they are confident that an ISP respects their preferences, allows them to make some choices about how their personal information is shared, and gives them the opportunity at any point to opt out of further data collection or use.

Governments also benefit from widespread use of privacy policies. Self-regulation is an effective mechanism in protecting privacy of online consumers when combined with a strong, effective, and clear underlying legal structure. By adopting the approach that the United States. has to date pursued, governments do not have to be concerned that outdated privacy laws will retard the growth of electronic commerce and they are still able to protect the privacy of their online consumers. The market is a powerful force, and as consumers begin to express their preferences toward data usage, businesses quickly comply. Those that do not, or those that betray their consumers' trust, will quickly be put out of business in a dynamic and interactive environment like the Internet.

Privacy Policy: Role

A privacy policy should accomplish three things: explain an ISP's information practices; identify choices that a consumer has in how his or her data is collected, used, or shared; and establish a mechanism for receiving, investigating, and resolving complaints.

Privacy Policy: Typical Example

Some privacy policies are very simple and some are far more complex. Policies vary widely among ISPs, and privacy policies reflect that differentiation. Visit *www.siia.net/govt/toolkit.asp* or *www.truste.com* for examples of privacy policies and more information.

Privacy Policy: Responsibilities

ISPs have a responsibility to develop a privacy policy that fully discloses their information practices, communicate these practices, in easy-to-understand language to consumers, and clearly identify what choices a consumer can make about the use of his or her information. ISPs also have an obligation to fully implement their privacy policies and ensure that employees fully understand the policy and to work with a third-party group to ensure compliance.

Consumers have a responsibility to look for privacy policies when online. Whether an individual is shopping or just browsing, everyone should read privacy policies and think carefully before sharing any information online with any site. If customers are not comfortable with the privacy policy of a given site, they should conduct their business elsewhere.

Security Policy: Role Technologies and Applications

The role of a security policy is to ensure that an ISP has established procedures that govern how it secures any sensitive or personal information it might collect. Although ISPs might have a comprehensive approach to security without such a policy, a security policy is an excellent addition to any ISP's operating procedures. Such an approach provides direction to staff, underscores the ISP's commitment to solid security practices, and reassures consumers.

A security policy should also identify for an ISP what types of data will be protected and in what manner. For example, will network access be protected only by password? Will all email be encrypted or only messages marked confidential? Will access to sensitive data be available to remote users? The development of such a policy will help an ISP identify its core assets, identify what types of data must be protected and in what manner, as well as which technologies and standards will be deployed throughout the site. The following is a list of technologies that can be used in the security of data:

- Cryptography.
- Certification and authentication.
- Single-sign on technologies and their role in monitoring network assets access. In other words, a single sign-on is designed with the mobile employee in mind. Users want a consistent authentication method regardless of their location and regardless of whether they have network connectivity.
- Human or individual authentication technology.
- Biometric technologies.
- Anonymity tools. [1]

Security Policy: Responsibilities

ISPs have a responsibility to develop a security policy that is comprehensive, takes into account all of the types of data stored and access allowed to its network, and leverages technology effectively to protect its assets. The ISP is also responsible for fully implementing the access policy that fully discloses their information practices, communicates these practices in easy-to-understand language to consumers, and clearly identifies the choices a consumer can make about the use of his or her information. E-businesses have an obligation to fully implement their security policies and ensure that employees fully understand the policy and to work with a third-party group to ensure compliance.

Response to a Breach

E-businesses and ISPs need to have clear policies about what to do in cases of a breach. In many cases, what an e-business or ISP does in the time immediately following a breach is critically important. E-businesses and ISPs must make sure that they not only shut down future attacks, but also that they do not destroy any evidence that could potentially help identify the source of the breach. E-businesses and ISPs that have experienced a disclosure of personal information might be under some obligation to notify their customers.

Government Action and Public Policy

This part of the chapter describes current public policy and possible areas for future attention.

Privacy Legislation

Currently, there is a wide range of privacy legislation pending in Congress. Some of this legislation would be quite restrictive when compared to current practices; other efforts are more targeted at particular types of information. It is unclear whether Congress will step in to regulate customer data any time soon, especially given the recent conclusion of safe harbor agreements with the European Union (EU).

Review of Current Public Information

There is a wide variety of information available to the public. This information can be categorized into three different areas:

1. *Public records* include the numerous records, files, databases, indexes, and other data maintained by local, state, and the federal government. These records, which are generally open for public inspection, include driver's license information, real estate records, business records, some professional certifications and licensing data, and other types of data collected by an official entity.

2. *Publicly available information* includes data that is available to the general public through nongovernment entities, such as phone books, classified ads, and newspaper reports.

3. *Open-source information* is a term that covers a wide variety of information that is generally available to the public, including newspaper archives, magazines, and other periodicals. [1]

Currently, Congress is considering limiting the amount of information that it collects from individuals, especially in the area of driver's licenses and vehicle information.

Review of Current Policies

Currently, there are few laws that govern the use of personally identifiable information. Whereas medical, financial, credit, and academic records are generally well-protected by statute and can only be released with the permission of the data subject, other data (including Social Security numbers, home addresses, and other personal information) are not so restricted. Given the rise in identify theft crimes in recent years, Congress is considering whether new legislation is necessary to directly address this growing problem. There are numerous bills currently pending that make identity theft a crime. Although it is unlikely that any of these bills will pass soon, their introduction has opened the discussion in Congress about the best way to combat identify theft.

Safe Harbor: Complete Existing Work

The safe harbor negotiations with the EU seem to have reached a successful conclusion. The Department of Commerce hopes to sign formal letters with the EU soon. Under the safe harbor provisions, U.S. companies will be required to provide notice, disclosure, choice, and access to customer information, in addition to a number of specific provisions for particular industries (e.g., head hunters, financial data, and others). E-businesses and ISPs will be required to self-certify annually that they are in compliance with the provisions of the safe harbor. A master list of e-businesses and ISPs that have self-certified will be maintained by the Department of Commerce, but they will not *verify* compliance. E-businesses and ISPs that are found to have violated the safe harbor process are subject to U.S. enforcement and could have their data flows from the EU suspended.

With regard to extradition and prosecution, the safe harbor negotiations with the EU have some unfinished business. They need to establish provisions for the following:

- Prosecution and extradition of individuals discovered using the identity of another.
- Criminal prosecution and extradition of individuals discovered in possession of multiple identities.
- Whereby the U.S. entity or any foreign entity in a member country will permit the civil prosecution of company found to have mishandled or failed to correctly store private information. [1]

Endnotes

[1] Tom Arnold, "Internet Identity Theft: A Tragedy For Victims," Cyber-Source Corporation, 1295 Charleston Rd., Mountain View, CA 94043 (The Software & Information Industry Association, 1730 M St. NW, Suite 700 Washington, DC 20036-4510), USA, 2002.

Chapter 5

PREVENTION METHODS FOR INTERNET SITE OPERATORS

I dentity theft is not particular to the Internet. It was around before the Internet and even now does not necessarily involve the Internet. It can be as simple as a waiter stealing your credit card number at dinner. What is different is the new ease of access that the Internet brings to your personal information. One Web site can help someone find your address and phone number; and another reveals your date of birth.

In other words, online networks enhance the opportunity of bad guys (e.g., criminals or terrorists) to quickly and efficiently aggregate the personal data of individuals, steal their identities, and cause havoc. Internet companies, including ISPs, ASPs and Web sites, are at the center of this issue, gathering large amounts of personal information and maintaining it on servers sitting on their networks like ducks—targets for the would-be bad guys. This chapter shows an ISP what to tell subscribers who have become victims, how to prevent identity theft, and what actions Internet companies should take to mitigate the risk of theft or improper release of the personal data they hold.

Inadequate Protection

A poorly designed government site, for example, such as a DMV site, can reveal a bit more personal information about you than it should. Before long, someone has developed a full and accurate profile of you. As an individual, you might be concerned with what personal information is available about you online. As an ISP or Internet network, you should be concerned with how you secure your confidential customer data and what to say to your subscribers if they fall victim to such a situation (see the sidebar "Prevention Methods for ISPs").

Prevention Methods for ISPs

The following are identity theft prevention methods for ISPs:

1. Limit the access to your customers' information within your organization.

2. Practice due diligence to ensure those who do have access are trustworthy (perform background checks).

3. Make sure your online transaction forms are as secure as you can make them.

4. Have one member of your staff, your privacy officer, responsible for your customers' data.

5. Educate your customers about the possible dangers of giving out personal information and make sure your staff is ready to help in the event that customers are victims of such an attack.

6. Know the law. When federal authorities come knocking, it will be helpful for you to know exactly what to give them and why.

Imagine a retail business that is open 24 hours a day but only has a staff for daytime hours, hires known shoplifters to work as clerks (comparable to airlines hiring criminals to check baggage), and leaves the day's cash receipts in an unlocked drawer. Absurd, you say? Perhaps, but that's how many e-commerce consumer-oriented Web sites are run today.

Believe it or not, there are people still sending credit card numbers and transactions in the clear over the Internet. You might as well be shouting out your credit card number in a railroad station. For example, many banking sites are still not encrypting their online applications.

In other words, ISPs and e-commerce solutions providers are not providing adequate identity theft and fraud protection for their customers. The biggest risks (to themselves, that is) are companies that try to build their own secure servers on their premises. This is a very bad move. The last thing a company should do is develop its own e-commerce site. It's like setting up an e-commerce site in your home office and being your own doctor.

Identity Theft Is Easy

Today hundreds of databases contain detailed information about your personal life, buying habits and other lifestyle characteristics. Various companies offer services that provide address, criminal, civil, and professional histories, as well as a list of assets and bank account numbers. Also available are your Social Security number, last six addresses, current phone number and names and phone numbers of neighbors. Some large, prestigious companies offering such information include Lexis-Nexis and West Publishing Company. Many smaller companies also provide similar services.

It's Quick

Identity theft is getting easier and faster. Today, you can steal someone's wallet or purse—or just find the right database on the Internet. This information is available in minutes with only a few mouse clicks. For example, there is an economical product known as Net Detective (*affiliates.jeanharris.com/cgi-bin/clickthru.cgi?pid=ND&sid=gobob&tid=ND*) that can quickly uncover detailed personal information.

Another investigative resource is Cyber-Detective Investigative Software (*www.ipsarion.com/*). This toolkit provides you with a complete how-to guide, a large selection of tools, and even databases that will aid you in just about any type of informational investigation. Not only does the kit provide you with sources and tools that are useful in gathering information on others, but it also provides you with an organized guide to what each source can provide and where it's located.

Create Your Own Identification

Nearly any document can be created if the content and form is known. You might be interested in visiting some sites that can rapidly produce IDs that can allow criminals to establish fraudulent credit accounts in your name. Although these sites advertise their document replicas as being for entertainment purposes only, these documents look real enough to be used for more nefarious purposes. Simply visit these sites:

- Fake-ID.org (*www.fake-id.org*).
- Fake ID.net (*www.fakeid.net/*)
- Photo ID Cards (*www.photoidcards.com/*).
- Fake IDs from Anarchy Underground (*www.silvatek.com/anarchywarez/fakeids.html*).
- ID SOFTWARE (*www.idsoftware.net/*).

The documents typically used to gather information to construct a fraudulent identity include the following:

- Social Security card
- Driver's license
- Credit cards or bank statements
- Telephone calling cards
- Birth certificates
- Passports

Battening Down The Hatches

ISPs have an important role (but not the only one) in preventing identity theft. If your systems are insecure (or if your customers' systems are) an intruder can break in and monitor traffic.

Inexperienced online businesses still use unencrypted sessions for orders including credit card data. Encryption does little good if a machine at either end can be compromised. This often happens because administrators fail to apply security patches in a timely way. However, if an operating system needs patching very often, it's time to switch before your administrators simply miss one.

Caution

It was probably this sort of hole that allowed a 19-year-old Welsh cracker to order large quantities of Viagra on Bill Gates's credit card—and have them delivered to the Microsoft CEO's home. Crackers' automatic vulnerability scans are quite efficient and will find holes you didn't patch.

Systems like Microsoft Passport, that aggregate all of your personal information and account information in one place are especially dangerous—not only because Microsoft systems are not known for their security, but because one breach will compromise all of your sensitive data at once. ISPs cannot prevent consumers from accessing insecure Web forms or from putting all of their eggs in one flimsy basket, but they can warn them about the potential consequences.

Not Just ISPs

Unfortunately, even if ISPs do everything they can, identity theft is still possible. The so-called Driver's Privacy Protection Act (which really should have been called the Driver's Privacy Prevention Act) requires your state to give personal information to virtually anyone who doesn't claim to be a marketer.

Tip

For further information, see www.networkusa.org/fingerprint/page1b/fp-dmv-records-18-usc-123.html. *Remember, URLs can change without notice.*

Another law, purporting to catch deadbeat parents, requires these records to contain your Social Security number. States' open records laws often require documents containing sensitive personal information to be available to the public. Need someone's Social Security number? Go to the courthouse—it's probably there.

Tip

For further information, see: www4.law.cornell.edu/uscode/42/666.html.

However, laws allowing consumers to clear their names are lax and allow for long delays. Unless voters overcome pressure from corporate lobbyists, data mongers and identity thieves will continue to have a picnic at citizens' expense.

Ironically, the danger of identity theft reaches even beyond the grave. Remember the sad story of Amy Boyer, the young woman who was killed after being tracked by a stalker using the Internet to find her? Just before she died, Amy lost her purse during an evening out. Six months after her murder, her grieving family was alarmed to discover credit charges being run up in her name. Even death had not saved her from the ravages of identity theft.

Online Identity Theft and Fraud Prevention

Online identity theft and fraud prevention are simply too complex. First, there's the physical security of the server in question. Putting a padlock on a door simply won't do. Then there's logical security—can a user with legitimate access to user account information gain unauthorized access to credit card numbers? There's also the question of network security, exposing valuable business information over the Internet. Also, hiring known hackers as security consultants (as many companies have done) is hardly the way to inspire confidence among customers and business partners. Unless you have studied security, you are not qualified. There are many different areas of security—cryptography, access control, risk management, and more—all of which require special skill sets.

Finally, there's the anonymous nature of the Internet itself. You don't have any trust in who you are dealing with. The Internet is fraught with people masquerading as someone who they are not.

If that isn't enough to scare you away from building your own e-commerce site, consider the Computer Security Institute/FBI 2000 Computer Crime and Security Survey. Although network security breaches are notoriously underreported, the survey found that losses from computer crime totaled $200 million for the fourth straight year. Twenty percent of survey respondents had detected unauthorized access or misuse of Web sites within the last 12 months—although 33% answered "don't know." Before you calculate how much money you're going to make from e-commerce sales, first figure out how much you can afford to lose. As a rule of thumb is, if you lost two days' worth of average daily sales volume, would that be a major impact on your company? There is opportunity in e-commerce, but there is also risk. Making an appropriate risk assessment is one of the most important things you can do.

At risk aren't just the goods and services of a company, but the credit card numbers of customers as well. Once a company goes online, it has an obligation not only to protect transactions, but the credit card information itself. Most often, the vendor, not the ISP, is responsible, unless there is a contract in place that says otherwise.

The first thing a business should inquire of an ISP or e-commerce solution provider is how the company handles credit card validation. The most popular method in the U.S. is to encrypt a credit card number (via Secure Sockets Layer [SSL]) and pass it along to a credit card authorization agency. If it is valid, the agency passes it back to the buyer to complete the transaction. All that happens by virtue of the ISP, the seller is not involved until after validation.

Nevertheless, preventing theft of credit card information and goods and services is only the beginning of e-commerce security. You also have to be able to fend off virus attacks. Many ISPs only have mirrored disks (delayed mirroring). However, if a virus hits disk A, it will also hit disk B. What an ISP really needs is offline (and off-site) backups. Delayed mirroring is a more advanced technique to do something similar, but the baseline is definitely offline backups. If the media is online, then it is at risk for tampering.

Tip

Delayed mirroring can also be used if you don't have another solution that is quickly available. It allows an ISP to determine that malicious code has entered, and restore the disk to where it was before the malicious code was there. However, this is difficult to do and if an ISP does it for you, they aren't going to be charging $19.95.

At the other extreme, less expensive ISPs and e-commerce hosting services (see the sidebar, "ISP Hosting Services") may offer bargains that put your business at risk. One of the most serious problems is that smaller ISPs and independent service providers don't understand security from a financial and electronic fraud standpoint. There is a difference between someone who hacks into your mail server and someone who is out to steal credit card information. Many ISPs keep their Web site outside their firewall—something that's an automatic disqualifier.

ISP Hosting Services

If you are trying to figure out how to securely host your Web site, you might be overwhelmed by all of the options and service plans available. To help you, let's look at the three basic types of site hosting services offered by

Web hosts and ISPs (shared, dedicated, and colocated), as well as the key security implications of each. An estimate of costs for each choice is provided; however, you should note that these can vary widely, depending on the e-commerce features and storage space you require.

Shared Hosting

With shared hosting, you rent space on a server you share with other organizations' Web sites:

- **Cost:** $15–$300 per month
- **Best for:** Businesses that are new to the Web or sites that won't have a lot of traffic.
- **Advantages:** Shared hosting is the cheapest and quickest way to launch a fully functional Web site. In addition, some ISPs offer special e-commerce packages, where basic shared hosting is bundled with extra features, such as shopping cart software, credit card processing, or merchant Internet accounts.
- **Disadvantages:** Shared hosting is the least reliable choice in terms of site stability. With shared hosting, your site can slow down or even shut down if another site on your server has a surge in activity.
- **Security Features:** Shared hosting packages almost always include SSL encryption, which encrypts data that's transferred over the Internet.

ISPs will sometimes add intrusion detection systems, which are used to detect intruders breaking into your system or any legitimate users misusing system resources. In addition, ISPs might also offer free Secure Shell login (SSH). SSH is a program to log into another computer over a network, to execute commands in a remote machine, and to move files from one machine to another. It provides strong authentication and secure communications over insecure channels. It is a replacement for telnet, rlogin, rsh, rcp, and rdist.

SSH protects a network from attacks such as sniffing, Internet Protocol (IP) spoofing, IP source routing, and Domain Name System (DNS) spoofing. An attacker who has managed to take over a network can only force SSH to disconnect. He or she cannot play back the traffic or hijack the connection when encryption is enabled.

When using SSH's slogin (instead of rlogin), the entire login session, including transmission of password, is encrypted; therefore it is almost impossible for an outsider to collect passwords. SSH is available for Windows, UNIX, Macintosh, and OS/2, and it also works with Rivest, Shamin and Adelman (RSA) authentication. However, even with these tools, you should be aware that everyone who shares your server has potential access to your database.

Dedicated Hosting

With dedicated hosting, you rent servers dedicated exclusively to your site.

- **Cost:** $200–$5,000 per month.
- **Suitable for:** Mission-critical, high-traffic, e-commerce sites. Unlike shared hosting, dedicated hosting usually requires some customization. If you're considering this option, you should have at least one reliable, Web-savvy technician either on staff or in a consulting relationship.
- **Advantages:** Dedicated servers are extremely reliable—there are no other sites on the server that can interfere with your site's stability. You can also set up devices that move traffic to a second computer when the first is overtaxed. In addition, because they can handle more advanced database and e-commerce applications, dedicated servers also offer more flexibility.
- **Disadvantages:** Although shared hosting gives you free or low-cost access to many common Web software solutions, you must license your own software for dedicated servers. In addition, it's usually harder for your Web host's support staff to fix problems on dedicated servers, due to their customization.
- **Security Features:** With dedicated hosting, you'll have to pay extra for each security feature you choose to add—these packages don't come bundled with any extras. Also, remember that there might be restrictions regarding the brands or types of security features you're allowed to install. Some Web hosts, for example, only support firewalls from one manufacturer. Before you commit to any contract, do your research about what features you require and ask your ISP if they're available.

Colocated Hosting

With colocated hosting, you buy your own servers and rent a physical space from a Web host or ISP equipped with a high-speed Internet connection.

Cost

- $500–$2,000 per month to rent space.
- Up to $1,000 per month to buy bandwidth.
- $5,000–$20,000 to buy server hardware. However, for a small business, this is unrealistic. Many start with sub-$2,000 server hardware, and build up over time.

Suitable for

Mission-critical, high-traffic, e-commerce sites. Colocated sites require the highest level of responsibility and maintenance from the site owner. If you're considering this option you should have (at minimum) 24-hour system administration coverage, as well as an entire IT department.

Advantages

Just like dedicated servers, colocated servers are very reliable—there are no other sites on the server to interfere with your site, and you can send traffic to a second server if the first is overtaxed. Colocated servers also give you the greatest control over their upkeep, maintenance, and support, while still allowing you to offset the costs of maintaining your Web site yourself. Because Web servers must be stored in climate-controlled, secure environments with strict fire prevention codes and 24-hour access, they are very expensive to store.

Disadvantages

You are completely responsible for your equipment. If for any reason your IT staff is unavailable, the Web host's on-site staff can maintain and monitor your servers, but they'll charge you high hourly rates.

Security Features

Like dedicated hosting environments, you're on your own when it comes to security. Colocated packages do not come bundled with security features the way shared hosting packages do—you'll have to pay extra for each feature you add. Unlike dedicated hosting, however, you have ultimate flexibility—you own the equipment, install everything, and pay for licensing yourself, so you are not limited in any way [1].

So, if many ISPs aren't up to snuff and the do-it-yourself approach is too risky, who can you trust? Fortunately for the e-commerce novice, there are several sources of certified security personnel. The International Information

Systems Security Certification Consortium, known as ISC2 (Shrewsbury, Massachusetts), has established the Certified Information System Security Professional (CISSP) program to ensure that consultants and other IT professionals have the necessary training and experience to do their jobs properly. The certificate is based on a rigorous exam on 10 different domains of knowledge. In addition to satisfactorily passing the exam, CISSPs need to maintain their certification, so there's a recertification every three years. They must accumulate 120 hours of continuing education or fulfill an experience requirement during those years.

A partial list of CISSPs can be found on the ISC2 Web site at *www.isc2.org*. In addition, the Computer Security Institute also maintains a list of references. Many of these professionals tailor their practices to medium-sized and small businesses, so any company that's able to invest in e-commerce should be able to afford the necessary security consultation. Moreover, the Institute of Internal Auditors has developed a WebTrust seal of approval to ensure that a site is secure, so it's easy to ask a prospective e-commerce hosting company if it meets the necessary requirements.

However, there will always be an element of risk. Even resource-rich Fortune 500 companies are struggling with e-commerce security issues. There is no cookie-cutter solution out there yet, so when it comes to e-commerce, both buyer and seller had better beware. The following questions are a guide for businesses considering e-commerce solutions:

1. Is anyone on the security team professionally certified to perform information security work?

Caution

Relying on certification is a dangerous business. Just because an individual has passed his or her certification exam doesn't mean that he or she has the hands-on experience needed to work on your organization's information security.

2. What kind of experience does your organization have in the field of Internet security?
3. What is your policy toward shared liability for stolen credit cards and fraudulent transactions?
4. Has there been a third-party review of the site's security and reliability?
5. What kinds of financial or regulatory exposure do you have by opening an Internet commerce site?
6. What kinds of fraud have you seen and what are you doing to mitigate the problem?

7. Does your site perform real-time authorization of credit cards or do you perform offline authorization?

8. Do you know that a card is valid when you submit the request for shipment of the order?

9. Will you provide any guarantees for credit information stored at your site?

10. What is your policy on user and client privacy and confidentiality? [4]

ID Theft and Fraud Protection Plan for E-Business

Electronic commerce can be a lucrative channel for small business owners. For many types of businesses, it makes a great deal of financial sense to take advantage of this outlet because it provides a way to reach millions of potential new customers anywhere in the world. However, e-commerce is not without its vulnerabilities. The inherent problem with doing business over the Web is that data traveling over public networks can be easily compromised. How does your business ensure the security of online communications, intellectual property, and commercial transactions?

The first part of your planning process should be to identify the most important security concerns for your e-commerce site and figure out how much implementing the necessary technology will cost. As part of your overall business plan, you will want to include the cost of protecting your e-business.

Common E-Commerce Security Infractions

When considering security, you should be familiar with the vulnerabilities that your Web site might fall victim to. Here are some of the more common hazards and recommendations for how to prevent them.

Hackers

Hackers use viruses and illegal programs to enter your Web site and funnel all kinds of information back to their own email addresses. There are many ways for a hacker to wreak havoc on your Web site.

Solutions For Keeping Hackers Out. Picture a building surrounded by fire. You can't go through it without a fireproof suit. This is how a firewall functions, except that the building is your Web server and the fireproof suit is the authentication that you need to gain access. A firewall checks users' IP addresses and determines if they should be allowed inside. Some more advanced firewalls can even fight back against intruders (see the sidebar, "Technology Firewalls").

 Tip

Not all firewalls perform IP-based authentication. Even those that do are susceptible to spoofing, and thus IP-based rules are not secure.

Technology Firewalls

As we all know, a firewall is like an online security gate—it prevents access to your private information, including customer financial and personal data, from the Internet. As a result, a firewall can help prevent future frauds by protecting the consumer data stored on your site. Here's how it works:

- Most firewalls consist of special software running on a computer that is dedicated solely to the firewall.
- All information flowing in and out of your network (e.g., email messages, requests for files, or Web pages) must pass through this computer.
- The software examines this traffic and blocks access or information transfer based on rules customized by an administrator (usually your Web host or your IT department, if you host your own site). These rules tell your firewall what it can and cannot do.

For example, your firewall can block all Web traffic from a certain known bad IP address or prevent any certain applications from entering your network. Different parts of your network will each have different rules.

What Kind of Site Needs a Firewall?

Any computer that is connected to the Internet needs a firewall. However, this is pure opinion, and will lead to holy wars on the topic of firewalls. There are people that believe that firewalls are a superfluous addition of unnecessary complexity, and cause more problems than they fix. These people also believe that the key to security is a combination of vigilance and smart policy ("Don't run services that you don't need or trust").

Nevertheless, most Web sites have a double firewall, in case one system goes down, and many large sites have several firewalls at different crucial points in the network. However, in some cases, there are single-firewall architectures that use two or more firewalls as a load-balancing and redundancy technique; this is not the norm. In two-firewall installations, the second firewall creates a demilitarized zone (DMZ), so that their Web presence can live in the DMZ, and their office machines can live behind the second firewall protected from the outside world. Also, some firewalls include intrusion detection systems to warn you when they may have been invaded.

What Are the Limitations?

A firewall only does what it is told; as a result, it is only as good as its rules. In addition, firewalls (as well as the computers they're located on) should be updated as the network changes or as patches and upgrades are released by the software developer.

Finally, there is no such thing as an absolute. Even a highly customized, well-maintained firewall can be vulnerable. As a result, merchants should ask their Web host, firewall administrator, or IT department for help in preparing a contingency plan.

How Much Does a Firewall Cost?

Setup and maintenance costs of a firewall depend on the complexity and size of the firewall system. Costs can range from less than $100 for off-the-shelf software to more than $100,000.

Note: There are free firewall implementations (such as IP tables in Linux) for those that are literate enough to deal with them (and who have a small enough scale that these make sense).

Most companies have their firewall systems developed and maintained by their Web host or e-commerce service provider. On average, a two-firewall system managed by a Web host costs about $1,200 to $1,800 a month. In addition, larger companies who host their own sites or provide their own site maintenance will usually develop or customize their own firewall systems. [3]

In addition to firewalls, intrusion detection software is also used as a solution for keeping out hackers. This security software alerts you to potential intrusion attempts by collecting information from a number of different sources on your network and analyzing the data for patterns that could indicate security breaches.

Credit Card Theft

Purchasing online makes life easier for customers. However, sites require credit cards, and there is always a danger that this information could be stolen.

Solutions for Preventing Credit Card Theft. Although using IP addresses to determine a user's identity works most of the time, it is still possible to fake an IP address. Partly because of the risk of imposture, most computer systems with highly sensitive data rely on a user authentication system.

User Authentication. User authenication software requests information from users to verify that they are who they say they are. The most common type of authentication asks for a name and password.

Encryption. Encryption is used to scramble important client information (e.g., credit card numbers). Data security between the user's browser and your server can be managed using the SSL protocol. It works by using a private key to encrypt data that's transferred over the SSL connection.

Public Key Infrastructures. Some organizations are also using public key infrastructures (PKIs) to solve e-business security issues. A PKI is a system of digital certificates, certificate authorities, and other registration authorities that verify and authenticate the validity of each party involved in an Internet transaction. Certificate authorities are third-party companies that issue digital certificates, digital signatures, and public–private key pairs. For e-businesses, these certificates serve as validation that a company or individual is who they claim to be, and not an imposter. Many companies are turning to digital certificates as a secure means of communicating and doing business with customers, employees, and suppliers.

Credit Card Fraud

Statistics show that fraud is more likely to take place online than in other kinds of commerce environments. According to Meridien Research, Inc., [2] less than 1% of credit card transactions in brick-and-mortar stores today are fraudulent, but nearly 10% of all Internet transactions are fraudulent. Meridien also predicts that by the end of 2003, online credit card fraud is expected to cost merchants $700 million, and overall consumer fraud is expected to cost online merchants $4.8 billion. Financial experts expect online fraud to only get worse.

Solutions for Preventing Credit Card Fraud. The most vulnerable enterprises are small and medium-sized businesses, because they can't afford expensive fraud detection products and services that compare new transactions against profiles of fraudulent ones. In fact, only 2% to 4% of Web merchants use such systems today. Providers of such fraud detection services typically charge one-time fees of tens of thousands of dollars on top of per-transaction fees. So what to do? Experts suggest developing an antifraud strategy before you launch your site. They also recommend studying how contracts work between online storeowners, bank and credit card companies. Before setting up shop online, carefully read the credit card agreement with the merchant bank, because once you ship the product, you're never going to see it again if the transaction turns out to be fraudulent.

Fraud Prevention Tools

What types of tools can help online merchants protect their businesses from fraud? The following five tools can help you:

1. Real-time credit card authorization
2. Address verification systems
3. Card verification codes
4. Rule-based detection
5. Predictive statistical model software [5]

The first three tools are services available from a bank or credit card company, and the last two are software packages you must purchase from software vendors. Table 5–1 shows merchant rankings of these tools by their cost-effectiveness and success at fraud prevention. [5]

Real-Time Credit Card Authorization. Obtaining a real-time authorization for a transaction from a credit card company is a good starting point for detecting and preventing fraudulent transactions. This will ensure that the credit card has not been reported as lost or stolen and that it is a valid card number.

However, an authorization does not tell you if the person using the card is authorized to use it. There are many other tools that a merchant can use to anticipate a fraud, such as those discussed next.

Address Verification Systems (U.S. Only). An address verification system (AVS) is a system that runs during the credit card authorization process. AVS will match the billing address provided by the customer with the billing address on file for that credit card.

This method is not foolproof, however. According to a recent analysis by ClearCommerce, [3] AVS returns a match in only about 40% of all transactions, when in reality a very small percentage of transactions are actually fraudulent. This means that many transactions that fail according to AVS are actually valid. Another important consideration is that 35% of the fraud cases examined by ClearCommerce matched addresses when run through AVS.

Card Verification Codes. Card verification codes (CVV2 for Visa, CVVC for MasterCard, and CID for American Express) are a fairly new way of verifying that a credit card is valid. For American Express, the code is a four-digit number that appears on the front of the card above the account number. For Visa and MasterCard, the code is a three-digit number that appears at the end of the account number on the back of the card. The code does not get printed on any receipts.

As a merchant, you can ask for this code on your online order form. In fact, MasterCard now requires that merchants collect this information.

Rule-Based Detection. With rule-based detection software, merchants define a set of criteria that each transaction must meet. Often called a *negative file*, this set of rules can be based on past experiences, price limits, names, addresses, and the knowledge of human experts, such as risk analysts (see the sidebar, "Fraud Detection System"). These criteria should always maintain not only stolen credit card numbers, but also bad shipping addresses and telephone numbers. The software will automatically screen incoming orders by these specific criteria and automate the decision to reject, review, or accept the order. For example, a merchant might screen for unusually high dollar transactions, billing and shipping addresses that do not match (these are not useful for businesses that cater more to gift-giving), an order for an unusually high number of one item, or names and credit cards that have been linked to fraud in the past.

Fraud Detection System

Like the name suggests, a rules-based fraud detection system compares each credit card transaction to a set of rules before the charge can be approved. Based on the rules, the system will then automate a response, such as approving the sale, declining the sale, or pulling the sale for manual review.

Also called *expert systems*, other types of rule-based systems have been in use for decades to do things such as diagnose blood disorders or predict stock prices. They are also often used to help detect network intrusions.

When used to prevent fraud, the rules will consist of a series of if–then statements geared to flag fraudulent sales. For example, if orders contain more than three of an item over $500, then review the sale, or if this credit card number is used, then decline the sale.

Rules work most effectively when they combine both expert research and the information gleaned from your own site. For this reason, many systems often work in conjunction with negative files that contain a list of names, credit card numbers, or other details that have been linked to fraud in the past.

What Kind of Site Needs a Rules-Based Detection System?

Although any business that encounters fraudulent sales might be helped by a rules-based system, they must first weigh the costs of the solution against the benefits they would receive. Any merchant with enough volume to make it impossible to manually review all incoming orders needs some automatic screening system.

A rule-based system is probably the place to start. Merchants processing more than 100 orders per day are probably a good fit.

In addition, merchants who sell high-risk merchandise should also consider using a rules-based system. These catagories include consumer electronics, computers, digital goods, calling cards, and high-ticket items like jewelry.

What Are the Risks and Limitations?

In a nutshell, rules-based fraud detection systems are only as smart as the rules they use. In other words, these systems execute the rules, but it is up to the merchant to define what the rules should be.

As a result, you will need to have an understanding of what types of fraud might actually occur on your site. You will also need to make sure the system is updated when you gain new knowledge.

In addition, a rules-based system should not be your sole method of detection. Instead, it should be one part of a plan that includes other methods of detection and manual reviews. These reviews are the key to ensuring you don't decline real customers.

How Much Does a Rules-Based Fraud Detection System Cost?

How much a rules-based system costs depends on whether you support it internally or purchase it from a vendor. It is usually quite time-consuming to develop and maintain a system inhouse. It's not the initial build that's difficult, but rather the maintenance.

It soon becomes a very demanding and resource-intensive task, because the risk management team will need to continuously refine the rules and add new ones. As an alternative, many companies offer the service and all maintenance for a yearly fee that can range from $40,000 to $70,000. [6]

Predictive Statistical Models. Predictive statistical model software analyzes data from millions of online sales to extract the profile of fraudulent transactions. Culling data from large, historical databases, the software develops a mathematical formula and applies it in real time to incoming transactions. Each transaction then receives a risk score based on its attributes.

Putting Them Together. All of the tools mentioned are complementary to one another, as they each inspect different components of a transaction. The best way to combat fraud is to use layers of fraud protection. When using fraud tools, one plus one equals three—using more than one tool will usually yield better results than using any tool alone.

Using a combination is also crucial for helping merchants reduce *insult rate*, or rejection of legitimate orders. Each time this happens, you risk losing that customer and possibly some of his or her friends.

Costs and Effectiveness. Although a combination of tools is always a superior solution to any single tool, according to ClearCommerce, [3] the overall effectiveness of each of these tools, as well as which tool is most cost-effective, is fundamental to any cost-effective solution. For example, ClearCommerce recently asked 30 online merchants (including both ClearCommerce customers and noncustomers) to rank the tools they were using to prevent fraud in the order of most effective to least effective. They also asked them to rank the tools they were using based on which one was the best value. The results of this poll are summarized in Table 5.1. [5]

Table 5.1. Merchant Rankings of These Tools by Their Cost-Effectiveness and Success at Fraud Prevention

Most Effective	Best Value
1. Rule-based detection	1. Rule-based detection
2. Real-time credit card authorization	2. Real-time credit card authorization
3. Card verification codes	3. Card verification codes
4. Statistical models	4. Address verification systems
5. Address verification systems	5. Statistical models

It's important to note that the costs for each of the tools listed in Table 5–1 vary according to your type of business. You should also remember not to exceed the costs of fraud to your business when you are considering these tools. For example, if you lose $75,000 to fraud per year, and you can only recover $30,000 through fraud management tools, don't spend more than $30,000 on those tools.

Don't Forget Human Intervention. Finally, when you're trying to develop fraud prevention procedures, it is important to recognize that you can't always rely on technology—there might be a need to manually review a small percentage of orders. As previously mentioned, merchants constantly balance the risk of accepting an order with the risk of losing the customer—in many cases, human intervention is still the best method. You should also remember (because the majority of transactions you receive will be valid orders) that this extra effort can be an excellent opportunity to help you build a customer relationship that lasts a lifetime.

Compromised Electronic Mail and Downloads

Intruders can also use email attachments and downloads to launch viruses, worms, and Trojan horses on your server, some of which can retrieve information from your system and automatically email it back to their creator.

A virus is a program that infects other programs and then spreads from program to program. A very harmful virus can take down an entire computer in a matter of minutes. Trojan horse programs fool a user into accepting a program into his or her computer, expecting it to be useful or interesting, when in fact the program turns out to be carrying a malicious payload. A worm usually spreads itself by email, sending itself to all of your contacts once you've opened it. A worm can carry a harmful payload in itself, or bring mail servers to a halt, simply overwhelming them by shuttling worthless mail between all the contacts across address books.

Safeguarding Your System. Everyone should own good virus detection software, just in case one of those harmful payloads does arrive with an email or inadvertently with a download. The best prevention against an email virus infection is an email filter that checks incoming messages for viruses and worms and screens for messages from unauthorized sources. Without email filtering, your system is also more vulnerable to distributed denial of service (DDoS) attacks.

Encrypting Database Contents. Typically, database systems encrypt and decrypt data in transport over the network, using industry-standard systems such as SSL. This system works well for client/server databases; the server is assumed to be in a trusted, safe environment, managed by a system administrator. In addition, the recipient of the data is trusted and is assumed to be capable of protecting the database. The only risk comes when transporting data over the wire, and data encryption happens during network transport only.

Dealing With Old Backups Securely. To prevent data loss, you must have reliable backup systems and tested backup and restore procedures.

Reliability means that your backup system provides error-free backups and restores. Accomplishing this requires a combination of reliable backup hardware and software and effective backup procedures. Problems caused by unreliable hardware cannot be fixed by software. Unless you have adequate backup procedures, chances are that at some point, critical data will not be properly backed up. So how do you maintain reliability? You should do the following:

- Monitor the number of times each tape is used, and replace or retire them early.
- Use a proper grade of tape.
- Tape drives should be used in a clean environment.
- Clean the tape drive and read/write heads regularly.
- Perform test restores on a regular basis.
- Verify your backups.
- Store the backup tapes under the proper environmental conditions.
- If you are using tape for archival storage, test and rewind each archived tape at least once a year.
- If you are keeping tapes for several years, copy old tapes to new ones periodically.

Disposal of "Dead" Hardware. With an anticipated 70 million computers slated for "retirement" in 2003, forget purchase price: The cost of disposal is becoming a major concern for PC owners. In a 2000 U.S. Census Bureau survey, 52% of households indicated they purchased a new computer in the past two years; only 15% were still using a machine more than four years old. Conclusion? PC users continue to cycle through hardware at light speed while unhealthy old technology piles up at landfills.

Why unhealthy? Because almost all PC hardware contains materials classified as hazardous waste by the Environmental Protection Agency, and only 17% of it will be properly recycled. With more than 4 billion pounds of computer carcasses headed for landfills in 2003, the disposal of old hardware is an increasing environmental and security problem for the PC industry. Lead glass from monitors and clock batteries on motherboards require proper disposal, and the longer you wait, the more expensive it will be to clean up.

Forget about dumping your dead hardware at the Salvation Army: Space-strapped charitable organizations are wary of high-tech hand-me-downs, because fewer than one in six donated PCs actually work. Although organizations such as the Computer Recycling Center (*www.educateusa.com*) use some broken hardware for vocational training, most charities don't have the resources to handle your trash. Share the Technology (*www.libertynet.org/*

share), a nonprofit organization that distributes computers to charities nation-wide, can provide information on how to donate a PC in your area.

Use the following rule of thumb when deciding what to do with an old machine: Sell at two years, donate at three, and be prepared to pay disposal costs at four. Corporate users should skip right to disposal. Disposal will probably be cheaper than resale when you factor in the cost of removing confidential company files from every PC. If you've got an entire office of 386s to get rid of, you might want to bring in a computer recycling specialist to help you make that outmoded technology disappear.

With circuit boards and memory chips selling for up to $4 per pound, consider precious-metal reclamation when planning your disposal strategy. How much gold, silver, and palladium is kicking around in abandoned PC hardware? No one has exact numbers, but assuming there's one-tenth of a gram of gold in each machine, that means we threw away more than $80 million in 2001.

DDoS Attacks

In a DDoS attack, the perpetrator takes over unprotected Internet nodes all over the world. The attack is hard to trace, because each node receives only limited information about who is initiating the attack or from where. The result affects the systems used in the attack as well as the targeted victim. The victim system (or server) receives simultaneous attacks from all the nodes at once. This floods the network normally used to communicate and trace the attacks and prevents legitimate traffic from using the network. Attackers often hide the identity of machines used to carry out an attack by address spoofing (falsifying the source address of the network communication). This makes it difficult to identify the source of the attack and often shifts attention to innocent third parties.

Fending off DDoS Attacks. Limiting an attacker's ability to spoof IP source addresses won't prevent attacks, but it will make it easier to trace an attack back to its origins. ISPs can ensure that traffic exiting or entering a Web site has a source address that matches the set of addresses for that site. Although this would still allow addresses to be spoofed within a site, it would at least allow tracing of attack traffic to the site from which it originated.

You should ensure that all packets leaving your own site carry source addresses within the address range of those sites. ISPs can provide backup to pick up spoofed traffic that is not caught by your filters. ISPs might also be able to stop spoofing by passing along traffic only if it comes from authorized sources.

Theft of Intellectual Property

Although everything on your Web page is supposedly safe under the law, your copyright, site content, images, Hypertext Markup Language (HTML) and are all easy to steal: Just copy and paste. Some people just don't care that the contents of your Web site are legally yours.

Preventing Theft of Intellectual Property. Start by posting a copyright notice at the bottom of each page on your site. Type short excerpts from your copy into popular search engines and see what they turn up. If you've determined someone else is using your content, contact him or her. If you don't get a response, notify his or her ISP. There is software that helps prevent image theft by making it hard for others to copy your images. Electronic verification services can help protect your work by time stamping and sealing it in a digital container that only you can access.

Corporate Espionage

It might be hard to believe, but in cases of espionage, about 85% of the time, employees are actually responsible. Your intranet firewalls might keep outsiders out, but do nothing to prevent insiders from exporting company secrets. In addition, unscrupulous programmers could build a secret back door, affording them repeated access to your business data.

Guarding Your Business From Corporate Espionage. Several of the same precautions against hackers and data theft can be used to combat corporate espionage. Antivirus solutions that include scanning for Trojan horses will help to eliminate data theft through back-door methods, and intrusion detection software will enable only those authorized to gain access to restricted areas of the network. It will also alert you to attempted intrusions so you can take appropriate action.

Despite all of your security precautions, there is always the possibility that an infraction could occur. It is important to be ready to respond immediately to any attack, intrusion, or other threat if it does happen. Hopefully the Web allows you to reach so many customers that it's worth the precautions that you need to take. Cover your security bases from the start, and not as an afterthought. In the long run, a strong security system will save your company money and solidify its reputation.

Preparing Your Site for Any Holiday

With predictions that the 2002 and 2003 holiday seasons could be gloomy for merchants, it's even more important to clamp down on losses due to e-commerce fraud. Now's the time to start preparing. To help you, the following sections provide a checklist of the basics.

Know Who's Naughty and Who's Nice

Before the holiday rush begins, read and understand all of the agreements provided by card issuers and by any third parties that process your site's charges. Once you understand your liability, you might be able pinpoint specific steps you can take to better prevent fraud.

Train Your Elves

During the holidays, there's twice as much to do in half the time, making it even easier for fraudsters to slip through the cracks. Before the season begins, take the time to educate your employees (especially the temporary holiday help) about the signs of fraud. In particular, remind them to pay more attention to items that are at a higher risk of fraud (see the sidebar, "Types of Merchandise That Are Most at Risk to Online Fraud").

Types of Merchandise That Are Most at Risk to Online Fraud

Let's face it—almost any kind of online inventory is a target for fraudsters. However, there are several types of e-commerce merchants that are more at risk—such as those who sell electronic goods or high-priced clothing. What follows is a list of the four kinds of merchandise that are most at risk to fraud.

Things That Can Be Resold on the Street

Clearly, anything that's easily convertible to cash is at risk for fraud. Vulnerable merchants include those who sell name-brand clothing, jewelry, athletic equipment, or high-priced electronic goods—especially DVD players or digital cameras. In short, fraudsters look for anything that can be easily fenced on the streets.

Direct Payments to Another Person

Web sites that support outbound payments are also at a greater risk for fraud. These Web sites include person-to-person payment sites (e.g., PayPal) or sites that allow you to purchase and send gift certificates online. Because the end result of these sites is financial reward, the risk of fraud increases.

Digital Goods

Digital goods are products or services that a customer can get immediately from a Web site with a credit card or other e-payment. Digital goods include electronically issued tickets or software and music files.

The fraud risk increases with digital goods, because they don't require a shipping address and can be delivered almost instantly. This means there's less time to review the transaction before the goods are delivered, and there's one less piece of information you can use to scrutinize a transaction.

Products That Have Been in the News

Products don't always have to be expensive to be at risk. If your product or organization has a lot of publicity (either good or bad), it can be a target for hackers.

For example, *hacktivists* could target your site to protest a controversial product. If your product is getting a lot of attention (e.g., the hype around Nintendo's Pokemon), the street value of your product (and your company's fraud risk) could increase.

Protecting Yourself

All e-commerce merchants face some risk of fraud, but those who sell the four kinds of merchandise discussed here, are at an even greater risk. As a result, it is even more important to follow the basics of fraud prevention: using address verification systems, reviewing cardholder identification numbers, implementing transaction screening software, or keeping negative files—a database of bad names and addresses from your own fraudulent sales. To read about the basics of fraud prevention, see the sidebar "Fighting Fraud."

It is also important to use some form of identification verification and transaction scoring software, which compares transactions to an industrywide database of information culled from millions of sales. This is often called a neural network or statistical modeling software. For more information, see Chapter 13, "Management of Ongoing Identity Theft Prevention and Protection Techniques."

These tools are important, because often the same people are doing it over and over. In addition, it is important to learn more about the e-commerce process. For example, you need to understand how fraud schemes work and how your product gets delivered. Then, you can use technology to evaluate the information that's coming in. [7]

Fighting Fraud

From building your site to shipping your goods, opportunities for fraud exist at every point in the online sales cycle. To better protect your business and your customers, follow these guidelines for security and fraud prevention.

Step 1: Building a Secure Site

Protect the Data Your Site Sends and Receives

Be sure your site uses the highest SSL technology. SSL is a protocol used to send information over the Internet that scrambles information to ensure it is transferred securely. Contact your IT department or the company that hosts your site to see if your site uses the most advanced version of SSL that your customers' Web browsers can support.

Use a firewall to prevent certain messages (e.g., ones that contain viruses) from entering or leaving your network if they don't meet your security standards. Firewalls can also detect and prevent any network intrusion. Talk to your company's IT department or a software vendor for more information about firewalls, or, if your site is hosted by an external vendor, ask them about their firewall procedures.

Store Your Data Safely

Don't store any customer data on a server connected to the Internet. This will help prevent hackers from getting access to your customers' personal, financial, and card account information.

Encrypt data files—including personal information, phone numbers, addresses, credit card numbers, and transaction records. Then, even if these records are accessed improperly, they can't be used without the key to translate the data. Talk to your site's host or a software vendor about using data encryption systems on your site.

Use intrusion detection systems that tell you when someone has accessed a private file or server as soon as it happens, in addition to preventing viruses or other troublesome messages from entering your network. Talk to your IT department or contact a software vendor for more information about these systems, or ask your site's host about their procedures.

Give data file access only to authorized employees by requiring users to enter a user ID and password. You should also monitor on a daily basis who is accessing these files.

Note: This is the minimum amount of security that you should provide. Biometrics, one-time-passwords, and strong authentication mechanisms should be mentioned.

Step 2: Making the Sale

Get All the Information You Need

Capture complete information from your customers, including the following:

- Their cardholder's name exactly as it appears on the card
- The card account number
- The card expiration date
- The card billing address
- The cardholder's home or business telephone number
- The cardholder's email address
- The name of the package recipient
- The shipping address
- A phone number at the shipping destination

Make sure your site uses a program that documents your site traffic, including the IP address of each customer, the date and time of order, and the duration of time the customer spends on your site, if possible. This information can be used to track criminals, especially in the theft of digital goods (files that can be downloaded directly), where there is no delivery address. Contact your site's host or a software vendor for more information about these programs.

Be Proactive

If you observe suspicious behavior, contact the customer before goods are shipped. Although some of these behaviors occur during normal transactions, some signposts include the following:

- Shipping and billing addresses that don't match. History has shown that these transactions carry a higher risk of fraud.

- Free email addresses that are easily established, such as Yahoo! and MSN Hotmail accounts, or email addresses that don't work.

- A large number of identical expensive items, such as 36 suits of the same size and color.

- A request for immediate or overnight delivery of higher value items.

- International or overseas delivery for higher value items. Outside of the United States, laws to protect merchants from fraudulent purchases might not be in place.

- An IP address that does not match the physical billing address of the customer, or multiple cards used from a single IP address.

- Several sales or attempted sales on card account numbers that vary by only a few numbers. These may be randomly generated by a system that tries to create valid credit card numbers.

- One delivery address used by multiple customers or cardholders. Thieves could have access to several stolen card numbers.

- One card that ships packages to several different shipping addresses. This might be a sign the card number has been sold to more than one person or is being used by an organization.

Ask for the name of the bank on the card. Although you will have to manually verify the bank name by calling the card issuer, only someone who has seen the card will know this information.

Verify addresses by using the card issuers' automatic verification systems. You can also work with vendors that have AVSs or software that can detect vacant buildings, disconnected telephones, or other suspicious information. In addition, there are also several directory services available on the Internet that allow you to look up names and addresses for free.

Consider buying fraud detection software that calculates the likelihood of a fraudulent transaction. These systems review email addresses, purchase information, and other data to help you determine if the risk is worth the reward of the sale. Some of these systems even provide guarantees or refunds for goods if their software approves a fraudulent transaction.

Use the shipping companies you trust. Contact them for their delivery policies or any tips they have to help online merchants combat fraud.

Step 3: Shipping The Goods

Use the shipping companies you trust. Contect them for their delivery policies or any tips they have to help online merchants combat fraud. Ask your shipping company if they will prevent high-value packages from being rerouted during delivery. This reduces the chances that someone can contact the shipping company, impersonate the customer, and change the shipping destination.

You should request a signature on delivery and a photo ID. This is for customers who want to pick up goods at shipping distribution centers or retail locations.

If your company is also a brick-and-mortar retail operation, consider implementing a program that gives customers some incentive to pick up high-value goods in person, such as reduced shipping rates.

Step 4: Preparing for the Future

Monitor the velocity of customer purchases. For example, if someone has stolen a credit card, they might order several high-value items from your site in rapid succession to try to reach the card's limit before it is reported as stolen.

Develop a database of bad addresses and verify them. Bad addresses include any locations where the goods have been shipped and lost due to a fraudulent sale.

Save all emails and transaction data. Continue to do this until you're sure the charges won't be disputed.

Add your toll-free customer service number to your customers' billing statements. This could help your customers report fraudulent purchases faster, giving you a better chance of tracking down stolen goods and criminals.

On your site, state that you intend to prosecute fraud. You should also follow up with law enforcement agencies when you believe a fraud has been committed. More information about agencies that can help you report and prosecute these crimes can be found in the sidebar, "Catching a Cyberthief".[8]

Catching a Cyberthief

Getting your money back from a fraudster might seem like a long shot, but merchants should still take the time to report the crimes. This sidebar explains why it's important and explains what you'll need to do.

Barriers to Prosecution

Catching a cyberthief is often a difficult proposition. For starters, the Internet is an anonymous and global environment that makes it easy for people to hide their identities.

What's more, victims are often in different cities, states, or countries than the criminals. This requires the cooperation of different law enforcement agencies. Making it even harder is the fact that the laws against e-commerce fraud vary from place to place, and don't exist at all in some countries.

Within the United States, for example, laws can differ from state to state, and each city's police department might have its own monetary threshold for investigating crimes based on their available resources. This means smaller crimes often slip through the cracks.

Why Reporting Cybercrime Is Important

As a result of these barriers, many merchants don't even bother to report fraud to authorities. However, according to fraud experts, it is just this behavior that prevents the prosecution process from improving. Businesses typically hesitate to report fraud. That's not a good thing.

Reporting crimes allows law enforcement and other agencies to keep of track of how large the problem is, allowing them to dedicate more resources to pursuing those types of cases. In addition, reporting crimes allows authorities to pinpoint new trends or types of scams, enabling them to develop precautions or warn the public.

In addition, reporting fraud is one of the only ways to find out if your case might be connected to a larger scam that is easier to prosecute. It might seem minor or small, but it could be part of a bigger ring.

Before You Report

Before you report a crime, you will need to do your homework. With no name, address, or other information about the criminal, law enforcement won't be able to help you. Some merchants even take depositions or hire private detectives or consultants, depending on the severity of the crime.

You should include as much detail as you can about the case, but present the information in a way that is clear and easily understood. The key to success for you as a merchant is to provide enough detail so that all the detective has to do is capture the criminal. Do as much of the research as you can.

This research should include everything you know about the transaction—emails, correspondence, addresses, phone numbers, and especially IP addresses, which can be used to track down the computer used and its physical location. In fact, to effectively trace and prosecute criminals you should always do the following:

- Save all email traffic between your site and your customers until you are certain that the charges will not be disputed. It is especially important to save the extended header information on an email that provides the sender's IP address.

- Make sure your site has a program that documents your customer traffic, including the IP address, date and time of order, and the duration of time a customer spends on your site, if possible.

- Retain explicit shipping information, including what was ordered, when it was ordered, the shipping address, and the name and credit card numbers used.

Reporting Crimes

Crimes That Involve the United States

According to the United States Secret Service, U.S. agencies will investigate and prosecute crimes where either the perpetrator or victim resides in the United States, or cases where the United States is being affected by the crimes. If your case fits these descriptions, you can start by the contacting the Electronic Crimes Task Force of the U.S. Secret Service at 202-406-5850, or by contacting the local police where the fraud occurred.

Note: You can find the correct contact information by going to an online yellow page service and typing in the zip code of the shipping or billing address used for the transaction. Then search for police.

The police will then contact the appropriate local, state, and federal agencies, such as the Secret Service, the FBI, or FTC. The Secret Service is usually the agency responsible for tracking credit card frauds.

Reporting Online: The IFCC

If the crime is U.S.-related, you can also turn to a new, centralized, Web-based resource for reporting and prosecuting frauds—the Internet Fraud Complaint Center (IFCC). Initiated in May 2000 by the FBI, the Department of Justice, and National White Collar Crime Center (NW3C), the IFCC site (*www.ifccfbi.gov/*) allows individuals and merchants to file e-commerce fraud complaints online.

Once a merchant submits a complaint to the IFCC site, it is reviewed by IFCC analysts and forwarded immediately to the appropriate local, state, and federal agencies. The complaint is also added to a database. Then, when new complaints come in, they are checked against existing entries. If complaints can be linked, information is compiled and provided to the agencies with jurisdiction. The IFCC can also track patterns and trends, provide analysis and historical data, and serve as a valuable hub for victims, researchers, and law enforcement.

Reporting Crimes Outside the United States

The path to prosecution may be less clear in other countries, partially due to the fact that Internet and e-commerce are not as widespread in some corners of the world as they are in the United States. You should always start with your local police.

In addition, in some areas where the Internet is widely used, initiatives to centralize both reporting and prevention information are underway. For example, the EU's European Commission includes the European Anti-Fraud Office (*http://europa.eu.int/comm/dgs/olaf/*), which is responsible for reviewing cybercrime issues in the EU.

In Canada, the government's Strategis Web site (*http://strategis.ic.gc.ca/engdoc/main.html*) is dedicated to business and consumer issues, including e-commerce fraud. The e-ASEAN Task Force (*http://www.e-aseantf.org/*) was developed to study e-commerce issues, including cybercrimes, across Asian countries.

In the Future

Although the global nature of the Internet currently makes reporting and prosecuting crimes difficult, new standards for international laws and law enforcement may soon be on the horizon. According to the Secret Service, law enforcement officers all over the world are already cooperating to bring cybercriminals to justice, and organizations around the globe are beginning to discuss ways to cooperate or develop international legislation.

For example, recently, more than 600 business executives and government officials from 40 countries met at the annual Global Internet Summit. The event's goals included tackling these types of issues.

Another organization at the forefront of the issue is the Global Information Infrastructure Commission (*www.giic.org/*), which is part of the Center for Strategic and International Studies based in Washington, DC. Dedicated to developing information networks and services on a global scale, the organization's site includes information on e-commerce around the globe.

Once partnerships are established, you should be able to point to one source for reporting and prosecution. Perhaps one day, the IFCC will be equipped to handle and track complaints from all over the world.

As soon as new standards are developed or new information and resources are available, the Worldwide E-Commerce Fraud Prevention Network will be the first to let you know. Until then, merchants should put most of their effort into protecting their businesses from e-commerce crimes in the first place. [9]

You should consider creating a quick facts card your employees can refer to when processing transactions or talking with customers. The card can cover the basics of finding fraud, or what to do if you discover a fraudulent sale. For help, see the sidebar "Discovering Fraud."

Discovering Fraud

Reviewing incidents of fraud after they occur can be just as important as preventing them. Next, let's discover how you can learn from your experience and get tips on how to use that knowledge to reduce fraud at your organization.

The Importance of Analyzing Fraudulent Orders

You've read a lot about preventing fraud before it occurs in this book, but don't forget the importance of finding fraud after it happens.

Detecting and tracking fraud after the fact can help you in many ways—and the faster you find it the better. Because professional fraudsters usually move in and hit their targets as many times as they can before they are detected, the faster you identify them, the less potential damage your business might suffer.

The sooner you report a fraud, for example, the better chance you have of finding the perpetrator. Finding fraud quickly will also help you stop further activity on a fraudulent card number.

What's more, fraud-finding can help you see what you're missing in your fraud prevention procedures. As a result, you can constantly fine-tune your fraud prevention tools and technologies.

Next, let's look at some tips for finding fraud, as well as what to do once you've found it.

Tip: Monitor Your Customer Calls

An unusual phone call to your complaint or customer service center is normally the first indicator of fraud. For example, someone might contact customer service about a bill for a purchase never made, or a bank might call to check suspicious activity on a cardholder's account.

These are both early warning signs that a credit card fraud may have occurred. To act on these warnings, you'll need to train the representatives taking phone calls to report these incidents to the right people.

You might consider developing a standard procedure for dealing with these types of calls. This would include how to report or track the incident, which calls require immediate assistance, and what to ask the caller to ensure that your staff is collecting the information that can help you in the long run. There are a few things your call staffers should do when they receive a call that might be related to a fraudulent sale.

Protect Your Process

Sometimes fraudsters will pose as concerned customers to try and glean information about your fraud prevention procedures. Don't reveal how you evaluate a transaction. Instead, tell the caller that you have a process, but that you can't reveal specific information, as it will jeopardize your customers' privacy and security.

Find out Who the Caller Is

Is the caller from a bank or a law enforcement agency? Is it the cardholder? Is it a repeat customer whose personal or financial data is stored in your database, or is it someone who has never bought from you before?

These details will be important to help you decide on a path of action—whether it is talking to your legal or fraud prevention department, contacting a cardholder to let him or her know about a credit card problem, reviewing your internal security policies and data storage for leaks, or calling in law enforcement.

Get the Facts

Be sure to get the caller's name, phone number, address, credit card number, the date of the sale, an account or invoice number of the sale (if he or she has this information), or any other information that can help you trace the transaction.

Ask How the Caller Found out About the Incident

Did a bill appear on the caller's credit card statement? Was the caller contacted by his or her bank? This information can help you as you evaluate your procedures. Determine if there are new things you need to screen as you process a transaction, or routine checks that can help you find frauds faster.

Don't Give the Caller Any Information About the Fraudster

Many callers will ask for this information because they want to track down the fraudster on their own, but you don't want them to be at risk. Instead, let them know you will work with law enforcement if the time comes, and encourage the consumer to file a police report.

Calm the Consumer

Because the customer will always associate the merchant with the fraud, you need to take the time to smooth the relationship. You should make the situation as easy as possible on your customers—recognize that they might feel violated and acknowledge those feelings.

You might want to offer information on how consumers can fight back. Consider keeping a list of consumer fraud reporting phone numbers or Web addresses on hand, such as the Identity Theft Data Clearinghouse (*www.consumer.gov/idtheft/*), the federal government's database for tracking identity theft complaints. By taking steps to make the caller feel better, you might even help to build some loyalty.

Ask for Permission to Follow up Later

Ask callers if it is acceptable to contact them for more information. This way, you'll have their consent to call if you need more information.

Tip: Review Your Chargebacks

Even though your chargeback advice might come weeks after a fraud has occurred, it is still important to determine which chargebacks are due to fraud. In addition to the fraud prevention insight you'll gain, you'll need the chargeback information as the statement of loss to present to law enforcement if you want to prosecute.

You can manually review your chargeback reports, which are usually sent by your credit card processor either electronically or in the mail. For an additional fee, many third-party processors will review the reports for you.

In some cases, chargeback reports also include the typology of the fraud, which is usually determined by the issuing bank for the credit card. The typology refers to the way the fraudsters got the information they needed to use the card—from a stolen card, for example.

This information is important to capture, because it can tell you if you need to screen for certain types of information that would alleviate these types of fraud. For example, if 80% of your fraud comes from stolen statements, you might consider collecting cardmember identification numbers, which aren't shown on the statement.

Tip: What to Do With Fraud Once You've Found It

Once you've determined which of your sales are fraudulent, you need to learn from them. For starters, you can look for ways to prevent the fraud you find. Ask this question: Are there things we could have done when the sale was coming in the door for the first time?

To do this, compare fraudulent transactions to legitimate sales to determine if there are significant differences. Then compare these transactions to each other to see what's identical. Some characteristics to look for include speed of delivery, product, price, whether refunds were eventually given, or if the cardholder is a repeat customer.

For instance, if you are seeing a lot of fraudulent sales after a customer has shopped with you, then you might have a problem with a vendor, internal staff, or perhaps your shipping procedures. In addition to helping you plug a hole in your process like the one previously discussed, your analysis will help you focus your time. If 80% of your fraud dollars involve a specific type of merchandise, for example, you need to spend your time there.

Tracking fraud will also help you keep tabs on what fraud really costs you. You can then use this data to help build an argument to buy fraud prevention software or increase your fraud prevention budget.

Tip: Using Account Numbers and a Database

To truly make the most of fraud tracking, you need to have access to all of the transaction data: credit card numbers, technical information such as IP addresses and email domains, and inventory, customer, and delivery information. It is critical that this information is secure and encrypted with access limited to those who deal with specific back-end processes.

For this reason, it is important to assign an invoice or unique number to a sale immediately. You will then, need to store all information associated with that number so that it can be accessed quickly and accurately or exported into a database.

This will allow you to reconstruct the transaction if you have to investigate it later. If all you have is the credit card number, you can't learn much about what went wrong.

The database will also make it easier for you to compare, analyze, and review transaction information to learn even more from your experience. In addition, you'll be able to track fraud patterns over time. As a result, you'll be able to prevent even more fraud in the future. [10]

Make a List

You should always save email or other correspondence between your site and your customers until you are certain that a charge won't be disputed. During a busy holiday season, you might want to extend this period. Retain explicit information, including what was ordered, when it was ordered, the shipping address, and the name and credit card numbers used. In addition, make sure your site has a program that documents your site traffic, including the IP address, date and time of order, and the duration of time a customer spends on your site, if possible. This detailed information not only helps in the pursuit of suspects, but also helps you build a case for prosecuting criminals.

Check It Twice

Normally, a transaction should receive more scrutiny if it is with a new customer or the shipping address does not match the billing address. Because both of these scenarios are very common during holidays, be sure to verify customer information—names, phone numbers, email addresses, billing addresses, cardmember identification numbers, card numbers, and expiration dates—before you ship orders. You can also work with vendors that have AVSs or software that can detect vacant buildings, disconnected telephones, or other suspicious information.

Beware of Changing Chimneys

Shipment rerouting is a new trick used by fraudsters. Using stolen credit card information, a thief will make a purchase and ask to have it shipped to the real cardholder's correct billing address. Once the package has left your warehouse, the fraudster calls the shipping company to have the package rerouted.

To prevent this, be sure to mask your shipping account numbers on your labels and work with your shippers to ensure that they follow more stringent procedures before authorizing a change in delivery location.

Prepare for Those Unexpected Holiday Visitors

Holiday shopping drives more users to the Web. Check with your IT department or Web site host to see if your hardware, software, and servers can handle the increased traffic and perform effectively.

Get the Latest and Greatest Gadgets

Always be sure to check with your IT department or Web site host to see if you are using the most recent versions, patches, and upgrades of SSL, firewall software, and any other network or fraud prevention software. Without the latest upgrades, your systems could be open to attacks from hackers, viruses, and worms.

In addition, keep negative files (a list of names and card numbers associated with fraudulent sales) and consider investing in fraud prevention software such as rule-based detection technology or neural networks.

Tip

Some of these tools are also available from transaction processors for a per-transaction fee.

Be Ready for the Grinch or Cyberterrorist

No matter what you do, your site could still be the victim of a hacker or cyberterrorist. If it happens during a holiday season, you might have to communicate the news more quickly and to a wider audience than normal. Plan how you'll deal with the situation, from pinpointing a company spokesperson to preparing a fact sheet on what's appropriate for comment.

As e-commerce matures, so do the risks associated with it. As a result, merchants and insurers are actively working to find solutions to this growing problem. In the next section, you'll find some background and basics about coverage and requirements.

Insurance and E-Commerce: Cyberliabilities

In the event of an e-commerce catastrophe, would you be protected by your business insurance? Probably not.

If lightning struck the warehouse where your servers are stored, you'd be covered. However, if hackers or cyberterrorists shut down those servers, you probably aren't because many traditional insurance policies don't specifically cover e-commerce issues.

Traditional business insurance plans (e.g., general liability) usually deal with physical catastrophes or specific named perils, including fire, flood, or burglary. Today, however, as e-commerce and Internet communication become commonplace, so do the risks—such as denial of service (DoS) attacks, loss of business due to downed servers, lawsuits from online customers, thieves breaking into your databases or email systems, and excess credit card fraud, to name just a few. As a result, insurance companies (and merchants) are searching for solutions.

A New Issue

Insurance policies that cover e-commerce issues have been available in some form for about two years, but the concept (like e-commerce itself) is still in its formative stages. At some point, traditional policies might be broadened to cover some of the issues raised by e-commerce. However, that debate is still being waged in the courts—and might not be settled for some time.

Meanwhile, a number of merchants have already learned the hard way that risks do exist and can be expensive. Several thousand companies have already purchased some kind of e-commerce policy, but most didn't until after the media focused on the billions lost due to the Love Bug virus in 2000, Yahoo! And eBay DoS attacks, and terriost attacks of September 11, 2001.

Even more important, e-commerce itself is both complex and new. Insurance companies do not have much data on e-commerce and its associated risks to rely on when calculating their policies. As a result, many of the larger insurers don't yet offer this type of insurance or have only recently launched their offerings.

113

New Policies

What types of insurance are currently available to cover e-commerce risks? Some insurers offer the option of adding e-commerce coverage to existing business policies that cover liability or credit card fraud. Others might offer specific e-commerce insurance, which is usually designed to protect against risks like hacking. For example, your insurance company might cover the following:

- Loss of business income or ad revenue if your site or systems go down
- The cost of public relations, attorneys, or security consultants
- The loss of intellectual property
- Claims from others if your security fails, if private or financial information is leaked, or if you have errors in your content
- The costs of any extortion schemes; for example, when hackers say they've found a problem with your site and offer to fix it for a price, or threaten to do damage to your systems unless they're paid
- The costs of prosecuting criminals or any costs of paying for information that leads to the capture of a criminal
- Some costs due to credit card fraud or nonpayment
- Damage or loss of goods during shipment

Remember, like any type of insurance policy, what's offered depends on the insurance company. For more information, contact your broker or insurance company. [11]

Requirements and Costs

Before you can get an e-commerce policy, your company and its e-commerce practices will most likely be scrutinized. For example, to be approved for coverage through Avan Trust, you must first complete a series of questions that assess your company's existing Web site security procedures.

Avan Trust sells Web site security insurance through a partnership with AIG, a major insurance company, and Dun and Bradstreet, an aggregator of business information. The Avan Trust assessment, which can be completed online, asks all kinds of questions, on everything from employee procedures to system setups. This assessment was developed with input from top security experts with knowledge of best practices in security and fraud prevention.

If your company requires coverage above a certain amount (usually in excess of $5 million to $10 million), Avan Trust requires a thorough on-site checkup. Avan Trust pays for the price of the checkup, which can cost up to $25,000.

How you fare on these assessments affects your eligibility for coverage and the costs of your premium. The better your existing security procedures and precautions are, the less your premium will cost.

Your coverage should normally equal the total of one year's revenue. At Avan Trust, complete coverage usually costs about $18,000 to $23,000 a year per million dollars in coverage.

In general, a company with revenues of $1 billion or less can expect to pay premiums of about $25,000 to $125,000 for a minimum of $25 million in coverage. Coverage of up to $200 million can also be obtained.

Avan Trust usually works with midsized to large companies, but as with all types of insurance, you can get fewer things for less money.

You should also remember that, like any type of insurance policy, requirements and premiums vary depending on your own company and the company providing the insurance. For specific information, you should check with your broker or insurance company.

Do You Need E-Commerce Insurance?

Whether or not you need some form of e-commerce insurance depends on many factors—from the type of customer data you store to your yearly revenue. In addition to talking to your insurance broker, legal consultant, and financial advisor, you should do two things before you make any decisions: Review your policy and see what you stand to lose.

Talk to your insurance company to see what you're covered for now. Chances are, you're not covered for hacking or anything like it. To assess what you stand to lose, consider this question: If your site goes down or your customer information is compromised, how devastating would that be? Determine what such losses would cost your company (from loss of revenue to consultant fees to possible lawsuits) and how those losses would affect your ability to stay in business.

Overall, most companies should at least review the options available to them. The entire world is becoming more dependent on technology. As a result, companies face new risks, and new risks call for new forms of protection.

AVSs are currently not an option for most international addresses. As a result, experts recommend that international merchants use a combination of fraud prevention solutions. Let's look at the issues and some recommended tips and tools.

International Addresses and AVSs

AVS is often listed as a key part of any online merchant's fraud prevention plan. Usually provided free by credit card processors during the card authorization process, AVS checks the billing address given by the customer with the one on record with the card issuer. The information is then provided to the merchant to help evaluate the risk of fraud for the sale.

Today, AVS is only available for credit cards issued by banks in the United States. AVS should also be available in the near future for cards issued in the United Kingdom, according to NatWest, a UK company that offers card processing services.

In addition, a few global card issuers and European banks offer some international AVSs, but the lack of consistency in addressing systems throughout the world usually means the service can be inaccurate. As a result, there's a large gap in protection for international merchants.

European AVS Software Vendors

To fill in those gaps left by card issuers, a few European vendors are now selling AVS services or software. However, these vendors cover only a handful of countries around the world. For example, AZ Bertelsmann Direct, a direct marketing firm in Germany, offers an address verification service called AZ Strada. The service is only available for Germany, Austria, and Switzerland.

Limitations of AVS

Even when AVS is available, there is no guarantee that a transaction is or isn't legitimate. In fact, many real transactions fail AVS if an address is entered incorrectly by the customer, and many fraudulent orders will match addresses if criminals have access to billing data.

Recommendations

Precisely because of these types of limitations, layering fraud prevention techniques is always recommended, even when AVS is available. All tools in fraud prevention bring incremental value, so AVS should not be used exclusively.

Tips and Tools for International Merchants

Without any complete solution, international e-tailers must look at layering other fraud prevention methods. Here are a few recommendations:

- As previously noted, ask for card verification codes (CVV2 for Visa, CVVC for MasterCard, and CID for American Express). For American Express, the code is a four-digit number on the front of the card above the account number. For Visa and MasterCard, the code is a three-digit number that appears at the end of the account number on the back of the card.

- Keep up with which countries are associated with high numbers of fraudulent transactions. Many fraud prevention Web sites catalog a list of stories or updates about current international frauds.

- Contact the customer when the transaction is high-risk or valuable. Some international merchants require that any customer making a high-value purchase fax in a copy of their credit card billing statement. Although customers might be irritated at first, you can explain that it will protect their own cards or accounts from fraud.

- Flag any transactions by international cards with other suspicious attributes for additional scrutiny. These characteristics include expensive items, large numbers of one type of item, free email addresses, overnight shipping, or any transaction where the billing and shipping address are from different countries. Remember, if the transaction is suspicious, always contact the customer before goods are shipped.

- Use rules-based detection: Keep your own negative files of card numbers, names, addresses, or other customer data associated with denied or fraudulent sales.

- Use predictive statistical model software. Available from vendors, this software compares each transaction to databases of fraudulent sales.

- Ask for the name of the bank on the card. Although you will have to manually verify the bank name by calling the card issuer, only someone who has seen the card will know this information. [12]

Finally, although it will be a while before marketplace standards and consumer awareness push e-signatures to everyday use, you should still be aware of this new technology and its potential for e-commerce.

The Future Benefits

E-signatures can legally be used to sign documents over the Internet. This means your customers can now complete contracts online (like life insurance applications or mortgages) by sending you their e-signature. As a result, expensive paperwork, postage, file storage, and administration time will all be reduced.

What's more, because each e-signature is unique, it can be used to better ensure a customer's identity to prevent fraudulent transactions, and could even replace the real signature merchants normally receive during a face-to-face transaction. Of course, without any standards in place, e-signatures are still just a minor aspect of e-commerce today. However, they should certainly be added to your portfolio of fraud prevention tools.

How E-Signatures Work

The U.S. Electronic Signatures in Global and National Commerce Act, also called E-Sign, was written with broad strokes to support new technologies as they emerge. Although there are a few restrictions (consumers must have the option to sign on paper, e-signatures aren't legal for documents such as wills, divorces, or adoptions, etc.), the Act makes most kinds of e-signatures legal, as long as consumer and merchant agree.

Since the Act was signed by President Clinton in October 2000, several companies have launched or are developing electronic signature products or services. Although few of these solutions have been tested either by public use or by the legal system, some ideas include image files of an individual's real signature, signing one's name on a tablet, entering a password or PIN, and using biometrics—eye, fingerprint, or face scanners (see Chapter 11, "Biometrics"). All of these types of e-signatures would most likely be sent to the merchant, who would then verify the e-signature with a third-party certification authority that has it on file.

Digital Signatures

One type of e-signature technology already in use is the *digital signature*—a term sometimes incorrectly substituted for electronic signature. A digital signature is generated from a digital certificate—a digital form of identification issued by a third-party certification authority, such as VeriSign, Equifax, or others. Digital certificates use public and private keys to ensure privacy and authenticity.

The technology works like this: With a private key that only you have access to, you create and lock your digital signature—an encrypted (or scrambled) mathematical code unique to you. Then, with your public key (which everyone has access to) the recipient unlocks your e-signature and verifies it with the certification company.

Smart Cards

Another option is the *smart card*, such as American Express's Blue credit card or the new cards offered by Visa. A smart card contains a computer chip that can hold information like a digital signature or other type of e-signature. With Blue, users use a card reader that plugs into their computer and a unique PIN. When they make a transaction, they insert their card into the reader and type in their PIN. This unlocks their digital certificate from the smart chip. The certificate is then sent over the Internet to American Express, who identifies the user as the authorized cardmember.

Lack of Standards

Although e-signatures stand to have a powerful influence on the prosperity of e-commerce, there are still many risks involved. For starters, the lack of standards, technical complexity, and expense make it difficult for consumers or merchants (especially smaller ones) to adopt e-signatures.

For example, to use digital signatures, each of your customers needs a set of keys and the ability to figure out how to use them. To use smart cards, your customers need the cards and the card readers. For other solutions, customers need eye scanners or electronic tablets. As a merchant, you need a way to collect and verify e-signatures.

Unfortunately, all the new legislation has done is make this process a legally binding one. It doesn't make it accessible to the user.

Fraud Risks

Yet, another concern is the same issue merchants have now: cybercriminals. Smart cards can be forged and public keys can be stolen. As with credit cards and customer data, e-signatures are targets on the consumer's PC, in transit, or in the merchant's database. As the tool gets more and more use, sooner or later, people will go after it.

The Future

The future of e-signatures is uncertain, but over time, technologies will be tested by consumers, merchants, and the courts. As in the past, the market will most likely move toward the few types of technology and verification systems that provide both ease of use and a secure reputation. For now, most people are just going to wait and see.

Are merchants going to need to know about this going forward? Yes! How will it be implemented? No one knows yet. The technical community and many others are standing back and waiting to see who's going to win.

Endnotes

[1] "Security and Your ISP," ClearCommerce Corporation, 11500 Metric Blvd., Suite 300, Austin, TX 78758, USA (Worldwide E-Commerce Fraud Prevention Network), 2001.

[2] Meridien Research, 2020 Commonwealth Avenue, Newton, MA 02466, USA, 2001.

[3] "Explaining Technology: Firewalls," ClearCommerce Corporation, 11500 Metric Blvd., Suite 300, Austin, TX 78758, USA, 2001.

[4] "Security for the Little Guy: If You Don't Have Fortune 500 Bucks To Spend How Do You Protect Your Business Online?" (Reprinted with permission from Bank Info) Thomson Financial, One State Street Plaza, 27th Floor, New York, NY 10004, 2002.

[5] Julie Fergerson, "Five Tools You Can Use to Prevent Fraud," ClearCommerce Corporation, 11500 Metric Blvd., Suite 300, Austin, TX 78758, USA, 2001.

[6] "Explaining Technology: Rules-Based Fraud Detection Systems," ClearCommerce Corporation, 11500 Metric Blvd., Suite 300, Austin, TX 78758, USA, 2001.

[7] "Ask the Expert," ClearCommerce Corporation, 11500 Metric Blvd., Suite 300, Austin, TX 78758, USA, 2001.

[8] "Fraud Fighting 101," ClearCommerce Corporation, 11500 Metric Blvd., Suite 300, Austin, TX 78758, USA, 2001.

[9] "To Catch a Thief," ClearCommerce Corporation, 11500 Metric Blvd., Suite 300, Austin, TX 78758, USA, 2001.

[10] "Finding Fraud," ClearCommerce Corporation, 11500 Metric Blvd., Suite 300, Austin, TX 78758, USA, 2001.

[11] "Cyberliabilities: E-Commerce and Insurance," ClearCommerce Corporation, 11500 Metric Blvd., Suite 300, Austin, TX 78758, USA, 2001.

[12] "AVS and International Addresses," ClearCommerce Corporation, 11500 Metric Blvd., Suite 300, Austin, TX 78758, USA, 2001.

Chapter 6

PROTECTING THE IDENTITY INFORMATION OF CUSTOMERS

C onfidentiality, integrity, and availability are of primary concern to an ISP in the installation and deployment of any identity theft protection solution. The goal has always been to balance business requirements and associated risks with necessary protection of customer identities. The modern enterprise, whether a vast global organization or a modest business, must contend with dynamic, diverse, and distributed environments that demand fluid connectivity. The World Wide Web provides a feature-rich medium for the inexpensive, convenient, and rapid exchange of information and commerce. Along with such advantages comes the significant challenge of securely integrating the Internet with the business infrastructure.

This chapter describes the adoption of the World Wide Web by consumers and corporations, provides an overview of the categories of risks and threats associated with identity theft protection, and illustrates how appropriate privacy policies and practices serve to mitigate the risks inherent in doing business on the Web. The intended audience for this chapter is ISPs, corporate officers, IT directors, security managers, risk managers, network supervisors, Web site managers, and business entities that are attempting to install and deploy identity theft protection for their customers on the Internet.

The Internet Itself

As you know, the Internet provides another opportunity for identity thieves to glean personal information. Thieves can design very official-looking email messages that imply they are from a major company, and successfully obtain personal information from trusting individuals.

Customer Email Policy

As an ISP or Internet company, you should have a customer email policy. You should have a message posted on your Web site that tells customers not to submit emails that contain sensitive or confidential information and not to use email for specific transaction-related requests. Your system should give you the capability of using autoresponders for any email submitted. You should also draft an autoresponder that thanks the sender for their message, acknowledges that it was received, and basically reiterates your policy about how they shouldn't be sending confidential or sensitive information or anything about a specific transaction or account. You might also want to add something like this statement: We will not act on email requests for funds transfers, stop payments, account closings, or fraud notifications. These must be done either in person, or by calling the phone number given.

Are the preceding recommendations a good approach, or is there a better way to handle this? Should you even consider posting an email address on your site at all, or just stop the email?

First of all, posting the additional notice is an excellent idea. In fact, unless you can take steps to independently verify the customer's identity, you might want to remove email links from your site altogether. The only true safe way to respond to a request that would involve sensitive or confidential information would be to require the customers to adopt some form of secure encryption for their email and utilize digital signatures to authenticate themselves to the bank.

Although you should do everything you can to tell customers that they should not send confidential information through an unsecured medium such as email, you probably won't be able to ignore them. Fraud notifications via email, once sent and received by a bank, have resulted in some liability for losses after that.

For example, the Federal Financial Institutions Examination Council Guidance On Electronic Financial Services And Consumer Compliance dated July 15, 1998 (Reg. E, under 205.6(b)(5)) states:

Notice to a Financial institution is given when a consumer takes steps reasonably necessary to provide the institution with the pertinent information, whether or not a particular employee or agent of the institution actually receives the information. The consumer may notify the institution in person, by telephone, or in writing. Written notice is considered given at the time the consumer mails the notice or delivers it for transmission to the institution by any other usual means. Notice may be considered constructively given when the institution becomes aware of circumstances leading to the reasonable belief that an unauthorized transfer to or from the consumer's account has been or may be made.

Additionally, the same document states:

Pursuant to §205.6, timing in reporting an unauthorized transaction, loss, or theft of an access device determines a consumer's liability. A financial institution may receive correspondence through an electronic medium concerning an unauthorized transaction, loss, or theft of an access device. Therefore, the institution should ensure that controls are in place to review these notifications and also to ensure that an investigation is initiated as required.

Clearly there is some burden on the bank. Although you might require additional verifications, it is only prudent to take some steps on notification of facts. That is, discourage the transmission of confidential information in a non-confidential medium, but don't ignore it if you get it.

The Internet Company

If you are an Internet company, be aware of the sensitivity of the information you have about your customers. Take care to ensure the security of this data. Think about who on staff has access to your customer information (see the sidebar, "Laws Dealing With Your Customers' Information"). Consider restricting access to a few who have a need to know. Perform due diligence on those who do have access. Criminal background checks are a reasonable option for those with access.

 Tip

Remember, if that new employee pockets a few thousand credit card numbers as a result of your sloppy information practices, you could be liable, as well.

Laws Dealing With Your Customers' Information

The following are some laws that deal with your customers' information:

- The FCC's Customer Proprietary Network Information rules prohibit telephone carriers from stealing this information from you when you order telephone service.

- The Electronic Communications Privacy Act governs when it is appropriate for you to turn information over to federal agents and what documents they have to present to you before you should supply that information. One online discussion recently recommended that you have an "in case of emergency, break glass" box that has inside specific instructions for your staff for when the FBI shows up, and perhaps a video camera or tape recorder to record their activity. It is not that you do not want to cooperate with your friendly local police officer; however, you have much to lose if they improperly or illegally take your subscribers' personal information.

- Any children's information collected online falls under the Children's Online Privacy Protection Act.

How is customer information secured and stored, and how do you dispose of it when it is no longer needed? Paper shredders now cost somewhere around $40 at the local office supply store. Safes and locking file cabinets are also very affordable.

Do you run Web sites for your customers or do you, yourself, conduct e-business? How secure are your online transaction forms? Could any terrorists' exploits defeat your security efforts and permit unauthorized users to rifle through your data?

Make sure someone on staff is responsible for the security of your network and your customers' data. Your security and firewall should be designed with the confidentiality of this data in mind. If your project is big enough, get your security tested. Consider subscribing to a voluntary trust program, like the Better Business Bureau or TRUSTe, that you can use to show your customers that you are taking the necessary precautions with their information.

Consider training your customer support staff to help victims of identity theft. After all, when customers have trouble with Netscape or Internet Explorer, who do they call? When customers worried about Y2K problems, who did they call? They called you.

Think about creating a list of frequently asked questions (FAQs) on your company Web site linking to the appropriate identity theft information. As your subscribers are going online with broadband connections and fixed IP addresses, they are increasingly vulnerable to intruders rifling through their hard drives. You should inform your subscribers, either on your Web site or in a flier with the material that you provide, about the dangers of exposing themselves to the barbarians online. Consider adding a firewall package to the service package you offer them. Recommend that they keep their sensitive data on removable media, like Zip disks, that are not always in their computers. When your customers are victimized online, it is an opportunity for your staff to shine with the best customer service in town.

What this discussion adds up to is the recommendation that you designate a privacy officer in your organization. Have one person on staff whose responsibility it is to watch over how customer information is handled. This individual should be at least familiar with privacy and information law. This person doesn't have to be an expert;. he or she just has to know that when federal agencies stick out their chests and demand information, you do not have to automatically turn it over—unless you want to be sued by the people whose information you turned over.

Consumer and Corporate Identity Theft Protection Implementation and Deployment

The Internet and the tremendous acceptance of the World Wide Web have taken the business-computing community by storm. Use of public-access networks is attractive to both the consumer and corporations. It is understandable that so many hardware and software vendors and promotions and media reports are geared toward promoting the Internet, espousing its use and acceptance, and protecting the identity of its customers.

The practicality of the Web is based on two open standards—HTML which facilitates document format and links to other document resources, and Hypertext Transfer Protocol (HTTP), a network protocol for delivering Web content. The combined result offers dynamic, seemingly boundless access and transmission of private information. This content-rich, platform-independent delivery mechanism, teamed with growing ease of access, yields an economical and convenient way for vendors and consumers to do business in private.

The consumer audience for the Internet is impressive. There are approximately 88 million Web browsers in use today with more than 70 million households connected to the Internet. Sun Microsystems has estimated that the number of Internet Web hosts is growing at a rate of 21% per month, and that the number of Web servers is growing at approximately 160% each month. Popular research indicates that 62% of consumers plan to make online purchases by the year 2003, which could amount to $80 billion in consumer-based electronic commerce.

By the year 2003, two-thirds of all businesses will be on the Web, and business-to-business (B2B) sales will reach $160 billion. It's estimated that over 82% of Fortune 1000 companies are taking advantage of Internet transport mechanisms for a variety of purposes, including email, employee and departmental collaboration, internal information exchange, mobile and remote access to sensitive corporate data, automated customer and supplier communication, and distribution of electronic information and products. According to IDC, business and commercial use of the Internet has expanded dramatically to become both a delivery vehicle and an execution platform for the next generation of client/server applications.

With the preceding in mind, the installation and deployment of identity theft protection on the Internet is becoming fast and furious. For some organizations, counting the number of Web sites, servers, managers, and contributors is nearly impossible. The following corporate Internet/intranet statistics shed some light on corporate Internet/intranet trends and possible identity theft risks (see the sidebar, "The Process of Implementing Identity Theft Protection"):

- 26% allow remote employee access.
- 38% utilize fewer than five employees to manage their Web site.
- 44% allow nonemployee access.
- 46% state that 50% of their employees use the Internet.
- 54% allow collection of corporate information.
- 55% implement sites on a departmental basis.
- 65% allow company database access.
- 80% will not allow security breaches to prevent the company from using the Internet. [2]

The Process of Implementing Identity Theft Protection

Let's take a moment to step back and look at protection of identity as a corporate strategy.

Protection of identity as a Corporate Strategy

A key component of the successful development and implementation of identity theft protection is the identification of a person who will be accountable for it within the organization. This designated individual could be your chief information officer (CIO), or you might designate this as the responsibility of another person within your organization. The designated person might also be responsible for the management and coordination of the information resources policies and procedures of the organization. In either case, the person in this position must have sufficient authority to be heard by your executive management and senior staff. This person must have a good general knowledge of the business functions and processes of your organization, in addition to knowledge of information management techniques and tools. This person will become the advocate for identity theft protection within your organization and for specific Web site applications.

Depending on the size and structure of your organization, the CIO or other designated person might assemble a team of people from across the organization to first develop and then implement identity theft protection. It is important that the team not be made up solely of staff with communications, technical, or production responsibilities. Establishing broad policies and procedures requires input from all parts of the organization. Members of the team bring knowledge of the functions and processes of their part of the organization and take back both information about identity theft protection and a commitment to making the principles work. Education of other staff members and customers will become an important part of their role.

The Corporate Planning Phase

As with any project, the planning phase is extremely important, and it is best to start with what is already known. Before identity theft protection principles can be successfully integrated into an organization's policies and procedures, a thorough understanding of those policies and procedures is essential. Any organization that has information gathering, processing, or distribution functions will undoubtedly have information handling policies and procedures, which will likely include some of the components of identity theft protection. It is vital at this point to identify the components in place and those that must be introduced. To do this successfully, the team must know and understand identity theft protection, particularly how it differs from such concepts as confidentiality and security.

Documenting the Identity Theft Protection Policies and Procedures Phase

Documentation is the most efficient and effective means of communicating the identity theft protection of an organization to customers and staff. It can also provide a clear and concise record of how the process of protecting information is to take place. The documentation should be in a form that makes it readily available to those who need it. This might mean brochure format for the customer, whereas the organization's staff is provided with a set of operational guidelines and procedures.

Maintaining the Identity Theft Protection Phase

To fully benefit from all the work you have done in the previous phases, you need to provide ongoing education for existing staff and training for new staff. You also need to periodically reinforce the importance of privacy to staff through such means as memos, internal newsletters, media clipping services, and internal case studies of both well-handled and poorly handled identity-theft-related issues.

Periodic reviews and audits of established policies and procedures give you an opportunity to acknowledge good practices and correct poor ones. A periodic review of your policies and procedures will reinforce your corporate strategy.

Customer satisfaction surveys can show you where you are succeeding and where you are not, providing you with an opportunity to fine-tune your procedures if necessary. A periodic report should be made by the individual designated with the responsibility for identity theft protection. Finally, a presentation to senior management on the status of the program should include the number of inquiries, the number of complaints, and the outcome of the complaints. [1]

Identity-Theft-Related Risks and Threats

The media have exhibited a remarkable affinity for Web-related issues. Articles highlighting momentous Internet and intranet security incidents are no longer relegated to the back pages of trade publications, but appear on the evening news and in the daily papers. Clearly, the preceding adoption statistics testify that businesses are willing to assume greater risks to immediately capitalize on the Web phenomenon. However, the process is not without its identity theft problems.

IT managers have always had the challenging task of determining identity theft risk areas within their enterprise and implementing both policy and technical measures to deal with them. However, the policies and safeguards now must not only defend internal resources, but also provide securely managed public access via highly visible Web resources as well. As the invisible hand of the market drives the complexity and glitz of Web sites upward, the task of properly implementing and maintaining the installation of identity theft protection grows expeditiously, often leaving the IT manager behind the curve as shown in Figure 6.1. [2]

Recent surveys suggest that great security flaws exist in corporate Internet sites. According to a recent Ernst & Young report that polled 1,026 commercial sites, over 51% had security breaches and 64% experienced losses exceeding $600 million. The Department of Defense reported that 93% of its sites had been penetrated in 2000. Recent International Computer Security Association (ICSA) Labs research showed that approximately 55% of U.S. Web sites are attacked or probed each month. [3]

It is not the intention of this chapter to imply that companies are not utilizing their security assets and tools to minimize identity theft liabilities. The emerging statistics indicate that despite the measures currently in place, the Web security picture is worsening. Security and identity theft issues must be systematically and consistently addressed for the Web to remain a viable and reliable medium for commerce.

The basic components of any secure operation are well-defined and enforced policies; adequate and secure hardware, software, and connectivity;

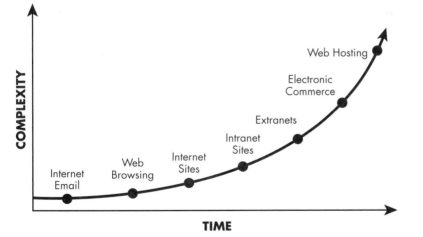

Figure 6.1 The Task of Properly Implementing and Maintaining the Installation of Identity Theft Protection Grows Expeditiously.

monitoring both routine and exception events; and well-designed and tested defenses against intrusion. Evidence has shown that although most internal and external Web sites have security and identity theft tools and measures in place, many are still exposed to significant inadvertent and inherent Web-related vulnerabilities.

Although in aggregate, 70% of companies use encryption, 100% use passwords, 100% use antivirus software, and 90% have firewalls, 70% still experience security breaches. Factors driving corporate Web security include the greater number of Internet connections, the popularity of remote access facilities, the vulnerabilities in popular Web site applications, the lack of end user awareness and the increased awareness, of identity theft protection threats.

What are some of the Web-based identity theft threats and how can such threats impact business? As mentioned earlier, most commercial sites experience attacks and probes on a regular basis. It would logically follow that the more visible or elaborate a Web site, the more likely that an internal or external Web server would be the target of identity theft intrusion attempts. However, identity theft threats do exist no matter what the size of the Web site, its location, or its use. In other words, most sites do not detect or respond to even blatant probes of their external networks.

Rapid implementation of identity theft protection, vague privacy policy, conflicting chains of command, and evolving network designs contribute significantly to Web-associated chaos, which intruders are all too ready to exploit. Installing identity theft protection techniques can provide unintended exploitation channels to users of a corporate system, or to the corporate systems themselves. The less than desirable possibilities are endless.

Many organizations treat their Web servers as simple information publishing tools and do not fully consider the content they deliver as vital or vulnerable to alteration and misappropriation. Without a proper operational security and identity theft protection policy and mechanism, it is possible for portions of a site to be modified with little or no record of change—having enormous ramifications. If a company incorrectly communicates timely information to its suppliers and distributors, the damage in terms of lost business, lost goodwill, and damages will almost assuredly exceed the cost of appropriate identity theft protection measures. Unfortunately, site administrators most often learn of such problems well after the fact, and the costs of both the damage and the solution must be borne.

Content integrity is of paramount importance to companies operating in regulated industries or offering timely information on which decisions are based. Placing appropriate identity theft protection controls on the modification of Web site content can be as important as locking the comptroller's filing cabinet.

The downside of the virtual marketplace can be readily observed in cases where it is necessary to contact the site operator by non-Internet means. In the event of a successful disinformation or graffiti attack, identity theft, chronic unavailability, suspected fraud, site spoofing, or other dissatisfaction, the ability to contact the site operator off line is directly related to continued commercial viability of the enterprise (see the sidebar, "Minimizing Online Identity Fraud and Theft"). Mechanisms for managing both host addressing information and administrative contact information are available. Unfortunately, in the heat of identity theft protection implementation, essentials such as maintaining current network information center contact phone numbers and clean DNS entries often remain on the to-do list long after the site is operational.

Minimizing Online Identity Fraud and Theft

Equifax Secure, the e-commerce division of Equifax, Inc., recently introduced a new standard of online identity fraud protection available through the Microsoft Passport service. The program is available to retailers participating in Equifax's consumer identity authentication technology, PayNet Secure™, which uses the Microsoft Passport single sign-in solution.

With the combined services, e-retailers are able to verify the identity of consumers in real time, reducing the risk of fraudulent transactions and boosting customer confidence in the safety and security of the transaction. Additionally, this integrated solution offers merchants enhanced e-payment capabilities, increasing the security, ease, and speed of the online purchasing process.

Under terms of the agreement, Equifax Secure has integrated Passport's single sign-in service for its online identity authentication and payment solution, PayNet Secure. PayNet Secure combines Equifax's patent-pending authentication technology with online check authorization services and management of a secure, private ID registry for authenticated consumers. Equifax Secure also resells Microsoft's Passport services to e-retailers.

Gartner Group recently reported that fraud is 12 times higher on the Internet than offline, based on a study of 160 retailers. According to the Boston Consulting Group, a strikingly high online purchase failure rate and fear of online fraud are preventing a sizable number of online shoppers from returning to the Web.

The combined Equifax and Microsoft Passport solution lowers the risk of fraudulent transactions for retailers supporting online transactions.Retailers can route purchasers through the PayNet Secure service during the purchase flow.

Once a consumer has signed into PayNet Secure using the Passport Single Sign-in service, he or she can verify his or her identity, thus increasing the integrity of the transaction. This agreement represents a significant milestone for Equifax, as well as online merchants. Through this agreement, Microsoft has demonstrated its ongoing commitment to work with the best available technology providers to ensure privacy and security while eliminating the risk of fraud in online transactions.

With an estimated 100 million registered Microsoft Passport consumers, Web retailers can now gain access to an installed base of customers to attract and retain while controlling operational costs through outsourcing back-end payment and fraud prevention services. The exponential growth in online fraud and the resulting costs challenge the profitability of online retailers.

The Passport/PayNet Secure solution advances a more secure environment for retailers in the online marketplace. Also recently announced, Paymentech, the nation's largest processor and acquirer of credit card transactions, has offered the Equifax PayNet Secure solution to improve transaction security and confidence for Internet merchants who have adopted its full-service credit card processing solutions.

In 2000 alone, Paymentech handled 6 billion transactions totaling $105 billion in bank card sales. The company also leads the transaction processing industry for card-not-present markets with almost half of all Internet point-of-sale transactions going through the Paymentech system for authorization and settlement.

About Microsoft Passport

Microsoft® Passport consists of two services: a single sign-in service that allows members to use a single name and password to sign in to a growing number of participating Web sites; and, an Express Purchase or wallet service that members can use to make fast, secure online purchases. Kids Passport, an optional feature of the single sign-in service, offers Web sites an easily implemented, turn-key solution for obtaining parental consent to collect or disclose a child's personal information.

Kids Passport facilitates a site's compliance with the parental consent requirements of the Children's Online Privacy Protection Act. More information on Microsoft Passport can be found at *www.passport.com*.

About Equifax PayNet Secure

PayNet Secure offers Equifax's authentication solution to participating retailers and Passport consumers. Because it instantly authenticates online users, PayNet Secure is the most advanced online identity verification solution available in the marketplace.

By obtaining a more complete and accurate user profile, Equifax authentication provides a superior shield against tampering and identity theft. The privacy of user information is protected through each step in the authentication process, which complies fully with the FCRA. Step by step, here's how Equifax's PayNet Secure works:

Step 1

The consumer completes and submits the enrollment form, providing the requested information. The information is encrypted and transmitted electronically to Equifax, with the privacy of the consumer protected every step of the way. Once the information reaches Equifax, the authentication engine compares and analyzes multiple elements in the furnished information against consumer data from Equifax and other consumer and business information sources.

Step 2

The authentication engine then displays a multiple-choice questionnaire compiled from information sources listed in the preceding step.

Step 3

The consumer answers the questions and clicks Submit. If the answers are verified, then the consumer is instantly authenticated. If the consumer's identity cannot be authenticated, then he or she will be instructed to complete the process manually. The authenticated individual is issued a Passport log-in ID and password that is re-usable at any Microsoft Passport or PayNet Secure retail site from any computer anywhere, anytime.

About Equifax Secure

Equifax Secure (*www.equifaxsecure.com*), the e-commerce division of Equifax, Inc., provides security, privacy, and transaction management solutions that protect consumers and enterprises from the risk of identity theft and fraudulent transactions. Equifax Secure authenticates online consumer identity, secures business applications, and manages digital certificates and directories for highly secure, private e-commerce over the Internet and other networks.

Equifax, Inc., serves the financial services, retail, credit card, telecommunications/utilities, transportation, information technology, and health-care industries and government. Equifax adds knowledge, expertise, convenience, and security to provide value-added solutions and processes for its customers wherever they do business, including the Internet and other networks. [4]

Implementation of identity theft protection measures (proper encryption methods, sensitive information handling, cache management, end-user advisories, and back-end transaction discipline) is an area of potential disaster in many commercial sites. Mechanisms and utilization standards exist in all of these areas; however, the impetus to implement a well-managed, consistent identity theft protection infrastructure and supporting policy is more often regarded as an expense or overhead, rather than a necessity of doing business.

The same ease-of-use issues that have fueled the e-commerce boom on the Web have improved the distribution channels for black-hat and white-hat players alike. Vulnerability warning information, exploitation tools and scripts, fixes, system patch announcements, and massive quantities of other related information is now the standard for staying informed about network identity theft protection issues.

Web site identity theft protection management is all too frequently considered a content issue. Massive changes in content, links to other sites, and frequently changing image issues are all part of the effort to promote business and increase Web site traffic. Due to lack of resources, revision control and configuration management are often nonexistent. In many cases, evidence of attacks and probes is recorded by the built-in logging facilities, but if such mechanisms are not regularly and consistently reviewed, no benefit is gained.

Explosive growth and the drive to get on the Internet has resulted in a new and sometimes dangerous class of Internet activity: the shrink-wrapped site. Despite public opinion to the contrary, installing identity theft protection techniques, operating systems, Web servers, and even firewalls right out of the box with default (or misunderstood) settings provides no assurance of security and identity theft protection whatsoever. There may be a false sense of security provided by using popular products that support all the buzzwords.

The fundamental issue is that configuration, design, and maintenance of an Internet site is a specialized and continuously changing area. Operating system installation and configuration, logging a review, management of permissions and rights, and server configuration and privacy policy implementation are all areas that must be executed properly at identity theft protection implementation and maintained throughout the operation of the site. The Darwinian nature of the Internet environment requires that the security posture of a site continually evolve and adapt to survive. Administratively inconvenient activities such as version upgrades, operating system patches, and site physical and operational security and identity theft protection reviews are essential components of a viable Internet presence.

Consumers are consistently willing to provide sensitive information in response to direct mail and telemarketing campaigns, although only 75% of Web-using consumers are willing to use the Web for making purchases. The gap in acceptance exists despite the fact that the public has no real information about the difference (or similarity) in enterprise security and identity theft protection posture between the direct mail vendor and the electronic commerce vendor. The perception of the lack of safety on the Internet has continued to plague electronic commerce. A recent study by TRUSTe and the Boston Consulting Group showed that consumers are not inclined to provide sensitive data or generic demographic data even with a familiar cyberretailer. The study also revealed that the simple declaration of a Web site's security and identity theft protection policy increased sensitive information disclosure by consumers up to threefold.

Many companies are choosing to implement Web sites at the departmental or business unit level, whereas others outsource the function to ISPs and Internet hosting providers. Whether hosted Web servers are dedicated, remotely managed, or shared, the degree of risk and adherence to security and identity theft protection policy can vary substantially from one department or hosting site to another. The gap between the desired security and identity theft protection posture, as dictated by a security and identity theft protection policy, and the actual security and identity theft protection practice does not often become apparent until a breach occurs. The hasty deployment of hot new identity theft protection capabilities only broadens this gap (see Figure 6–2). [2]

Whether browsing or managing an Internet or intranet Web site, there currently exist limited and dynamic baseline standards for availability, integrity, and confidentiality. Furthermore, the range of identity theft vulnerability and risk areas is both broad and complex. Web-based attacks—exploitation of

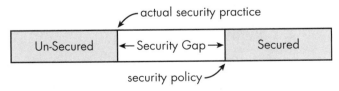

Figure 6.2 The Security Gap.

operating system flaws, Web servers, common gateway interface (CGI) code, and identity theft—are also responsible for the following:

- *Internal intrusion*: Physical security issues, seizure of administrative access

- *Receipt or distribution of malicious code:* CGI/CxE code review, change management issues, virus scanning of downloadables, and so on

- *Attack exposure:* Effectiveness of network security mechanisms, enforcement of policy, physical security, version upgrades, security patches, and so on

- *DoS and availability issues:* Environmental, power protection, redundancy, recoverability, intrusion defection, attack detection, log review and reporting, and so on

- *Negligence and due diligence:* Handling of sensitive information, encryption key handling, authentication, access and transaction logging, and so on

- *Misrepresentation and authentication problems:* User identity, access to private content, fraudulent transactions, administrative policy failure, site spoofing, or site data corruption

- *Loss of trust:* Due to graffiti attacks, content corruption or inaccuracy, disclosure of customer or corporate proprietary information [2]

Web Site Identity Theft Provisions

Applying information security disciplines and techniques in the Web arena can be a painful cross-cultural experience. Complex integration issues associated with a commercially attractive Web presence, internal network security, identity theft protection, and importance of defending sensitive information are difficult to manage. If ignored, these areas can yield significant supplier, customer, and shareholder confidence implications. The network aspect of securing a Web site is comprised of four primary components:

1. Perimeter defenses, such as properly configured firewalls or screening routers. Firewalls and filtering routers provide access control and monitoring functions at the border of the enterprise.

2. Elimination of unnecessary services and protocols. Conservative configuration enables only those services and protocols that are essential to the business requirements. Disabling all others eliminates unnecessary toeholds that can be used by intruders.

3. Maintenance of system components and software. Version upgrades, patches, and vulnerability workarounds must be addressed as they occur to avoid becoming an easy target.

4. A consistently enforced policy that addresses the management, usage, and procedures associated with the configuration. A well-constructed, enforceable policy allows all of the Web players in the enterprise to understand the purpose, procedures, and constraints associated with the endeavor. [2]

The need for harmony among these elements cannot be overstressed. Even if perfection is achieved in three of these areas, failure of the fourth element can undermine the entire effort.

As with the network security components and identity theft protection techniques, Web site administrative concerns can be divided into a number of interdependent categories:

- *Operational security:* Creating and enforcing organizational policies regarding personnel changes, physical and facility security, separation of production and development environments, appropriate management of cryptographic keys, and other areas.
- *Availability:* Taking appropriate measures to ensure that systems are consistent with the needs of both the customer and the site availability operator.
- *Confidentiality:* Handling of both customer and corporate sensitive and proprietary data in an appropriately secure manner. This is of particular concern as it applies to connections with corporate back-end systems.
- *Recoverability:* Ensuring that adequate backup and recovery mechanisms are in use to ensure that the site can be restored in the event of a catastrophe, whether a natural or technical disaster.
- *Accountability:* Proper registration of a site's DNS, having current domain contact information registered with the network information center, and offline contact information for the site all contribute to the ability of an end-user to locate and contact a site operator in the event of difficulties. [2]

Web site pages that can contain or accept sensitive data (e.g., name, address, customer ID) require special handling to improve security and identity theft protection. Although current Web technology places control of many related issues beyond the site operator (in the browser), there are both technical and informational practices that serve to mitigate the exposure. Server parameters can be set to suggest to intermediate caches (which can occur at the ISP or enterprise) that certain pages should not cached—clearly an appropriate measure, although intermediate caches might ignore the advisory and store copies of the pages in any case. Appropriate use of session encryption can reduce the exposure of such information to on-wire observers. Similarly, persistent client state mechanisms, commonly called *cookies*, that allow the server to instruct the user's browser to remember certain data, are inappropriate for saving sensitive data. Informing site visitors about sensitive information risks and the mechanisms and techniques in place to minimize these risks allows users to make informed decisions about the use of the site and configuration of their browser. Additionally, informing site visitors of how sensitive data will be used, what suitable defenses the user can employ, and what security policies are in place contributes to their understanding and perception of the site's security and identity theft protection.

As an extension of traditional access controls, properly implemented file-and session-based encryption can dramatically reduce the threat of identity theft and unauthorized data interception. Session encryption mechanisms such as SSL, Secure HUP (SHUP), Secure Electronic Transactions (SET), Secure Internet Mail Encoding (S/MIME), and other emerging standards can responsibly safeguard the transmission of sensitive data in a variety of forms. By offering users the confidence of transmitting their sensitive information in a secure manner, one can enhance the safety perception of one's site as follows:

- SSL secures connections at the IP socket level that provide encryption, authentication, and validation of all protocols supported by an SSL-enabled Web browser such as Netscape Navigator or Microsoft Internet Explorer.
- SET enables effective authentication of those parties involved in a purchase transaction.
- S/MIME allows the transparent handling of encrypted files. Although the addition of encryption to an insecure system does not magically solve its problems, properly implemented encryption mechanisms are a key component of a viable commercial Web site. [2]

Web technology is equally adept at delivering both useful information and malicious code. Given the choice between having dancing pigs and not, users will choose dancing pigs every time. With such a user propensity to click on anything, the proper control and review of site content is incumbent on the site operator who wants to retain user confidence. Virus-infected content, potentially subversive or faulty Java applets, or ActiveX components are particularly insidious in that a Web server can blithely serve them up without harm to itself, with the damage, inconvenience, and loss-of-service problems occurring directly on the end user's system. Providing assurance to users that a site's operational practices include measures to review client-executable content is both good Net citizenship and smart business.

Another threat category associated with Web sites is that of CGI scripts and programs. CGI is a standard means of handing off information sent from a browser to programs other than the Web server for processing. The most common example of an application is that of a search engine, where a user's query is sent to the Web server and then passed to a database system for processing. Because CGI involves execution of programs that process arbitrary data sent by an end user, great care must be taken to avoid exploitation of the CGI code, as unauthorized access to the operating system could result. Fortunately, the matter has received much study and safe CGI coding standards have been published.

Unfortunately, the standards are not consistently followed. Because CGI is an imperfectly understood mechanism, many sites are at risk due to improperly constructed CGI, whether developed in house or included with the Web server software. Some CGI-related issues include the following:

- *Code origin:* Where the code came from, whether in house, distributed with the server software, or obtained from a third party.
- *Configuration management:* Knowledge of the business purpose and maintenance status of all accessible CGI programs on the server.
- *Coding standards adherence:* Review of all CGI for which source code is available to ensure that standards were followed in development.
- *Integrity management:* Use of digital signatures (e.g., MD5 hashes) to allow detection of unauthorized changes to CGI programs. For example, commercial versions of Tripwire (a product that also allows detection of unauthorized changes) are available for the Solaris, Windows NT, HP-UX, and IBM AIX operating systems, as well as Tripwire Manager from Tripwire, Inc. To find out more, visit *www.tripwire.com.* [2]

Last but not least, you must plan for physical threats such as water, fire, natural disaster, equipment theft and failure, vandalism, and unauthorized entry and access. Sites that fail to meet traditional physical security requirements, such as access-controlled areas and available emergency contact information, have ample exposure to DoS attacks and security breaches.

Web Identity Theft Protection Verification

A company can undertake many identity theft protection provisions, in terms of tools and actions, to reduce the inherent risks associated with building and maintaining a Web site. It is in any company's best interest to employ such identity theft protection mechanisms as firewalls, encryption technology, anti-virus products, password controls, physical safety inspections, transaction monitoring, and security assessment (see Figure 6–3). [2] Establishing, documenting, enforcing, and promoting operational and logical security policies, coupled with staff and end-user education, provides a basis for identity theft threat reduction. However, individual products only offer components of what is required in a holistic approach to Web site identity theft protection.

Verification by an independent third party strengthens Web identity theft protection mechanisms and contribute's to management's due diligence efforts and responsibilities. Whereas accounting auditors assure that proper and accepted principles are exercised, certification from security professionals confirms that the proper configuration of tools and implementation of procedures meet desired security requirements. However, just as accounting auditors cannot guarantee accepted principles are adhered to or will, in fact, protect the financial stability of a company, no ICSA Labs Web certification program can provide absolute identity theft protection or completely eliminate negligence. [3] Certification will, however, dramatically reduce risks.

The ICSA Labs Web certification program provides an independent verification of technical and policy-based identity theft protection provisions, with the goal of improving the standards of practice and reducing areas of risk. [3] As an annual process, the program tracks identity theft protection threats and standards of practice to provide an increasingly stringent baseline for commercial Web site operation. The standard is intended to be concise and attainable, providing end users with an indication that a site operator has an ongoing commitment to good practice.

The unique ICSA Labs identity theft protection program is comprised of a detailed on-site evaluation, remote assessment, random inspection, and an evolving set of industry-endorsed standards and best practices. ICSA Labs will

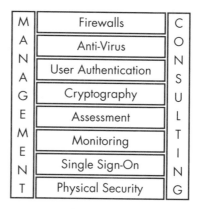

M	Firewalls	C
A	Anti-Virus	O
N	User Authentication	N
A	Cryptography	S
G	Assessment	U
E	Monitoring	L
M	Single Sign-On	T
E	Physical Security	I
N		N
T		G

Figure 6.3
Identity Theft Protection Mechanisms.

continue to evolve its ICSA Web certification criteria based on research of expert and vendor material; interviews with ISPs, Webmasters, and computer security experts; and ongoing input from the staff of ICSA Labs.

ICSA Web site certification provides the site operator and the end user with a meaningful baseline of identity theft protection practices and is a step in the right direction toward reducing your company's Web site exposures and liabilities.

Endnotes

[1] Information and Privacy Commissioner/Ontario, 80 Bloor Street West, Suite 1700, Toronto, Ontario, M5S 2V1, 2001.

[2] "Web Site Security: Adoption, Risks & Prevention," ICSA Labs, International Computer Security Association, 1200 Walnut Bottom Road, Carlisle, PA 17013, (TruSecure Corp., 13650 Dulles Technology Drive, Suite 500, Herndon, VA 20171) USA, 2001.

[3] ICSA Labs, 1200 Walnut Bottom Road, Carlisle, PA 17013, USA, 2001.

[4] Equifax Secure, Inc., P.O. Box 740341, Atlanta, GA 30374-0241, USA.

[5] Federal Trade Commission, 600 Pennsylvania Ave, NW, Washington, DC 20580, USA, 2001.

Chapter 7

Internet Site Operator Testing and Performance of Identity Theft Protection Techniques

T he key to an ISP successfully installing and deploying identity theft protection (discussed in Chapter 6, "Protecting the Identity Information of Customers") on a Web site is to consider it as part of the central design and testing criteria. This ensures that identity theft protection is built into the Web site right from the start, thereby eliminating the difficult and expensive task of retrofitting identity theft protection into an existing Web site. Before looking at ISP identity theft design and testing techniques, let's first look at the principles involved in protecting against identity theft.

Identity Theft Protection Principles

Many of the concerns expressed by consumers about identity theft relate to the manner in which personal information is collected, used, and disclosed. When organizations collect information without the knowledge or consent of the individuals to whom the information relates, use that information in ways that are unknown to those individuals, or disclose the information without the consent of the individuals, informational identity is violated.

Today, the online world is creating exciting new commercial opportunities for businesses. Consumers are drawn to electronic commerce not only because of the products and services available, but also because of the convenience and savings possible with online transactions.

However, there are strong indications that the growth of e-commerce is being impeded by consumers' fears about their identity and privacy online. One recent survey revealed that eight out of 10 consumers were concerned about protecting their identity when participating in online activities, and that 40% did not believe that online companies honored their posted privacy policies.

Consumers' fears about identity theft are not without foundation, and are reinforced by frequent media stories about irresponsible online practices and unauthorized access to online data. A recent study of commercial Web sites showed the following:

- Half of the surveyed sites did not have a privacy policy.
- 40% did not indicate if they shared the information they collected with a third party.
- 26% of the sites used cookies, but did not reveal that to users.
- Over half of the sites did not provide contact information.
- More than 60% did not allow users to access information they had submitted. [1]

One of the more troubling conclusions of this study was that U.S.-based sites performed much worse in terms of identity theft than sites outside the country that target U.S. users. Clearly, the need to establish and maintain the trust of customers or potential customers is a significant challenge for online businesses, and a key to lasting commercial success. Protecting users' identity information is an essential component of building that trust.

In addition to consumer pressures, businesses are facing an evolving legislative framework for identity theft protection in the private sector. To respond to the dual incentives of developing consumer trust and compliance with legislation, companies that wish to succeed in the online world are working to make identity theft protection an integral part of their business initiatives.

Online businesses need to move quickly to understand their responsibilities to respect their customers' privacy. They need to recognize the following:

- If they collect, use, or disclose personal information, they must do so responsibly.
- They must maximize customer control over their own personal information online.
- They must ensure that their information practices are open and transparent to the consumer. [1]

Beyond compliance with the law, identity theft protection is critical to competitiveness online. Effective identity theft protection is now a necessary part of doing business. There are significant risks and consequences (both commercial and legislative) for businesses that do not adequately address identity theft.

To encourage ISPs to examine their online practices, and to more fully integrate privacy into those practices, Table 7.1 examines a set of best practices for online identity theft protection. [1] These best practices outline areas that should be addressed to effectively protect the identity of online customers. They are overlapping and interrelated in nature, which means that to adequately protect an identity, all areas must be considered. However, these practices are not intended to be adopted in their entirety—they consist of a list from which you can select those items most appropriate to your circumstances.

Table 7.1. Best Practices for Online Identity Theft Protection Checklist Form

How to Protect Against Identity Theft Online
ID Theft Online Protection Checklist Form
Date: _____

It is recommended that those ISPs who design Web sites that use advanced identity theft protection technologies or those who market Web sites commit to the following best practices or principles. These are best practices steps to effectively protect the identity of online customers. (Check all tasks completed.)

Respect for Privacy

❑   1. Conduct business in the least intrusive manner possible.

❑   2. Understand and comply with applicable identity theft legislation, agreements, and standards.

❑   3. Understand that personal information includes all information about, or linked to, a personally identifiable individual. This includes such information as name, address, credit card number, income, purchase preferences, and transactional data. Email addresses, as well as data collected from automatic tracking methods, may constitute personal information if linked to an identifiable individual.

❑   4. Recognize that personal information is about individuals who have the right to exercise reasonable control over that data.

❑   5. Assess the impact on privacy of any proposed online practice, service, product, or technology prior to implementation.

❑   6. Take special care when dealing with children. If there is a reasonable likelihood of collecting, using, or disclosing personal information from or about children, follow appropriate privacy practices.

147

Table 7.1. Best Practices for Online Identity Theft Protection Checklist Form (Continued)

Openness

❑ 7. Develop identity theft policies and practices requiring personal information to be handled in an open and accountable manner.

❑ 8. Be open and informative about your organization's policies and practices involving personal information.

❑ 9. Ensure your stated policies and practices are factual, accurate, and complete. Do not misrepresent your company's identity or information practices.

❑ 10. Inform individuals, on request, of any records your organization maintains containing their personal information, how you use it, and what data you disclose.

❑ 11. Provide individuals with sufficient information for them to understand their privacy rights, and give them the opportunity to exercise those rights quickly, effectively, and without prohibitive cost. Information should include the name or title and contact information of the person or area responsible for your identity theft policies and practices, as well as details about how individuals can access their personal information in your control.

❑ 12. Prepare and post an identity theft policy on your Web site. Your policy should clearly explain all your responsibilities and information practices. Specifically, your policy should be designed so it is:

    ❑ a. Easy to find, easy to read, easy to print, and easy to understand (use examples to explain and demonstrate your practices).

    ❑ b. Accessible from every Web page, not just the home page.

    ❑ c. Written in the same language as the Web site to which it is attached.

❑ 13. Do not change your stated identity theft policies and practices without providing enough time and information for affected individuals to make informed decisions and take appropriate action.

❑ 14. Inform individuals of:

    ❑ a. All applicable identity theft legislation and agreements, and provide links to the Web sites of the authorities responsible for the administration and enforcement of these instruments.

    ❑ b. All professional codes of practice, seals, or other programs you must be in compliance with, and provide links to the full text of these agreements and the Web sites of the organizations responsible for their proper implementation and enforcement.

    ❑ c. The consequences to your organization for noncompliance with your privacy policies and practices, and with all other relevant programs and legislation (audit,

Table 7.1. Best Practices for Online Identity Theft Protection Checklist Form (Continued)

penalties or sanctions, revocation of seal, loss of professional membership, complaint forwarded to an oversight body for investigation, or publication of name for noncompliance).

❏   d. Their recourse if they believe you are not complying with your policies and practices, or with any other relevant programs or legislation.

❏   15. Explain your use of any type of Web-based tools to collect personal information that might not be readily apparent to a user. This should include use of automatic tracking software, clickstream data, cookies, and clear GIF files (Web bugs).

❏   16. Explain your solicitation practices (email and other means), as well as what personal information you rent, sell, or exchange to third parties for marketing or other purposes.

❏   17. Inform individuals:

❏   a. If data you collect, use, and disclose online is handled differently offline and why. If it is, specify how, and inform them how they can interact with your organization through other means (mail, in person, fax, or telephone).

❏   b. Of any security or privacy violations involving their personal information as soon as possible, as well as what action they can take to remedy the problem or minimize the risks.

Accountability

❏   18. Ensure identity theft protection is a priority for all levels of your organization. Top-level commitment to privacy policies and practices is critical for success.

❏   19. Understand that if you collect personal information, you accept the responsibility to handle that data in accordance with your stated privacy policies and practices, and to make that information available to the individual to whom it relates.

❏   20. Train your staff and make them accountable for adherence to your privacy policies and practices.

❏   21. Designate a specific individual or position responsible for protecting identity and complying with your privacy policies. In larger organizations, it might be necessary to have a team or group involved in developing and implementing your policies, with varying levels of responsibility, but there always should be someone with final accountability. Provide sufficient resources and authority to discharge this responsibility in an effective and timely manner.

❏   22. Publicize the identity of the responsible individual on your Web site, along with information about how they can be reached online and offline, and your days and hours of operation, if applicable.

Table 7.1. Best Practices for Online Identity Theft Protection Checklist Form (Continued)

❑ 23. Establish procedures for reviewing your privacy policies and practices to ensure they remain accurate, timely, and complete.

❑ 24. Develop a process to verify your compliance with your stated privacy policies and practices, and to publicly demonstrate that compliance.

❑ 25. Define your obligation to undertake all necessary action to correct any problems that arise out of your noncompliance with your own policies and practices, or with any legislative requirement.

❑ 26. Include identity theft protection requirements, comparable to your own policies and practices, in your contracts with business partners or third parties who will have access to personal information collected or controlled by you. This is particularly important if you will be sending personal information to jurisdictions without comparable identity theft protection regulation. Take all reasonable steps to ensure the contracted party follows the identity theft protection measures stipulated in your contracts (e.g., site visits, audits).

❑ 27. Understand that if you collect personal information, you accept the responsibility to handle that data in accordance with your stated privacy policies and practices, and to make that information available to the individual to whom it relates.

Purpose Specification

❑ 28. Define the purposes or reasons you need each piece or type of personal information (name, address, email address, clickstream data, age, gender, income, etc.) to complete a specific, legitimate business transaction. When identifying potential purposes, consider the following:

    ❑ a. If nonidentifiable information (coded, anonymous, pseudonymous, or aggregated) could fulfill the purpose.

    ❑ b. How the personal information needs to be collected (directly from the individual through a subscription, automatic collection of clickstream data, or from a third party) and why.

    ❑ c. Who will need to use the information (within and outside the organization), and why.

    ❑ d. To whom the information will need to be disclosed, and why.

❑ 29. Identify any additional reasons to collect, use, or disclose personal information not strictly related to the specific business transaction (incentive programs, target email marketing services, data mining, etc.).

❑ 30. Understand that your defined purposes should be reasonable in the context of your business.

Table 7.1. Best Practices for Online Identity Theft Protection Checklist Form (Continued)

❏ 31. Do not define your purposes so broadly as to make them meaningless to the individual from whom you want to collect personal information.

❏ 32. Document your purposes so that your staff and the individuals to whom the personal information relates can know what they are.

❏ 33. Identify any new purpose for using previously collected personal information prior to its use.

Individual Knowledge and Consent

❏ 34. Obtain consent prior to collecting individuals' personal information, whenever possible. Ensure that individuals understand the purposes for which you will be collecting, using, and disclosing their personal information prior to obtaining their consent.

❏ 35. Use express consent provisions whenever possible. Set the defaults on consent options to be the most privacy protective (do not use a negative option such as pre-checked boxes on registration pages that require individuals to take action to indicate what they do and do not consent to).

❏ 36. Consider the sensitivity of the personal information involved when determining the appropriate type of consent. As a general rule, more sensitive data (medical or financial information) should have express rather than implied consent.

❏ 37. Define narrowly the exceptional circumstances when consent is not possible or may be inappropriate. In very limited circumstances you might need to collect, use, or disclose personal information without any type of consent (for law enforcement purposes or when the individual is a minor, seriously ill, or mentally incapacitated).

❏ 38. Provide individuals with clear and adequate information for them to make an informed decision about giving their consent, including the consequences, if any, of refusing or withdrawing consent. Individuals should be able to withdraw consent at any time, subject to legal or contractual restrictions and reasonable notice.

❏ 39. Provide individuals with a simple, clear, and secure online mechanism to indicate their consent, refusal, or withdrawal of consent, regarding the:

    ❏ a. Collection, use, and disclosure of their personal information.

    ❏ b. Storing, altering, or copying of any information on their computers.

    ❏ c. Use of any type of automatic tracking software, by you or a third party, including the automatic disclosure of clickstream data to third parties.

    ❏ d. Receipt of any online or offline marketing or promotional communications, from you or third parties.

❏ 40. Do not mislead or pressure individuals to obtain their consent.

Table 7.1. Best Practices for Online Identity Theft Protection Checklist Form (Continued)

❑ 41. Do not make the supply of your product or service conditional on individuals consenting to purposes unrelated to the supply of that product or service.

❑ 42. Do not withdraw previously accessible services or products if individuals do not consent to the use or disclosure of their personal information for new and unrelated purposes.

❑ 43. Inform individuals of exactly what is and what is not covered by your consent provisions (collection by your Web site only or also by a third party), and if their consent is time-limited.

❑ 44. Ensure that individuals understand when you will not be asking for consent and why (after initial consent is given, and until such time as individuals take contrary action or notify you of a change in their wishes, permission to use persistent cookies will not be solicited each time they revisit your site).

❑ 45. Take reasonable steps to verify that the individual providing the consent is authorized to do so (i.e.,is the individual to whom the personal information relates or is the authorized representative).

❑ 46. Take reasonable steps to ensure that the individual is old enough to give legal consent when your product or service likely involves children. When appropriate, obtain explicit and verifiable consent by a child's parent or authorized guardian prior to the collection, use, or disclosure of any personal information related to that child.

❑ 47. Obtain consent from the individual to whom the personal information relates, prior to using their data for a new and unrelated purpose, unless that purpose is required by law.

❑ 48. Do not assume that because individuals have visited your site or even made a purchase they consent to solicitation.

❑ 49. Do not require individuals to call or write to express their lack of consent for your use of their personal information collected online. At the time of consent, ask individuals if you can follow up with them and how they want to be contacted, if at all. Maintain a record of consent and make it accessible to individuals for their review.

❑ 50. Do not revoke opt-in/opt-out options or change time limitations without prior and adequate notice to the individual.

Collection Limitation

❑ 51. Do not collect personally identifiable information whenever possible (permit the individual to visit your Web site without capturing clickstream data, or let the individual deal with you anonymously or pseudonymously).

❑ 52. Collect only the amount and type of personal information necessary and relevant for the identified purpose(s), or as required by law.

Table 7.1. Best Practices for Online Identity Theft Protection Checklist Form (Continued)

❑ 53. Collect personal information by lawful and fair means, and from reliable sources.

❑ 54. Do not collect personal information in a covert or coercive manner, or through misleading or deceptive practices.

❑ 55. Inform individuals, at or before the time of collection, of the type of personal information you intend to collect, including data you collect by automated means.

❑ 56. Inform individuals at or before the time of collection if the personal information to be collected is required by law and, if so, fully explain the specific requirement.

❑ 57. Collect personal information directly from the individual to whom it relates, except in limited and defined circumstances.

❑ 58. Inform individuals of the types and sources of personal information you collect indirectly for the purpose of providing services or products (data collected from third parties).

❑ 59. Also indicate why direct collection is not possible or appropriate.

❑ 60. Do not allow third parties to collect personal information or cookies through your Web site unless they are contractually bound to a comparable privacy standard.

❑ 61. Avoid collecting unique identifiers (Social Security number or driver's license number) unless their use is required by law, or express consent is obtained from the individual. If required to collect unique identifiers (for tax requirements), explain reasons to the individual at or before the time of collection.

❑ 62. Comply with relevant legislative restrictions on the collection of personal information (human rights legislation might limit what can be collected on employment applications).

Use and Disclosure Limitations

❑ 63. Do not use personal information except in the manner and for the purpose(s) identified to the individual at the time of collection, unless the individual to whom the personal information relates consents, or by authority of law.

❑ 64. Do not disclose, distribute, or make personal information available in any way, except for the purpose(s) and to the sources identified to the individual at the time of collection, unless the individual to whom the personal information relates consents, or by authority of law.

❑ 65. Take all reasonable steps to ensure that the personal information you use and disclose is relevant and necessary to fulfill the identified purpose(s) or the requirements of law.

❑ 66. Use both policy and technical restrictions to control unauthorized and unrelated uses and disclosures.

Table 7.1. Best Practices for Online Identity Theft Protection Checklist Form (Continued)

❑ 67. Limit use of persistent cookies to where they are needed for a continuing purpose. The expiry date of a cookie should be consistent with the purpose.

❑ 68. Inform individuals of any legal requirements you have to disclose personal information, and to whom. Include these requirements in your privacy policies.

❑ 69. Inform individuals of the circumstances when disclosure can take place without their prior knowledge or consent (serious and imminent threat to public health or safety). Include these reasons in your privacy policies.

❑ 70. Do not knowingly disclose or transfer personal information to third parties without adequate privacy safeguards.

❑ 71. Establish appropriate and effective controls and schedules for information retention and destruction. Ensure that all practices are fully documented.

❑ 72. Retain personal information in identifiable form only as long as it is relevant and necessary to fulfill the purpose(s) for which it was collected, as required by law, or as needed to give the individual to whom the information relates an opportunity to access or correct the data.

❑ 73. Destroy, erase, or permanently deidentify any personal information no longer needed for its identified purpose(s) or to meet legal requirements.

❑ 74. Maintain a record of disclosure so you can update third parties who have previously received personal information from you, as required (in cases when disclosed data is corrected due to inaccuracy).

Accuracy

❑ 75. Do not knowingly collect, use, or disclose inaccurate personal information.

❑ 76. Take all reasonable measures to ensure personal information is accurate, complete, and up-to-date, having regard for the nature of the data the purpose(s) for which it is collected, used, and disclosed; and the interests of the individual to whom the data relates.

❑ 77. Take all reasonable steps to minimize the chances of inaccurate data being used to make a decision about an individual. In determining what measures you should adopt, consider the extent of potential harm to the individual should you use or disclose inaccurate information.

Security

❑ 78. Protect all personal information in your control from loss or theft, and from unauthorized access (within and outside your organization), use, alteration, copying, disclosure, and destruction.

Table 7.1. Best Practices for Online Identity Theft Protection Checklist Form (Continued)

❏ 79. Establish security safeguards appropriate and proportional to the sensitivity of the personal information, and the nature of the possible risks. In gauging sensitivity, consider the potential harm (financial loss, loss of benefits or opportunities, discrimination or stigmatization, public embarrassment) to the individual should the information be misused or disclosed in an unauthorized manner.

❏ 80. Implement effective physical, technical, and procedural measures to secure personal information on your Web site and linked computer systems.

❏ 81. Develop policies and practices restricting employee access (including IT staff) to personal information for unrelated and nonbusiness reasons. Include appropriate disciplinary measures for violation.

❏ 82. Inform individuals of the security measures you will undertake to protect their personal information. Include an outline of these measures in your privacy policies.

❏ 83. Inform individuals of the steps they should take to conduct online transactions safely and securely.

❏ 84. Establish appropriate access and verification procedures, audit trails, and record integrity controls.

❏ 85. Take all reasonable steps to ensure communications or transactions through your Web site do not result in unauthorized access to individuals' computers or personal information, or unauthorized modification or destruction of their data.

❏ 86. Establish secure disposal procedures to ensure personal information cannot be re-created or reconstructed after destruction, and the individual cannot be identified or linked to that data in any way.

❏ 87. Maintain a record of destruction documenting how and when personal information is destroyed and the necessary authorization to do so.

❏ 88. Take all reasonable steps to ensure third parties involved in a transaction (those renting or leasing the data, as well as any party contracted to your organization to conduct such activities as data processing or data mining) have adequate security.

Right of Access and Correction

❏ 89. Design your information management systems and practices to facilitate individuals' right to access their own personal information, and to challenge the accuracy and completeness of their personal information in your control.

❏ 90. Inform individuals of their right to access and correct their own personal information, and how that right may be exercised.

❏ 91. Establish a simple, clear, and secure online mechanism for individuals to find out:

   ❏ a. What personal information relating to them you have, both online and offline.

Table 7.1.   Best Practices for Online Identity Theft Protection Checklist Form (Continued)

❑   b. The purposes for the collection, use, and disclosure of that information.

❑   c. To whom it has been disclosed.

❑   d. The full cost of access (costs should be reasonable and demonstrable).

❑   e. The sources of the personal information (whenever possible).

❑   f. The name and location of the person in charge of the information.

❑   92. Provide individuals with a simple, clear, and secure online mechanism to access their personal information, on request, review and correct their personal information, if necessary.

❑   93. Ensure access is provided to individuals in an understandable format, and without undue delay or expense (at no or minimal cost), whenever reasonably possible.

❑   94. Establish clear and limited criteria for why individuals' requests for access or correction can be denied. Include these reasons in your privacy policies.

❑   95. Verify the identity of the individual before granting access to or correcting any personal information.

❑   96. Correct or destroy personal information found to be incorrect, incomplete, irrelevant, or inappropriate as quickly as is reasonably possible.

❑   97. Provide individuals with the following, if you deny their request to access or correct their personal information:

❑   a. The reasons for that decision, in a timely and understandable manner.

❑   b. An opportunity to prepare a statement of disagreement and have it, along with your reasons for denial, attached or linked to the data in question, in the event that their challenge remains unresolved.

❑   c. An opportunity to clarify their request.

❑   d. A fair opportunity to challenge the decision.

❑   98. Take all reasonable measures to inform third parties who have used or accessed personal information within the last year of the relevant corrected information or unresolved challenges. Provide them with copies of corrected information or the record of unresolved challenge, if possible.

Complaints and Dispute Resolution

❑   99. Develop procedures to receive, investigate, and respond to complaints and questions about all aspects of compliance with your posted privacy policy and practices. Permit as much secure online interaction as possible.

Table 7.1. Best Practices for Online Identity Theft Protection Checklist Form (Continued)

❏ 100. Ensure your complaint and dispute resolution processes are effective, fair, impartial, confidential, understandable, easy to use, and timely. They also should be cost-effective for all parties involved, to the extent reasonably possible.

❏ 101. Respond to complaints and take corrective action, as appropriate, in a timely manner.

❏ 102. Ensure your process for receiving and responding to inquiries and complaints, along with the individual's recourse, is fully described and easily found on your Web site.

❏ 103. Do not charge individuals for the opportunity to exercise their right to challenge your denial of access decisions.

❏ 104. Inform individuals of any third-party investigative and dispute resolution procedures available to them.

❏ 105. Direct individuals to the relevant authorities (a privacy or identity theft protection commissioner, industry association, or seal program) if you cannot resolve the complaint to the individual's satisfaction. Alternatively, make available third-party dispute resolution mechanisms on an optional basis. Such processes should be accessible, affordable, fair, and impartial for all parties

Design and Testing Techniques

The components or best practices in Table 7.1, make up the identity theft testing assessment checklist. Some components apply during the development of a Web site, whereas others are more applicable during the implementation stage and actual use of the Web site. Many of these components apply throughout all stages of design, development, implementation, testing, and usage.

Actions you should take are shown in boldface and italics in Table 7.2. [1] Background information has been included to assist you in preparing your answers. Table 7.2 serves as a guide to the components needed to develop an identity theft protection program, rather than a complete record of the program. Certain components might require the development of separate documents to completely describe and document the component. In those cases, the checklist will serve as a reference list for these documents. The checklist will also serve as an overview of the program that can be distributed to staff and customers to better inform them of the organization's commitment to privacy.

Table 7.2. Identity Theft Protection Testing Assessment Checklist

Step	Details
Description of the Proposed Web Site *[Describe the proposed Web site requiring the collection of personal information:* What are the important features? For example, what categories or groups of individuals you will be or are you gathering information from and what classes or types of information are being gathered? What methods of collection, storage, and transmission of the information are being used? How will the information be organized? For example, is the information for an individual retained together or stored separately by type, such as identifying information in one location, and transaction or functional information in another location?]	
Description of the Personal Information to Be Collected *[List and describe the personal information to be gathered:* What type of personal information is to be collected? How is the information obtained (directly from the source or indirectly)? Is any third-party information involved? If the information is to be collected indirectly the reasons why this is necessary should be clearly outlined. What differences, if any, are there for different types of customers? Does the information pertain to one individual or to a group of individuals? What is the extent of the information to be collected (one record or several)?]	

Table 7.2. Identity Theft Protection Testing Assessment Checklist

Step	Details
Purpose of the Collection	

[Identify the purposes for the collection of personal information: Why is the personal information necessary and relevant to the application? Why must the personal information be collected in identifiable form? Why is personal information required as opposed to anonymous or pseudonymous information? What, if any, are the consequences of not collecting the personal information? Is the information required for functional or administrative purposes or both?]

How Is Notice of Collection Given and Informed Consent Obtained?

[Design the notice to be authorized by the customer and attach: How is notice of the collection given? How is consent obtained? If consent is inferred from some action of the customer rather than expressly given, indicate why this approach is necessary. What is the process by which the individual is informed and provides consent? Attach such documents as the Web site form used to seek consent, the customer response card that gives consent, a listing of the oral information provided when information is collected, and so on. Is the information to be shared with other organizations or linked with their databases? If so, are fair information practices also in place there?]

Table 7.2.   Identity Theft Protection Testing Assessment Checklist

Step	Details
Method of Collection	
[Describe how information will be collected and, if appropriate, how it will be linked to previously collected information: What is the process of collection? How is the collected information transferred and stored? Is there any linking or matching with previously collected information? If so, how is this accomplished? What controls are in place to ensure the validity of the information during the various steps of this process?]	
Duration of the Collection of Personal Information	❏ One time
	❏ Unlimited
[Identify the period of time over which the data will be collected: Is the collection for this one time only, is it limited in duration or ongoing? Particularly important to note are the reasons why the collection is ongoing, as this leads into issues of data integrity.]	❏ Limited
	Start date:_____
	End date:_____
Accuracy	
[Outline the steps to be taken to ensure that information is accurate at all stages of the application: What steps will be taken to ensure the accuracy of the collected information both at the time of collection and over time if the information should change? Is a verification process part of the overall process?]	
Method of Storage	
[List each method by which the personal information is stored, including the original collection form, computer files and copies, backup copies, on the Web site, and so on: What is the storage method and process for the Web site and associated components in the overall Web site?]	

160

Table 7.2.   Identity Theft Protection Testing Assessment Checklist

Step	Details
Key Personnel	Chief Information Officer
[List by name and title all personnel responsible for the privacy of this Web site: Who serves as the focal point for the identity theft protection process of the organization (the CIO)? Who are the people who have roles in the access and correction process? From the perspective of those inside the organization, it is useful to list persons who have key roles in the functions of collection, use, retention, and disclosure of the information.]	Other Key Personnel Name _____, Function_____ Name _____, Function_____ Name _____, Function_____
Description of Procedures for Access and Correction	
[Describe the process to be used by individuals to view and request changes to their data: What procedures are or will be put in place to permit customers to gain access to their personal information? What are the procedures for requesting correction of information? This might include reference to more detailed documents that describe the process at greater length. A document that is suitable for distribution to the customer is very useful as is a document for internal use to outline the steps of the access process and correction process for staff.]	
Procedures for Complaints and Appeals of Denial of Access or Correction	
[Describe the procedure to be followed by an individual who wishes to lodge a complaint about his or her data or problems in accessing or correcting that data: What procedures are in place for a customer to voice a complaint about how his or her personal information is being collected and used? What procedures exist if access to this information or correction of it has been denied? How are concerns resolved? What time frames exist for resolution?]	

Table 7.2. Identity Theft Protection Testing Assessment Checklist

Step	Details
Security	
[Describe the security measures that will apply to the information at all stages of its existence (see "Method of Storage"): What security measures are to be used to ensure the protection of personal information, restrict the possibility of unauthorized use, and track authorized use? These measures should reflect the sensitivity of the data and should have the flexibility for customers to select security measures for their data that reflect their perception of the sensitivity of their data.]	

Identity Theft and Your Web Site

Each time you design a new Web site or modify an existing one you should assess the impact of the Web site on privacy. It can become a natural part of your systems design and testing process and will work well with your existing procedures. It starts by looking at each piece of data and determining who can access it and what they can do with that data element.

During the Design, Development, and Testing of the Web Site

You first start by identifying each piece of data that will reside on the computer or the Web site. You will find a checklist in Table 7.3 [1] that you can copy and use during this phase of your Web site design. On the checklist, *communicate* refers to transmitting data over a communications port. If your Web site was to gather frequent flyer points for a loyalty program, your checklist might include the fields as shown in Table 7.4: [1] Let's say the Web site hosts a health care card. Your fields might include those shown in Table 7.5. [1]

Table 7.3. Data Field Checklist

Data Field	Accessed By	Read Only	Add Data	Change	Delete	Copy	Print	Communicate

Table 7.4. Data Fields for Web Site Frequent Flyer Checklist

Data Field	Accessed By	Read Only	Add Data	Change	Delete	Copy	Print	Communicate
Card owner name	Card owner	Y	N	N	N	N	N	N
	Issuer (Airline)		Y	Y	Y	Y	Y	Y
	Travel agent	Y	N	N	N	N	N	N
Frequent flyer number	Card owner	Y	N	N	N	N	N	N
	Issuer (Airline)		Y	Y	Y	Y	Y	Y
	Travel agent	Y	N	N	N	N	N	N
Card owner name	Card owner	Y	N	N	N	N	N	N
	Issuer (Airline)		Y	Y	Y	Y	Y	Y

Table 7.5.   Data Fields for the Web Site Health-Care Card

Data Field	Accessed By	Read Only	Add Data	Change	Delete	Copy	Print	Communicate
Patient name	Patient	Y	N	N	N	N	N	N
	Issuer		Y	Y	Y	Y	Y	Y
Drug allergies	Doctor		Y	Y	N	N	Y	Y
	Nurse	Y	N	N	N	N	N	N

It is important to identify each piece of data, but equally important is to identify it by location; that is, if you specify the access rights of the field on the central computer, you must do the same for that data field on the Web site, and also for any backup. Only then can you be assured that you have protected privacy relative to each piece of data.

When you have completed both this checklist and the identity theft protection testing assessment checklist, you will have carefully and systematically planned for the protection of informational privacy for your application—and you will also have documented it! Congratulations—you're way ahead now.

Endnotes

[1]   Information and Privacy Commissioner/Ontario, 80 Bloor Street West, Suite 1700, Toronto, Ontario, M5S 2V1, 2001.

Part III

IDENTITY PROTECTION FOR CORPORATIONS

Chapter 8

PROTECTING THE IDENTITY INFORMATION OF CUSTOMERS AND EMPLOYEES

I dentity theft victims frequently turn to their ISPs and financial institutions to help resolve some of the issues associated with this crime. Every institution must plan for and have an information security program in place that describes the measures that the institution takes to protect data— and to investigate reports of misuse.

As you know, the term *identity theft* is relatively new, but imposters who use another person's identity to commit offenses have been practicing their schemes for decades. The difference now, however, is that federal and state laws (and industry-standard security practices) have been enacted and developed to address these special crimes. Financial institutions and their customers both suffer when someone steals the customer's identity: The customer experiences a loss of money, reputation, and a positive credit history; and the institution experiences an increase in fraudulent new accounts, phony loans, thefts from safety deposit boxes, and forgeries.

Customers usually do a poor job of planning and protecting themselves from well-recognized sources of identity theft. Financial institutions and ISPs don't always do much better in protecting their customers (or their employees') sensitive data. This chapter addresses identity theft from two perspectives: the planning measures that institutions should take to protect and secure their own, their customers' and their employees' data; and the information protection planning measures that institutions can recommend to their customers and employees.

This planning process logically requires the participation of every insider. This chapter addresses the planning (strategic and tactical) methods to consider and the most effective planning methodologies for creating identity theft prevention and investigation practices. When planning to prevent identity theft, the following topics must be addressed:

- A brief review of the identity theft provisions of the Gramm–Leach–Bliley Act (see the sidebar, "Protecting Consumer Information From Identity Theft" later in the chapter).
- The types of crimes that rely on identity theft—and how those crimes work.
- The types of offenders who steal identities and their motives.
- Which customers are most at risk for identity theft.
- Where both internal and external offenders look for identity theft opportunities.
- What information protection measures are commercially reasonable and available. [3]

Identity Theft Crimes

A diamond-studded tennis bracelet, a set of wedding rings, a camcorder, and more rang up on the cash registers of Cincinnati retailers. All of these purchases were charged to the credit cards of Lynette Vandenberg. Hundreds of miles away in a small Pennsylvania town, Vandenberg had no idea that $8,000 worth of merchandise was being purchased using her credit. It didn't take long to realize that her identity had been stolen by someone who had moved into the Indianapolis apartment she had vacated some time ago. The woman simply filled out and sent in a preapproved credit card application she discovered in her mailbox that had been addressed to Vandenberg.

This can easily happen to anyone. As you know, it is the phenomenon known as identity theft. As previously stated in earlier chapters, it is one of the fastest growing consumer credit crimes today. In an increasingly cashless society, identity theft has become almost the perfect crime, called by some a 1990s kind of crime. The rapid growth of the crime results from the ease with which people can commit the crime and the low risk of being apprehended and prosecuted. It is so common and easy that a simpleton could commit identity theft.

Identity theft is a vibrant and growing criminal enterprise, and consumer advocates have called it the easiest crime because we live in a society where cash is seldom carried and most wallets are filled with plastic. By posing as someone else, thieves have found that they can steal in a way that leaves victims powerless and police uninterested.

It is difficult to say just how widespread identity theft is because there is no standard definition of the crime. However, sometime around 1994, the number of complaints to government, business, and consumer groups began to explode. Credit reporting firms say fraud inquiries have soared from less than 12,000 annually in 1992 to more than 700,000 today. The biggest problem with statistics on identity theft is that cases can go for years and years before being detected.

Identity theft encompasses a variety of different crimes—credit card fraud, stealing an ATM card, using someone's Social Security number, or confiscating someone's driver's license. The perpetrators use this information to buy everything from cars to toys, leaving the person's credit rating in ruins. Imposters have even been known to commit crimes, then give their fake identity to police when they're arrested.

Several states, (e.g., California, Wisconsin, Massachusetts, Georgia, and Arizona) have enacted identity theft statutes, making the crime a felony. Congress recently voted on a bill that makes identity theft a federal felony, punishable by up to 15 years in prison. Another bill recently introduced would give consumers more control over who has access to personal information, such as Social Security numbers.

However, in many states, including Virginia, stealing someone's identity is still the perfect crime because there is little that can be done to prosecute it. These states simply do not have any separate statutes addressing identity theft. Most states have provisions for prosecuting obtaining a birth certificate under false pretenses, credit card fraud, forgery, and so on, but no provisions or recourse for identity theft. The crime is prevalent nationwide and the consequences of it are immense.

Identity Theft Offenders

Identity theft is one of the fastest growing crimes in the country, and the Internet certainly makes it easier. Some IT planners argue that sequestering personal information from the Web is the only solution, but that approach would prove a complete disaster.

As you know by now, identity theft is the stealing of another person's identity, usually to leverage the victim's credit rating to obtain personal loans, credit cards, or instant credit, and run up debts that are never repaid. Some identity thieves go even further and siphon money directly from a victim's existing bank accounts.

There's also the rare identity thief who isn't after financial gain. For those who enter the United States illegally, using another person's Social Security number might facilitate obtaining employment, renting an apartment, and activating utilities like telephone service and electricity. There are also those who have no credit or negative credit histories that borrow another person's Social Security number to establish a line of credit without any intention of defrauding the real owner. For those master criminals who have been profiled on such shows as *America's Most Wanted*, stealing an identity (from the living or dead) might help them avoid being captured before the first commercial break.

Regardless of motives, what makes all this thievery possible is the system by which people are issued identification documents and the practices of verifying identity. The perpetrator only needs to learn a few personal details about his or her target. The credit industry accepts a certain level of risk in doing business, and creditors are more than willing to service anyone who can verify personal information against the details already on file with major credit reporting agencies.

The unsuspecting public might assume that those details, like their mother's maiden name, Social Security number, and driver's license information, are secret and protected from public disclosure. However, numerous governmental and private organizations (like ISPs) keep so-called private information in widely accessible databases, and many opportunities exist for identity thieves to obtain it. Thieves can learn most personal identifiers through low-tech methods, like mail theft and dumpster diving. More sophisticated attackers might break into government or private-sector databases to retrieve the data. Thanks to the World Wide Web and its plethora of databases, search engines, and public records, getting this information is now easier than ever.

Roots of the Problem

Several genealogical sites provide research tools to help you trace your family tree. These sites have collected an enormous amount of data from many different sources, including birth, death, and marriage records.

One site, *www.rootsWeb.com*, allows Web surfers to search and retrieve data from California's birth and death records index, which are public information in the state. This might be a valuable tool for a genealogist, but it's also a potential gold mine to an identity thief. For example, financial institutions typically ask customers doing business over the phone to give their mother's maiden name to prove their identity. If you were born in California, anyone with access to the Internet can find out that information.

The potential for abuse escalates when records can be easily cross-referenced with other data. Ambitious thieves could even employ identity-stealing bots that comb through the vast array of information on the Web and assemble dossiers on potential victims.

Such a program would begin by searching through online alumni records, or professional referral services that catalog doctors, lawyers, or accountants, with the primary objective of targeting affluent people who are likely to have stellar credit profiles. After acquiring a target, the bot would scour through any and all online resources in search of personal identifiers. For example, if the target was born in California, the program might visit RootsWeb to acquire the target's date of birth and mother's maiden name. Next, it would search online telephone directories or other databases to locate the target's home address. Once it identified the address, the bot would connect to an online information broker, such as *www.merlindata.com*, to run a credit header search, which would identify the victim's previous addresses and his or her Social Security number. The program would also repeat itself as necessary.

Send in the Clones

Identity theft offenders (assumers) who are looking for long-term cover, typically deadbeat parents or fugitive felons, often take on the names of people who died as infants. Although morbid, this technique gives thieves a blank slate—an identity that has no established paper trail.

The Web can prove useful here as well: The thief can create a bot that would scour death record indexes and the obituary sections of newspaper Web sites, then cross-reference the information with birth records. Once identity thieves have the information they need, they can seize existing customer accounts through the old change of address trick: The imposter makes a request of the Postal Service via phone or mail and change a victim's address to a mail drop or post office box. This delays tipping off the victim and allows the imposter to intercept credit cards, bank statements, and credit applications.

Sophisticated identity assumers will sometimes clone a living person's identity by either counterfeiting or obtaining a certified copy of the victim's birth certificate. Anyone with the right information and a few dollars can obtain anyone else's birth certificate through the mail. An applicant only needs to know the target's full name, date of birth, place of birth, and mother's maiden name. Once the imposter receives the birth certificate, he or she can easily obtain traditional forms of identification, including a driver's license and Social Security card.

Social Insecurity

It's clear the system is broken. These dated forms of authentication should have been abandoned ages ago. The continued use of these practices will result in even more cases of identity theft and in the future, anyone could be the target of an identity-stealing bot. It's always amusing when banks and utility companies verify an identity by asking for the last four digits of a Social Security number. It's no wonder identity theft is so easy.

Some privacy planning advocates argue that certain personal identifiers should be restricted from disclosure; and there are a number of bills pending in Congress to strengthen individual privacy. Will enacting laws that proscribe the dissemination of Social Security numbers, for example, be effective?

The answer to the preceding question is a resounding no! As the old saying goes, the cat is already out of the bag. Once information is freed, it cannot simply be controlled. Should research tools that are available on genealogical Web sites be restricted from legitimate use just because unscrupulous people can exploit them? That would be analogous to outlawing motor vehicles because they can be used in a bank heist.

Databases available to Web surfers should not be outlawed or restricted, even though they might reveal our traditional personal identifiers. Instead, the government and the private sector (like ISPs) must adopt new planning strategies and practices when verifying an individual's identity. Your mother's maiden name is not a password and your Social Security number is not a PIN.

Federal, state, and local governments must work hand in hand with private enterprise to plan for an overhaul of the identity verification system, and begin to immediately implement accurate and effective methods of authentication. One major step along the way is to strip the value of known personal identifiers so the information is worthless to an imposter. Then, and only then, can we all become a shadow in the eyes of the identity-stealing bot.

Which Customers Are at Risk?

You might not be able to prevent identity theft, but you can take steps to make yourself less vulnerable. In other words, hope for the best, but plan for the worst.

Each one of the following statements represents a possible avenue for an ID theft and which customers are at risk. If you agree with any of them, you are at risk:

- You receive several offers of preapproved credit every week, but you do not shred them before putting them in the trash.
- You carry your Social Security card in your wallet. You do not have a post office box or a locked, secured mailbox.
- You drop off your outgoing mail at an open, unlocked box or basket.
- You carry your military ID in your wallet at all times.
- You do not shred or tear banking and credit information when you throw it in the trash.
- You provide your Social Security number whenever asked. You provide it orally without checking to see who might be listening.
- You are required to use your Social Security number as an employee or student ID number.
- Your Social Security number is printed on an employee badge that you wear.
- Your Social Security number or driver's license number is printed on your personal checks.
- You are listed in a Who's Who guide.
- You carry your health insurance card in your wallet and it contains your Social Security number or your spouse's Social Security number.
- You have not ordered a copy of your credit report for at least two years.
- You do not believe that people would root around in your trash looking for credit or financial information.

Internal and External Identity Theft Offenders

The Internet provides an ideal operating environment for internal and external identity theft offenders. It makes it much harder to plan for identity theft protection, because:

- It is much easier to disguise intent and present your scheme in a positive light.
- It is easier to disguise the identity and location of a perpetrator.
- It makes monitoring, detection, and prosecution problematic for law enforcement.

The identity theft frauds that can occur in this system are essentially similar to those in the traditional model—they are simply being committed in a new environment, requiring new security considerations. Identity theft fraud could take the form of information theft or diversion, where the fraudster (internal or external) could intercept and manipulate electronic customer orders or delivery and transportation details to steal goods or redirect payments. Ultimately, the risk will be determined by the checks and balances within any given system.

The potential threats from the Internet to law enforcement are in the speed and ease with which illegal transactions can be conducted anonymously and the difficulty of obtaining reliable evidence. Identity verification procedures are currently not sufficiently secure to ensure that anyone operating on the Internet is who they say they are. The Internet provides a medium through which anonymity can be actively exploited. There is a lack of security in data transfer and storage and poor use of electronic security systems in general.

There is the potential for internal systemic manipulation of information to perpetrate identity theft fraud. The shift to almost entirely electronic systems has made it easier in one sense for insiders to commit internal fraud, in that it can be achieved instantaneously and sometimes anonymously.

On the positive side, automation of business processes offers the potential for dramatic reductions in costs, as well as reductions in errors and cross-checking of information, which could reduce the risk of internal identity theft fraud. Preventive remedies include encrypting transmissions, or using PKI to ensure that the correct message is received by the authorized person. Many electronic systems produce an audit trail that can be used together with some analysis of employee behavior to track down the suspect if the attack is internal.

In the race to compete in the e-commerce market, businesses can neglect security concerns. Many organizations are implementing new systems rapidly and only considering the risks once the systems are operational. The IT staff can be stretched beyond their level of capability in managing new systems. They might effectively be increasing their exposure to identity theft fraud, while not ensuring effective protection against new risks.

Recent DoS attacks on Internet Web sites have highlighted the vulnerability of Web-based systems. That most ISPs or World Wide Web-based companies failed to download the free software tool made available around that time by the U.S. National Infrastructure Protection Center indicates that many companies might not be taking the risks seriously.

Criminals could exploit the confusion and lack of familiarity with new processes and new technology in this time of transition and perpetrate identity theft frauds that might go unnoticed or that could be interpreted as mistakes. At the leading edge, hacking and protective skills will continue to develop in competition with each other and it seems unlikely that one will establish an insurmountable lead over the other. Systems that are not on the leading edge will always be vulnerable to attack. Leading edge security systems themselves are likely to be vigorously challenged and ultimately rendered vulnerable.

It is important that preventative measures and control systems keep up with and adapt to continuous change; otherwise, opportunities for identity theft fraud could be created in the new systems and remain undetected. Although law enforcement is likely to seek stronger and stronger computer forensic powers, both legal and technical, ultimately the most effective remedy is increased awareness of the level of risk and encouraging a preventative approach within the private and public sectors.

Increased Scope for Fraudulent Exploitation of Identity Theft

Technology has weakened the integrity of many identifiers currently in use—birth certificates can be reproduced using desktop publishing software and counterfeit passports and counterfeit smart cards can be purchased over the Internet. Easy access to these false identifiers facilitates a range of fraudulent behavior, including tax evasion, immigration malpractice, and fraudulent claims against Social Security and health insurance companies. It also assists in hiding the proceeds of frauds.

However, the transfer of some paper-based records (e.g., birth certificates) to electronic form can strengthen identity authentication processes. Data mining techniques will enable better checking of data integrity and identification of suspicious identity profiles. Already, banks have experimented with online access to birth, death, and marriage records, to check customer identity claims.

The use of biometric information, such as digital fingerprints, coupled with online access to other confirmatory information, such as digital photographs, also has the potential to improve the security of identification authentication methods. None of these methods will provide absolute proof of identity, however. These technological developments need to satisfy privacy requirements before they could be brought into widespread use.

Outsourcing

In response to the pressure of competition and to become more efficient, many organizations in the private sector, and especially in government, are streamlining operations and outsourcing many functions. The trend in the public sector over the past few years has been to outsource a range of activities, such as IT, payment centers, recruitment, and project management. The risk of identity theft fraud depends on the quality of the contract and strength of the contract management. A well-managed, strong outsourced contract could actually reduce the risk of internal identity theft. However, poor contract management could lead to increased opportunities for identity theft fraud against the government or organization, either by internal or external sources, if adequate controls are not in place. The contractor could commit fraud, for example, by not delivering the service that was paid for or by abusing access to information. The identity theft fraud could be perpetrated by the contract manager in the distribution of funds, for example.

Identity Theft Information Protection Measures

Based on today's legal, cultural, and social conditions, this part of the chapter describes some identity theft prevention measures and best practices. It is clear that prevention is currently the only viable approach to resolving the problem of stolen identities being used online because postloss enforcement and property recovery is difficult and rare due to the limited number of trained Internet fraud investigators. This part of the chapter also gives the reader a set of best practices to consider that could help reduce the risk of loss. For example, for e-business, companies should do the following:

- Develop and publish a privacy policy.

- Follow your privacy policy. Above all, ensure that your employees are trained about the policy.

- Monitor the privacy policy and your compliance. To this extent, appoint a security and privacy coordinator for your organization. Make that person's contact information known. Research and respond to any consumer complaints.

- Store only data elements that you absolutely need to have. Maintaining a database with purchase and address information is fine to facilitate one-to-one marketing, but maintaining a database of payment information is not necessary. Once the payment is completed, this data should be removed.

- Verify that the payment system you implement (even when outsourcing) deletes temporary data files with payment records and that the outsourcing entity has strict security and privacy policies as well.

- Make certain server log files do not inadvertently store customer payment information.

- Compartmentalize access to payment systems. All employees don't need access to databases or payment application software.

- Monitor employees who have access to sensitive data or payment systems. Perform spot checks and verify that employees are working within the scope of their jobs.

- Immediately report any security breach or loss of computer systems to police.

- Provide an audit trail system for any database so that you can monitor the logs of the audit system to look for suspicious behavior or tell what a malicious employee did after the fact.

- Only ask customers for information that is absolutely necessary to complete the transaction. [2]

Service institutions (especially Internet-based service institutions) must also perform the following actions to ensure that planned identity theft protection measures are in place:

- Establish and publish a privacy policy, including appointing a consumer privacy coordinator responsible for implementation of the policy, monitoring and researching any consumer complaints.

- Have a security policy that is clearly documented, understood by employees, monitored, and modified as appropriate.

- Encrypt sensitive data, like credit card account data, in databases or storage area networks (SANs). Sensitive data, whether it resides inside or outside a database or SAN, should be encrypted. SANs or databases by themselves do not provide any added security to sensitive data in a system. Encrypting uses cryptographic methods to scramble data so that only an authorized application in possession of a special key can read the data.

- Manage encryption keys. This includes all key management best practices, including obsolescence and reissuance of keys.

- Use sufficiently large key lengths and strong enough cryptographic technology to ensure integrity of private data over the life of storage. Most people don't know what a proper secure key length should be. Currently, a 2048-bit key would be a good size. In the future, anything less than a 4096-bit key is just pretending that your data will be secure.

- Understand storage of sensitive data and implement an electronic shredding policy.

- Verify that backup tapes and other offline systems correctly store sensitive data.
- Monitor access to sensitive information.
- Constantly review security policy compliance and periodic review and update of procedures.
- Carefully observe internal staff capable of handling sensitive data.
- Manage terminating employees. [2]

Information and marketing companies consist of data miners, spammers, information brokers, and market research companies. They should also perform the following actions:

- As with the preceding e-business identity theft protection tasks, businesses in this area must have a strong privacy policy. If your policy is to use, abuse, share, or sell information, publish this as your policy and follow it.
- Designate a privacy coordinator, responsible for implementation of the policy, monitoring and researching any complaints.
- Remember that companies must adhere to the policies and agreement between the initial business collecting the data and the end user.
- Provide a mechanism for end users to challenge the use of information by one of these companies. To this extent, some U.S. companies might be governed by the FCRA. Those not covered by the FCRA should have some mechanism to collect, investigate, and resolve end user complaints.
- Encrypt sensitive data, like credit card account data, in databases. Better yet, avoid using or storing this information. If a marketing company receives a data set containing sensitive consumer information, this data should be destroyed or electronically shredded. The sender of the information should be notified not to send such data in the future. A certificate of destruction should be kept on record to respond to any potential consumer challenge.
- Manage encryption keys. This includes all key management best practices, including obsolescence and reissuance of keys.
- If you must store private data, use sufficiently large key lengths to ensure integrity of private data over the life of storage.
- Understand the storage of sensitive data and implement an electronic shredding policy.
- Verify that backup tapes and other off line systems correctly store sensitive data.
- Monitor access to sensitive information.

- Constantly review security policy compliance and periodically review and update procedures.
- Carefully observe internal staff handling of sensitive data.
- Properly manage the termination of employees. [2]

Role of Privacy and Security Policies

Privacy and security policies are important steps in protecting consumers from fraud. Companies should have both privacy and security policies to ensure that there are clear rules to which the company and its employees adhere and that consumers understand the operations of a company with which they choose to do business.

Tip

Security and privacy policies often go by the wayside after a company goes bankrupt. It kind of makes one wonder what happened to the employees' identity protection over at what is left of the defunct Enron. Who has control of those identities and how are they being used?

Developing a good privacy policy helps a company examine and analyze its own information practices. Companies often find that in the process of writing and implementing a privacy policy, they might be able to change how the firm collects data, what data is collected, how data is stored or used, and where consumer choices can be introduced. By taking a comprehensive approach to writing a privacy policy, companies are forced to examine their own practices and, in the process, could modify their current practices to be more consumer friendly. The result is generally a raised awareness within a company about consumer privacy concerns, a greater sensitivity to consumer preferences about personal data, and greater attention to the security of personally identifiable data. For businesses, there is the additional benefit of improved consumer perceptions as companies work with their customers to identify consumers' concerns and preferences about privacy.

For consumers, the benefit is a greater sense of trust and security when doing business online or providing personally identifiable information to Web sites. Individuals are far more likely to share information if they are confident that a company respects their preferences, allows them to make some choices about how their personal information is shared, and gives them the opportunity at any point to opt out of further data collection or use.

Governments also benefit from widespread use of privacy policies. Self-regulation is an effective mechanism in protecting privacy of online consumers when combined with a strong, effective, clear underlying legal structure. By adopting the approach that the United States has to date pursued, governments do not have to be concerned that outdated privacy laws will retard the growth of electronic commerce while still being able to protect the privacy of their online consumers. The market is a powerful force, and as consumers begin to express their preferences about data usage, businesses quickly comply. Those that do not, or those that betray their consumers' trust, will quickly be put out of business in a dynamic and interactive environment like the Internet.

Privacy Policy: Role

A privacy policy should accomplish three things: (a) explain a company's information practices; (b) identify choices that a consumer might have in how his or her data is collected, used, or shared; and (c) establish a mechanism for receiving, investigating and resolving complaints.

Typical Example.   Some privacy policies are very simple; some are far more complex. Policies vary widely from company to company, and privacy policies reflect that differentiation. Visit *www.siia.net/govt/toolkit.asp* or *www.truste.com* for examples of privacy policies and more information.

Responsibilities.   Companies have a responsibility to develop a privacy policy that fully discloses their information practices, communicates these practices in easy-to-understand language to consumers, and clearly identifies what choices a consumer can make about the use of his or her information. Companies also have an obligation to fully implement their privacy policies, ensure that employees fully understand the policy, and work with a third-party group to ensure compliance.

Consumers have a responsibility to look for privacy policies when online. Whether an individual is shopping or just browsing, everyone should read privacy policies and think carefully before sharing any information online at any site. If customers are not comfortable with the privacy policy of a given site, they should conduct their business elsewhere.

Security Policy: Role

The role of a security policy is to ensure that a company has established procedures that govern how it secures any sensitive or personal information it might collect. Although companies might have a comprehensive approach to security without such a policy, a security policy is an excellent addition to any company's operating procedures. Such an approach provides direction to staff, underscores the company's commitment to solid security practices, and reassures consumers.

A security policy should also identify for a company what types of data will be protected and in what manner. For example, will network access be protected only by password? Will all email be encrypted or only those messages marked as confidential? Will access to sensitive data be available to remote users? The development of such a policy will help a company identify its core assets, what types of data must be protected and in what matter, and which technologies and standards will be deployed throughout the company.

Technologies and Application. The following technologies should or can be used in the security of data:

- Cryptography
- Certification and authentication
- Single-sign on technologies and their role in monitoring network asset access
- Human and individual authentication technology
- Biometric technologies
- Anonymity tools [2]

Responsibilities. Companies have a responsibility to develop a security policy that is comprehensive, takes into account all types of data stored on and access allowed to its network, and leverages technology effectively to protect its assets. The company is also responsible for fully implementing the policy and access policy that fully disclose their information practices; communicating these practices in easy-to-understand language to consumers, and clearly identifying what choices a consumer can make about the use of his or her information. Companies also have an obligation to fully implement their security policies, ensure that employees fully understand the policy, and work with a third-party group to ensure compliance.

Response to a Breach

Companies need to have clear policies about what to do in case of a breach. In many cases, what a company does in the time immediately following a breach is critical. Companies must make sure that they not only shut down future attacks, but also that they do not destroy any evidence that could potentially help identify the source of the breach. Companies who have experienced a disclosure of personal information might be under some obligation to notify their customers.

Now, watch out, companies and online merchants: Here comes the law. Legal challenges and legislation are poised to chink the armor protecting people from identity theft: There are no legal consequences for companies that fail to protect their customers' and employees' personal information, such as credit card numbers.

Planning for Identity Theft Liability

Hackers and identity thieves can be prosecuted—if they're caught. Whereas credit card companies pay up when swiped numbers are used, and victims of fraud suffer financially and emotionally, there is not yet a law covering how companies guard private customer data.

Meanwhile, private lawsuits brought against companies with security lapses will soon constitute a new breed of high-profile legal cases, and interest in federal and state laws is spreading. Any commercial entity that puts you in jeopardy because of their lack of keeping up with technology and because of their negligence should be liable. A legal vacuum surrounds data security, but in the absence of laws, people stung by security lapses will increasingly turn to private lawsuits.

The issue of data protection grows more urgent with each electronic break-in. One case recently involved conference registration service site RegWeb.com (run by Cardinal Communications), which had a security flaw that revealed more than 400 customers' credit card numbers.

States including California and Wisconsin are starting to address identity theft. Merchant liability in hacking cases is among the topics under discussion by lawmakers representing banks, businesses, and government agencies. As states craft a hodgepodge of laws, a standard federal law will be required to eventually protect consumers against inappropriate compromise of their information.

Identity theft has become a hot topic because of the booming popularity of online credit card data theft and other forms of identity theft. Chat rooms are monitored daily by companies and ISPs looking for stolen credit card numbers and reporting them to credit card companies. Roughly 4,000 stolen credit card numbers are traded in chat rooms each month.

Recently, federal regulators issued a proposed rule setting standards for how financial institutions protect private consumer information. The Safeguards Rule, proposed under the 1999 Gramm–Leach–Bliley Act that forced financial institutions to deal more systematically with consumer privacy issues, will inject a strong dose of regulatory oversight into information security practices within financial institutions (see the sidebar, "Protecting Consumer Information From Identity Theft").

Protecting Consumer Information From Identity Theft

The Gramm–Leach–Bliley Act directs the Federal Reserve Board (otherwise known as the Board) and other federal agencies to ensure that financial institutions have policies, procedures, and controls in place to prevent the unauthorized disclosure of customer financial information and to deter and detect fraudulent access to such information. Consistent with section 525 of the Gramm–Leach–Bliley Act (15 U.S.C. 6825), this sidebar addresses how member banks and other banking organizations that provide products or services to the public or that maintain customer account information should protect customer information against identity theft. Included in this sidebar is an explanation on completing a Suspicious Activity Report (SAR) when reporting offenses associated with identity theft and pretext calling. In addition, banking organizations are reminded that a guidance was recently issued by the Board and other banking agencies concerning the safeguards that institutions can put into place to ensure the security of customer information.

Background

The fraudulent use of an individual's personal identifying information, such as Social Security number, date of birth, or bank account number, to commit a financial crime like credit card, check, loan, or mortgage fraud (commonly referred to as identity theft) is a growing problem. One way that wrongdoers improperly obtain personal information of bank customers to commit identity theft is by contacting a bank, posing as a customer or someone authorized to have the customer's information, and convincing an employee of the bank to release customer identifying information. This practice is known as *pretext calling*.

There are several federal criminal statutes that address illegal conduct associated with identity theft and pretext calling. These include the following:

- Section 1028 of the Federal Criminal Code (18 U.S.C. 1028) makes it a crime to knowingly use, without lawful authority, a means of identification (e.g., an individual's Social Security number or date of birth) of another person with the intent to commit a crime.

- Section 523 of the Gramm–Leach–Bliley Act (15 U.S.C. 6828) makes it a crime to obtain customer information from a financial institution by means of false or fraudulent statements to an officer, employee, agent, or customer of a financial institution.

- Section 523 of the Gramm–Leach–Bliley Act also makes it a crime to request another person to obtain customer information at a financial institution if the requester knows that the information will be obtained by making a false or fraudulent statement. This would mean that a banking organization requesting customer information that is then obtained by pretext calling could be subject to criminal sanctions if the institution knows how the information would be obtained.

Protecting Customer Information

Banking organizations can take various steps to safeguard customer information and to reduce the risk of loss from identity theft. These include the following:

- Establishing procedures to verify the identity of individuals applying for financial products.
- Establishing procedures to prevent fraudulent activities related to customer information.
- Maintaining a customer information security program.

Verification Procedures

Verification procedures for new accounts should include steps to ensure the accuracy and veracity of the application information. These could involve using independent sources to confirm information submitted by a customer, calling a customer to confirm that the customer has opened a credit card or checking account, or verifying information through an employer identified on an application form. A financial institution can also independently verify that the zip code and telephone area code provided on an application are from the same geographical area.

Fraud Prevention

To prevent fraudulent address changes, banking organizations should verify customer information before executing an address change and send a confirmation of the address change to both the new address and the address on record. If an organization receives a request for a new credit card or new checks in conjunction with a change of address notification, it should verify the request with the customer.

When opening a new account, banking organizations should check to ensure that information provided on an application has not previously been associated with fraudulent activity. For example, if a banking organization uses a consumer report to process a new account application and the report is issued with a fraud alert, the banking organization's system for credit approval should flag the application and ensure that the individual is contacted before it is processed. In addition, fraud alerts should be shared across the organization's lines of business.

Information Security

In early 2001, the Board and the other federal banking agencies issued Interagency Guidelines Establishing Standards for Safeguarding Customer Information. These guidelines can be obtained on the Federal Reserve's Web site at *www.federalreserve.gov/boarddocs/press/boardacts/2001/20010117/*. The guidelines require banking organizations to establish and implement a comprehensive information security program that includes appropriate administrative, technical, and physical safeguards for customer information. To prevent pretext callers from using pieces of personal information to impersonate account holders to gain access to their account information, the guidelines require banks and other financial institutions to establish written policies and procedures to control access to customer information.

Other measures that might reduce the incidence of pretext calling include limiting the circumstances under which customer information may be disclosed by telephone. For example, a banking organization cannot permit employees to release information over the telephone unless the requesting individual provides a proper authorization code (other than a commonly used identifier). Banking organizations can also use caller identification technology or a request for a callback number as tools to verify the authenticity of a request.

Banking organizations should train employees to recognize and report possible indicators of attempted pretext calling. They should also implement testing to determine the effectiveness of controls designed to thwart pretext callers, and might consider using independent staff or third parties to conduct unscheduled pretext phone calls to various departments.

Reporting Suspected Identity Theft and Pretext Calling: SARs

Current regulations require state member banks and other banking organizations supervised by the Federal Reserve to report all known or suspected criminal violations to law enforcement and the Board on SARs. Criminal activity related to identity theft or pretext calling has historically manifested itself as credit or debit card fraud, loan or mortgage fraud, or false statements to the institution, among other activities.

As a means of better identifying and tracking known or suspected criminal violations related to identity theft and pretext calling, a banking organization should, in addition to reporting the underlying fraud (e.g., credit card or loan fraud) on an SAR, also indicate within the SAR that such a known or suspected violation is the result of identity theft or pretext calling. Therefore, when identity theft or pretext calling is believed to be the underlying cause of the known or suspected criminal activity, the reporting institution should, consistent with the existing SAR instructions, complete an SAR in the following manner:

- In Part III, Box 35, of the SAR, check all appropriate boxes that indicate the type of known or suspected violation being reported and, in addition, in the "other" category, write in "identity theft" or "pretext calling," as appropriate.

- In Part V of the SAR, in the space provided for the narrative explanation of what is being reported, include the grounds for suspecting identity theft or pretext calling in addition to the other violation being reported.

- In the event that the only known or suspected criminal violation detected is the identity theft or pretext calling, write "identity theft" or "pretext calling," as appropriate, in the "other" category in Part III, Box 35, and provide a description of the activity in Part V of the SAR.

Consumer Education and Assistance

Banking organizations should provide their customers with information about how to prevent identity theft and the necessary steps to take in the event a customer becomes a victim of identity theft. An excellent source of information for consumers is the FTC's Web site at *www.consumer.gov/idtheft/*.

Banking organizations should also assist their customers who are victims of identity theft and fraud by having trained personnel to respond to customer inquiries, by determining whether an account should be closed immediately after a report of unauthorized use, and by prompt issuance of new checks or new credit, debit, or ATM cards. If a customer has multiple accounts with the institution, it should assess whether any other account has been the subject of potential fraud. [1]

The definition of *financial institution* in the regulation is broad and includes, for example, retailers that issue inhouse credit cards to shoppers. However, it still leaves untouched the vast majority of institutions (from online retailers to newspaper Web sites to Internet services like Microsoft's Passport) that regularly collect and store credit card information.

Meanwhile, the three major credit card companies (American Express, MasterCard International, and Visa International Service Association) all have programs aimed at giving merchants more online security muscle. In 2001, MasterCard unveiled its Site Data Protection Service, a set of security products and measures offered to its merchants. MasterCard also has rules for merchants to follow when processing and storing credit card information. There are penalties and consequences if you don't process properly. You can lose your license to process. Unfortunately, the incidents of hacking are on the rise.

Recently, Visa launched its Cardholder Information Security Program, which requires vendors that collect and store credit card information remotely to meet a set of security standards, from installing firewalls to encrypting stored data. In 2000, American Express started using VeriSign's Payflow, which gives merchants the option to let American Express process and store all American Express charges.

RegWeb is also storing the numbers for 877Chicago.com, a site that's run for the Chicago Convention and Tourism Bureau by a third party called McCord Travel Management. Recently, a link to a hacker Web site listing stolen credit card numbers from the site was emailed to major media organizations across the country.

RegWeb also switched Web hosts and a file containing credit card numbers got left behind on the old server. When RegWeb learned of the security hole, they immediately notified the credit card companies and later told the FBI. The credit card companies told RegWeb not to notify cardholders directly, but to let them notify banks. Cardinal Communications is bringing in an outside security company to audit RegWeb's operations. Notification should always occur. If companies were doing what was right, they would notify the businesses and consumers that they're doing business with that there's a potential that their privacy has been violated.

Cases like RegWeb's also illustrate the need for laws that hold companies accountable for exposing all of us to identity theft. Merchant liability in such cases is murky. There is a big question mark out there: How does negligence apply in computer security contexts? Unfortunately, there is no answer to that question.

187

Endnotes

[1] Federal Reserve Bank of San Francisco, San Francisco Office, 101 Market Street, San Francisco, CA 94105, USA, 2001.

[2] Tom Arnold, "Internet Identity Theft: A Tragedy for Victims," The Software & Information Industry Association, 1730 M St. NW, Suite 700 Washington, DC 20036-4510, (InfoSpace, Inc., 601 108th Ave. NE, Suite 1200, Bellevue, WA 98004), USA, 2001.

[3] "Identity Theft: How I Became You," Netopia, Inc., 2470 Mariner Square Loop, Alameda, CA 94501, USA, 2002.

Chapter 9

GUIDELINES FOR PROTECTING THE IDENTITY AND CONFIDENTIALITY OF PERSONAL INFORMATION WHEN WORKING OUTSIDE THE CORPORATE OFFICE

I n the course of performing their duties, employees might be required to work outside their employer's conventional office space. This could include transporting records by car, bus, subway, train, or airplane; working on assignments or projects at home; attending meetings at hotels and conference centers; appearing at court or tribunal hearings; conducting investigations; making visits to clients or recipients of services; and representing their organization at ceremonies or public gatherings.

Records containing personal information can be in either paper or electronic format. The purpose of these testing guidelines is to test how employees should protect the identity and confidentiality of such records when working outside the office.

Other Sensitive Information

In certain circumstances, employees who are working outside the office might be dealing with other confidential records that do not necessarily include personal information, such as records subject to solicitor–client privilege, or records containing advice to the organization. Although these testing guidelines apply to personal information, they are equally applicable to records containing other types of sensitive information.

Identity Theft Legislation

When working both inside and outside the office, government employees must comply with the identity theft legislation. One purpose of identity theft legislation is to protect the privacy of individuals with respect to personal information about themselves held by government.

Personal information is defined in identity theft legislation as recorded information about an identifiable individual, including his or her race, age, family status, address, telephone number, medical or employment history, and other information. Identity theft legislation contains privacy rules governing the collection, retention, use, disclosure, and disposal of personal information held by an organization.

Removing Records From the Office

Employees should only remove records containing personal information from the office when it is absolutely necessary for the purposes of carrying out their job duties. If possible, only copies should be removed, with the originals left in the office.

Depending on their positions, employees might be required to obtain approval from their manager before removing records containing personal information from the office. Records containing personal information that are being removed from the office should be recorded on a sign-out sheet that includes the employee's name, a description of the records, the names of the individuals whose personal information is being removed, and the date the records were removed.

Paper Records

Paper records containing personal information should be securely packaged in folders, carried in a locked briefcase or sealed box, and kept under the constant control of the employee while in transit. When an employee travels by car, paper records should always be locked in the trunk. There have been cases, however, where records have been stolen from employees, even from the locked trunk of a car. Consequently, unless there is no alternative, paper records should never be left unattended in a car trunk while the employee goes elsewhere. Also, paper records should not be opened or reviewed while traveling on public transportation such as a bus, subway, train, or airplane.

When working at home, employees should store paper records in a locked filing cabinet or desk drawer when they are not being used. The cabinet or desk should only contain work-related records.

When working at other locations outside the office, employees should keep paper records under their constant control, including during meals and other breaks. If this is not possible, the records should be temporarily stored in a secure location, such as a locked room or desk drawer.

Electronic Records

Electronic records containing personal information should be stored and encrypted on a password-protected disk or CD rather than the hard drive of a laptop or home computer. To prevent loss or theft, a disk or CD should be carried in a locked briefcase and kept under the constant control of the employee while in transit. When used at home, a disk or CD should be stored and locked in a filing cabinet or desk drawer after use.

When working at other locations outside the office, employees should keep a disk or CD under the constant control of the employee, including during meals and other breaks. If this is not possible, the disk or CD should be temporarily stored in a secure location, such as a locked room or desk drawer.

Laptop and Home Computers

Access to laptop and home computers should be password-controlled, and any data on the hard drive should be encrypted. Other reasonable safeguards, such as antivirus software and personal firewalls, should also be installed. Employees should only use software that has been approved by their institution's IT department.

Laptops should be kept under the constant control of the employee while in transit. When an employee travels by car, a laptop should always be locked in the trunk. There have been cases, however, where laptops have been stolen from government employees, even from the locked trunk of a car. Consequently, unless there is no alternative, a laptop should never be left unattended in a car trunk while the employee goes elsewhere.

If it is necessary to view personal information on a laptop screen when working at locations outside the office, ensure that the screen cannot be seen by anyone else. Personal information should never be viewed on a laptop screen while traveling on public transportation.

When working at home or at other locations outside the office, user should log off and shut down a laptop or home computer when not in use. For added protection, laptops should be locked to a table or other stationary object with a security cable. To the maximum extent possible, the employee should maintain constant control of the laptop, particularly when working at locations outside the office. If this is not possible, it should be temporarily stored in a secure location, such as a locked room or desk drawer. Also, do not share a laptop that is used for work purposes with other individuals, such as family members or friends.

Laptop Security

There's been a tremendous amount of attention recently to the problems of laptop security while traveling, especially in light of the September 11, 2001 terrorist attacks. With an increased number of international business travelers carrying computers through airports, hotels, and other public areas, the security checkpoint in general has become the target of a scam aimed at separating you from your laptop. Actually, the scam has been around since the mid 1990s, but, the problem has now become so widespread that it has reached epidemic proportions.

The scam works something like this: You place your computer on the conveyor belt at the security checkpoint—whether it be an airport, office building, or other public area. Someone in line in front of you sets off the detector. He or she goes back through, empties the change from pockets, and tries again. Again he or she triggers the metal detector. More stuff is placed into the tray and this time the person passes through fine. You follow, and go to pick up your bag and your computer, but it's too late. Your computer is long gone, snatched up by the partner of the person who delayed you coming through the checkpoint (see the sidebar, "How to Avoid Being a Victim").

How to Avoid Being a Victim

How do you avoid being a victim? Check out the following tips:

1. Don't put your computer on the conveyor belt until the person in front of you has cleared the detector.

2. Make sure the computer has disappeared into the scanner before you pass through the detector; otherwise someone on the outside can grab it before it goes through.

3. Don't carry your computer in a clearly definable computer carrying case. Use a briefcase with a computer sleeve inside or a bag that does not scream "There's a computer inside of me!"

4. If you set off the detector, ask to be checked with the wand inside security where you can watch your computer. If you go back out, a computer that has already passed through the scanner can disappear.

At some security checkpoints, security personnel will make you take out laptops and turn them on before you go through the checkpoint. If they do this, insist that they carry the computer around and hand it to you after you have cleared security. Otherwise, they have just put a sign on your computer bag that says "Steal me."

TrackIt Security *(businesstravel.about.com/gi/dynamic/offsite.htm?site= http://www.trackitcorp.com/)* offers alarm systems that go off if your laptop is moved away from you. There are many other systems on the market that are mentioned later in this chapter.

Overall, the best protection may be vigilance! Happy traveling, and keep your eye on that laptop.

So, how do you really protect your laptop from being stolen while traveling? The simple answer is to lock it up! This part of the chapter describes methods you can use to protect your laptop device against physical and data theft.

Locking Down the Laptop

Laptop computers have become a prime target of thieves who are not only targeting these devices for the value of the device itself, but also for the sensitive data contained therein.

Laptop security can be broken down into three phases: physical security, data security, and access control/authentication and tracking/recovery (see the sidebar, "Securing Laptops"). However, the biggest challenge might be changing users' attitudes and habits.

Securing Laptops

Mobile mania, like anything else, has its pros and cons. On the pro side, laptops cater to today's peripatetic work world. However, the downside is clear: Untethered desktops render corporate assets highly vulnerable.

The answer, according to solution providers, analysts, and vendors is layered security. Don't just lock up your laptop with a cable. Use a high-tech authentication system to gain access, then go a few steps further: Encrypt your data and arm your notebook with an intelligent tracking agent. Then maybe your data will be safe from thieves.

It's absolutely essential to layer security solutions. For example, Computrace, a tracking system from Absolute Software, Vancouver, British Columbia, is one such solution. A low-level client installed on a PC's hard drive, Computrace automatically contacts a central monitoring center at scheduled intervals to transmit data about the PC's location, hard drive status, and memory usage. Computrace might be Absolute's signature product now, but the company has a loftier goal in mind: to be a one-stop security shop for laptop users.

With that in mind, let's say a crook does make off with your laptop. If you've done a good job of layering security, the wrongdoer won't be able to get at your data anyway. That's where access control comes in, and a number of technologies are gaining popularity in this area, including biometrics.

Biometrics has been around for a while, but it hasn't been used very much until now, except in law enforcement. The benefit of fingerprint reading is that you don't need to carry another device; your finger's always there.

Chipmaker Intel aims to give biometrics a kick-start with its Intel Protected Access Architecture (IPAA), a specification for incorporating BIOS-level authentication capability in notebooks. Hundreds of thousands of notebook computers are stolen every year, which represents nearly one-quarter of the notebooks sold, a statistic too high to ignore. The risk of losing the important and sometimes personal data on the notebook makes it imperative that measures be taken to prevent this from occurring to you. The hot spots for notebook theft are offices, airports, cars, and hotel rooms. Notebook computers are ideal targets for a thief because they are portable, valuable, easy to pawn off, and difficult to recover.

Whether using a security device or not, everyone should be sure to back up the data on the notebook regularly. Never leave your notebook unattended. As previously mentioned, when going through airport security, don't put your notebook on the conveyer belt until it's your turn to walk through the metal detector. Keep you notebook in an inconspicuous case rather than an obvious notebook or laptop case. Record your notebook serial number, or place an Ultraviolet mark on it so you can identify the notebook if it is ever recovered. Laptop theft is not something to be taken lightly. The insurance company can replace the computer, but the data that is inside can be priceless and sometimes damaging to an individual or organization in many cases.

Nevertheless, Intel has also been working with vendors of BIOS software and developers of biometric security devices so that IPAA can be built into laptops that are biometrics-ready, enabling road warriors to use smart cards, fingerprint readers, or USB tokens to authenticate themselves to notebooks before they boot. Laptops with IPAA are expected to be rolled out in 2002, but these things always take time to become ubiquitous.

Most vendors—Acer, Dell, Hewlett-Packard, IBM, and Toshiba among them—already incorporate security features into their laptops, but you can expect the technology to become increasingly sophisticated over time. For example, Toshiba jumped on the biometrics bandwagon in 2001 with the release of PC Fingerprint Readers, which the company made available through distributors and Value Added Resellers (VARs).

Xyloc, a wireless solution from Ensure Technologies, is gaining momentum, too. With Xyloc, the user carries a badge that acts as a radio. When an authorized user approaches a laptop, it recognizes the user and logs him or her onto the network. The notebook logs off or shuts down when the authorized user walks away.

Ensure sells Xyloc through about 36 resellers nationwide. Also, Ensure is not looking for players that want to earn a quick buck or push boxes. The company wants resellers that know how to integrate security solutions and take care of customers.

Other token-based security solutions have been available for some time. RSA Security's SecurID, for example, employs two-factor authentication, requiring users to hold a token and enter a password.

The end result? Laptop thieves beware.

It's been more than two years since an unattended laptop disappeared from the U.S. Department of State's Washington, DC, headquarters. Two top-level administrators were fired and four others received career-ending reprimands for losing a notebook computer that contained sensitive nuclear weapons proliferation data. Despite an intensive investigation and a $58,000 reward, the FBI has still been unable to recover the missing laptop.

The State Department administrator who had his laptop stolen in a crowded conference room was doing nothing different than what thousands of executives do everyday—hauling a notebook computer from appointment to appointment. However, these portable devices—rich in computing power and communications capabilities, and often loaded with sensitive data—are big targets for opportunistic thieves and industrial spies.

Laptop theft is a huge problem, according to security industry and insurance company statistics. Safeware (*www.safeware.com*), an Ohio-based insurance firm specializing in PC policies, reported that nearly 540,000 laptops valued at $1 billion were stolen in 2001, a 7% increase over the previous year. The trend is mirrored by the expansion of the laptop security market, with some manufacturers reporting 60% to 70% annual growth rates.

Criminals are definitely targeting laptop systems, especially systems that cost more than $5,000. In 2001, notebook computers accounted for 90% of all of Safeware's total computer theft claims, compared to 75% in 1999.

As in most computer-related crimes and security breaches, insiders (regular staff, temporary workers, and contractors) are at least partially responsible for many notebook computer thefts. About 60% of the systems stolen occur when a person is in the office. Many times it's coworkers who are taking the computers.

Few bandits are interested in the digital treasures contained on the laptop hard drives; they just want the quick profit from selling the devices on the black market. There are plenty of buyers out there searching for the power and convenience of a laptop at a bargain basement price.

If anything, the software loaded on a stolen device enhances the machine's value, whereas the personal and business files have little practical use to end recipients. This is not to say that industrial spies and enterprising thieves do not seek out the digital bounty held in these portable computers. Should a notebook bandit sneak off with the right laptop, he or she could find himself or herself in possession of proprietary secrets, confidential product development information, or sensitive financial data. The value of the information depends on how much the victim's corporate rivals are willing to pay for a competitive advantage, or how much the thief can extort for the information's return.

One of the biggest nontechnical problems involved in securing laptops is the mindset of the laptop owners themselves. It's common for CEOs and other corporate executives to assume their communications and files aren't interesting to anyone but themselves—and, therefore, they don't go to extreme measures to protect them.

Although there's no changing the elements that make laptops easy to steal (and altering CEOs' mindsets might prove even more difficult), there are several ways to physically and electronically secure these devices. Locking down the laptop can be approached in three phases: pretheft physical security, posttheft access control to protect against unauthorized access to sensitive files and information, and posttheft tracking devices that help in recovery.

Physical Security

Physical laptop protection primarily consists of attaching a locking security cable to the universal security slot (USS) on your laptop. The security cable is wrapped around an immovable object and connected to the laptop to provide excellent physical security protection. For those laptops that do not have a USS (approximately 80% of laptops have a USS), there are adhesive connectors that mount directly to your laptop casing, which provide a way to attach the security cable. These security cables can use either keyed or combination locks to secure them to your laptop. If there isn't a large immovable object accessible to wrap the security cable around, anchoring devices are available that enable you to attach the cable to cubicle walls and other stationary objects. There are also systems available that, when attached to your laptop, sound an alarm if the laptop is moved. These types of devices are useful when you'll be traveling with your laptop and have to put it down (e.g., while sitting in the airport awaiting your flight).

Physical Security Importance. Protecting your laptop while you are traveling with it requires vigilance and care, but with some simple software, a stolen laptop can be recovered. For example, Lucira Technologies (*www.lucira.com/corporate/products.htm*) makes software that will facilitate recovery of your laptop by contacting the police if your laptop is stolen. Lucira can track the location of your stolen laptop once it is online either through a dial-up connection or a LAN Internet connection. The only way that this system can be defeated is if the hard drive is removed and replaced.

Laptops on desks are also easy prey. Often workers leave their desk for the day and leave their laptop sitting on the desk. Even if the office is locked, cleaning staff have easy access to offices and the contents within. Kensington and other companies make hardened cables that attach to the security port found on most laptops and then securely bolt down to the desk or another equally difficult-to-move object. Kryptonite makes a device called the Kryp-toVault that offers dual security. On the road, it securely locks the laptop closed so that you cannot open it without destroying the laptop in the process. In the office, the laptop can be anchored to the desk so that it cannot be removed.

One other method for securing your laptops is to put them in a secure room like the server room or even a safe. When you're not traveling with your laptop, it should be safely stored in a secure location. The server room, if it is properly secured, is a good place for laptops that are staying in the office. A safe offers one more level of security that the server room does not offer, a fire-resistant environment. Not only is your laptop safe from thieves, it is also reasonably safe from fire and smoke damage. Lockable desks or file cabinets are not usually secure enough, but if that is your only solution, it is better than nothing. At least if the laptop is stored in a locked desk or filing cabinet, it is out of sight and it will take a thief a little longer to get at it.

When traveling, you must take extra precautions with your laptop. Don't ever let it out of your sight. When you go through the security checkpoint at the airport, don't let yourself get distracted. Keep tabs on your laptop throughout the process. When you are at the ticket counter, do not set your laptop down even for a second. Clever thieves are watching for just such an opportunity. If you have to make a phone call from a phone booth, step through the laptop bag strap so a fast-moving thief cannot grab your bag and run. By no means should you ever check your laptop bag through baggage. Chances are it will not arrive at the same destination that you will. You should also encrypt all of your personal and proprietary information. It is bad enough to lose a $3,000 laptop, but it is another thing to give some thief your bank account and credit card information along with all of the company's business secrets that reside on the laptop hard drive. Finally, make frequent (daily) backups of all of the important data stored on your laptop. This way, if it is lost or stolen, you will at least still have your data to work from.

Physical security is one of the most overlooked aspects of network or computer security, but it is also one of the easiest to implement. It requires no complicated configuration, no high-priced certified engineer, or no regular and expensive software updates and patches. Simply lock it up.

Physical Security Devices

Vendors have crafted a variety of physical security devices that diminish the threat of laptop thefts. Many of these products tie a system down to a heavy object, such as a desk or workstation, so a thief can't simply pick it up and walk away. Other manufacturers offer alarms and sensors for alerting users that someone is tampering with their notebook computers. These devices are designed to stop the opportunistic thief, someone who is not a criminal, but seizes on the chance to get a free laptop.

Cable Locks.   Retailing for $40 to $50, laptop cable locks are similar to the locks used on bicycles. A steel clip provided by the manufacturer is installed on a security slot, either on the back or side of the laptop. A steel cable is threaded through the clip and wrapped around an immovable object, such as a desk leg or support pole. If the laptop does not contain a security slot or the desk does not provide a location for suitable anchorage, special adhesive pads containing an anchoring slot are available. The two ends of the cable are secured with a padlock.

Different versions of cable locks are manufactured by AnchorPad International (*www.anchorpad.com*), Kensington Technology Group (*www.kensington.com*), Computer Security Products, Inc. (*www.computersecurity.com*), PC Guardian (*www.pcguardian.com*), Targus Group International (*www.targus.com*), and Kryptonite (*www.kryptonitelock.com*), among others.

Although inexpensive and easy to use, many cable locks are easily defeated with tools from any hardware store. Any thief with a bolt cutter can break the cable and then walk off with your laptop system.

Cable locks are most effective when used in the office or home, where computers are rarely moved. However, laptop owners still have to use them if they're to have any effect. Laptop thieves often target conventions and conferences because laptop owners feel comfortable in a group of their peers, particularly when they're using the same conference room for two or three straight days.

Even if the conference center or convention floor has a convenient place to attach a cable lock, users have a tendency to use the locks less and less the longer they're in any one location. Maybe they'll use them during coffee or bathroom breaks during the first day or two, but as they get more comfortable with their surroundings, they tend to get lax. This is when opportunistic thieves make their rounds. The lesson is that it's important to help users make laptop locking a routine part of setup and operation—as routine as plugging it in and booting it up.

Alarms and motion detectors.   These devices are more sophisticated physical security measures that alert owners when someone tampers with or tries to move a laptop. Products range from simple motion detectors to sensors that detect the unplugging of cables to high-pitched sirens that sound similar to car alarms.

An alarm system offered by TrackIT (*www.trackitcorp.com*) is basically a proximity device. A transmitter installed in or attached to the laptop case maintains continuous radio contact with a mobile receiver carried by the user. If the laptop is moved beyond a set distance from the user, an alarm sounds on the laptop and the mobile unit alerts the owner.

Targus offers the Defcon family of alarm units, which are basically cable locks with alarms. Defcon I is a sensor circuit that sounds an alarm if anyone breaks the security loop on the laptop or cuts the cable lock. Defcon III is essentially the same unit, except it emits a warning tone when the notebook is moved slightly and a louder alarm if movement continues.

Minatronics (*www.minatronics.com*) has developed a fiber-optical alarm system that acts similar to Targus's cable sensor. A fiber-optic cable is passed through a security tab or any available opening on a laptop and is anchored to a stationary monitoring unit that sends continuous light pulses through the line. An alarm sounds immediately if the pulses are interrupted.

Whereas cable locks are designed to stop the opportunistic thief, alarms and motion detectors are intended to make a laptop bandit so conspicuous that he or she aborts the crime. Because thieves don't want to draw attention to themselves, they'll likely drop a computer rather than risk getting caught. Sure, the laptop will probably sustain some damage in the process of being discarded, but at least its digital contents won't be compromised.

Data Security

Data protection can be broken down into three distinct categories: operating system security, sensitive data storage practices, and data encryption. Operating system security covers the normal operating system (and services) security best practices.

The data on your laptop might be more valuable to the thief than the device itself. Therefore, it's always best to use good judgment when storing sensitive information on your machine (see the sidebar, "Be Deliberate in Securing Your Data"). You should do the following:

- Keep the amount of institutional data stored on your machine to a minimum.

- Not use any option that remembers your password so that you do not have to reenter it the next time you connect.

- Use data encryption tools to protect those sets of data that you must have stored on your laptop.

Be Deliberate In Securing Your Data

Laptops are commonplace today and so is their theft. However, losing the computer often doesn't matter as much as losing the data it contains.

Case in point: Qualcomm's chairman and CEO recently gave a speech to the Society of American Business Editors and Writers at the Hyatt Regency Hotel in Irvine, California. After his speech, numerous journalists gathered around to ask questions. During that brief time, he was never more than 30 feet from his laptop, yet someone managed to steal it. The laptop contained some of Qualcomm's most valuable trade secrets (reported to be worth millions), which are now in the thief's hands.

News reports indicate the laptop was running a Microsoft operating system and required a password to access its files, but the operating system had no file encryption in place. In one report, the executive openly commented that he hoped Microsoft's password protection would prevent access to the laptop's data. Certainly someone can access the laptop's files without a password. For example, a person can use an NTFS boot disk if the laptop uses that file system, or someone can simply install a new operating system, boot it, log on, and access the data.

Note: NTFS, short for NT File System, is a file system for the Windows NT operating system (Windows NT also supports the FAT file system). NTFS has features to improve reliability, such as transaction logs to help recover from disk failures. To control access to files, you can set permissions for directories or individual files. NTFS files are accessible from other operating systems such as DOS. There's an NTFSDOS device driver. Linux has read/write support for NTFS4 and read-only for NTFS5. For large applications, NTFS supports spanning volumes, which means files and directories can be spread out across several physical disks.

The need to protect portable computing platforms is obvious in this light. Not only must you guard the device at all times, you should also consider some form of disk encryption to protect against a worst case theft scenario.

If you prefer the Windows platform, consider adopting Microsoft Windows XP for systems that store sensitive information. The new operating system contains an Encrypting File System (EFS) that uses public key technology to guard files. Without the private key, users can access the file system only through an account that has been authorized as a private key recovery agent.

Note: EFS is easy to manage and completely transparent. All you do is use a private key, generated by Windows XP, to encrypt only those files or folders that need protection. Users without the private key can't access the data.

Also, be aware of a nuance with the EFS utilities. EFS documentation states that read-only files won't be encrypted. However, it's been found that read-only files are encrypted. If you use the Properties dialog box in Windows Explorer to mark a folder encrypted, a message asks whether you want to encrypt all subfolders and files. If you choose not to do so, all files in the selected directory, including any read-only files, will be encrypted. This does not occur with the command -line EFS utility Cipher.exe.

Finally, consider using a laptop cable lock to secure the device when you can't guard it closely. In addition, you might want to install a utility such as Stealth Signal (*www.stealthsignal.com/web/main.asp*) that can phone home when connected to the Internet to report a system's IP address, which you can use to help locate a stolen system.

Access Controls and Authentication

Although cable locks and motion detectors will deter physical theft, owners must still consider barriers to disable or make their laptop inaccessible should it fall into the wrong hands. Most laptop computers were designed with basic access control features, including an easily defeated BIOS password system. However, these password systems have limited effectiveness, as users will often choose easily cracked PINs and will not perform proper maintenance. On the other hand, organizations with stringent security policies are often burdened by the increased number of calls to their help desks by users who forget their constantly changing and difficult-to-remember laptop passwords.

Traditionally, multiple form-factor authentication applications have been confined to high-security desktop client/server networking environments and, more recently, in single workstation/multiple user environments (e.g., hospital nursing stations or manufacturing floors). Today, several applications combining something you have with something you know have been ported to the laptop environment.

Smart cards are still used sparingly in laptop environments. Few, if any, laptops have built-in smart card readers, although vendors such as SPYRUS (*www.spyrus.com*) manufacture portable serial port readers. More conveniently, digital certificates and other identifying credentials can be stored on USB tokens from vendors such as SPYRUS, Rainbow Technologies (*www.rainbow.com*), and Aladdin Knowledge Systems (*www.ealaddin.com*).

Although older laptops may not be USB-compatible, most notebooks (and PCs) manufactured after 1998 include USB ports.

Authentication tokens such as the Secur-ID from RSA Security (*www.rsasecurity.com*) and the DigiPass line from Vasco (*www.vasco.com*) are common in remote-access environments. Similar remote log-in tools are offered by CRYPTOCard Corp. (*www.cryptocard.com*). These tokens remotely synchronize with back-office authentication servers (RSA's is called the ACE/ Server) to provide users with one-time passwords. However, although ideal for secure network authentication from a laptop or other portable computer, these devices do little to secure the laptop's otherwise unprotected hard disk from the peering eyes of a dedicated adversary.

As previously discussed, biometrics provides another means for blocking access by only allowing users who authenticate their identity with their physical characteristics, such as fingerprints, voice patterns, or retina scans. All biometrics systems work basically the same way: A user scans his or her identifier with a capture device, which stores the pattern in a database. To access data, the user presents his or her identifier, and the biometrics system will grant him or her access if it matches the stored pattern. Unlike passwords or tokens, biometrics identifiers are extremely difficult to duplicate, crack, or exploit through a replay attack.

The first biometrics units were expensive and designed primarily for desktops, but the expanding security market and improved technology has made the technology affordable for portable devices. Using scanners hooked into peripheral or USB ports, built-in laptop microphones and even laptop cameras, finger-, face- and voice-recognition biometric vendors have made strong inroads into the laptop authentication market. For instance, the U.are.U security system, manufactured by Digital Persona (*www.digitalpersona.com*), uses a USB-compatible sensor to capture finger scans.

Perhaps the most interesting biometric applications for laptops combine multiple biometrics for added security. For example, Keyware's Layered Biometric Verification (LBV) system (*www.keyware.com*) combines spoken passphrases with optional finger scanning. The beauty of LBV is that it operates in thin-client mode, eliminating the need for client-side readers or software to store credentials and protocols. Using the LBV toolkit, developers can customize a Java- or ActiveX-based applet, which is presented to users requesting access via a Web browser to a secured page or application. Once enrolled, the user enters his or her ID or passphrase and, using the built-in microphone on most laptops, speaks a designated passphrase. The toolkit will extract voiceprint minutia from the passphrase and transmit it along with the ID or PIN to the NT-based LBV authentication server. The server then compares the data to stored credentials, and permits or denies access to the requested page or file. The toolkit's applet can be configured to sense whether or not the client has a fingerprint reader installed, and if so, to require fingerprint verification by itself or in conjunction with a voiceprint.

Other systems combine a single biometric with a hardware device. Trinity, a system produced by Ankari (*www.ankari.com/*), offers optional packages that bundle biometrics with smart cards, tokens, and password applications for multifactor authentication. Ethentica (*www.ethentica.com*) offers a fingerprint verification system on a swappable Type II PCMCIA card, called the Ethenticator MS 3000.

Two-factor authentication applications are designed to keep the bad guys out, but data encryption systems protect information stored on computers should other access control mechanisms be defeated. In addition to traditional data encryption and digital signature software from companies such as Network Associates Technology, Inc. (*www.pgp.com*), F-Secure (*www.f-secure.com*), RSA Security, and PC Guardian, several vendors are offering notebook encryption hardware via PCMCIA cards. For instance, Global Technologies Group (*www.gtgi.com*) offers the CryptCard, a Type II PCMCIA card with Triple-DES hard-disk encryption capabilities. In addition, operating-system-specific encryption applications, such as the Windows 2000 EFS, are growing in popularity in laptop environments.

Tracking and Recovery Systems

Luck, until recently, was the determining factor in recovering stolen laptops. Thieves could unload or use machines with near impunity because there was little chance of getting caught. However, a new generation of technology is providing users with the ability to track stolen notebook computers. Similar to the LoJack vehicle retrieval system, alarm and tracking software residing in an undetectable file on the hard drive will periodically contact a monitoring service via the Internet. The service verifies the missing computer's location, which is generally sufficient for police to obtain a search warrant.

Through its monitoring center, Absolute Software Corp. (*www.compu-trace.com*) routinely updates its security application running on subscribers' laptops with new call-in schedules. Should a machine be reported stolen, the system is programmed to increase the time between calls, which allows for a faster trace and recovery. Similarly, Lucira Technologies (*www.lucira.com*) markets Secure PC, an application that traces stolen laptops once they're connected to the Internet. The company's monitoring center will notify the local police of the laptop's location and even provide them with a map. The company plans to improve future versions by offering data and file retrieval without the thief's knowledge. It will not, however, wipe the hard drive clean.

CyberAngel, by Computer Sentry Software (*www.sentryinc.com*), provides both monitoring and retrieval capabilities. Should anyone attempt to access the Internet with the laptop, CyberAngel will immediately alert the owner via fax or email. The Computer Sentry Software operations center will use the initial notification to trace the laptop's location. After the alert, the program locks the modem port to prevent access to a corporate LAN, the Internet, or other remote operations. An optional software module can also lock out the keyboard and mouse, making the machine virtually useless.

The recovery rate with these tracking and locator systems is about 90% when police lend their assistance, according to industry experts. However, each jurisdiction places a different priority on stolen computers, and some police departments might not want to allocate resources to recover a single machine. Even with the help of authorities, recovery is a slow process, averaging about three months.

Finally, let's discuss laptop theft prevention and protection when traveling internationally. Since the events of September 11, 2001, this has become an area of heightened concern among government and military personnel alike.

Laptop Vulnerabilities While Traveling Internationally

Your information and valuables are far more vulnerable to theft while traveling abroad than when you are in the United States. Principal targets for theft include the following:

- Government and business documents of interest to the local intelligence service.
- Personal documents (passport and other ID and travel documents) of interest to criminal organizations, including those that arrange illegal immigration to the United States.
- Laptop computers are of interest to everyone—for the information on them, for resale, or for personal use.
- Expensive jewelry, cameras, and any other items that are easy to sell.

You have special vulnerabilities in your hotel room and elsewhere in your hotel, as well as at the airport or on the train (with sensitive equipment in transit), and in any office to which local foreign nationals have unrestricted access.

Hotel Rooms and Vaults

Bag operations are typically conducted by the host government's security or intelligence service, frequently with cooperation of the hotel staff. Hotel security staffs commonly maintain close contact with the local police and government security service.

 Tip

> Bag operations *is the term commonly used to describe surreptitious entry into hotel rooms to steal, photograph, or photocopy documents; steal or copy magnetic media; or download from laptop computers. Bag operations are common. In fact, they are routine procedure in quite a few countries.*

It is common for retired government security and intelligence officers to obtain employment in the security offices of major hotels and corporations. Bag operations might also be conducted by the corporation you are dealing with or by a competitor. They might be done during the day while you are out of the room or at night while you are asleep. (Yes, they do take the risk of coming into your room while you are sleeping!)

Government and business travelers often report that their belongings were searched while they were absent from their hotel room. In some cases, they have returned to their room soon after departing to retrieve a forgotten item, finding persons in their room claiming they are there to repair a broken TV, or using another excuse. Seldom is anything missing; the purpose is only to copy documents or download information from a traveler's laptop computer. Sometimes there is little effort to conceal the search. Other times it is more subtle. If done correctly, the traveler will not be aware of the search.

Leaving sensitive government or company information in your hotel room, even in a locked briefcase or the safe provided in your room, is an invitation for material to be copied or photographed while you are out. Hotel vaults are not much better. In most cases, foreign intelligence officers can gain access to hotel lockboxes or vaults without you being aware of the compromise.

Never leave a laptop computer with sensitive information on it in a hotel room unattended. Keep it in your personal possession at all times or don't take it on the trip. If you must take a laptop, use encryption to protect sensitive files and perform regular backups to ensure no loss of vital information in case of theft.

Suitcase and attaché case locks might delay the trained professional for a few minutes, but will not protect your sensitive information. Nevertheless, it is wise to keep your luggage locked whenever you are out of the room. Although locks will not inhibit the professional thief or intelligence agent, they will keep the curious maid honest. Curious hotel employees are even more likely to remain honest if combination locks are set so that the combination for each piece of luggage is different. For attaché cases with two combination locks, use different combinations for each lock.

The only solution to the security problem is to take as little sensitive information as possible when traveling overseas and to carry what you must take on your person, possibly on computer media. Computer diskettes and CD-ROMs must also be carried with you at all times. If you must carry sensitive information, the following suggestions might be helpful.

When Carrying Sensitive Information

While asleep or in the shower, engage both the deadbolt and the privacy latch or chain on the hotel room door. A hotel's emergency keys can override the deadbolt locks, so the latch or chain is your principal source of security.

 Tip

> *Many hotel rooms have a door to a connecting room. This is a potential vulnerability, as these doors do not normally have a privacy latch or chain.*

Utilize a portable or improvised burglar alarm while asleep. Two ashtrays and a water glass are quite effective as an alarm when placed on the floor in front of the door into your room. Place a water glass in one ashtray and balance the second ashtray on top of the glass. If a straight chair is available, place it next to the door and put the ashtray and water glass alarm on the edge of the chair where it will fall with enough racket to wake you.

When leaving the room, make a mental or written note of how your suitcase or other personal property that would not normally be touched by the cleaning personnel was left. Any movement might suggest that others were in the room to examine your belongings. The same procedure is even more effective to check for surreptitious entry while you were asleep.

Jewelry or other valuables should normally be left at home, but you might need to protect a substantial amount of money. Guidelines for protecting money from thieves are different from those for protecting sensitive information from the local intelligence or security service. Money should not be kept on your person. It should be kept in a safe in a local office or in the hotel's safe deposit box or safe. This is safer than a room safe and could also make the hotel liable for any loss. Liability laws in many countries provide that the hotel is not liable for the loss of guest property unless it is in the care, custody, and control of the hotel. Additional protection might be gained by double-enveloping all valuables, initialing across the seams, and then taping all edges and seams (over the initials).

If you determine that an item is missing, conduct a thorough search prior to reporting the incident to hotel security. Do not expect to receive a copy of the security report, as it is an internal document. The incident should be reported to the local police, the security officer at the nearest U.S. Embassy or Consulate, and your insurance carrier. Hotel security can provide a letter verifying that you reported property missing.

Elsewhere in the Hotel

There are a number of areas in your hotel where you are particularly vulnerable to theft. Let's look at few in the following section.

Rest rooms. Female travelers should be careful about placing purses on hangers on the inside of the lavatory doors or on the floor in stalls—two frequent locations for grab-and-run-thefts. On occasion, unauthorized persons use rest rooms for other types of theft or to deal drugs or engage in prostitution.

Public telephones. Areas around public telephones are often used by criminals to stage pickpocket activity or theft. Keep briefcases and purses in view or *in hand* while using phones. Safeguard your telephone credit card numbers. Criminals sometimes hang around public telephones to gather credit card numbers and then sell them for unauthorized use.

Hotel bars and restaurants. Purse snatchers and briefcase thieves are known to work hotel bars and restaurants waiting for unknowing guests to drape these items on chairs or under tables, only to discover them missing as they are departing. Keep items in view or *in hand*. Be alert to scams involving an unknown person spilling a drink or food on your clothing. An accomplice might be preparing to steal your wallet, briefcase, or purse.

Pool or beach areas. Pool or beach areas are fertile areas for thieves to take advantage of guests enjoying recreation. Leave valuables in the hotel. Safeguard your room key and camera. Sign for food and beverages on your room bill rather than carrying cash.

The red light district. Prostitutes take advantage of travelers around the world through various ploys, including use of drugs and theft from the victim's room. Avoid engaging persons you do not know and refrain from inviting them to your room.

Airports and trains. Airports, railroad terminals, and trains are easy targets for pickpockets, thieves, and terrorist bombers. Unattended baggage is an obvious risk. Checked baggage is also at risk and should never contain valuables such as a camera or sensitive papers. It is not unusual for government and business travelers to report broken suitcase locks and rearranged contents.

Theft from sleeping compartments on trains is surprisingly common. Train thieves spray chemicals inside sleeping compartments to render the occupant(s) unconscious then enter and steal valuables. Using this technique, valuables can be stolen from under a sleeping person's pillow. A locked door might be helpful, but is no guarantee.

☞ **Tip**

Laptop computers are a prime target for theft everywhere, but they are especially vulnerable in airports. They are stolen for the value of the information on them, as well as for the value of the computer.

According to Safeware (*www.safeware.com/*), an insurer of personal computers, 10% of all laptop thefts occur in airports. Airports offer an inviting atmosphere for thieves due to large crowds, hectic schedules, and weary travelers. Laptop thefts commonly occur in places where people set them down—at security checkpoints, pay phones, lounges and restaurants, check-in lines, and restrooms. Two incidents at separate European airports demonstrate the modus operandi of thieves operating in pairs to target laptop computers.

Airport security at Brussels International Airport reported that two thieves exploited a contrived delay around the security X-ray machines. The first thief preceded the traveler through the security checkpoint and then loitered around the area where security examines carry-on luggage. When the traveler placed his laptop computer onto the conveyer belt of the X-ray machine, the second thief stepped in front of the traveler and set off the metal detector. With the traveler now delayed, the first thief removed the traveler's laptop from the conveyer belt just after it passed through the X-ray machine and quickly disappeared.

While walking around the Frankfurt International Airport in Germany, a traveler carrying a laptop computer in his roll bag did not notice a thief position himself to walk in front of him. The thief stopped abruptly as the traveler bypassed a crowd of people, causing the traveler also to stop. A second thief, who was following close behind, quickly removed the traveler's laptop computer from his roll bag and disappeared into the crowd.

All travelers, both domestic and international, should be alert to any sudden diversions when traveling, especially in transportation terminals. If victimized, travelers should report the thefts immediately to the authorities and be able to provide the makes, model information, and serial numbers of their laptop computers, or any other items of value.

Sensitive Equipment in Transit

Sensitive equipment might be stolen so that it can be copied through reverse engineering. For some purposes, it might be sufficient to gain access to the equipment for only a brief period.

209

For example, a company participated in an airshow that took place overseas. The company shipped over an operational $250,000 multimode radar system that can be used on fighter aircraft. At the conclusion of the airshow, the radar system was packaged for return shipping by company personnel, and the radar assembly was actually bolted to the shipping container. The shipping container was routed through a third country with the customs seals intact.

When company personnel opened the package, they discovered that the radar was no longer bolted to the shipping container. As a result, the radar system was damaged beyond repair. It was determined that the radar was properly bolted down at the time it was prepared for shipment. It also was determined that the country that sponsored the airshow was keenly interested in the radar's technology. It is not known whether the intruder's failure to rebolt the radar was an oversight or was done deliberately to destroy evidence of whatever was done to examine the radar.

Lesson learned: The company did not really need to take the entire radar assembly to the airshow. A mock-up without the internal mechanisms could have been set up along with photographs of the internal components.

Overseas Offices

Offices of U.S. government agencies and U.S. businesses in foreign countries are vulnerable both to burglary and to theft of information by local national employees. For example, the Western European office of a large American corporation was burglarized in an obvious case of industrial espionage. Located on the sixth floor of a 12-story office building, it was entered from the outside window ledge by breaking the window. The thieves ignored the company's expensive computers and other valuable items and went directly to their target—the company's marketing and business data, client and business contact lists, and banking information.

Foreign offices of U.S. government and business organizations are staffed, in part, by local citizens. In many countries, some of these employees cooperate voluntarily with the local security or intelligence service or are pressured or coerced into doing so. In one allied Western European country, collecting proprietary information from the offices of American and other foreign corporations with offices in that country is known as *economic patriotism*. Collected information is provided routinely to local competitors of the U.S. companies. In many countries, local national employees are also debriefed for assessment data about the American personnel.

Foreign intelligence interest is not necessarily determined by an employee's rank in the company. Researchers, key business managers, and corporate executives can all be targets, but so can support employees such as secretaries, computer operators, technicians, and maintenance people. The latter frequently have good, if not the best, access to competitive information. Additionally, their lower pay and rank can provide fertile ground for manipulation by an intelligence agency.

Protection of sensitive information is very difficult under these circumstances. Discussion of all the physical and technical security requirements for protection of proprietary technologies and sensitive commercial information is beyond the scope of this chapter.

Additional Tips and Ideas

Thieves are everywhere. They like cash, cameras, and jewelry, of course, but they also love portable computers. You should not go anywhere without at least one computer in tow. In conclusion, the following are a few tips and ideas on how to protect it. A number of these tips and ideas have been mentioned in passing already.

Always Lock It up. Get a Kensington lock. It might not look like much, but it will really deter a thief or at least slow the thief down if he or she decides to go after your computer. The most important thing is that the cable be attached to something unmovable. Attachment points you might consider in your hotel room are your bed, the pipes under the bathroom sink, or the base of the toilet.

Secure It in Your Car Trunk. The problem with locking your laptop in your hotel room is that it alerts the cleaning staff that your computer is something worth stealing. Instead, you might consider attaching the lock to the trunk door hinge and locking it in your rental car trunk. Always be sure, of course, to park your car in a shady (i.e., cool) area, although your trunk and your computer case are likely to shield your computer from the heat.

Make it Your Constant Companion. Of course, whenever possible, you should keep your computer with you. This isn't difficult to do if the model you use is light and its case is comfortable to carry. If you plan to spend your trip engaging in sports or outdoor activities, however, keeping the laptop with you all the time is probably not practical.

Consider Using the Hotel Safe. Many hotels make safes available in each room or at the front desk. Although most of these safes are not very large, they are generally roomy enough to provide a secure place large enough for the average laptop. Room safes with combination locks are preferable to those with keys, but because many hotels guarantee the security of your valuables (up to a certain dollar value) if you use the safe, you can be relatively certain that your computer is protected from the average thief.

Exercise Extra Caution at the Security Gate. Many computers get stolen at airport X-ray machines (which, by the way, will not hurt your computer). If you are traveling alone, put the computer on the conveyor belt and then do not walk through the metal detector until the computer has passed well into the machine (i.e., out of the reach of a thief at the security checkpoint). Once you go through the metal detector, quickly pick up the computer. If you set off the metal detector, keep walking anyway and pick up your laptop. Demand that one of the security people hold it while you go through the metal detector for a second time.

If you are traveling with someone else, the second person to go through security should hold the computer(s). Don't put them on the belt until the first person has gone through and is ready to catch the computer(s) coming out of the X-ray machine.

You might also consider taking your hard drive out of your laptop and asking the security staff to hand check it. That way, if someone does walk off with your computer, you'll at least still have your data files.

Leave Your Laptop in Suspend Mode . Many airports will make you turn on the computer to prove it isn't a bomb in disguise. If your computer is in suspend mode, you will save yourself a few minutes of waiting at the security area. This could be important if you are running late. Also, the longer you are distracted by your computer, the easier it is for someone to steal your other luggage.

Protect Yourself With a Password. Always make use of password protection. If your data is the real goal of a thief, this will help protect your information. If they are just after your hardware, this will be your way of cheating them out of a victory at your expense.

Guard Your Connection. Never use the save password feature of any dial-up connection. That way, if someone steals your computer, they won't have instant access to your ISP or worse, your company data.

User Security Comes First. To summarize, security products provide effective theft deterrents and access controls, but ultimately it's up to individual users to prevent laptop theft. Users need to be particularly careful in public locations, such as airports, hotels, and conference centers, and take appropriate steps to ensure someone doesn't try to snatch their machine.

When traveling, owners should keep their notebooks in bags sporting bright colors or large tags. Because thieves don't want to draw attention, they will often avoid stealing bags that stand out.

Unfortunately, few laptop users exercise such caution. According to industry experts, organizations need to do a better job of educating laptop users about physical security. Laptop security is an issue that has been percolating from the bottom up in large enterprises. IT departments usually have a pretty good understanding about the potential problems, but it isn't a top concern for management—although it has been getting better after recent high-profile cases and the terrorist attacks of September 11, 2001.

Organizations should determine the appropriate security levels for different employees. A $50 physical cabling device is a no-brainer for all users. Stronger access controls, like authentication and file encryption, would be appropriate for managers who store confidential information on their machines. Depending on the value of the data on the hard drive, an organization might want to explore using a tracking service.

Regardless of the approach, the security method chosen by an organization must blend into the users' regular routines. Surveys have found that laptop users will not use security systems that inconvenience them.

Despite the progress in security products and applications, the threat of laptop theft continues to grow. Telecommuting, wireless Internet access, and business travel will continue to put laptop computers within arms' reach of would-be thieves. Physical and electronic security systems are no guarantee of protecting a notebook computer from theft, but they will decrease the odds of it happening.

Wireless Technology

Employees should protect the identity and confidentiality of personal information stored on wireless devices such as PDAs and cell phones. Access to such devices should be password-controlled, and any stored data should be encrypted.

To prevent loss or theft, a wireless device should be carried in a locked briefcase or closed purse and kept under the constant control of the employee while in transit. Never leave a wireless device unattended in a car. If it is absolutely necessary to view personal information on a wireless device while in public or when traveling on public transportation, ensure that the display panel cannot be seen by anyone else.

When working at locations outside the office, the employee should maintain constant control of wireless devices. If this is not possible, they should be temporarily stored in a secure location, such as a locked room or desk drawer. Do not share wireless devices that are used for work purposes with other individuals, such as family members or friends.

Telephones and Voice Mail

When in transit or working outside the office, employees should avoid using cell phones to discuss personal information. Cell phone conversations can

213

be easily overheard or intercepted by individuals using scanners or other devices.

If an employee works at home on a regular basis, a separate phone line and password-controlled voice mailbox should be set up. Do not disclose the password to family members or roommates.

Email, Faxes, and Photocopies

When working at home or at other locations outside the office, employees should avoid sending personal information by email or fax. Ideally, employees should undertake the faxing or photocopying of personal information themselves. However, in some locations outside the office, fax and photocopy machines for individual use might not be readily available. If employees must submit records containing personal information to a third party for faxing or photocopying, they should ask to be present when these tasks are being done.

Conversations Outside the Office

Employees should not discuss personal information in public locations such as buses, commuter trains, subways, airplanes, restaurants, or on the street. If it is necessary to do so, move to a location where other persons cannot overhear your conversation.

Reporting Requirements

Finally, the loss or theft of personal information should be reported immediately to an employee's immediate manager and senior management. If personal information has been lost through theft, the police should be notified as well. At the outset of an investigation, it is recommended that the institution (ISP) notify any individuals whose personal information has been lost and take steps to contain the loss of the information.

Chapter 10

MANAGEMENT OF ONGOING IDENTITY THEFT PREVENTION AND PROTECTION TECHNIQUES

Financial institutions lose billions of dollars annually to new account, credit card, and other types of fraud. They also lose face by allowing their legitimate customers to be hurt by this fraud. Even though individuals who are the victims of identity theft might not suffer a monetary loss, they will be presented with the burden of completing affidavits, answering merchant demand letters, contacting credit bureaus, and clearing their once-cherished good names.

The simplicity of obtaining the necessary identification to open fraudulent accounts, together with regulatory restrictions, provide wrongdoers the ability to reap huge monetary benefits. The verification instruments that everyone uses (credit reports, Social Security number and name verifications, employment verification, address and phone number verification) are the targets that criminals aim for to establish false identities.

The banking industry needs to thwart those criminal efforts by teaching their own employees about identity theft. The employees need to pass along that valuable information to customers.

The question to ask IT managers about their institution's training programs is this: are they providing their line staff, managers, and clients with the information they require for fraud awareness? Actually, they are not! They teach techniques designed to protect the financial institution against potential monetary loss from undesirable account relationships. However, they are not denying fraudsters the one important tool necessary for the fraud to occur:

and identity. If potential criminals cannot develop the name, Social Security number, or identification of a true individual, their attempts will be futile. Information available for training employees to recognize and prevent such fraud is plentiful, yet some banks fail to take advantage or to keep up-to-date on the latest trends.

To defraud a financial institution, a perpetrator has to obtain the personal identification information of a real individual. Very few fraudsters will use their own identification. Bank employees need to understand how fraudsters obtain those identities and how to guard against identity theft. By incorporating the measures shown in Table 10.1 into fraud training programs, you can teach your employees how to make the white-collar criminal work harder to develop identifications.

Table 10.1. Individual Fraud Prevention Tips Checklist

How to Prevent Fraud
Individual Fraud Prevention Measures Checklist
Date: _____

It is recommended that banks should train their employees to make sure that customers need to (check all tasks completed):

❑ 1. Review credit reports every six months. Unauthorized credit information should be detected and reported as quickly as possible.

❑ 2. Destroy preapproved credit card applications. Don't just discard them—burn or shred them. Otherwise, discarded applications can be retrieved from the garbage, completed, and submitted with a different cardholder address. Once one card is obtained, others are much easier to get.

❑ 3. Obtain from merchants and destroy voided credit applications. Again, burn or shred them. The word void does not make the individual data any less readable or beneficial to the criminal. Individual merchants are not selective or concerned with disposal techniques.

❑ 4. Don't use publicly accessible containers for any pertinent information used for financial verification, such as preapproved credit applications, canceled checks, old bank statements, or voided credit applications. Dumpster divers obtain a majority of their information from accessing trash containers. Once the trash has been placed at the curb, the contents can be obtained by anyone.

❑ 5. Raise questions when bank statements are late, do not arrive, or are missing certain items. A majority of bank statements contain account holder Social Security numbers. Canceled checks contain identification (driver's license numbers). Some state drivers' license numbers are Social Security numbers. Thieves will remove mail from mailboxes, copy documents, and then reseal and return them to previously delivered addresses.

Table 10.1. Individual Fraud Prevention Tips Checklist (Continued)

❏ 6. Never place paid bills in an unsecured residential or business mailbox or facility. Legitimate checks can be removed from the envelopes, chemically washed clean of payee name, and made payable to unauthorized individuals or businesses.

❏ 7. Credit cards should not be used after hours at non-point-of-sale service stations. Leaving credit cards with station attendants while gas is being pumped provides potential thieves the opportunity to record the card holder's name, account number and expiration date.

❏ 8. Individual bank account numbers should not be recorded on the reverse of items deposited into personal accounts, such as refund checks or payroll checks. The depositor cannot know the storing and disposal process of canceled checks by the drawee bank. The canceled item will contain the depository bank name, individual name and account number, and depository bank routing number.

❏ 9. Caution should be used when responding to advertised job announcements. Phony office fronts have been established in an effort to obtain completed job applications from unsuspecting job seekers. Resumes should never be mailed or faxed in response to blind announcements. The sender is unable to verify if the resume went to a legitimate receiver.

❏ 10. All sensitive items and documents should be mauled via a secure container at U.S. Postal Service locations.

❏ 11. All receiving mail should be received via a post office box (which is most secure), residential door mail slot, or secured receiving postal device.

Management of electronic records presents interesting challenges for many public and private-sector organizations that are concerned with managing ongoing identity theft prevention and protection techniques. Let's now look at some of the difficulties that organizations can encounter if electronic records are not managed in a systematic way.

Management of Electronic Records

With the advent of information technologies, the variety of ways that information can be created, stored, and manipulated has increased many fold in comparison to the days when information was produced almost solely through the medium of paper. In devising a strategy to deal with the theft of electronic records, organizations might need to consider this issue in the wider context of managing their global information requirements and the diverse forms of IT that now exist.

Electronic records exist in an environment that encompasses various forms of hardware, software, and information or data. Moreover, an electronic record can exist simultaneously in a variety of mediums—on paper, on a CD-ROM, on tape, or on hard disk. In fact, no single medium can hold all the records that reflect an organization's activities or functions. Electronic records, however, can be subject to alteration, correction, and deletion once a transaction or decision is complete, thereby weakening their authenticity and subsequent usefulness as evidence of the original transaction or decision. Important information about who created the records, when, and for what purposes can be lost or stolen.

The computer, which just a few years ago was used almost exclusively by technical specialists, is now being employed by nearly everyone in an organization. As a consequence, individual users are often in control of what happens to the records that they create. Given such a decentralized framework for assembling information, corporate standards are essential to effectively maintain an organization's records holdings.

For many users of desktop systems, electronic records are created and used in real time, and once they are sent by email or read, there might seem little reason to keep them or file them according to some systematic criteria, as was done for paper records. This scenario is less likely to be played out where records are stored in highly structured, closely managed information systems. Problems are more likely to arise with records that deal with administrative, policy formulation, and decision-making processes in the organization.

Let's now look at a compelling irony—the information age could be the least documented period in human history. In the past, decisions on whether or not to retain documents were typically made months or years after the record was created and temporarily filed. Today, these determinations are often made by individuals soon after the electronic record has been created or within a few days or months, but certainly not years. What is being destroyed or stolen are not just historical records, but contemporary ones as well.

Records cannot be accessed by an identity thief if they do not exist. If contemporary electronic records are being destroyed or stolen, an then revised or otherwise affected so that they cannot be retrieved in their original form (even if records are retained), inadequate provisions are made to ensure that records remain readable and retain their full value as evidence of decisions or transactions. Changing technologies could render records unreadable or alter their original structure or appearance as documents or data. The management of recorded electronic information can, therefore, be viewed as integral to the operation of an organization.

The best management practices for electronic records discussed next are arranged so that a suggested practice is cited first, followed by a brief discussion of the reasoning behind the practice. Organizations should take into account their own particular circumstances.

Best Practices

Government and private organizations today are experiencing a transition period, as more and more of their operations become computerized, and the way they do business increasingly involves the creation of electronic records. Although this IT assists in the delivery of programs and services to the public, it has presented government and corporate managers with many new challenges. The best practices suggested here assume that an organization is only beginning the process of dealing with the potential theft of electronic records.

Best Practice 1

Because electronic records might not necessarily take material form (hard copy), a record should be viewed as being an all-inclusive term that encompasses every conceivable way that information, including data, text, image, or sound, can be created, stored, and retrieved electronically. You have been used to thinking that what is printed on paper is a record, because it possesses physical properties. More and more government and private organizations, however, now utilize various forms of IT, principally the personal computer, to assemble and present information. The records or other electronic images created using this technology might not in many instances be stored as such on the computer. The data or text might only exist as stored memory that can be assembled and retrieved later to form a coherent document or image, or a sound playback. It can also be immediately erased without ever being printed on paper or any other form, or it can be stored electronically, (e.g., on a hard disk or diskette).

 Tip

Throughout this part of the chapter, the term electronic records *includes data, text, images, and sound. If one of these descriptors is not present, no change in meaning is intended.*

Best Practice 2

Email that records communications relating to the mandate or functions of the organization and is in the custody and control of the organization should be considered a record. Within the context of describing electronic records, special mention should be made of electronic messages.

The use of email is widespread in government and the private sector. However, government and corporate employees might not always consider this form of communication to constitute a record, because the form of this communication might appear transitory, personal, or unimportant. There is no doubt that in some cases email bears no relation to the mandate or functions of the organization (e.g., personal messages) or is so inconsequential that it does not need to be retained for operational purposes. However, electronic messages that document communications relating to the organization's mandate or functions should be considered records for the purposes of freedom of information legislation. Such messages chronicle electronic exchange of views on the activities and functions of the organization or document business activities.

The practice of some people in some organizations is to automatically print a copy of such messages for a paper file. Although this is not a long-term solution, it might be necessary until the retention capabilities of information technologies have been further developed. Otherwise, important emails should be systematically saved to subject- or program-based directories.

Best Practice 3

Software created by a government or organization should be treated as potentially constituting a record. A software program is an essential tool for the creation, organization, and storage of records. Information or data cannot ordinarily be retrieved without the application of a software program. Viewed from this perspective, a software program can form an integral part of a record. In some cases, the organization itself may have produced the software and, as a result, the information might only be accessible through the use of this particular software. In many cases, when using commercial software, the record cannot be accessed in its original form without using the software with which it was created.

 Tip

Based on proposals being advanced in the United States, a software program developed by the government or an organization (as distinct from a commercially acquired, off-the-shelf program) would be considered a record for purposes of freedom of information legislation.

Best Practice 4

Data and records viewed online and not subsequently stored on an individual workstation or database are generally not considered a record. A government or organization might subscribe to an external commercial online email service or bulletin board, or might be connected to a wide area network, such as the Internet. In these cases, individuals will often view electronic documents, publications, and other materials online with no permanent record of the information being kept by the institution. Although this issue has not been specifically adjudicated, the approach adopted in the United States is that information, text, or data viewed online (but not downloaded and stored) is not a record for purposes of legislation. If, on the other hand, the information or data was copied and stored either in an electronic version or as a hard-copy printout, it should be considered a record.

Best Practice 5

A good strategy for management of electronic records starts with a review of an organization's functions and business processes to determine what records need to be created and retained, and a review of existing records management practices to determine their continuing effectiveness. After an organization determines that the management of its electronic records should be reviewed, a good strategy would start with an analysis of the organization's functions and business processes. Such an analysis would seek to determine whether the records that are being created document these activities accurately and completely. In preparing the analysis, it might be useful to consider the following points:

- The creation of an interdisciplinary team consisting of systems specialists, archivists, record managers, and program managers probably represents the most effective way to undertake this type of investigation, and then to develop workable program documentation and records management strategies.

- Any review should consider the proper management of all forms of records, irrespective of the way in which they are stored, such as electronically, on paper, on microfilm, and so on.

- In determining what records need to be created and retained, public organizations should take into account various laws and practices that require documentation for accountability purposes or as evidence of decisions made. [1]

Best Practice 6

Once a need to change existing records management practices has been identified, available options for managing the system should be considered. In particular, serious consideration should be given to integrating the management of paper and electronic records. An integrated electronic and paper system would entail ensuring that records in paper and electronic form were carried over to the electronic filing system. There are increasingly powerful records management and document management systems that can assist in this integration.

Best Practice 7

Government organizations should take records management considerations into account when designing information systems and when planning for upgrades to existing systems. When organizations consider designing or upgrading information systems or software applications, they should carefully consider their ongoing records management needs. These include ensuring the ongoing accessibility of information and its prompt disposal when no longer required. Unless records management needs are specifically addressed, it is unlikely that they will be incorporated effectively into the new system.

Best Practice 8

Prior to acquiring new IT, government organizations should ensure that technical or other solutions are in place to support easy, ongoing access to records placed on a system and ready for conversion to other convenient formats, as required. As governments and organizations increasingly acquire more sophisticated technologies, they will be faced with choices about the kind of hardware and software to obtain. Governments and organizations should incorporate in their analysis of options the access and retention capabilities of the technology they intend to acquire. The technology, whether hardware or software, should be capable of providing easy storage and retrieval of information and data.

 Tip

IT is used broadly to include computers and telecommunications devices that allow for local area and wide area networks, as well as any other machine-readable technology that processes information or data.

Access could be thwarted, for example, if a particular software program does not permit information to be transferred to a new or different application or media format. In many instances, utility programs exist that can handle this conversion (e.g., from a particular word processing format to another text format governed by Standard Generalized Markup Language).

Best Practice 9

Government organizations should include in their IT planning a strategy for preserving information, data, or text for extended periods of time. One of the disadvantages of electronic records is that they are stored on media (usually magnetic tapes or disks) that deteriorate over time, in some cases within just a few years. Although no new technology has yet been created to fully rectify this problem, steps can be taken to ensure that the information, data, or text that these records hold is preserved for longer periods of time. That is, they need to be retrievable and usable over the information's life cycle from creation to final disposition. The use of CD-ROM technology does provide greater capability. The important point is to periodically migrate electronic records to new tapes or disks before decomposition sets in, or, if appropriate, to new technologies.

The need to ensure that records can be transferred to other media and software applications has already been discussed. Given rapid technological obsolescence, this consideration has particular urgency for records with long-term value. Moreover, some electronic records have archival value. If they will eventually be transferred to an archive, an agreement should be developed with the archive regarding the medium and format in which they will be transferred.

Best Practice 10

The quality of electronic records can be enhanced if "contextual" information that allows the original purpose or context of a record to be determined becomes part of the records management system. For an electronic record to be of use as evidence of decisions, or transactions made, it must contain certain elements that make it understandable to someone who did not originally create the record. In a paper context, a record would ordinarily include details that placed the content of the document in a particular context (letterhead, addresses and titles, etc.).

Such a record would also be filed according to some system of record keeping, indicating that the document had been produced by a certain person in a certain department within the organization. It should also be filed with other related documents that allow the larger context in which the record was created to be understood (e.g., the issue that prompted a particular memo or email message to be written).

In an electronic environment, a record might consist only of its text or data contents without its author being identified. The information is often key to preserving the record's value as evidence, whether for legal or more standard operational reasons. In addition, other important contextual information might be absent, including the following:

- The date and time when the record was created
- Its origins within the organization
- The person or persons to whom it may have been sent
- The date and time when it was sent [1]

In some cases, it might not be evident why a record was created, or documentation might be lacking to permit the integrity and completeness of records stored on a database to be assessed. Finally, the record might exist in a number of different locations and might not be filed according to a system that places the record and related records in distinct files and file series following a recognized classification system that permits ready location of required records.

Tip

Key information would include information about the agency and the persons who created it; the time, place, and reasons for its creation; and its relationship to other records.

In addition, to ensure that a record can be retrieved later (and in a manner that retains its evidentiary character), it might be necessary to preserve the software that was used to create it, as well as important information on the technical characteristics of the storage media and system and any guides or protocols that describe and control how records were filed as data on the system or its storage media. Otherwise, the record might need to be transferred to another storage medium that better preserves its accessibility and evidential value.

Governments and organizations should also consider mechanisms to ensure that records that reflect a final position, decision, or transaction are made tamper proof. Restrictions should be placed on the people who are able to alter, change, or delete the record. Often, a number of copies of the same record exist. To avoid any confusion, organizations should find a way to identify the authoritative version. Finally, it is important to email messages, attachments, and other transferred files to be integrated into and stored in the organization's record-keeping system (see Best Practice 6).

Best Practice 11

IT managers should determine uniform protocols for storing electronic records in consultation or collaboration with records managers so that such information can be easily retrieved as required. All documentation about the system should be retained for easy access.

Governments and organizations should develop and adhere to standard methods of identifying and storing information, data, and text to ensure that they can be easily stored and retrieved. This will mean developing systems documentation and data management protocols. It could also include development of file classification plans for paper and electronic records by records management specialists.

Best Practice 12

Records in all media, including electronic media, should not be destroyed without appropriate official authorization. Before the advent of IT, a record was typically thought of as a piece of paper that proceeded through a defined and predictable life cycle. It was created and used, filed, and then destroyed, or, if of long-term value, given to the organization's archives. Today, however, the record is often not a piece of paper, but information recorded by the use of a computer. Erasable immediately after it is created, the information exists in electronic form in the memory of a computer and becomes material (hard copy) only when a printout is made.

Those who work with various information technologies invariably make decisions about whether to retain information at the moment that it is either created or received. Thus, for example, an email message relating to the mandate or function of the organization is sent, and once read, often deleted by users. This might occur because technical or operational procedures for retaining and storing email or other computer-generated information have not been adopted. The record, in any event, is not saved.

Best Practice 13

When new software or hardware is introduced, organizations should use their best efforts to convert their active stored information, data, and text to the new systems or retain the ability to access it. Another aspect of retaining electronically created records is maintaining and modifying the software systems documentation and other data management tools so that information, data, or text can be easily retrieved at some later date. This is particularly important because IT changes so rapidly. This requires that institutions regularly purchase new hardware and upgrade existing software programs. Unless the stored data or information that has long-term value is converted to the new systems, it might become very difficult, if not impossible, to obtain access to that data stored under older technology. Over time, the development of open systems and standards will help as more information and data will be accessible without complex conversion.

Best Practice 14

Governments and organizations should integrate electronic records into their record retention scheduling process. When paper records were the norm, the question of what records to keep or destroy was usually made some time after the documents were created. In this respect, retention schedules were developed to indicate how long records were to be maintained by a particular department before they were destroyed or transferred to a records center and archived.

Schedules should similarly be developed for electronic records. Early in the development of electronic information systems, each department should determine the retention period for related groups of email messages, reports, database files, and so on, and see that they are scheduled accordingly. This approach will help ensure that electronic records are kept as long as they are needed and that the permanent portions of electronic records can be selected and preserved by archives.

Best Practice 15

The vulnerability of electronic records to a variety of security breaches needs to be addressed through appropriate security procedures. Without proper precautions, electronic records are vulnerable to unauthorized access and tampering. Among the strategies organizations can apply to minimize the chance of a security breach are the following:

- Levels of security and authorized access can be formalized for the organization through the use of passwords and sign-on identifiers.
- Confidential information can be encrypted when stored or transmitted.
- Records should also be secured from system failures and physical disasters.
- An appropriate backup system is required.
- A disaster recovery plan needs to be devised. [1]

Best Practice 16

Whenever feasible, governments and organizations should provide individuals with the electronic records that they seek in the format requested. When a request for access to a record is made, the government or organization will ordinarily provide a paper copy of the record or give the requester the opportunity to view the original. Where the request is for an electronic record, there are a variety of ways that the request can be fulfilled, depending on what the requester wants and the capabilities of the technology in use by the institution.

Where the information is stored on a videotape or audiotape, the organization could provide a copy of the tape, if such is the request, or give the requester the opportunity to listen to or view the tape. Ordinarily, to provide a copy of an audiotape or videotape is neither time-consuming nor unduly expensive.

With the increasing use of various forms of IT, it is often practical to provide access to an electronic record in the format requested. Thus, an institution might hold requested information in a database that is accessible by means of a commercially available software package. The requester could ask that the information be copied to a disk. A request of this kind neither entails difficult procedures nor much time and should be responded to routinely.

Best Practice 17

Governments and organizations should attempt to modify their software to provide access to a requested electronic record where it is reasonable to do so. Organizations should be flexible in determining what is reasonable.

Electronic records might not exist in paper form. A record could be data or text assembled in a particular way through the use of a software program. A discrete record or file might not exist, but could be created with the assistance of software or technical knowledge available to the government or organization.

Such a scenario would arise where a government or corporate database held raw data or statistics, and the government or organization had a computer software program that allowed the data to be manipulated in a variety of ways. A request could be made for the data to be assembled in a way not anticipated by the organization. How should the organization respond?

The organization should modify the software program as appropriate, provided that doing so would not unreasonably interfere with the organization's operations. IT has developed to the extent that relatively little time and effort are often required to make such modifications.

Less problematic are requests for access to videotapes or audiotapes, microfilm, and microfiche. More challenging is a request for access to a record online; that is, where the institution has, for example, created a database comprising discrete pieces of information and the requester would like to have direct access to that database through his or her home or work computer.

Best Practice 18

Finally, electronic records, like other records that contain information of general interest, should be routinely disclosed and distributed to the public. Some government and corporate information is now provided through information kiosks at various public locations.

Neural Networks

A *neural network* is a computerized system that examines the details of an online transaction. The neural network compares these details to historical patterns about fraudulent sales, and then assigns a score to each transaction that predicts its risk of fraud.

 Tip

In other words, neural networks can be used to examine details of an online transaction but they are actually information processing systems that are modeled on the way biological nervous systems operate.

Because neural networks can analyze vast amounts of data, they are also used by insurance companies to predict risk and by financial companies to predict stock trends. Here's how they work to help prevent fraud and identity theft.

First, the development of a neural network begins with a historical database of transaction information—usually at least six months of data—that can include hundreds of thousands of online transactions. This data includes the attributes of the sale—area code, time, geographical location, item size, price, credit card number, and so on. This database also notes whether or not the transaction was fraudulent.

Based on the information in the database, the neural network develops profiles of fraudulent transactions. These profiles take the form of a mathematical formula. The neural network then applies the formula to each transaction as it is being processed. Using the formula, each attribute of the transaction is given a certain weight. The weighted sum of all attributes represents the transaction's risk of fraud.

Neural networks, which can also be called fraud scorers, screeners, or predictive statistical models, are often used in conjunction with rule-based detection systems (see the sidebar, "Rule-Based Detection"). Whereas neural networks review historical data to develop a risk score, rule-based detection systems compare sales to a set of yes–no questions.

Rule-Based Detection

With rule-based detection software, merchants define a set of criteria that each transaction must meet. Often called a negative file, this set of rules can be based on past experiences, price limits, names, addresses, and the knowledge of human experts, such as risk analysts. These criteria should always maintain not only stolen credit card numbers, but also bad shipping addresses and telephone numbers. The software will automatically screen incoming orders by these specific criteria and automate the decision to reject, review, or accept the order. For example, a merchant might screen for unusually high dollar transactions, billing and shipping addresses that do not match (these are not useful for businesses that cater more to gift giving), an order for an unusually high number of one item, or names and credit cards that have been linked to fraud in the past. [2]

Because the neural networks rely on authentic, historical data about fraud and ID theft, and because they can review many interrelated factors to determine the risk of a sale, they can be very accurate. When you overlay it on all your transactions, it is amazing how effective it can be.

What Kind of Site Needs a Neural Network?

Many experts laud neural networks as an invaluable tool for e-commerce sites. However, as with any fraud and identity theft prevention tool, you'll need to weigh your potential fraud and identity theft losses against the cost of the tool before you invest in it.

This cost comparison should include three factors: the start-up costs to build or purchase the system, the costs of the resources to maintain the system, and the effectiveness of the solution. This final factor includes both the reduction in the number of transactions to be manually reviewed and the potential financial impact of losing revenue from turning away good customers.

You should look at all these issues, and then ask yourself this, Would I be spending more than I would be losing to fraud? If the answer is yes, then you probably don't need a neural network. If you choose not to implement fraud screening, you must monitor your business for signs of an emerging fraud pattern, as an unidentified problem could be fatal to some businesses.

What Are the Risks and Limitations?

Like all fraud and identity theft prevention tools, a neural network is just one component in a plan, rather than a complete solution. In addition, you should review the factors covered in the following sections when evaluating the benefits of the software.

Data

The first limitation of a neural network is its data—a neural network is only as good as the database it is based on. For this reason, data should be as accurate as possible, refreshed at least every six months to account for new trends, and based on a large sample of sales.

Human Resources

A risk of any fraud and identity theft prevention tool is false negatives, or turning away good customers. For this reason, you'll need real people to manually review the sales flagged by the neural network to determine which are actually fraudulent and determine a course of action. A lot of people miss this step.

You also need to evaluate the time you have to review a sale: The less time you have, the more people you need. If you are selling CDs or stuffed animals, you have more time to review a transaction than if you are selling a plane ticket, for example.

Customization

For the most part, the more customized a neural network, the better it is. You'd want a database with data from your industry, your target audience, and, if possible, your own company. If you sell children's clothing to Europe, for example, you don't want data about selling videos in the United States.

Customization will also allow you to more efficiently pinpoint fraudulent sales. An off-the-shelf neural network with minimal customization might flag as much as 10% of sales as risky.

If you process 30,000 transactions a day, that's 3,000 sales to review—far too many to handle unless you have a huge staff. A more customized system will reduce that percentage to something much easier to handle.

How Much Does a Neural Network Cost?

Like many fraud and ID theft prevention technologies, the cost of a neural network depends on its complexity and whether or not you have the resources to build it in house. Because neural networks are so highly sophisticated and require database customization, they can be expensive to develop.

The initial costs are largely dependent on your volume. If you push through a significant number of transactions, a vendor might provide customization and implementation for little to no cost. If you have low volume you can pay $20,000 to $30,000 for setup, or maybe more.

A transactional fee is then assessed, ranging from a few cents to more than a dollar per transaction, depending on the type and level of scoring performed. In addition, you'll also have to consider the costs of updating and maintaining the neural network with good information, and the cost of the staff required to review the system's findings.

Next, let's look at the aftermath of fraud. What are you supposed to do when fraud occurs?

Postfraud

One question merchants always ask is this: What am I supposed to do when fraud occurs? No one person has the answer, but there are a number of best practices that merchants typically use if they are the victims of fraud:

- Review the fraudulent order
- Document the fraudulent order
- Create a negative file
- Prepare your case
- Determine how to report a crime
- Learn what happens to your case when you report it
- Learn about other best practices
- Get your money back. [3]

Review the Fraudulent Order

When fraud occurs, don't just write it off and consider it a cost of doing business. You must review the fraudulent order internally and determine your plan of action. Why do you have to review the fraud? It will help you better prevent future fraudulent transactions. Once a fraudster figures out that he or she can successfully commit fraud on your Web site, he or she will continue to do it until stopped. He or she will teach all his or her friends how to commit fraud against you as well.

Repeated frauds on the same site should increase a fraudster's chance of getting caught, but what actually happens in this situation? The fraudster learns that you have limited resources to fight fraud. If one person commits fraud against you, you might be tempted to try to catch that person. However, if 100 of his or her closest Internet buddies commit fraud against you, you are spread so thin that you won't be able to keep up with the volume of fraud. When a merchant is targeted by groups of fraudsters, the outlook is grim. Large-scale fraud could actually force a merchant to shut down a business.

Document the Fraudulent Order

It is imperative to document every fraudulent order. Documentation will allow you to build a criminal case, track fraud within your business, and find the root cause to determine how to prevent it from happening again.

The critical elements of the order you should record are the shipping address, the shipping telephone number, and the IP address. Try to collect a signature at the time of delivery for an even stronger piece of evidence. When you ship via UPS or FedEx, you can require a signature on delivery.

Create a Negative File

The most effective thing a merchant can do is create a negative file—essentially a history of fraudsters. The negative file should contain credit card information, fraudulent names, shipping addresses, and IP addresses.

Used properly, this list will become one of your most powerful tools against fraud. Compare each incoming order against the negative file and if there is a match or close match, mark the order for internal review.

Never automatically reject an order based on your criteria because you might inadvertently reject a valid customer. These wrongful rejections are known as *insult orders* in the industry.

Do not share negative files with other merchants. Another merchant's negative file could contain valid customers who had bad experiences at the store and simply charged back the order. If you rejected that customer, you would have an insult order on your hands.

Prepare Your Case

Who should you call to report fraud? What steps are involved in reporting fraud? When should or shouldn't you report fraud? These are extremely complicated questions that only your organization can answer.

First, establish in-house guidelines about fraud and how to handle fraud cases. For example, if the fraud is less than $1,000, you might want to simply document the case in your negative file and continue business as usual. If the fraud is greater than $1,000, you might want to invest two hours of research time to try building a case against the fraudster. Of course, the dollar amount you use as a cutoff must be tailored to your business.

When you prepare your case to report to the authorities, make it easy for law enforcement officials to absorb. Place the most important details (especially the IP address and shipping address) near the top of the page. Include as much detail as you can about the case, but present the information in a way that is clear and easily understood.

Determine How to Report a Crime

Visit a yellow pages search engine, such as Yahoo! Yellow Pages. Click Change Location. Enter the zip code of the fraudulent shipping address and in the Search box, type *police*.

Call the local police and ask to speak with a detective. Explain your case to the detective and send him or her the summary information. Remember, detectives are measured by the number of cases they can solve. The more detail you provide, the easier you make it for them, and the bigger your chance of catching the fraudster.

Manage your own expectations. A detective in a New York City police department probably won't be chomping at the bit to go after a case where someone defrauded you for $100 on a couple of DVDs. On the other hand, expect police in smaller towns to be more aggressive against smaller crimes.

The key to success for you as a merchant is to provide enough detail so that all the detective has to do is capture the criminal. Do as much of the research as you can.

Learn What Happens to Your Case When You Report It

First, the detective builds the case. Then he or she either captures the fraudster or involves the Secret Service or other appropriate federal agencies. After the fraudster is caught, the case is presented to the district attorney. It is up to the law enforcement folks to "sell" the case and get the district attorney to actually bring the case to court.

Learn About Other Best Practices

Make someone your in-house fraud expert. Do not allow customer service representatives to automatically contact customers about fraudulent or suspicious activities. It is best to have a single person (or group of people) handle these situations. After a while, your chosen fraud expert will develop an instinct for recognizing patterns in fraud cases. This cultivated "gut feeling" will help in your fight against fraud.

Go after attempted fraud, too. When the police are creating a case, they can convict on attempted fraud as well as actual fraud.

Be helpful to the detective. Respond to all questions in a timely manner. Not only does this help catch the fraudster, but it also means you will be first on the detective's mind.

Once the case is resolved, put the fraudster on a payment plan. Experts say you are more likely to get your money back if you work out some sort of payment plan with the fraudster. Most online fraud is committed by people who simply thought they could get away with it.

Get Your Money Back

Current restitution rates are quite disappointing. It is estimated that you may only see 10% of your money. In fact, you will probably spend more than that on investigating the fraud.

If that's the case, is it even worth fighting fraud? Absolutely. The alternative is simply too risky. Once fraudsters figure out that you do nothing to combat fraud, you become an easy target. Take action against fraud, and you can protect your business and your customers' IDs.

Now, if you are thinking about adding e-commerce features to your site, but you keep reading about online fraud, what information should you collect from your customers to protect yourself? Are you leaving your customers or yourself open to identity theft? Let's briefly take a look.

Processing Internet Charges

To decrease the risk for fraud and identity theft when processing Internet charges, make sure you get complete information from your customers:

- Their cardholder's name exactly as it appears on the card
- The card account number
- The card expiration date
- The card billing address
- The cardholder's home or business telephone number
- The cardholder's email address
- The name of package recipient
- The shipping address
- A phone number at the shipping destination. [4]

Once you have this information, use the card issuers' AVS to determine whether the customer is who they say they are. In addition, some vendors offer software that can detect vacant lots or other suspicious information like abandoned buildings used as addresses. For very small merchants on a budget, there are also free services online that allow you to check names and addresses.

If the address is incorrect, or you still feel nervous about the transaction, simply call the customer and verify the transaction. Of course, if the phone number is wrong, don't ship the goods.

Next, let's look at a new challenge for online merchants: shipment rerouting, an emerging scheme that allows fraudsters to evade online fraud detection screening methods. How do you prevent it?

Rerouting Shipments

The inevitable destiny of every mechanism designed to spot potentially fraudulent orders is to become obsolete. In fact, as fraudsters devise new schemes to circumvent the checks that merchants put in place, the traditional red flags begin to lose their effectiveness as screening tools.

One of the most commonly used indicators for online fraud detection is the one that flags orders being shipped to an address that is different from the credit card billing address. Shipment rerouting is an emerging scheme that allows fraudsters to evade this type of screening method. With that in mind, this part of the chapter covers the following:

- How shipment rerouting works
- What merchants can do
- Working with shipping companies
- Masking the tracking number
- Verifying shipment records [5]

How Shipment Rerouting Works

Although the vast majority of orders with different billing and shipping addresses are legitimate, there are several good reasons for taking a closer look at this segment of orders. First, if a fraudster manages to steal the identity of the cardholder (including the legitimate billing address), the merchandise must be delivered to some other address where the fraudster can collect it. Second, although the issuer validates the billing address when the transaction is authorized (via AVS), the shipping address, if different from the billing address, cannot be validated.

Because most merchants have put in place stringent order validation procedures for orders shipped to alternative addresses, fraudsters have quickly learned to avoid notice with the shipment rerouting scheme. Using this scheme, orders are initially placed with same billing and shipping address, so as not to trigger potential fraud warnings.

Next, after the order is approved, the fraudster attempts to change the delivery address by either calling the merchant's customer service department or, more frequently, calling the shipment company directly. The fraudster then collects the merchandise at the new delivery address, while the merchant, in most cases, isn't even aware of the switch.

This scheme is an effective workaround not only for fraud screening based on alternative shipping addresses, but also for screening based on high-risk shipping addresses. For example, if the merchant has set up a block on certain delivery addresses, such as those related to prior chargebacks, this scheme would also render those validations ineffective.

What Merchants Can Do

How can merchants defend themselves against this emerging scheme? As mentioned earlier, the fraudster will request a change of delivery address by calling either the merchant or, after the goods have been shipped, the shipment company directly.

Merchants can put procedures in place to control at least the first situation. Specifically, if the merchant has implemented fraud screens that occur when the order is first received, it is important to ensure that any subsequent updates to the order (including changes in shipping address) trigger a reexamination of the order via the fraud screens. The merchant should also attempt to validate the new delivery address by requesting and verifying a phone number for the delivery, for example.

When the fraudster contacts the shipping company directly, merchants have definitively less control over the situation; therefore, this is the most problematic case for online commerce. Most shipment companies have policies that allow only the shipper to request a change of delivery address when a package is en route.

Unfortunately, these policies provide very little defense against fraudulent activities because call center representatives rarely validate the identity of the person on the other end of the phone. Thus, if asked, the fraudster simply acts as a representative from the company shipping the product. The real merchant is obviously completely unaware of the situation, and often the scheme is uncovered only several weeks later, when a chargeback notification arrives and shipment records are researched.

Working With Shipping Companies

Merchants have begun working with shipping companies to try to find a solution to the problem. Some shipping companies have begun to put in place new control policies by which the caller requesting a delivery address change must provide the shipper's account number, which should only be known to the merchant. Unfortunately, for these new policies to become effective, shippers will need to educate thousands of call center representatives and ensure that the new policy is strictly enforced.

Some merchants have little faith in the ability of shipping companies to properly implement these new policies. These are very big organizations. There are no system-level controls behind this, and it also works against their customer culture.

One incentive to properly implement these procedures might be liability. Some online merchants believe that the shipper should be made accountable for the loss if the shipper does not follow the prescribed procedure of requiring the account number. Of course, holding the shipper accountable is easier said than done, but it is doable. Until shippers are liable for authorized rerouting of merchandise, merchants need to be alert and consider all possible countermeasures.

Masking the Tracking Number

What can merchants do to defend themselves from shipment rerouting requested via the shipper? The only way to manage this is to mask the tracking number. Most merchants provide customers with the shipment tracking number as soon as the merchandise has been shipped, but some merchants are pursuing alternatives. The tracking number provides the fraudster with an easy way to identify the package with the shipper and place a rerouting call at the right time.

To provide legitimate customers with the same level of convenience without disclosing the actual tracking number, some merchants now offer shipment-tracking services at their own Web sites. The user simply enters the merchant order number and the status of the shipment is fetched directly from the shipper and displayed to the consumer.

This is possible thanks to the communication protocols that shippers such as FedEx and UPS now offer to their customers. Tracking number masking is only a partial remedy, as a fraudster might be brave enough to call the shipping company even without a tracking number—inquiring by the recipient's name and address. However, it definitively provides some level of defense against this scheme.

Verifying Shipment Records

Finally, online merchants should at least be aware of what could happen after goods leave their fulfillment centers and, if possible, monitor the final delivery address of their shipments. Specifically, online merchants should verify shipment records for chargeback orders that were originally shipped to an AVS-validated billing address, because these might be orders that were rerouted. This data can help merchants detect if they have been victimized by this new scheme.

Internet Privacy Policies

How do you show your customers how to develop Internet privacy policies before real problems like identity theft arise? In other words, most companies argue that profiling helps them create a very customized experience on the Web, and that's all well and good if the individual has consented to that activity. However, as part of their self-regulation, merchants should allow individual users reasonable access to correct, supplement, and augment whatever information they've acquired about them to make sure that picture is accurate.

On one side are frustrated marketers with a slew of technology for cookie planting, invisible GIFs, and Web log analysis, hoping that the next breakthrough in customer insight will shake revenues out of the doldrums. On the other side is a consumer base growing increasingly edgy about invasions of digital privacy, both perceived and real.

With numerous government and industry initiatives in this country lining up to complement and contradict each other, and Canada and the EU already enacting more comprehensive codes of conduct, privacy is no longer simply a matter of posting a cookie-cutter policy. Yet it's still not easy to see exactly what will drive consistent, coordinated standards for consumer privacy.

Demand alone seems unlikely to carry the day. Despite pockets of outcry over low points such as Toysmart.com's aborted sale of its customer database and DoubleClick's overly ambitious campaign to unify online and offline customer profiles, public pushback has not given rise to an Internet-wide privacy agenda. Part of that is a lack of money talking.

Consumers haven't shown themselves willing to pay for privacy, which is only compounded by the stigma of serving the market in the first place—early adopters are perceived to have something to hide. People who want to be anonymous on the Internet are often not the most savory people.

Everything to Hide

At best, privacy has been a sideline feature for some of the larger names in personal Internet security, and a value-added proposition for solution providers. Citing low subscription rates, Montreal's ZeroKnowledge recently abandoned its Freedom Network pseudonym browsing system in favor of more conventional desktop privacy and security software. The writing was on the wall for some time. Before the shutdown, Toronto-based communications integrator Conexys bundled the Freedom pseudonym browsing system from ZeroKnowledge in its portal, but noted that it was far from the key feature that drives customers to sign the dotted line.

Whether they are willing to pay to make a difference or not, consumer privacy choices can have a real impact on a corporation's bottom line. For example, some Web site operators make up to half of their revenue on renting customer data and log file analysis.

Although marketers publicly speak at great lengths about wanting to respect customer privacy above all, there is also a great deal of frustration over new-found resistance to decades-old practices that typically met with little organized resistance in the offline world. Among some marketing minds, a transaction between customer and producer implies permission for equal and essentially unfettered attempts to learn more about the other side. Contrary to its intention, such attitudes usually only provide more grist for the proprivacy mill.

Heightened awareness has led to an intricate dance between marketing and online data. Indeed, marketing service bureaus now spin themselves as privacy intermediaries. Optas, Inc. of Wakefield, Massachusetts, which specializes in the pharmaceutical industry, describes the new order as "bubble marketing" to reflect the precarious nature of consumer confidence in another's ability to collect and share sensitive information about them. In keeping with this theory, Optas positions itself not as a cold calculator of propensity to buy the latest drug, but as a secure conduit that allows ostensibly trusted health sites to pass offers to consumers based only on aggregated information.

The pharmaceutical companies get the zip code and demographics, but the Web site has full control over the privacy of the relationship and what level of detail gets passed back. The organization that has the trusted relationship ultimately has to have tools to protect that relationship. In that, at least, both sides of the issue are in agreement. If you're going to hold personal information, the burden is on you, not the consumer, to protect that information.

Still, key questions remain: How much data needs to be disclosed to provide service? At what point does data disclosure merely serve to grease the marketing machines?

Depending on the forum, if somebody is asking for very personal advice, you might be uncomfortable giving out information without knowing who you're talking to. However, if you're at a party and having a conversation with someone, do you ask to see his or her driver's license? People need to have that kind of choice, especially when conversations are being archived.

Even without looking for third-party vendor relationships, larger corporations still typically have an impressive array of data-sharing options at their disposal, and such relationships tend to come under less scrutiny even from privacy advocates. When you give up data, it's implicit that it's shared across the whole company—especially in the customer service department, where they have everything on you. Yet, the conglomerates with the largest market research departments often have disparate, nonobvious subsidiaries, and there is virtually no requirement that a company disclose which of its subsidiaries and divisions will have access to consumer data.

Hypothetically speaking, it might seem obvious to an AOL Time Warner director that information provided to Time magazine should also be visible to sister business units such as AOL's online service and New Line Cinema.

However, a consumer will not necessarily draw the same conclusion. Although some analysts have assumed that the technology involved in making consumer data that transparent across an enormous enterprise would be an equally enormous headache, that could be a passing problem, which means it could become a sore point before long.

Opening the Data Vaults

Much has been said about how U.S. privacy standards differ significantly from those in the rest of the world. One of the major differences is the principle of one's right to access and correct the data stored about him or her. Even among firms that cheerfully refrain from data sharing, even going so far as to offer opt-in instead of opt-out, such in-depth access is a rare find. Aside from an obvious desire not to let individuals delete the most valuable items from their databases, information collectors face a serious challenge—positively identifying someone who, by definition, wishes to remain rather private and anonymous with enough authority to let them make a sensitive change.

Rationally, there's no reason to expect information collectors and aggregators to open up their files to individuals for review and correction online, despite (or because of) the fact it would be an extremely convenient way for consumers to review the extent of their data profiles. Consider the DMA's response to the efficiency of the Internet. Its Mail and Telephone Preference Service opt-out lists traditionally allowed consumers to send a letter of request to have their name placed on a master do-not-contact list, provided to DMA member companies. The DMA now offers a Web form as well, which is faster and more convenient for all involved—and comes with a $5 fee. Allegedly, this charge is justified by faster service (although the database is still only updated quarterly, regardless of how the request is submitted), but could also be considered a thinly veiled disincentive to use the one-click convenience of a Web page opt-out.

Coming up Short

Current market proposals to clear up the privacy question are not living up to expectations. Despite the ubiquitous logos proudly stating compliance on a vast number of popular Web destinations, privacy seal programs, which purport to certify and validate the privacy practices of member companies, do less than many realize. Typically, U.S.-based privacy seal organizations hold their recipients to only the barest minimum standard of conduct. By and large, the

241

seals only establish that a company has written a privacy policy using complete sentences.

Organizations such as TRUSTe and BBBOnLine dictate very little about what the privacy policy should say. Instead, they serve primarily to provide some assurance that the text of the privacy policy (whether it provides iron-clad privacy, or rampant resale and integration of personal data with myriad outside vendors and data customers) matches a firm's actual business practices. Because of the notable lack of substance behind these reassurances, their value as a marketing tool may be short-lived.

Not only is enforcement questionable, but a company that buries information about third-party data in a slew of legalese is placed on the same level as one that clearly states up front that it has no intention of transmitting data. In general, those policies don't amount to much more than a 10-page legal document, which states that they're going to take your information and sell it when it's in their best interest.

Although some speak with hope about the prospects for the Platform for Privacy Preferences Project (P3P), which enables a P3P-aware browser to read a supporting Web site's privacy practices and match them against a user's stated privacy preferences, there is considerable suspicion that its impact will be minimal. It doesn't really do too much; it just allows consumers to put in preferences and doesn't really require anything as far as corporate compliance is concerned.

Many worry that P3P will prove as impotent as end-user cookie management. Cookie blockers haven't worked because some sites deny service in part or in whole if a myriad of cookies are not accepted and retained on a user's computer. Cookies are far too convenient and prevalent in Web design to eliminate entirely, which (not coincidentally) is why privacy advocates typically scoff at suggestions to exercise their right to shut off the feature.

Legislative Action, Present and Future

To gauge the true extent of public interest and concern over privacy, everyone with a stake in the matter is watching the impact of the Gramm–Leach–Bliley Act, which governs new professional and data practices in the financial services industry. Among other things, the laws require a more concise and consistently presented outline of a firm's data practices, including a clearly labeled opt-out procedure.

No one knows yet whether the flurry of privacy policy alerts financial institutions were required to send out in 2001 has soothed or stoked broader consumer concern. If there is any backlash brewing, however, it's slow in coming, and early reports put opt-out rates stemming from the mandatory announcements below 1%.

However, consumer privacy guerrillas are already earning their stripes on the margins. Even outside the domain of consumer advocates, suspicion is starting to build that optional industry regulation might fail to materialize. It is highly unlikely that organizations will actually implement transparent policies and practices on any significant scale. If spending on privacy protection indeed means the higher costs and lower profits marketers bemoan, voluntary participation could be foolish indeed.

Some feel that good privacy can be good business, not just profit-harming lip service. There are two questions: There's the risk of an enforcement action or a public relations nightmare, and there's also long-term sustainability, as well as a pragmatic look at public sentiment. If your business model is predicated on practices that are deplored by the public, it's not likely to survive.

A full legislative answer is not likely to arrive soon. The FTC recently dismissed calls for new consumer privacy laws, and the commission's formal privacy agenda now calls for tighter enforcement of existing law, such as the Gramm–Leach–Bliley Act. The FTC also intends to use its powers to ensure actual privacy practice matches stated policy under both normal operating conditions and liquidation or merger transactions. Research firms including Forrester and Gartner now peg the likely introduction of any significant new privacy legislation in the 2005–2006 time frame.

Choose up Sides

That said, there are indeed companies making a serious investment in boosting the precision, accuracy, and potentially the respectful relevance with which they collect, track, and share customer data. According to Zona Research, it is not uncommon to find companies with billion-dollar revenues slating $36 million per year for their privacy infrastructure in the immediate future.

The money is in companies that review Web site privacy policies and set them up. With Gramm–Leach–Bliley in full swing, and Health Insurance Portability and Accountability Act (HIPAA) coming into effect before the end of 2003, expect those opportunities to grow.

Without additional legislative imperatives, however, building a more efficient marketing database is still likely to draw a bigger crowd than a remarkable privacy solution. Certainly, there are companies that provide products and services to protect the environment, but there's much more money to make by damaging the environment, and companies, if allowed to, will make the decision to do so.

Despite the resistance from companies worried that an entire way of doing business could be coming to an end, pundits still hope that the taste of the medicine will be the only sting. One of the most ironic implications of privacy legislation could be forcing companies to put some money and resources into thinking about what their marketing really is.

If most forms of data collection and ensuing contact must be explicitly approved by a customer, you have to have a good value proposition if you expect customers to opt in. That could bring a level of discipline that would help organizations around the world. Companies should audit their privacy procedures now, rather than face a court order or major crisis.

Carelessness and red tape might be the biggest threat. With all the mergers and acquisitions, the real issue is that there is somebody who doesn't know about a data-sharing arrangement. Say the deal was done years ago (two acquisitions ago); there could still be some autorenewal clause of third-party sharing that nobody knows about.

It's surprising to see firms waiting for legislation to tell them to get their data practices in order. If you look online, advertising networks collectively have lost $600 million, so at least in the online world, the more you collect on people, the more you can sell is proving wrong.

In data-sharing relationships, watch for the other shoe to drop. So far, most of the attention has been focused on preventing companies from selling or sharing the information collected. Cutting off demand, by creating situations where consumers can force a company to stop soliciting information about them from other sources, could be the next target. If the hue and cry so far has been deafening, wait until that question is raised. Direct marketing would be put out of business if such a rule came to pass.

If, by chance, consumers win most of their victories, the next battleground will be over how consumers' rights change during working hours. The Privacy Foundation estimates that 25 million souls are under some surveillance on the job.

Tracking an employee's online behavior costs less than $20 per year. As a pragmatic investment against internal espionage or otherwise illicit communication, it seems a small price to pay as a hedge against wrongdoing, but the ensuing databases and profiles will inevitably come under fire as highly sensitive information.

With no end to the debate in sight, be prepared to integrate privacy challenges into business as usual, rather than taking a reactive stance to the legislative proposal of the week. Those focused on compliance are missing the financial benefits of finding ways to make privacy part of a customer value proposition. There's no competition in complying better than someone else.

Endnotes

[1] Tom Wright, "Electronic Records: Maximizing Best Practices," Information and Privacy Commissioner/Ontario, 80 Bloor Street West, Suite 1700, Toronto, Ontario, M5S 2V1, 2001.

[2] Julie Fergerson, "Five Tools You Can Use to Prevent Fraud," ClearCommerce Corporation, 11500 Metric Blvd., Suite 300, Austin, TX 78758, USA, 2001.

[3] Julie Fergerson, "The Aftermath of Fraud," ClearCommerce Corporation, 11500 Metric Blvd., Suite 300, Austin, TX 78758, USA, 2001.

[4] "Ask the Expert," ClearCommerce Corporation, 11500 Metric Blvd., Suite 300, Austin, TX 78758, USA, 2001.

[5] Daniele Micci-Barreca, "A New Challenge for Online Merchants: Shipment Rerouting," ClearCommerce Corporation, 11500 Metric Blvd., Suite 300, Austin, TX 78758, USA, 2001.

Part IV

Identity Theft Future Solutions and Technologies

Chapter 11

BIOMETRICS

Since the terrorist attacks of September 11, 2001, biometrics, once a backstage, niche technology has been put in the spotlight, as jittery companies and government agencies search for ways to secure their physical facilities and electronic data. Biometrics solutions identify people by physical traits, such as fingerprints, faces, irises, voice, and now DNA.

Tip

Biometrics, generally, is the study of measurable biological characteristics. In computer security, biometrics refers to authentication techniques that rely on measurable physical characteristics that can be automatically checked. Examples include computer analysis of fingerprints or speech. Although the field is still in its infancy, many people believe that biometrics will play a critical role in future computers, and especially in electronic commerce. Personal computers of the future might include a fingerprint scanner where you could place your index finger. The computer would analyze your fingerprint to determine who you are and, based on your identity, authorize you different levels of access. Access levels could include the ability to use credit card information to make electronic purchases.

The terrorist attacks opened the eyes of a lot of people to the technology. Some people view biometrics as the silver bullet for solving the terrorist threat and identity theft problem, but the technology can only minimize it.

Companies can enhance all kinds of security, be it physical security or access to databases. You need a higher level of security than passwords everywhere.

Fingerprint scanners are the most popular biometrics technology at this point, and government agencies are showing the greatest interest in them. DigitalPersona, a Redwood City, California-based company that provides fingerprint-recognition technology, for example, has seen interest in biometrics grow at a faster clip in the government sector than in any other.

Microsoft Windows XP is stimulating demand for DigitalPersona's technology as well. The company worked with Microsoft to integrate support for its U.are.U personal fingerprint-scanning system in the new operating system. This has been a big launch of biometrics capabilities in a PC. Biometrics is becoming mainstream; it's not just for airports or Fort Knox.

Biometrics represents a vast improvement over passwords, the traditional means of user authentication. People forget passwords, and they're vulnerable to hackers. In addition, at less than $90 per access point, a fingerprint-scanning authentication system is more cost-effective than a password system, which requires continuous support.

PEC Solutions, a solution provider based in Fairfax, Virginia., is implementing a biometrics solution to automate the criminal-booking process for the Department of Justice. The $2 million project, which began as a pilot program before September 11, allows fingerprints to be captured electronically, replacing the old system of taking fingerprints in ink.

As previously explained, because biometrics-based authentication offers several advantages over other authentication methods, there has been a significant surge in the use of biometrics for user authentication to prevent identity theft in recent years. It is important that such biometrics-based authentication systems be designed to withstand identity theft attacks when employed in security-critical applications, especially in unattended remote applications such as e-commerce. This chapter specifically details the inherent strengths of biometrics-based authentication, identifies the weak links in systems employing biometrics-based authentication, and presents new solutions for eliminating some of these weak links. Although, for illustration purposes, fingerprint authentication is discussed throughout the chapter, the discussion also extends to other biometrics-based methods. Before delving too deeply into biometrics-based authentication itself, let's first briefly take a look at how biometric systems work and the types of biometrics that are currently available.

How Biometric Systems Work

A biometric is the actual characteristic or trait, and a biometric system is the computer hardware and software used to recognize or verify an individual. Although there are many variations in how specific products and systems work, there are a number of common processing elements.

Collection

As a first step, a system must collect or capture the biometric to be used. One essential difference between the various techniques is the characteristic (body part or function) being analyzed. Obviously, this influences the method of capture.

All biometric systems have some sort of collection mechanism. This could be a reader or sensor on which a person places his or her finger or hand, a camera that takes a picture of his or her face or eye, or software that captures the rhythm and speed of his or her typing.

To enroll in a system, individuals present their "live" biometric a number of times so the system can build a composition or profile of their characteristic, allowing for slight variations (e.g., different degrees of pressure when they place their finger on the reader). Depending on the purpose of the system, enrollment could also involve the collection of other personally identifiable information.

Extraction

Commercially available biometric devices generally do not record full images of biometrics the way law enforcement agencies collect actual fingerprints. Instead, specific features of the biometric are extracted. Only certain attributes are collected (particular measurements of a fingerprint or pressure points of a signature). Which parts are used is dependent on the type of biometric, as well as the design of the proprietary system.

This extracted information, sometimes called raw data, is converted into a mathematical code. Again, exactly how this is done varies among the different proprietary systems. This code is then stored as a sample or template. The specific configuration of a system will dictate what, how, and where that information is stored. Regardless of the variations, all biometric systems must create and retain a template of the biometric to recognize or verify the individual.

251

Although the raw data can be translated into a set of numbers for the template, commercial biometric systems are generally designed so that the code cannot be reengineered or translated back into the extracted data or biometric.

Comparison and Matching

To use a biometric system, the specific features of a person's biometric characteristic are measured and captured each time they present their "live" biometric. This extracted information is translated into a mathematical code using the same method that created the template. The new code created from the live scan is compared against a central database of templates in the case of a one-to-many match, or to a single stored template in the case of a one-to-one match. If it falls within a certain statistical range of values, the match is considered to be valid by the system.

Types of Biometrics

Police forces throughout the world use Integrated Automated Fingerprint Identification Systems (IAFIS) or Automated Fingerprint Identification Systems (AFIS) to process criminal suspects and match finger images. Various other forms of biometrics are used to secure prisons, secure police detention areas, enforce home confinement orders, and regulate the movement of probationers and parolees.

Around the world, governments at all levels use biometrics for both recognition and verification purposes. Employers also utilize biometrics to help protect the safety and security of their staff and physical assets. In addition, biometrics are used to record the attendance and movement of employees.

These types of applications are not, however, the focus of this chapter. Instead, the growing commercial use of biometrics is examined. So far, consumer applications are limited to the verification of identity, many in the context of access control to secure locations, equipment, and information. Biometric technology continues to evolve and expand, with new developments and applications announced regularly. Next I provide a brief overview of the main categories of biometrics in use today.

Eye

There are two main types of biometric analysis of the eye. One involves the iris, which is the colored ring that surrounds the pupil, and the other uses the retina, which is the layer of blood vessels at the back of the eye.

Iris

Each iris has a unique and complex pattern such that even a person's right and left iris patterns are completely different. It has been claimed that the system is foolproof because artificial duplication of the iris is virtually impossible due to its properties and the number of measurable characteristics. The iris is stable throughout one's life and is not susceptible to wear and injury. Contact lenses do not interfere with the use of this biometric identifier. Iris recognition technology involves the use of a camera to capture a digital image of the eye, from which data is extracted. This type of biometric technology can be used for one-to-one verification or one-to-many recognition. Examples of iris recognition applications used by consumers are as follows:

- A tae kwon do chain in the United States uses iris recognition to speed up its daily sign-in and information processing procedures. A one-second glance into a camera for verification of identity is necessary each time a student enters a class.

- Some ATM manufacturers include iris scans as an alternative to passwords or PINs. Recently, Bank United of Texas became the first bank in the United States to offer iris recognition at ATMs. Several other American banks are expected to unveil iris identification ATMs soon. In addition, the technology is already used by 22 different banks outside of the United States.

- The Royal Bank of Canada and the Canadian Imperial Bank of Commerce recently tested an ATM with iris scanning capabilities in Toronto. [2]

Retina

As with the iris, the retina forms a unique pattern that begins to decay quickly after death. Unauthorized access to a retinal system is reported to be virtually impossible. With this type of system, a one-to-many identification is usually the comparison performed.

A precise enrollment procedure is necessary. A user must focus on a specific point and then the system uses a beam of light to capture the user's unique retinal characteristics. The downside of retinal scanning is people's reluctance to have light shone into their eyes to gather information. Retinal biometrics usually are found in high-security applications where inconvenience and user comfort are not important considerations.

Face

There are two main types of facial recognition systems; the most common uses video, and the other uses thermal imaging. Video face-recognition technology analyzes the unique shape, pattern, and positioning of facial features. A video camera is used to capture an image from a distance of a few feet away from the user. A number of points on the face (position of the eyes, mouth, and nostrils) are usually mapped out. With other systems, a three-dimensional map of the face can be created. Most systems feature a face-locating function that searches for faces within the field of view. This permits people of different heights to use the system while standing. Face-recognition systems are designed to compensate for expressions, glasses, hats, and beards.

A facial thermogram uses an infrared camera to scan a person's face and then digitize the thermal patterns. Apparently no two people, not even identical twins, have the same facial thermogram. The patterns are created by the branching of blood vessels in the face. As the blood is hotter than the tissue surrounding it, it radiates heat that can be picked up at a distance. Plastic surgery does not change a thermogram unless it involves the rerouting of the flow of blood. In addition, time does not alter a thermogram. However, it is thought that alcohol consumption can radically change a person's thermogram.

Whereas face recognition is being used in a one-to-many capacity by law enforcement and government, commercial applications use this technology for one-to-one verification. The use of video-based face recognition for consumer applications has grown considerably in the last few years. Some American banks, gas stations, and convenience stores are using this technology to identify and record check-cashing transactions. One American ATM system automatically takes a biometric picture every time a customer cashes a check. The customer first has to enroll in the system, but no bank account or driver's license is needed. To cash a check, customers key in their Social Security numbers. This information, combined with the biometric, creates a real-time, irrefutable, permanent record of the transaction.

German banks have been using face-recognition technology to give customers unattended, 24-hour access to their safety deposit boxes. Customers request their boxes at a self-service computer terminal, which includes a video camera. The camera captures and processes the customer's facial image. System software verifies the person's identity and authority to receive the requested safety deposit box. If the person is authorized, the box is retrieved by robots and delivered to the owner by an automated handling system.

A Malaysian company is using this technology to create an airport security system that tracks passengers' baggage with an image of their face. Only when passengers actually enter the plane will the system allow their baggage to be loaded.

There also are applications that replace passwords for computer login. The primary advantage is that face recognition is able to operate "hands-free." With a camera positioned on a computer monitor, the user's identity is verified simply by staring at the screen. Access to sensitive information can be disabled when the user moves out of the camera's field of vision.

Facial recognition can be done on a more remote basis so a person will not know his or her face is being analyzed. For example, some casinos are using face recognition as a way of identifying suspicious players. A surveillance camera captures an image of the individual's face and then compares it to a digitized photo database of known cheaters. Globally, airports have expressed interest in another system that can pick a moving face out of a crowd. They hope to use this technology as a way of identifying terrorists and other criminals.

Finger Scanning

As previously noted, use of the fingerprint by law enforcement for identification purposes is commonplace and widely accepted. However, the technology has diversified, migrating away from law enforcement toward civil and commercial markets. In the context of commercial applications, the preferred term is *finger scanning*, which is the process of finger image capture.

There are a number of different types of finger-scanning systems on the market. Some analyze the distinct marks on the finger called *minutiae points*. Others examine the pores on the finger that are uniquely positioned. Finger image density or the distance between ridges also can be analyzed. The way in which the image is captured also differs among vendors. None involve the inking of the fingerprint as traditional law enforcement procedures often entail.

Finger scanning can be used for both verification and recognition purposes. At present, the one-to-many identification IAFIS or AFIS applications are confined to law enforcement, government programs, and the military. However, there is mounting pressure to expand identification applications.

In the areas of financial transactions, network security, and controlling the movement of individuals, finger scanning is considered to be a highly mature biometric technology with a range of proven installations. Examples of consumer applications include the following:

255

- Recently, the Bank of America started a pilot program that uses finger scans to give customers access to their online banking services. Before using the system, the customer enrolls a finger scan on a chip attached to a multiapplication smart card. Authentication is completed by the customer placing a finger on a scanning device attached to his or her personal computer. The software matches the finger scan from the scanner against the image stored in the smart card.

- Canadian banks are looking at thumbprinting check-cashing, nonaccount customers. Reportedly, banks in all 50 American states have some version of a finger-scanning system.

- Recently, one American hotel chain announced that it will start collecting fingerprints as part of its check-in procedure.

- A number of vendors have developed finger scanners resembling a computer mouse. Scanners built into computer keyboards also have been produced. Recognition of a finger scan takes place in an average of two seconds on a personal computer or one second on a workstation, with accuracy claimed to be 99.9%. [2]

Hand Geometry

The hand geometry technique uses a three-dimensional image of the hand and measures the shape, width, and length of fingers and knuckles. A user places a designated hand on a reader, aligning fingers with specific positioned guides. A camera is used to capture both a top view, which gives length and width information, and a side view, which gives a thickness profile.

In Ontario, Canada, hand geometry is used at nuclear power-generating stations. Perhaps the best known government application is the U.S. Immigration and Naturalization Service's Passenger Accelerated Service System, which uses hand geometry readers to verify air travelers' identity, and is currently operating at Toronto's Pearson International Airport.

Hand geometry is predominantly used for one-to-one verification. It is one of the most established biometrics in commercial use today. Applications continue to grow because it is easy to use and convenient. It is also fast, with one vendor reporting a 1.2-second scan. Applications include the following:

- The 2002 Winter Olympic Games in Salt Lake used hand geometry to identify and secure approximately 260,000 athletes, staff, and other participants.

- The University of Georgia uses the technology to control access to its student cafeteria. When students visit a cafeteria, they swipe their identity cards through a reader and have their hands verified before entering the food service area.

- An American elementary school uses the technique to identify individuals picking up children. Anyone authorized by the parents can enroll in the system. To be able to pick up a child from the school, a person first must be verified by a hand geometry reader.

- In Toronto, hand geometry is used by a racquet and fitness club to verify identity of 12,000 club members and staff. Initially, it was introduced at only one location to test acceptability. Now it has been expanded to all locations. [2]

Finger Geometry

The finger geometry technology operates on similar principles as hand geometry, but utilizes only one or two fingers. Measurements of unique finger characteristics, such as width, length, thickness, and knuckle size are taken.

Finger geometry systems can perform one-to-one verification or one-to-many identification. The main advantage is that these systems are fast and designed to accommodate a high throughput of users. According to one company, its system confirms identity within one second. Finger geometry systems are considered very durable and able to cope well with external conditions. As an example, Disney World uses three-dimensional two-finger geometry to verify the identity of season-ticket holders in the United States.

Signature Verification

This behavioral biometric involves the analysis of the way in which a person signs his or her name. Signature biometrics are often referred to as dynamic signature verification (DSV). With this technique, the manner in which someone signs is as important as the static shape of the finished signature. For example, the angle at which the pen is held, the time taken to sign, the velocity and acceleration of the signature, the pressure exerted, and the number of times the pen is lifted from the paper can all be measured and analyzed as unique behavioral characteristics. As DSV is not based on a static image, forgery is considered to be difficult.

Signature data can be captured via a special pen or tablet, or both. The pen-based method incorporates sensors inside the writing instrument, whereas the tablet method relies on sensors embedded in a writing surface to detect the unique signature characteristics. Recently, another variation has been developed known as acoustic emission. This measures the sound that is generated as an individual writes his or her signature on a paper document.

A few years ago, the Chase Manhattan Bank tested DSV to identify corporate clients initiating transactions. Today, a number of American hospitals, pharmacies, and insurance firms use this biometric technique to authenticate electronic documents.

Speaker Verification

Voice-related biometrics should not be confused with speech-recognition computer software that recognizes words as they are spoken. Biometric systems involve the verification of the speaker's identity based on numerous characteristics, such as cadence, pitch, and tone. Speaker verification is considered a hybrid behavioral and physiological biometric, because the voice pattern is determined, to a large degree, by the physical shape of the throat and larynx, although it can be altered by the user.

One-to-one verification is the preferred application. The technology is easy to use and does not require a great deal of user education. However, background noise greatly affects how well the system operates. Speaker verification works with a microphone or with a regular telephone handset. It is well suited to telephone-based applications where identity has to be verified remotely.

Recently, more than 8,000 personal computers with speaker verification systems were sold on the Home Shopping Network. Voice recognition also is being integrated into security systems for online banking and electronic commerce. One European automobile manufacturer even investigated the possibility of incorporating speaker verification into its ignition systems.

Keystroke Dynamics

Typing biometrics are more commonly referred to as keystroke dynamics. Verification is based on the concept that how a person types, in particular his or her rhythm, is distinctive. Keystroke dynamics are behavioral and evolve over time as users learn to type and develop their own unique typing pattern. The National Science Foundation and the National Bureau of Standards in the United States have conducted studies establishing that typing patterns are unique. The technique works best for users who can "touch type." The health and fatigue of users, however, can affect typing rhythm.

This technology has experienced a recent resurgence with the development of software to control computer and Internet access. One system creates individual profiles according to how users enter their passwords, accounting for factors such as hand size, typing speed, and how long keys are held down. Reportedly, the technology can be used with any keypad, from computer keyboards to ATM machines to telephones. Previously, differences in keyboards had been one of the problems that had limited the implementation of keystroke dynamics.

Other Developments

Some other techniques are currently being used by law enforcement and the military. It is not inconceivable that use of these will eventually filter down, but it is unlikely that the consumer will see them in commercial applications in the near future.

Palm Print

The palm print is a physical biometric that analyzes the unique patterns on the palm of a person's hand, similar to fingerprinting. Palm biometrics are predominantly used for one-to-many identification. Like fingerprinting, latent or ink palm images can be scanned into the system.

Vein Patterns

This physical biometric analyzes the pattern of veins in the back of a person's hand. One proprietary system focuses on the unique pattern of blood vessels that form when a fist is made. The underlying vein structure, or vein tree can be captured using a camera and infrared light.

Ear Shape

A lesser known physical biometric is the shape of the outer ear, lobes, and bone structure. Apparently, police are able to capture earprints of criminals left when they listen at windows and doors. The technology has been used to obtain convictions in the Netherlands. One French company is working on the Octophone, a telephone-like biometric device that captures images of the ear.

Body Odor

Body odor is a physical biometric under development that analyzes human body smell. Sensors are capable of capturing body odor from nonintrusive parts of the body such as the back of the hand. Each unique human smell is made up of chemicals that are extracted by the system and converted into a template. Reportedly, the University of Cambridge worked on an "electronic nose" that can identify people by their body odor.

DNA

DNA is an abbreviation for deoxyribonucleic acid. It is a unique, measurable human characteristic, and is currently considered a biometric technology. In other words, analysis of human DNA, now possible within seconds is sufficient to rank DNA as a biometric technology. Technology has now advanced so that DNA can be matched automatically, almost in real time, so it has emerged as a significant contender against the existing biometric industry.

The use of DNA in the areas of forensics and law enforcement has been much in the news with several high-profile cases where DNA played a critical role in determining guilt or innocence. Recently, there has been a growing demand to expand the use of DNA. In 1998, after a Swissair plane crash off the coast of Nova Scotia, the Royal Canadian Mounted Police and prominent forensic experts called for the creation of a global system of DNA samples for airline crews and possibly frequent fliers. The Florida Department of Law Enforcement offered parents a free children's DNA identification program in some of its school districts. In addition, Florida is encouraging parents to take DNA samples from their newborns.

Privacy-Enhanced Biometrics-Based Authentication

Reliable user authentication to prevent identity theft is becoming an increasingly important task in the Web-enabled world. The consequences of an insecure authentication system in a corporate or enterprise environment can be catastrophic, and could include loss of confidential customer and employee information, denial of service, and compromised data integrity. The value of reliable user authentication is not limited to just computer or network access. Many other applications in everyday life also require user authentication, such as banking, e-commerce, and physical access control to computer resources, and thus could benefit from enhanced security.

The prevailing techniques of user authentication to prevent identity theft, which involve the use of either passwords and user identifiers, or identification cards and PINs, suffer from several limitations. Passwords and PINs can be illicitly acquired by covert observation. Once an intruder acquires the user identifier and password, the intruder has total access to the user's resources. In addition, there is no way to positively link the usage of the system or service to the actual user; that is, there is no protection against repudiation by the owner. For example, when a user identifier and password is shared with a colleague, there is no way for the system to know who the actual user is. A similar situation arises when a transaction involving a credit card number is conducted on the Web. Even though the data is sent over the Web using secure encryption methods, current systems are not capable of assuring that the transaction was initiated by the rightful owner of the credit card. In the modern distributed systems environment, the traditional authentication policy based on a simple combination of user identifier and password has become inadequate.

Fortunately, automated biometrics in general, and fingerprint technology in particular, can provide a much more accurate and reliable user authentication method to prevent identity theft. Biometrics is a rapidly advancing field that is concerned with identifying a person based on his or her physiological or behavioral characteristics. Examples of automated biometrics include fingerprint, face, iris, speech, and DNA recognition. User authentication methods can be broadly classified into three categories as shown in Table 11.1. [1] Because a biometric property is an intrinsic property of an individual, it is difficult to surreptitiously duplicate and nearly impossible to share. Additionally, a biometric property of an individual can be lost only in case of serious accident.

Biometric readings, which range from several hundred bytes to over a megabyte, have the advantage that their information content is usually more detailed than that of a password or a pass phrase. Simply extending the length of passwords to get equivalent bit strength presents significant usability problems. It is nearly impossible to remember a phrase that long, and it would take an inordinately long time to type such a phrase (especially without errors). Fortunately, automated biometrics can provide the security advantages of long passwords while retaining the speed and characteristic simplicity of short passwords.

261

Table 11.1. Existing User Authentication Techniques to Prevent ID Theft

Method	Examples	Properties
What you know	User identifier	Shared
	Password	Many passwords easy to guess
	PIN	Forgotten
What you have	Cards	Shared
	Badges	Can be duplicated
	Keys	Lost or stolen
What you know and what you have	ATM card + PIN	Shared
		PIN a weak link (writing the PIN on the card)
Something unique about the user	Fingerprint	Not possible to share
	Face	Repudiation unlikely
	Iris	Forging difficult
	Voiceprint	Cannot be lost or stolen
	DNA	Duplication impossible (unless the person is a clone)

Even though automated biometrics can help alleviate the problems associated with the existing methods of user authentication to prevent ID theft, hackers will still find weak points in the system, vulnerable to attack. Password systems are prone to brute force dictionary attacks. Biometric systems, on the other hand, require substantially more effort for mounting such an attack. However, there are several new types of attacks possible in the biometrics domain. This might not apply if biometrics is used as a supervised authentication tool. However, in remote, unattended applications, such as Web-based e-commerce applications, hackers might have the opportunity and enough time to make several attempts, or even physically violate the integrity of a remote client, before detection.

A problem with using biometric authentication systems to prevent identity theft arises when the data associated with a biometric feature has been compromised. For authentication systems based on physical tokens such as keys and badges, a compromised token can be easily canceled and the user can be assigned a new token. Similarly, user IDs and passwords can be changed as often as required. Yet, the user only has a limited number of biometric features (e.g., one face, 10 fingers, two eyes). If the biometric data is compromised, the user will quickly run out of biometric features to be used for authentication.

Later in the chapter, a more detailed discussion of the problems unique to biometric authentication systems to prevent identity theft is presented, as well as proposed solutions to several of these problems. As previously mentioned, although the chapter focuses on fingerprint recognition throughout, the analysis can be extended to other biometric authentication methods. With that in mind, the next part of the chapter details the stages of the fingerprint authentication process.

Fingerprint Authentication

Fingerprints are a distinctive feature that remain invariant over a persons lifetime, except for injuries. As the first step in the authentication process, a fingerprint impression is acquired, typically using an inkless scanner. Several such scanning technologies are available. Figure 11.1 shows a fingerprint obtained with a scanner using an optical sensor. [1] A typical scanner digitizes the fingerprint impression at 500 dots per inch (dpi) with 256 levels of gray per pixel. The digital image of the fingerprint includes several unique features in terms of ridge bifurcations and ridge endings, collectively referred to as minutiae.

The next step is to locate these features in the fingerprint image, as shown in Figure 11.1, using an automatic feature extraction algorithm. However, due to sensor noise and other variability in the imaging process, the feature extraction stage might miss some minutiae and generate spurious minutiae. Further, due to the elasticity of the human skin, the relationship between minutiae may be randomly distorted from one impression to the next.

In the final stage, the matcher subsystem attempts to arrive at a degree of similarity between the two sets of features after compensating for the rotation, translation, and scale. This similarity is often expressed as a score. Based on

Figure 11.1
Fingerprint recognition: (A) input images (B) features.

this score, a final decision of match or no-match is made. A decision threshold is first selected. If the score is below the threshold, the fingerprints are determined not to match; if the score is above the threshold, a correct match is declared. Often the score is simply a count of the number of minutiae that are in correspondence. In a number of countries, 12 to 16 correspondences (performed by a human expert) are considered legally binding evidence of identity.

The operational issues in AFIS are somewhat different from those in a more traditional password-based system. First, there is a system performance issue known as the *fail-to-enroll rate* to be considered. Some people have very faint fingerprints, or no fingers at all, which makes the system unusable for them. A related issue is a Reject option in the system based on input image quality. A poor quality input is not accepted by the system during enrollment and authentication.

Tip

Poor-quality inputs can be caused by noncooperative users, improper usage, dirt on the finger, or bad input scanners. This has no analog in a password system.

In addition, in a biometric system, the matching decision is not clear-cut. A password system always provides a correct response—if the passwords match, it grants access, but otherwise it refuses access. However, in a biometric system, the overall accuracy depends on the quality of input and enrollment data along with the basic characteristics of the underlying feature extraction and matching algorithm.

For fingerprints, and biometrics in general, there are two basic types of recognition errors, namely the *false accept rate* (FAR) and the *false reject rate* (FRR). If a nonmatching pair of fingerprints is accepted as a match, it is called a false accept. On the other hand, if a matching pair of fingerprints is rejected by the system, it is called a false reject. The error rates are a function of the threshold, as shown in Figure 11.2. [1] Often the interplay between the two errors is presented by plotting FAR against FRR, with the decision threshold as the free variable. This plot is called the receiver operating characteristic (ROC) curve. The two errors are complementary in the sense that if one makes an effort to lower one of the errors by varying the threshold, the other error rate automatically increases.

In a biometric authentication system to prevent identity theft, the relative FAR and FRR can be set by choosing a particular operating point (a detection threshold). Very low (close to zero) error rates for both errors (FAR and FRR) at the same time are not possible. By setting a high threshold, the FAR error can be close to zero, and by setting a significantly low threshold, the FRR rate

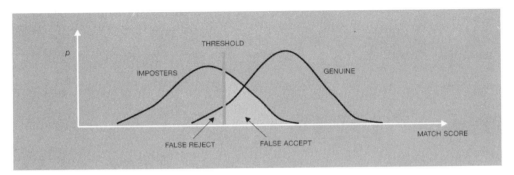

Figure 11.2 Error trade-off in a biometric system.

can be close to zero. A meaningful operating point for the threshold is decided based on the application requirements, and the FAR versus FRR error rates at that operating point might be quite different. To provide high security, biometric systems operate at a low FAR instead of the commonly recommended equal error rate operating point where FAR is equal to FRR. High-performance fingerprint recognition systems can support error rates in the range of 10^{-6} for false accept and 10^{-4} for false reject. The performance numbers reported by vendors are based on test results using private databases and, in general, tend to be much better than what can be achieved in practice. Nevertheless, the probability that the fingerprint signal is supplied by the right person, given a good matching score, is quite high. This confidence level generally provides better nonrepudiation support than passwords.

Vulnerable Points of a Biometric System

A generic biometric system can be cast in the framework of a pattern recognition system. The stages of such a generic system are shown in Figure 11.3. [1]

The first stage involves biometric signal acquisition from the user (the inkless fingerprint scan). The acquired signal typically varies significantly from presentation to presentation; hence, pure pixel-based matching techniques do not work reliably. For this reason, the second signal processing stage attempts to construct a more invariant representation of this basic input signal (in terms of fingerprint minutiae). The invariant representation is often a spatial domain characteristic or a transform (frequency) domain characteristic, depending on the particular biometric.

During enrollment of an individual in a biometric authentication system to prevent identity theft, an invariant template is stored in a database that represents the particular individual. To authenticate the user against a given iden-

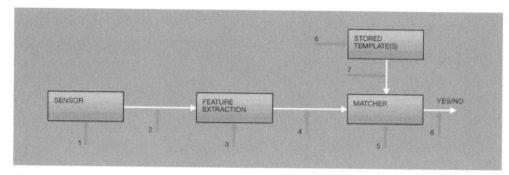

Figure 11.3 Possible attack points in a biometric-based system.

tity, the corresponding template is retrieved from the database and matched against the template derived from a newly acquired input signal. The matcher arrives at a decision based on the closeness of these two templates, taking into account geometry, lighting, and other signal acquisition variables.

 Tip

Password-based authentication systems can also be set in this framework. The keyboard becomes the input device. The password encryptor can be viewed as the feature extractor and the comparator as the matcher. The template database is equivalent to the encrypted password database.

Figure 11.3 identifies eight places in the generic biometric system where attacks can occur. In addition, the numbers in Figure 11.3 correspond to the items in the following list:

1. Presenting fake biometrics at the sensor. In this mode of attack, a possible reproduction of the biometric feature is presented as input to the system. Examples include a fake finger, a copy of a signature, or a face mask.
2. Resubmitting previously stored digitized biometrics signals. In this mode of attack, a recorded signal is replayed to the system, bypassing the sensor. Examples include the presentation of an old copy of a fingerprint image or the presentation of a previously recorded audio signal.
3. Overriding the feature extraction process. The feature extractor is attacked using a Trojan horse, so that it produces feature sets preselected by the intruder.
4. Tampering with the biometric feature representation. The features extracted from the input signal are replaced with a different, fraudulent feature set (assuming the representation method is known). Often the two stages of feature extraction and matcher are inseparable and this mode of

attack is extremely difficult. However, if minutiae are transmitted to a remote matcher (say, over the Internet) this threat is very real. One could "snoop" on the Transmission Control Protocol/Internet Protocol (TCP/IP) stack and alter certain packets.

5. Corrupting the matcher. The matcher is attacked and corrupted so that it produces preselected match scores.

6. Tampering with stored templates. The database of stored templates could be either local or remote. The data might be distributed over several servers. Here the attacker could try to modify one or more templates in the database, which could result either in authorizing a fraudulent individual or denying service to the persons associated with the corrupted template. A smart-card-based authentication system, where the template is stored in the smart card and presented to the authentication system, is particularly vulnerable to this type of attack.

7. Attacking the channel between the stored templates and the matcher. The stored templates are sent to the matcher through a communication channel. The data traveling through this channel could be intercepted and modified.

8. Overriding the final decision. If the final match decision can be overridden by the hacker, then the authentication system has been disabled. Even if the actual pattern recognition framework has excellent performance characteristics, it has been rendered useless by simply overriding the match result. [1]

There are several security techniques used to thwart attacks at these various points. For instance, finger conductivity or fingerprint pulse at the sensor can stop simple attacks at Point 1. Encrypted communication channels can eliminate at least remote attacks at Point 4. However, even if a hacker cannot penetrate the feature extraction module, the system is still vulnerable. The simplest way to stop attacks at Points 5, 6, and 7 is to have the matcher and the database reside at a secure location. Of course, even this cannot prevent attacks in which there is collusion. Use of cryptography prevents attacks at Point 8.

The threats outlined in Figure 11.3 are quite similar to the threats to password-based authentication systems. For instance, all the channel attacks are similar. One difference is that there is no "fake password" equivalent to the fake biometric attack at Point 1 (although, perhaps if the password was in some standard dictionary it could be deemed "fake"). Furthermore, in a password- or token-based authentication system, no attempt is made to thwart replay attacks (because there is no expected variation of the "signal" from one presentation to another). However, in an automated biometric-based authentication system, one can check the liveness of the entity originating the input signal.

Brute Force Attack Directed at Matching Fingerprint Minutiae

This part of the chapter analyzes the probability that a brute force attack at Point 4 in Figure 11.3, involving a set of fraudulent fingerprint minutiae, will succeed in matching a given stored template. Figure 11.4 shows one such randomly generated minutiae set. [1] In a smart card system where the biometrics template is stored in the card and presented to the authentication system, a hacker could present these random sets to the authentication system assuming that the hacker has no information about the stored templates.

 Tip

An attack at Point 2 of Figure 11.3, which involves generating all possible fingerprint images to match a valid fingerprint image, would have an even larger search space and consequently would be much more difficult.

Wavelet Scalar Quantization-Based Data Hiding

In both Web-based and other online transaction processing systems, it is undesirable to send uncompressed fingerprint images to the server due to bandwidth limitations. A typical fingerprint image is on the order of 512×512 pixels with 256 levels of gray, resulting in a file size of 256 KB. This would take nearly 40 seconds to transmit at 53 Kbps. Unfortunately, many standard compression methods, such as Joint Photographic Experts Group (JPEG), have a tendency to distort the high-frequency spatial and structural ridge features of a fingerprint image. This has led to several research proposals regarding domain-specific compression methods. As a result, an open wavelet scalar

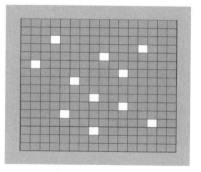

Figure 11.4
Example of a randomly generated minutiae set.

quantization (WSQ) image compression scheme proposed by the FBI has become the de facto standard in the industry, because of its low image distortion, even at high compression ratios (over 10:1).

Typically, the compressed image is transmitted over a standard encrypted channel as a replacement for (or in addition to) the user's PIN. Yet, because of the open compression standard, transmitting a WSQ compressed image over the Internet is not particularly secure. If a compressed fingerprint image bitstream can be freely intercepted (and decrypted), it can be decompressed using readily available software. This potentially allows the signal to be saved and fraudulently reused (Point 2 in Figure 11.3).

One way to enhance security is to use data-hiding techniques to embed additional information directly in compressed fingerprint images. For instance, if the embedding algorithm remains unknown, the service provider can look for the appropriate standard watermark to check that a submitted image was indeed generated by a trusted machine (or sensor).

The approach is motivated by the desire to create online fingerprint authentication systems for commercial transactions and identity theft prevention that are secure against replay attacks. To achieve this, the service provider issues a different verification string for each transaction. The string is mixed in with the fingerprint image before transmission. When the image is received by the service provider, it is decompressed and the image is checked for the presence of the correct one-time verification string. The method proposed here hides such messages with minimal impact on the appearance of the decompressed image. Moreover, the message is not hidden in a fixed location, which would make it more vulnerable to discovery, but is instead deposited in different places based on the structure of the image itself. Although the approach here is presented in the framework of fingerprint image compression, it can be easily extended to other biometrics such as wavelet-based compression of facial images.

The information hiding scheme presented here works in conjunction with the WSQ fingerprint image encoder and decoder, which are shown in Figure 11.5. [1] In the first step of WSQ compression, the input image is decomposed into 64 spatial frequency subbands using perfect reconstruction multirate filter banks based on discrete wavelet transformation filters. The filters are implemented as a pair of separable identity filters. The two filters specified for Encoder 1 of the FBI standard are plotted in Figures 11.6 and 11.7. [1] The subbands are the filter outputs obtained after a desired level of cascading of the filters as described in the standard. For example, subband 25 corresponds to the cascading path of 00, 10, 00, 11 through the filter bank. The first digit in each binary pair represents the row operation index. A zero specifies low pass filtering using $h0$ on the row (column), whereas a one specifies high pass filtering using $h1$ on the row (column). Thus, for the 25th subband, the image is first low

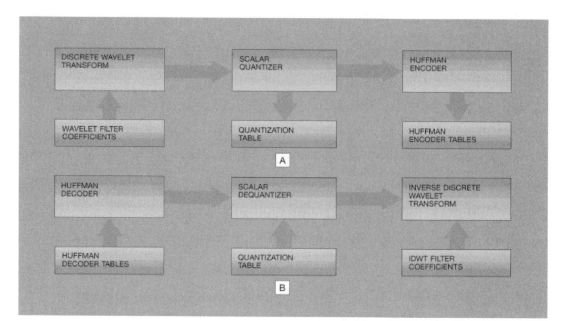

Figure 11.5 WSQ algorithm: (A) compression (B) decompression.

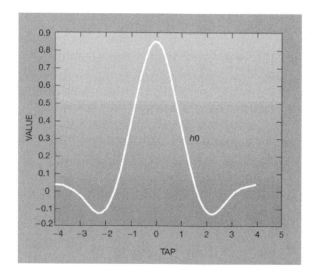

Figure 11.6
Analysis filter *h*0.

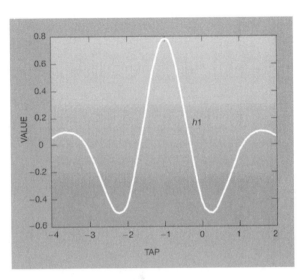

Figure 11.7
Analysis filter h1.

pass filtered in both row and column, followed by high pass filtering in rows, then by low pass filtering in columns. The output is then low pass filtered in rows and columns, and finally high pass filtered in rows and columns.

Tip

There is appropriate down sampling and the symmetric extension transform is applied at every stage as specified in the standard. The 64 subbands of the grayscale fingerprint image shown in Figure 11.8 are shown in Figure 11.9.

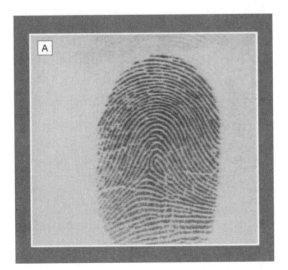

Figure 11.8
WSQ data-hiding results: Original image.

271

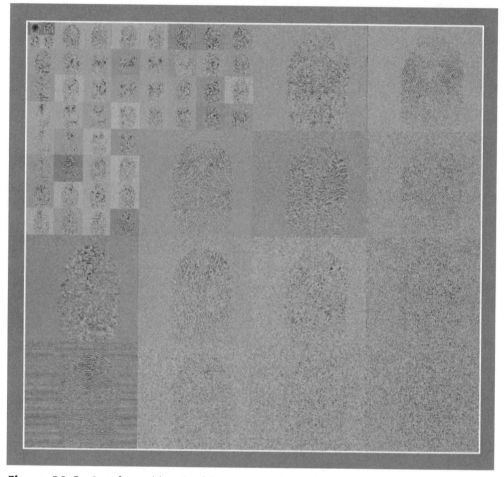

Figure 11.9 Sixty-four subbands of the image in Figure 11.8.

Image-Based Challenge/Response Method

Besides interception of network traffic, more insidious attacks might be perpetrated against an automated biometric authentication system for the prevention of identity theft. One of these is a replay attack on the signal from the sensor (Point 2 in Figure 11.3). A new method is proposed here to thwart such attempts based on a modified challenge/response system. Conventional challenge/response systems are based either on challenges to the user, such as requesting the user to supply the mother's maiden name, or challenges to a physical device, such as a special-purpose calculator that computes a numerical response. The approach here is based on a challenge to the sensor. The sensor is assumed to have enough intelligence to respond to the challenge. Silicon fingerprint scanners can be designed to exploit the proposed method using an embedded processor.

Tip

Standard cryptographic techniques are not a suitable substitute. Although these are mathematically strong, they are also computationally intensive and could require maintaining secret keys for a large number of sensors. Moreover, the encryption techniques cannot check for liveness of a signal. A stored image could be fed to the encryptor, which would happily encrypt it. Similarly, the digital signature of a submitted signal can be used to check only for its integrity, not its liveness.

This system computes a response string, which depends not only on the challenge string, but also on the content of the returned image. The changing challenges ensure that the image was acquired after the challenge was issued. The dependence on image pixel values guards against substitution of data after the response has been generated.

The proposed solution works as shown in Figure 11.10. [1] A transaction is initiated at the user terminal or system. First, the server generates a pseudorandom challenge for the transaction and the sensor.

Tip

It is assumed here that the transaction server itself is secure. The client system then passes the challenge on to the intelligent sensor. Now, the sensor acquires a new signal and computes the response to the challenge that is based in part on the newly acquired signal.

Because the response processor is tightly integrated with the sensor (preferable on the same chip), the signal channel into the response processor is assumed to be iron-clad and inviolable. It is difficult to intercept the true image and to inject a fake image under such circumstances.

Some examples of responder functions include computing a checksum of a segment of the signal, a set of pseudorandom samples, a block of contiguous samples starting at a specified location and with a given size, a hash of signal values, and a specified known function of selected samples of the signal. A combination of these functions can be used to achieve arbitrarily complex responder functions. The important point is that the response depends on the challenge and the image itself.

273

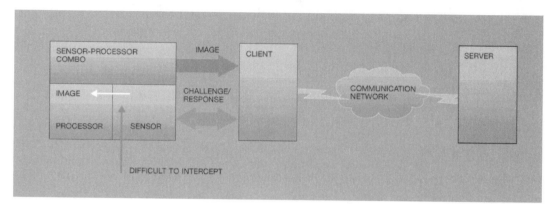

Figure 11.10 Signal authentication based on challenge/response.

Cancelable Biometrics

Deploying biometrics in a mass market, like credit card authorization or ATM access, raises additional concerns beyond the security of the transactions. One such concern is the public's perception of a possible invasion of privacy. In addition to personal information such as name and date of birth, the user is asked to surrender images of body parts, such as fingers, face, iris, and even DNA. These images, or other such biometric signals, are stored in digital form in various databases. This raises the concern of possible sharing of data among law enforcement agencies or commercial enterprises.

The public is concerned about the ever-growing body of information that is being collected about individuals in our society. The data collected encompass many applications and include medical records and biometric data (see the sidebar, "Are You Guarding Your Biometric DNA Data?"). A related concern is the coordination and sharing of data from various databases. In relation to biometric data, the public is, rightfully or not, worried about data collected by private companies being matched against databases used by law enforcement agencies. Fingerprint images, for example, can be matched against the FBI or Immigration and Naturalization Service databases with potentially ominous consequences.

Are You Guarding Your Biometric DNA Data?

Seven vials of blood is a lot. That was Janice Avary's first thought when she heard that her husband Gary's employer, the Burlington Northern Santa Fe (BNSF) railroad, was requiring that amount of blood to be taken after he filed claims for a carpal tunnel injury. As a registered nurse in Alma, Nebraska, her internal alarm was tripped. When she called the company for an explanation, Avary was stunned to hear the words "genetic test."

Her queries led a railroad workers' union to sue, seeking an end to the allegedly secret testing. BNSF indicates it has stopped the pilot program, but Gary Avary thinks that if his wife hadn't asked, it would still be going on. Unless you have a medical background, you wouldn't know to ask these questions. Let's see what really happened at BNSF.

Railroad Workers Allege Secret Sampling

John Wiebelhaus, a fourth-generation railroad man, makes his living with his hands, laying miles of track, repairing heavy steel rails, and picking ice from the track's switches. It's tough work, but Wiebelhaus loves it. It's in his blood.

That might not be all that's in his blood, which is why, the track maintenance foreman claims, his employer, the BNSF, has been secretly testing the blood of workers with carpal tunnel syndrome. The railroad wants to be able to state: "You were a time bomb. Because you are genetically predisposed to the disease, you would've gotten it whether you were a soda jerk or running a jackhammer." Harry Zanville, an attorney for the railworkers' union, recently filed a lawsuit, along with Wiebelhaus, to force the company to stop the alleged covert testing. He claims that 125 workers recently gave blood samples and that at least 18 were subjected to gene tests without their consent. The reason: Money! The company hopes to avoid paying out millions in medical bills and disability to workers who develop the painful musculoskeletal disorder on the job.

The federal court lawsuit, the first of its kind against a private company, charges that the furtive testing violates the Americans with Disabilities Act and several state laws barring DNA testing by employers. The U.S. Equal Employment Opportunity Commission (EEOC) filed a separate petition, also in a federal court in the Northern District of Iowa. The EEOC alleges that the Fort Worth-based railroad required blood samples from workers who had submitted claims arising from carpal tunnel injuries. The blood was then allegedly tested for a genetic defect that might predispose a person to some forms of the ailment. Athena Diagnostics, the lab that allegedly conducted the tests, is also a defendant in the union's case.

Hidden Reason

As previously mentioned, Gary Avary, a BNSF employee, indicated that he discovered the alleged covert screening after he received a letter from his employer directing him to get his blood tested. The Nebraska track laborer had recently returned to his job after successful carpal tunnel surgery. The lawsuit alleged that when his wife, a registered nurse, inquired about the test, the secret intentions of BNSF were inadvertently revealed. After Avary refused to take the test, the company informed him that he would be investigated for failing to cooperate. A railroad spokesperson indicated BNSF doesn't require workers to submit to genetic testing, but that some employees were asked to take a test.

The railroad employees are encouraged by a federal court's approval recently of a settlement in a case involving the genetic privacy rights of workers at Lawrence Berkeley Laboratory. These workers for decades were tested without their knowledge for syphilis, pregnancy, and the genetic trait for sickle cell disease. Former President Clinton, banned genetic discrimination against federal employees in 2000, but Congress has not extended the rule to the private sector. It's important for the public to have confidence that genetic tests will be used for their benefit. Unfortunately, this case suggests that companies are still in the dark ages of employment-based testing.

Geneticists in particular question the legitimacy of the carpal tunnel test. They point out that the disease is a common workplace disability and mutations of it are extremely rare.

DNA Bias

In any event, the lawsuit—the first of its kind against a private employer—was filed just as scientists first published the map of the human genetic code. Genetic advances will likely lead more patients to seek cures for inherited diseases, but they are also increasing worries among legal experts and patient rights groups about how genetic data will be used, both in the workplace and elsewhere. There's no question some employers are testing. As more tests are developed and the price drops, the market is expected to grow. Even so, there are ways to protect your privacy in the workplace, or if you choose to be tested on your own.

A big concern among genetic experts is that results from such tests could be used to block someone from being hired or promoted, or to deny insurance. Already, there are hundreds of documented cases alleging genetic discrimination by employers and insurers. For example, preliminary results from a survey by the Genetic Alliance, a coalition of patient advocacy groups, show that 42% of 220 respondents claimed health insurance discrimination. Sixteen percent cited bias at work and in the military. The survey included such cases as a woman who alleged she was denied long-term disability insurance because the company indicated she had a predisposition for Alzheimer's disease. Its decision was based on a doctor's scribbled notation in her medical record that her father might have the condition. In another instance, after a first grader was diagnosed with a genetic developmental disorder, his mother's employer eliminated the child's health-care coverage, saying the diagnosis qualified as a preexisting condition.

Protect Yourself

Although federal workers are legally protected against genetic bias in health insurance and employment, private employees are not. Representative Louise Slaughter, a New York Democrat, indicated that support is building for legislation she cosponsored that would ban such discrimination. Each of us has bad genes, and eventually they'll all be identified with diseases. Even some genetic experts who advocate responsible testing, like Vivian Weinblatt, president of the National Society of Genetic Counselors, are advising patients to consider waiting for Congress to pass such a law before getting screened. Ask yourself: Will knowing the results make my life better? Will I make different life choices? Can I wait a year? If results will help you to treat or prevent a condition for which you're currently at risk, like colon cancer, testing might be wise. If not, or if the results could be inconclusive, then it's probably not worth the risk of a permanent flag on your medical record.

If you decide to test, experts offer this advice: Express any concerns to your physician or a genetic counselor and ask who would have access to your records. Find out whether your employer is self-insured, meaning your boss might get the bills. Consider buying life, health, and disability insurance before getting screened.

Question whether you really need to be tested. In some cases you might consider making the same lifestyle changes you'd make if you tested positive. Those with a family history of breast cancer, for example, might forgo genetic testing and instead be vigilant about regular breast exams. Also, be aware you might learn something you could later regret knowing. For instance, one of the tests for predisposition to heart disease might also reveal a risk for Alzheimer's.

Finally, become familiar with the mechanics of testing. If your employer requires blood samples, get a list of the tests to be run. Ask what happens with the blood afterward: Is it stored or destroyed? The railroad workers are still waiting to find out; their test called for only two blood samples. What did they do with the other five vials? Were other tests planned?

These concerns are aggravated by the fact that a person's biometric data is given and cannot be changed. One of the properties that makes biometrics so attractive for authentication purposes (invariance over time) is also one of its liabilities. When a credit card number is compromised, the issuing bank can just assign the customer a new credit card number. When the biometric data is compromised, replacement is not possible.

To alleviate this problem, the concept of cancelable biometrics is introduced here. It consists of an intentional, repeatable distortion of a biometric signal based on a chosen transform. The biometric signal is distorted in the same fashion at each presentation, for enrollment and for every authentication. With this approach, every instance of enrollment can use a different transform, thus rendering cross-matching impossible. Furthermore, if one variant of the transformed biometric data is compromised, then the transform function can simply be changed to create a new variant (transformed representation) for reenrollment as, essentially, a new person. In general, the distortion transforms are selected to be noninvertible. So even if the transform function is known and the resulting transformed biometric data is known, the original (undistorted) biometrics cannot be recovered.

Example Distortion Transforms

In the proposed method, distortion transforms can be applied in either the signal domain or the feature domain. That is, either the biometric signal can be transformed directly after acquisition, or the signal can be processed as usual and the extracted features can then be transformed. Moreover, extending a template to a larger representation space via a suitable transform can further increase the bit strength of the system. Ideally, the transform should be noninvertible, so that the true biometric of a user cannot be recovered from one or more of the distorted versions stored by various agencies.

Examples of transforms at the signal level include grid morphing and block permutation. The transformed images cannot be successfully matched against the original images or against similar transforms of the same image using different parameters. Although a deformable template method might be able to find such a match, the residual strain energy is likely to be as high as that of matching the template to an unrelated image. In Figure 11.11, the original image is shown with an overlaid grid aligned with the features of the face. [1] The adjacent image in Figure 11.12, shows the morphed grid and the resulting distortion of the face. [1] In Figure 11.12, a block structure is imposed on the image aligned with characteristic points. The blocks in the original image are subsequently scrambled randomly but repeatably.

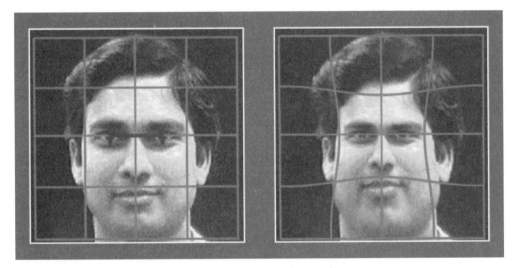

Figure 11.11   Distortion transform based on image morphing.

Figure 11.12   Distortion transform based on block scrambling.

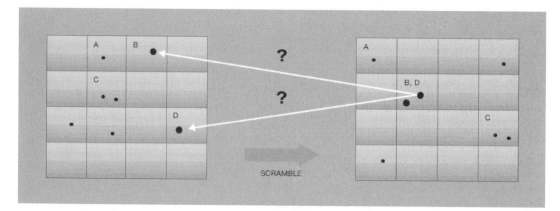

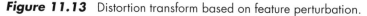

Figure 11.13 Distortion transform based on feature perturbation.

An example of a transform in the feature domain is a set of random, repeatable perturbations of feature points. This can be done within the same physical space as the original, or while increasing the range of the axes. An example of such a transform is shown in Figure 11.13. [1] Here the blocks on the left are randomly mapped onto blocks on the right, where multiple blocks can be mapped onto the same block. Such transforms are noninvertible, hence the original feature sets cannot be recovered from the distorted versions. For instance, it is impossible to tell which of the two blocks the points in composite block B, D originally came from. Consequently, the owner of the biometrics cannot be identified except through the information associated with that particular enrollment.

Tip

For the transform to be repeatable, you need to have the biometric signal properly registered before the transformation. Fortunately, this problem has been partially answered by a number of techniques available in the literature (e.g., finding the "core" and "delta" points in a fingerprint, or eye and nose detection in a face).

Encryption and Transform Management

The techniques presented here for transforming biometric signals differ from simple compression using signal or image processing techniques. Although compression of the signal causes it to lose some of its spatial domain characteristics, it strives to preserve the overall geometry. That is, two points in a biometric signal before compression are likely to remain at a comparable distance when decompressed. This is usually not the case with distortion transforms.

This technique also differs from encryption. The purpose of encryption is to allow a legitimate party to regenerate the original signal. In contrast, distortion transforms permanently obscure the signal in a noninvertible manner.

When employing cancelable biometrics, there are several places where the transform, its parameters, and identification templates could be stored. This leads to a possible distributed process model as shown in Figure 11.14. [1] The "merchant" is where the primary interaction starts in the model. Based on the customer ID, the relevant transform is first pulled from one of the transform databases and applied to the biometrics. The resulting distorted biometrics information is then sent for authentication to the "authorization" server. Once the user's identity has been confirmed, the transaction is finally passed on to the relevant commercial institution for processing.

 Tip

> *An individual user might be subscribed to multiple services, such as e-commerce merchants or banks.*

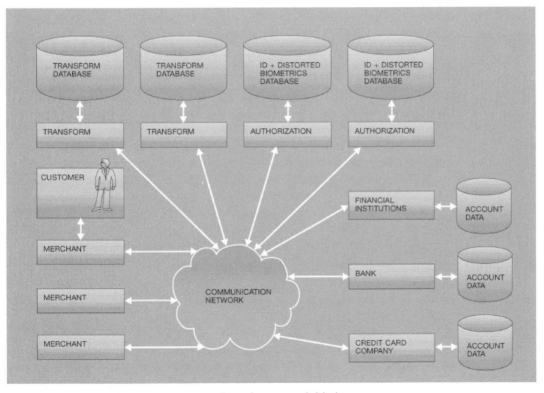

Figure 11.14 Authentication process based on cancelable biometrics.

The authentication for each transaction might be performed either by the service provider itself, or by an independent third party. Similarly, the distortion transform might be managed either by the authenticator or by another independent agency. Alternatively, for the best privacy, the transform might remain solely in the possession of the user, stored, say, on a smart card. If the card is lost or stolen, the stolen transform applied to another person's biometrics will have very little impact. However, if the transform is applied to a stored original biometrics signal of the genuine user, it will match against the stored template of the person. Hence "liveness" detection techniques (as described earlier) should be added to prevent such misuse.

Specialized Biometrics Enterprise Deployment

As previously explained, in view of recent advances, biometric technologies have become more reliable and cost-effective for specialized enterprise deployment (see the sidebar, "Specialized Enterprise Successful Deployment"). The cost savings that can be achieved by removing (or even decreasing) the use of passwords is often tremendous.

Specialized Enterprise Successful Deployment

The travel and immigration, health care, and financial services sectors—industries that require ubersecurity to protect sensitive data and confirm individuals' identities—will get the most benefit from biometric technologies. In other words, the travel and immigration industries have started to apply biometrics in some of the most interesting ways. The Immigration and Naturalization Service Passenger Accelerated Service System, a pilot program working in several U.S. airports including San Francisco International and New York's JFK, allows travelers to bypass immigration lines by using biometric terminals. Airlines are also considering using biometrics to help identify passengers before boarding.

Working to become compliant with Health Insurance Portability and Accountability Act (HIPAA) regulations, health care companies are seeking more secure solutions. Although the technology is not specifically required by HIPAA, many organizations are looking at biometric techniques to secure access to confidential patient data. Some are also using biometrics to authenticate drug prescriptions. Doctors who enter prescriptions online use biometrics to identify themselves to the system and authorize the transaction.

Financial services companies are also turning to biometric technologies. Some are considering using biometrics at ATM machines, but others use biometrics in only the most sensitive situations, such as when allowing access to vaults or approving the execution of huge transactions.

Nevertheless, despite recent advances, biometrics are still not ideal for all companies. Biometrics have a definite use in certain industries and security-sensitive areas, but the technologies will not become ubiquitous in the enterprise for at least seven years, if ever. Prices must continue to fall dramatically and privacy issues must be addressed. The next part of the chapter addresses these issues and concerns.

Biometrics and DNA at Work: Are They Cost Prohibitive for Identity Theft Protection?

James Bond, *Star Trek*, and countless other stories of intrigue and science fiction have long heralded the use of biometrics—the ability to scan for specific life signs at great distances through DNA scanning. Now, in 2001, we're finally getting a glimpse of how easy advanced security can be when an individual's unique physical characteristics are electronically stored and scanned. Recent advances have made biometrics more reliable, accurate, scalable, and cost-effective for the enterprise. Nevertheless, the technologies remain too expensive for most organizations to deploy widely, so biometrics are ideal only for environments with the highest of security needs.

Fingerprint identification, hand geometry, voice verification, retina or iris scanning, and facial recognition are the biometric techniques most likely to be used in an enterprise, but not the only ones. Extreme methods, including DNA, ear lobe, and typing pattern recognition, can now be used in circumstances that require extremely high security measures, such as monitoring access to a missile launching system.

Deploying any method of biometrics can offer a greater sense of security, but the high cost of purchasing the hardware, installing and integrating it into enterprise systems, and training end users is still prohibitive, and often not offset by the increased security levels. General day-to-day issues, such as how to enroll a new finger in the system if a user injures his or her authentication finger, are easy to overlook.

Mapping the Body

Although many parts of the human body can provide data for electronic identification, users remain most comfortable offering their fingertips. As previously mentioned, fingertip scanners are the most commonly used form of biometrics, and the least expensive and easiest to deploy, but not all scanners are the same. Some match the ridges in a thumbprint, others are straight pattern-matching devices, and still others take unique approaches such as ultrasonics.

As previously explained, a more accurate system is hand geometry, led by Recognition Systems' HandKey II. Because this area has not seen the dramatic price decreases of fingerprint scanners, however, hand geometry is usually deployed only in the most sensitive areas of the enterprise, such as vaults or data centers.

Banks are great candidates for voice verification. Simply allowing customers to change their PINs by voice could save banks hundreds of thousands of dollars. Despite its potential for improving customer service, voice verification techniques are largely limited to use on internal networks. The variability of telephone handsets and line quality creates significant challenges for deploying it over public networks.

As previously explained, one of the most advanced but most intrusive biometrics is retina scanning, which scans the unique patterns of the retina with a low-intensity light source. By contrast, iris scanning uses a camera and requires no intimate contact with the reader; its ease of use and system integration have traditionally been poor, but they are improving dramatically with recent developments. Nevertheless, its high cost will continue to limit iris scanning to extremely sensitive areas.

Facial recognition, which compares a user's facial characteristics with the stored results of an algorithm calculation (similar to a data hash), offers the ultimate security. Some systems match two static images, and others claim to be able to unobtrusively detect the identity of an individual within a group.

As previously explained, facial recognition could be used (has been used in the United Kingdom for the last 10 years) indiscriminately through the application of covert video surveillance (hidden camera devices) in airports and on the street. This application would help law enforcement identify known wanted criminals or terrorists, whose photos are contained in a network-attached storage system (or database) for easy access and comparison. In other words, once the video surveillance system identifies a target or person, that person's face or facial characteristics are frozen and matched against a digital stored photo of the wanted suspect. However, here in the United States, facial recognition has had only very limited success in enterprise applications, such as access to nuclear facilities, because of its cost and complexity.

Getting Under Its Skin

When deciding to add biometrics to your mix of enterprise security, selecting the type of technology to use is only half the battle. You must also consider identification versus verification, template storage, and network impact.

Cost, processing speed, and fewer false positives make verification systems the popular choice. Most biometric products use verification: The user's biometric template is retrieved from storage by a PIN, token, or smart card and quickly compared to a live sample. Identification solutions, on the other hand, compare the live sample to the entire database. If the comparison parameters are loosely defined, the search might match more than one live user to the same data. Identification works well with a small group of users, but when you get into the thousands, the time, processing power, and cost needed to scan the entire database can be excessive.

If you choose a biometric verification solution, you'll next have to figure out how to store the templates, which contain data defining the users' characteristics. If templates or the database containing the templates are compromised, attackers could easily inject unauthorized templates to gain access to the protected network, system, or application. Templates are frequently stored on a centralized database, but they can also be kept on the biometric reader or in a portable token.

Centralized databases create many security risks and can add a substantial amount of traffic to your network. If the database is compromised, your entire biometric solution could also be compromised. Storing the template locally decreases processing time but might introduce difficulties if users move from machine to machine. Using smart cards might be the best way to go because they give the user portability and do not require centralized storage. However, if the token goes missing, the user must reenroll, which can be a costly, time-consuming process.

If your company has decided to use biometrics to defray costs, you might require a different biometric technology than a company that primarily wants to boost security. Because the average corporation spends $150 to $200 per user, per year resetting passwords, the initial setup costs for biometrics can quickly be recovered by the annual savings of not resetting passwords. If this is your reasoning, your biometric solution should be easy to use and not very intrusive. However, if you are implementing biometrics for security reasons, your comparison parameters should be biased to deny access.

Biometrics are still in the early-adopter stage, but significant technological advances are beginning to make them a viable, if costly, solution in particular areas of the enterprise. Standards that allow interoperability among readers, increased accuracy and reliability, and lower costs will make biometrics a more practical alternative someday, and someday is now. There is now an urgency to implement all types of biometrics, no matter what the cost. The benefits now outweigh the costs. Let's take a look at some of the reasons why.

Benefits

Biometric technology offers a number of benefits to both businesses and consumers. It is these benefits, in addition to the factors noted earlier, that are driving their increased usage and acceptance.

Positive Identification

Companies are looking to biometrics because they see the positive identification provided by the technology as a way to control fraud and abuse, build nonrepudiation into electronic commerce transactions, and enhance customer service. It can be reasonably argued that each one of these potential corporate benefits also benefit the customer.

In today's business environment, many organizations can no longer rely on their employees to recognize individual clients. Companies are looking for means whereby individuals can be recognized reliably, at a distance, over a period of time, without reliance on human memory, and, in some cases, despite the preference by the person not to be recognized.

Financial institutions have long been evaluating the merits of biometrics. This interest has increased significantly with the rise in electronic banking and the concern over possible terrorist attacks. It is estimated that over 89% of all banking transactions are now done electronically.

ATMs and transactions at the point of sale are considered to be particularly vulnerable to fraud and breaches in security. Emerging markets such as telephone and Internet banking also need to be secured for bank customers and bankers alike.

Biometrics are ideally suited for electronic commerce and other online applications because they can automatically "prove" the identity of a person and assure that no one else can impersonate them. The benefit of positive identification is strengthened by the fact that biometrics can connect an actual person to a transaction. By linking a verified individual to a particular transaction (much like a digital signature), repudiation by a party after the fact, on the grounds that the identification was forged, becomes very difficult. Biometric authentication systems can be built using an online signing service to accept the biometric measurements, and if the identification is positive, to use the secret key on behalf of the user to generate the cryptographic binding of the document to the identity of the user.

Combatting Credit Card Fraud

A significant subset of the identification issue is credit card fraud. Stolen credit card numbers are routinely posted and swapped on Internet bulletin boards and real-time chat lines. On the Internet, credit card numbers come from traditional offline sources (stolen wallets and discarded receipts), as well as from poorly secured Web servers that store credit card information.

Now there are computer programs that fraudulently generate valid credit card numbers. All credit card numbers end with a checksum digit that is generated from the other digits using an algorithm. That formula is used by these programs to create unauthorized numbers that can fool a simple authorization check.

 Tip

A recent U.S. survey found that nearly one-third of consumers who have purchased products on the Internet have experienced fraud or misuse of credit card information.

Requiring positive identification of the cardholder prior to authorizing a transaction (either in person or online) has obvious appeal to sponsoring financial institutions, as well as to individual businesses. MasterCard International estimated the use of biometrics could reduce credit card fraud by 93%.

Preventing Identity Theft

The need for accurate identification is as important an issue for consumers as it is for businesses. Although there are many ways to combat identity theft, some consumers see biometrics as an effective and convenient way to diminish the problem. Biometrics can fight identity theft by eliminating PINs and passwords, by verifying the identity of parties in a remote transaction, by authorizing credit card or check transactions, and by securing personal assets like computers, as well as personal information. In this capacity, a biometric can be seen as an identity protector.

One new service, called *e-dentification*, is designed to help allay consumer concerns about participating in electronic commerce for fear of identity theft or misuse of their personal information. It is set up so that each individual identity record is biometrically "passworded" and encrypted, with the key remaining in the consumer's control. The identity record is legally owned and controlled by the individual consumer and cannot be accessed without the biometric consent of the consumer.

With the rise of identity theft, the imperative for identity authentication has changed from just being a corporate concern to one shared equally by consumers. Now, more than ever before, it is critical for consumers to be able to prove their identity. For individuals to protect their own identify from theft or misuse, they need a secure form of portable identification that they control. Biometrics offers this potential.

Restoring Identity

Biometrics offers another potential benefit to consumers in that they can verify their identity should their identifying papers be lost or stolen. The technology addresses the "chicken or egg" question of how a person gets identification if he or she has no identification. An example illustrating the utility of biometrics can be found in Oklahoma, where authorities issued new driver's licenses with a thumbprint to replace documents lost in tornadoes. The biometric was seen as a deterrent to criminals, and a way to protect the public by ensuring that the new licenses were given to their rightful owners. Should these licenses be lost in the future, the biometric will reestablish identity so the appropriate person can be issued the necessary documentation quickly and easily. This benefit is equally applicable to membership cards or credit cards.

Enhanced Security

The changing nature of business has created significant new security concerns. With customers increasingly interacting with companies through some form of IT (telephone, kiosk, or computer), traditional security methods are being challenged. Opening up access to computer systems and networks might enhance customer service, but it also increases the potential for security breaches. A recent survey on computer crime in the United States indicated that almost one-third of respondents reported that outsiders had penetrated their computer systems in the past year, most frequently through an Internet connection. The most serious losses occurred through the theft of proprietary information and financial fraud.

As noted earlier, traditional authentication methods involve something the user knows, such as a password or PIN, or something the user has, such as a card, key, or token. Now companies are questioning the reliability of these security measures to protect their interests, as well as those of their customers.

Cards or keys can be forgotten, given away, lost, stolen, duplicated, or forged. Passwords can be shared, guessed, observed, stolen, or forgotten. One example of the limits of passwords is that a group of hackers from Europe broke into the email system at Stanford University in California, stole thousands of student and staff passwords, and went undetected for three weeks.

Another recent survey found that even experienced computer users tend to choose the same passwords. The most popular were dates of birth (15%), and names of partners, children, or pets (49%), and 20% of the men surveyed chose their favorite football team. Eighty percent of respondents justified choosing simple passwords because they were afraid of forgetting more complex words and number combinations.

New computer viruses can capture keystrokes so that as a person types a password or PIN, including encryption keys, the software collects and transmits that information to unauthorized parties without the user's knowledge. Keystroke recorders or loggers are designed to record and play back all keyboard and mouse actions. These programs are widely available, yet difficult to detect, with some having the ability to penetrate conventional firewall protections.

Some industry experts predict that the use of passwords for email, corporate networks, and the Internet will come to an end in the next few years. Passwords are far too vulnerable, whereas biometrics are seen, by some, as offering superior security.

Biometric companies are promoting their products as security systems that cannot be stolen, forgotten, shared, or intercepted. Additionally, biometric characteristics can only be linked to a single identifiable individual. The technology offers two significant advantages over other authentication methods: The person to be identified is required to be physically present at the point of identification, and identification based on biometric techniques eliminates the need to remember a password or PIN or to carry a token.

Some industry supporters consider biometrics the most effective information security tool because biometric systems verify the person, not the card or the code. This advantage has led vendors to call the technology "proof-positive" security. Biometrics is considered particularly effective when several techniques are layered (voice verification and finger scan) or combined with traditional security measures.

The potential for enhanced security offered by biometrics to businesses regarding their computers and networks has a flip side for consumers. A customer is just as concerned about the validity and security of an online transaction.

Data Authentication

To prevent the unauthorized altering of information (deliberate or unintentional) during online transactions, some form of data authentication becomes necessary. This ensures that the information sent and received is complete and not tampered with or intercepted in transit.

The use of encryption to secure both business and personal communications is on the rise. Encryption is a mathematical process that changes data from plain text (that which can be read) to an unintelligible form. To reconstruct the original data or decrypt it, the key to the algorithm used must be known.

Certain newer biometric systems can be used to encrypt data—the process is called biometric encryption. Information extracted from biometrics can be used as the key to scramble and unscramble data. As an example, the unique pattern in a person's fingerprint could be used to code his or her PIN for accessing a bank machine. The coded PIN has no connection whatsoever to the finger pattern. What is stored in the database is only the coded PIN. The finger pattern acts as the coding key. The actual fingerprint pattern is not stored anywhere during this process. Biometric encryption ensures that the information encrypted with the biometric key cannot be decrypted without the live biometric. Another potential benefit to this system is that the operation of successfully decoding the PIN authenticates that person's eligibility for the service without revealing any personal identifiers. Most important, biometric encryption cannot serve as a unique identifier, eliminating many fears commonly associated with the use of biometrics.

Physical Access Control

Initially, biometric access controls were limited to high-security areas such as nuclear power plants and military facilities. Now, these access control systems are used in theme parks, hotels, and health clubs. Some industry commentators believe there is no limit to the kinds of organizations that could use biometrics to secure the physical movement of people, particularly as prices continue to fall and public acceptance grows.

Automated access control systems using biometrics offer certain advantages over keys, cards, or security guards in terms of convenience, security, and operating costs. Forgotten passwords and lost keys or cards are a nuisance for users and a major expense for the company. With the existing demographics of an aging population, memory loss can only be expected to escalate.

From a business perspective, the benefits of a biometric access control system are that access can be limited by person, by location, by time, and by the system that keeps an accurate record of exactly who is given access and when. Biometric systems are viewed as being reliable and constant, because machines never get distracted, tired, or affected by the "psychological defects" that might affect people working as security guards.

From a consumer's perspective, biometric systems designed for large-scale access control are fast and easy to use. In addition, consumers can benefit from customized service and the convenience of 24/7 access. If you think of all the PINs, passwords, and cards you use throughout the day to access an office, computer, bank account, or health club, it is easy to understand why biometrics are appealing to many people: There is nothing to remember and nothing to carry. A person simply presents his or her biometrics to be authenticated and is given access.

Another potential consumer benefit to the technology is that it can give people control over their own assets and information. In certain circumstances, such as with the previously noted biometric encryption, individuals can use biometrics as their own access control measures. This means they can put their own confidential information somewhere, both offline and online, and then secure it with their biometric. No one but they can gain entry.

Some Final Thoughts

Finally, the potential application of biometric technology for the prevention of identity theft is infinite. Any situation that allows for an interaction between man and machine is capable of incorporating biometrics. The benefits of biometrics will make the technology's use, and consequently, its acceptance, inevitable.

Despite the very real benefits to both businesses and consumers with relation to identity theft, as discussed in this chapter, the public acceptance of biometrics is not necessarily inevitable. It will only come if the privacy concerns associated with the technology are effectively addressed.

Whether biometrics are privacy's friend or foe is entirely dependent on how the systems are designed and how the information is managed. Although the biometrics industry has made some positive initial steps, without private-sector data protection legislation, companies are still free to use biometric data without restriction.

It must be recognized that the use of biometrics needs to conform to the standards and expectations of a privacy-minded society. The responsibility to ensure that this new technology does not knowingly or unknowingly compromise consumer privacy lies not only with businesses, but also with consumers.

Businesses must acknowledge and accept their obligation to protect their customers' privacy. Prior to introducing any biometric system, the impact that such an application might have on consumer privacy should be fully assessed. To appropriately and effectively balance the use of biometric information for legitimate business purposes with the consumer's right to privacy, companies should adopt and implement the fair information practices and requirements discussed in this chapter. Voluntary adoption of such practices is essential if there is to be meaningful privacy protection of consumers' biometric data in the private sector.

Consumers need to advocate for their own privacy rights. They can make a difference by only doing business with companies that follow fair information practices and make use of the privacy-enhancing aspects of biometrics in the design of their information management systems and identity theft protection techniques. Consumer preferences will be key in defining the appropriate uses and protection of biometrics. Consumers have the power—they need to use it wisely.

Endnotes

[1]   N. K. Ratha, J. H. Connell, and R. M. Bolle, "Enhancing Security and Privacy in Biometrics-Based Authentication Systems," IBM Corporation, 1133 Westchester Avenue, White Plains, NY 10604, USA, 2002.

[2]   "Consumer Biometric Applications," Information and Privacy Commissioner of Ontario, 80 Bloor Street West, Suite 1700, Toronto, Ontario, M5S 2V1, 2001.

Chapter 12

DIGITAL SIGNATURES: SMART, OPTICAL, AND OTHER ADVANCED CARDS

As you know, online identity theft has become too easy. Offline, you prove that you are who you are with paper documents like birth certificates, driver's licenses, and passports—none of which can be easily squeezed through a modem.

Online, most of you want to be anonymous the majority of the time. You don't particularly like the idea of Web sites knowing who you are, except when there's money involved. Although Web browsers and commercial Web sites can encrypt information you send out on the Internet, that doesn't prevent someone who got your credit card number offline from using it online. That's where a new kind of electronic ID, often called a digital ID, can make online transactions more secure with a digital or electronic signature, for both buyer and seller.

In the offline world, rip-off artists have devised hundreds of clever ways to steal your credit card information or obtain credit cards fraudulently using your name and Social Security number. Remember the New York busboy who was charged with using cyberspace to try to steal identities and millions from 217 of the richest Americans, including Steven Spielberg, Martha Stewart, H. Ross Perot, and Warren Buffett?

Your biggest online risk is probably entering your credit card information into a Web site that you're unfamiliar with and haven't taken the time to research—especially sites selling pornography. Although buying online is quick and convenient, it horrifies people. People are leaving themselves wide open to fraud whenever they buy online.

 Tip

> *My advice is simple: Don't.*

One solution is to require purchasers to attach a digital signature each time they buy something on the Web. That would make committing online credit card fraud difficult, if not impossible. A thief with your credit card information won't be able to use it unless he or she also has the key to your digital signature, which can be a password or, still more secure, a fingerprint or retinal scan.

 Tip

> *A digital signature is comprised of a digital code that can be attached to an electronically transmitted message that uniquely identifies the sender. Like a written signature, the purpose of a digital signature is to guarantee that the individual sending the message really is who he or she claims to be. Digital signatures are especially important for electronic commerce and are a key component of most authentication schemes. To be effective, digital signatures must be unforgeable. There are a number of different encryption techniques to guarantee this level of security.*

Three Levels of Security

Digital IDs are issued by a variety of companies. For example, VeriSign, [1] the biggest issuer of digital IDs, offers three levels of security.

Class 1

Class 1 is not terribly useful. It won't identify you legally, for example, as Rudy Lancaster. It just tells the recipient of an email you sent or the operator of a Web site that this ID is associated with a particular email address.

Class 2

According to VeriSign, the Class 2 level of security is for small, low-risk transactions. This type of digital ID provides reasonable, but not foolproof assurance of a subscriber's identity. The company verifies your identity by checking your answers to some detailed questions against information contained in third-party databases. That's what you signed up for.

Class 3

Class 3 is the real thing. It requires the applicant to go to a notary or some other local registration authority to physically verify that you are who you are.

The key that protects your digital ID from unauthorized use is a string of numbers, ones and zeroes. The key, which also unlocks emails you choose to encrypt, is protected by a password at the lower levels of security. For Class 3 IDs, VeriSign recommends installing a hardware token on your PC, so that only users of that machine can access your private key. However, you can't attach a digital signature to an online book purchase yet, and you can't buy airline tickets with a digital signature yet.

The primary users of digital IDs today are people doing business—contracts, sales, and legal documents. The signature saves time because you don't have to mail or fax a document. You're assured of its authenticity at a level you find acceptable.

A Few Kinks to Work out

The sale of a home would be a natural candidate for the use of digital signatures, and there have been some attempts to make them work. Two sales were closed not long ago in Rochester, New York, that were entirely electronic. What's preventing the idea from spreading is that every state has its own set of real estate laws and procedures, and standardizing the required disclosures and documents is tricky at best.

There are other problems. First of all, uniform standards on digital signatures haven't been agreed on. EU nations are trying to develop yet another set of standards that might not conform to standards being developed in the United States and Canada.

295

Second, you have to go through the trouble of downloading the software, which takes several steps and a bit of time. For the highest level of security, you also have to physically verify your identity.

Third, for anyone who's been involved in e-commerce, you know it can take a lot to get an online user to spend money. So, unless a consumer sees a real crisis, he or she might not be willing to spend even the $7.95 you spent to buy the digital signature.

Of course, no system is completely bulletproof. Not long ago, someone tricked VeriSign into issuing two digital certificates in Microsoft's name. Theoretically, the certificates could be used to identify software containing viruses as real software from Microsoft.

At best, then, a digital ID is something you might one day use as part of your personal toolkits. However, there's a bit of warning that must be injected right here: Although digital IDs will help to protect your credit cards from unauthorized use (at least online), they won't make online commerce foolproof. You can still be ripped off by someone whose name and digital ID number you know.

Now let's look at how advanced digital ID cards use technologies with capabilities that surpass the currently used magnetic stripes you find on many of the cards you carry in your wallet. These smart, optical, and capacitive cards are in use around the world. The technology allows more information to be stored and transported than do the existing magnetic stripes, which contain very little information. Each of the new technologies can be used for applications that might benefit a privacy assessment, so that developers can build privacy protection into advanced card technology applications.

In other words, this part of the chapter helps the developer or marketer design and implement advanced card applications that build privacy protection into the application and surrounding components of the process. It also helps you assess privacy protection in a systematic way, leads you through the overall process that surrounds your advanced card technology application, and helps you analyze the individual pieces of data that you might need to collect and use.

Smart, Optical, and Other Advanced Cards

Think of your own privacy for a minute. Who knows what about you? If you begin with your wallet and the cards you carry, you start to realize that a lot of companies, government, and other organizations know, and likely have stored somewhere, your personal information. Now, let's take that a step further. Are you sure that you know every organization or company that has your personal information in its possession? If a company that you gave information to sold it to another company, you might not know, in which case, you would find it very difficult to identify the new companies who now have your personal information, to check the completeness and correctness of that data, and correct any errors or omissions.

Your information belongs to you—maybe not the paper file it resides in or the disk it is stored on, but the information itself is truly yours. Therefore, you have a right to determine who has access to it, to authorize what it is used for, and to be provided with a mechanism to review the data and make any necessary corrections.

Yet, as you go about your everyday life, you are frequently asked to provide information about yourself to others. Joining a video or book club, using a preferred customer card, and getting money from the bank all produce a set of electronic records that singly and in combination provide insight into you and your habits. Such information is a valuable commodity that is regularly bought and sold, usually without your knowledge.

Now, let's look at this from a business perspective, rather than a personal perspective. Information is a fundamental commodity in today's business world. In today's information economy, the quality and integrity of information is of paramount importance. Customer service, in terms of identifying and meeting their needs and expectations, is one of the central tenets of today's business environment. Your customer is a source of valuable information that must be respected and protected. Today's customers are increasingly aware of and concerned about their privacy and the control of their information. When businesses become sensitive to this customer concern, their ability to successfully market their products and services will be greatly enhanced.

The Impact of Computer Technology on Privacy

As previously explained, technology allows information to move quickly and often invisibly. In the past, some comfort could be taken from the fact that your personal information was buried in paper files and would be very difficult for unauthorized parties to retrieve. Today's databases, networks, and the Internet, however, remove that procedural protection.

In mainframe computer applications, privacy was often a subset of security. Your salary information was available only to authorized persons because the payroll application was designed to meet the security needs of the company. The same was true of human resources information. As you moved from mainframes to PCs, you started to look at the computer, and therefore the security, differently. Information stored on your PC is often viewed as personal. It is your correspondence, your spreadsheets, your databases, and basically the information you use to do your work. You started to view the data as being yours, as opposed to belonging to the company. Because you thought of it as yours, you often give it to coworkers if you feel they need it for their work. Another security weakness is that data on one's PC is relatively easy to access. Just turning on someone's PC will often give you the ability to access their computer files.

Advanced cards allow individuals to carry more information in their wallets than they did formerly. Smart cards are basically a PC on a credit-card-sized piece of plastic. They are capable of storing data and performing computations. This technology is being introduced to consumers in the form of prepaid phone cards and stored value cards. Optical cards are also capable of storing massive amounts of data on a credit-card-sized piece of plastic. They work in much the same way as CDs.

In each of these applications, there is personal information that should be protected, but that information is a part of the overall system, not just linked to the card or the application. In the case of electronic value, people want to know who will have access to their purchase information. With customs information, people want to know who will have access to their travel and declaration data. With transit, people want to know who will know where and when they have traveled. This is all coupled with the desire to have all the convenience and benefits offered by these cards.

Now, let's return to systems designs that give thought to who is permitted access to each piece of data. Who can see the data, add to it, change it, or even delete it? How is the information protected when it is on a PC or on a smart, optical, or capacitive card? How do you treat the information when it is initially collected? Do you collect it on paper and then enter it into the application? If this is the case, how do you treat the forms after the data have been entered? How do you ensure that the data isn't copied and given to others who were never intended to have access to it?

Protection of privacy must be viewed systematically at each stage from collection to destruction. As previously stated, the purpose of this part of the chapter is to provide developers and marketers of applications using advanced card technologies with the background information and necessary tools to successfully meet the customer service goal of privacy protection. By understanding privacy principles and by following the process discussed in this part of the chapter, you will be able to incorporate privacy protection into your applications, processes, and procedures.

As information becomes more readily available through computers and the increasing use of the Internet, the public becomes more concerned about who has access to their information. In some cases, they are also worried that stored information about them might be incorrect and if so, they would have no means of correcting it. Although these concerns have always existed, even when information was written by hand on paper, computers have made the collection and distribution of information much easier and faster, escalating most people's concerns.

As smart, optical, and capacitive card applications have been introduced, questions have been asked that are indicative of some of the misunderstandings about how advanced cards work. The aim of this part of the chapter is not to teach you about card technology, but rather how to build privacy protection into your applications. Before looking at the system design elements, let's first look at the principles involved in protecting privacy, often referred to as *fair information practices*.

Privacy Protection Principles

Many of the concerns expressed by consumers about privacy relate to the manner in which personal information is collected, used, and disclosed. When organizations collect information without the knowledge or consent of the individual to whom the information relates, use that information in ways that are unknown to the individual, or disclose the information without the consent of the individual, informational privacy is violated.

Concern about informational privacy in Europe in the early 1970s gave rise to the need for data protection, which focuses on people's personal information and the ability to maintain some degree of control over its use and dissemination. What followed from the concern for data protection was the development of a set of practices commonly referred to as fair information practices. There have been several attempts to develop a complete and comprehensive set of fair information practices.

More recent significant efforts to protect privacy have been the EU's Directive on the Protection of Personal Data with Regard to the Processing of Personal Data and on the Free Movement of Such Data. Table 12.1 lists a set of privacy practices that combines the use of personal information for business purposes with an individual's right to privacy protection. The practices that follow reflect these business practices, modified to fit the circumstances relating to advanced card technologies. Those who design applications that use advanced card technologies or those who market them are encouraged to commit to these principles.

Table 12.1. Privacy Practices Checklist

Privacy Practices
Combination of Personal Information for Business Purposes With an Individual's Right to Privacy Protection Checklist
Date: _____

Those who design applications that use advanced card technologies or those who market them need to (check all tasks completed):

❑ 1. Recognize that your customers are the owners of their personal information, to be consulted in the development of policies or practices that could potentially impact their privacy.

❑ 2. Adopt privacy protection practices and apply them when handling all customer personal information.

❑ 3. Assess, prior to implementation, the impact on privacy of any proposed new policy, service, or product.

❑ 4. Adopt a policy of redress or restoration so that if any service alters the privacy status quo, you will provide a means to restore that privacy at no cost to the customer.

❑ 5. Communicate your privacy protection policies and practices to your customers in a manner that enables customers to exercise their rights.

❑ 6. Ensure there is an openness about your policies and practices relating to your customers' personal information, and that the existence of any record-keeping systems containing your customers' personal information is not kept secret from them—they should be transparent.

❑ 7. Develop and publicize a process for addressing and responding to any customer inquiry or complaint regarding the handling of his or her personal information.

❑ 8. Identify the purposes for which your customers' personal information is to be collected, used, or routinely disclosed, before it is collected.

❑ 9. Do not withdraw access to services or products if a customer subsequently refuses to permit the use of his or her personal information for a purpose not identified at the time of collection, including the exchange or sale of that information to a third party for marketing purposes.

❑ 10. Only collect personal information about your customers that is necessary and relevant for the transaction(s) involved.

❑ 11. Collect personal information about your customers directly from the individuals concerned, whenever reasonably possible.

❑ 12. Collect customers' personal information with the knowledge and consent of the customers, except in very limited circumstances, and inform the customer of these

Table 12.1. Privacy Practices Checklist (Continued)

circumstances at, or prior to, the time of collection.

❏ 13. Notify your customers at, or before the time of collection, of:

    ❏ a. The purposes for which the personal information is to be used or/and disclosed.

    ❏ b. The source(s) from which the personal information is to be collected, if not directly from the customer.

❏ 14. Only use personal information for the purposes identified to the customer at the time of collection unless the customer explicitly consents to a new use, or the activity is authorized by law.

❏ 15. Establish a right for customers to have access to their personal information, subject to clear and limited exceptions (if such access would constitute an invasion of another person's privacy).

❏ 16. Provide customers with access to their personal information in a form understandable to them, without undue delay or expense.

❏ 17. If they are denied access, you should inform the customer of the reasons why and provide them with a fair opportunity to challenge the denial.

❏ 18. Establish a right for customers to challenge the accuracy of their personal information.

❏ 19. Amend customer's personal information if it is found to be inaccurate, incomplete, irrelevant or inappropriate.

❏ 20. Make note in the customer's file of any discrepancies regarding the accuracy or completeness of their personal information.

❏ 21. Take all reasonable measures to inform third parties who also use your customers' personal information, of corrections or changes that have been made.

❏ 22. Take all reasonable and appropriate measures to ensure that the personal information you collect, use and disclose, meets the highest possible standard of accuracy, completeness and timeliness.

❏ 23. Obtain customers' consent prior to disclosure of their personal information, except where authorized by law or in exceptional circumstances. These limited, exceptional circumstances should be identified and customer informed of them at, or prior to, the time of collection.

❏ 24. Obtain your customers' consent prior to renting, selling, trading or otherwise disclosing their personal information to a third party.

❏ 25. Retain personal information only for as long as it is relevant to the purposes for which it was collected, or as required by law.

Table 12.1. Privacy Practices Checklist (Continued)

☐ 26. Dispose of personal information in a consistent and secure manner, or remove all references that would link the data to a specific identifiable person (thereby rendering it anonymous), once it has served its purpose.

☐ 27. Adopt appropriate and comprehensive measures to ensure the security of your customers' personal information against loss or unauthorized access, use, alteration, disclosure, or destruction.

☐ 28. Communicate your privacy policies and practices to all staff, and make your staff accountable for adherence to those policies and practices.

☐ 29. Conduct periodic reviews of your privacy policies and practices to ensure that they are in keeping with your customers' expectations, as well as international developments.

☐ 30. Stipulate right in your contract:

    ☐ a. The privacy protection measures to be adopted by business partners or third parties using your customers' personal information.

    ☐ b. The purposes for which your customers' personal information may be used and disclosed by business partners or third parties.

☐ 31. Reduce, to the greatest extent possible, the collection and retention of identifiable transactions (transactions in which the data in the record could be readily linked to an identifiable individual). This can be achieved through the use of either:

    ☐ a. Anonymity: Ideally, there should be no personal identifiers involved in the transaction —you have "de-identified" it.

    ☐ b. Pseudonymity: Where the functional or administrative needs of the application require some link between transactional data and identity, it is often possible to use pseudonymous techniques. These include such procedures as storage of partial identifiers by two or more organizations, both of whom must provide their portions of the transaction trail in order for the identity of the individual to be constructed; storing of an indirect identifier with the transactional data which serves as a pointer to the personal identifiers; and storing separately a cross-index between the indirect identifier and the individual's true identity.

The practices listed in Table 12.1 are pertinent to your system as a whole. The next part of the chapter contains checklists that should be completed for every new application or revision to an existing application. These checklists will not only assist you in assessing whether your application adheres to fair information practices, but by completing them, you are also creating documentation that will substantiate your application's protection of privacy.

Privacy Assessment Checklist

The key to successfully implementing privacy protection in an application is to consider it one of the central design criteria. This will ensure that privacy protection is built into the application from the start, thereby eliminating the difficult and expensive task of retrofitting privacy protection into an existing application.

The components covered in the following sections make up the privacy assessment checklist. Some apply during the development of an advanced card application, whereas others are more applicable during the implementation stage and actual use of the application. Many of these components apply throughout all stages of development, implementation, and usage.

The action you should take is described next. Background information has been included to assist you in preparing your answers. A checklist that should prove helpful in completing this portion of the project can be found in Table 12.2. [5] It serves as a guide to the components needed to develop a privacy protection program, rather than a complete record of the program. Certain components might require the development of separate documents to completely describe and document the component. In those cases, the checklist will serve as a reference list for these documents. The checklist will also serve as an overview of the program that can be distributed to staff and customers to better inform them of the organization's commitment to privacy.

Table 12.2. Privacy Protection Assessment Checklist

Step	Details
Description of the Proposed Application *Describe the proposed application requiring the collection of personal information:* What are the important features? For example, what categories or groups of individuals will you be or are you gathering information from and what classes or types of information are being gathered? What methods of collection, storage, and transmission of the information are being used? How will the information be organized? For example, is the information for an individual retained together or stored separately by type such as identifying information in one location and transaction or functional information in another location?	

Table 12.2.   Privacy Protection Assessment Checklist (Continued)

Step	Details

Description of the Personal Information to Be Collected

List and describe the personal information to be gathered: What type of personal information is to be collected? How is the information obtained (directly from the source or indirectly)? Is any third-party information involved? If the information is to be collected indirectly the reasons why this is necessary should be clearly outlined. What differences, if any, are there for different types of customers? Does the information pertain to one individual or to a group of individuals? What is the extent of the information to be collected (one record or several)?

Purpose of the Collection

Identify the purposes for the collection of personal information: What are the reasons why the personal information is necessary and relevant to the application? Why must the personal information be collected in identifiable form? Why is personal information required as opposed to anonymous or pseudonymous information? What, if any, are the consequences of not collecting the personal information? Is the information required for functional or administrative purposes or both?

How Is Notice of Collection Given and Informed Consent Obtained?

Design the notice to be authorized by the customer and attach: How is notice of the collection given? How is consent obtained? If consent is inferred from some action of the customer rather than expressly given, indicate why this approach is necessary. What is the process by which the individual is informed and provides consent? Attach such documents as the application form used to seek consent, the customer response card that gives consent, a listing of the oral information provided when information is collected, and so on. Is the information to be shared with other organizations or linked with their databases? If so, are fair information practices also in place there?

Table 12.2. Privacy Protection Assessment Checklist (Continued)

Step	Details
Method of Collection *Describe how information will be collected and, if appropriate, how it will be linked to previously collected information:* What is the process of collection? How is the collected information transferred and stored? Is there any linking or matching with previously collected information? If so, how is this accomplished? What controls are in place to ensure the validity of the information during the various steps of this process?	

Duration of the Collection of Personal Information
 	
Identify the period of time over which the data will be collected: Is the collection for this one time only, is it limited in duration, or is it ongoing? Particularly important to note are the reasons why the collection is ongoing, as this leads into issues of data integrity.
	❑ One time
	❑ Unlimited
	❑ Limited
	    Start date:_____
	    End date:_____

Accuracy *Outline the steps to be taken to ensure that information is accurate at all stages of the application:* What steps will be taken to ensure the accuracy of the collected information both at the time of collection and over time if the information should change? Is a verification method part of the overall process?	
Method of Storage *List each method by which the personal information is stored, including the original collection form, computer files and copies, backup copies, on the advanced card, and so on:* What is the storage method and process for the advanced card application and associated components in the overall application?	

Table 12.2. Privacy Protection Assessment Checklist (Continued)

Step	Details
Key Personnel	Chief Information Officer:
List by name and title all personnel responsible for the privacy of this application: Who is the person who serves as the focal point for the privacy protection process of the organization (the CIO)? Who are the people who have roles in the access and correction process? From the perspective of those inside the organization it is useful to list persons who have key roles in the functions of collection, use, retention, and disclosure of the information.	_____ Other key personnel: Name _____, Function _____ Name _____, Function _____ Name _____, Function _____

Description of Procedures for Access and Correction

Describe the process to be used by individuals to view and request changes to their data: What procedures are or will be put in place to permit customers to gain access to their personal information? What are the procedures for requesting correction of information? This might include reference to more detailed documents that describe the process at greater length. A document that is suitable for distribution to the customer is very useful, as is a document for internal use that outlines the steps of the access process and correction process for staff.

Procedures for Complaints and Appeals of Denial of Access or Correction

Describe the procedure to be followed by an individual who wishes to lodge a complaint about his or her data or problems in accessing or correcting that data: What procedures are in place for a customer to voice a complaint about how his or her personal information is being collected and used? What procedures exist if access to this information or correction of it has been denied? How are concerns resolved? What time frames exist for resolution?

Table 12.2. Privacy Protection Assessment Checklist (Continued)

Step	Details
Security	
Describe the security measures that will apply to the information at all stages of its existence (see "Method of Storage"): What security measures are to be used to ensure the protection of personal information, restrict the possibility of unauthorized use, and track authorized use? These measures should reflect the sensitivity of the data and should have the flexibility for customers to select security measures for their data that reflect their perception of the sensitivity of their data.	

Description of the Proposed Advanced Card Application

Particular mention should be made of the privacy implications of the application on both the positive and negative sides. The actual technology involved should be described as much as possible, in plain, nontechnical language to make it accessible to your customers. Although sufficient detail should be included to identify all the key components of the application, it should not reveal any information that would provide a competitive advantage. It is important to include whether the application could potentially affect the privacy of your customers and, if so, what methods will be introduced to minimize the intrusion and restore any lost degree of privacy.

Description of the Personal Information to Be Collected

Personal information is information about an identifiable individual, for example, information related to a person's health, finances, entitlement to social benefits, travel plans or preferences, purchasing patterns, club memberships, or anything that links information to a specific, identifiable person. It includes, but is not limited to the following:

- Information relating to the race, national or ethnic origin, color, religion, age, sex, sexual orientation, or marital or family status of the individual
- Information relating to the education or the medical, psychiatric, psychological, criminal, or employment history of the individual or information relating to financial transactions in which the individual has been involved

- Any identifying number, symbol, or other particular assigned to the individual

- The address, telephone number, fingerprints, or blood type of the individual

- The personal opinions or views of the individual except where they relate to another individual

- The views or opinions of another individual about the individual

- The individual's name where it appears with other personal information relating to the individual or where the disclosure of the name would reveal other personal information about the individual. [5]

The description of the personal information to be collected should also include such details as these:

- Does the information pertain to one individual or to a group of individuals?

- What is the approximate number of records to be collected for each customer?

- Is any third-party information involved? [5]

Purpose of the Collection

Purpose of the collection helps the organization to clearly focus information collection on only what is necessary to fulfill the requirements of the application or the function it serves. Limiting the collection to only this necessary information simplifies the process and adheres to fair information practices. Consideration should be given to the use of anonymous and pseudonymic techniques to alleviate the need to collect personal information.

How Is Notice of Collection Given and Informed Consent Obtained

Individuals must always be told when their personal information is being collected. Consent for the collection should be obtained before or at the time of collection. Sufficient information must be communicated about the purpose and process of the collection, retention, use, and disclosure of the information for the individual to understand what is actually involved. It is also vital to highlight whether the personal information will be shared with other organizations or linked to other databases.

Ideally, consent should be given expressly by the individual, but at times it can be reasonably implied by the fact that the individual has undertaken some action. For example, a consumer applying for a frequent flyer card could reasonably expect that all flights taken relating to that program will be noted and reported.

It is also key to ensure that the customers' consent is voluntary and informed. The customer must be knowledgeable enough to be able to weigh the advantages and disadvantages of providing the information in question. This ensures that consent is informed, and thus valid.

Method of Collection

Normally, personal information will and should be collected directly from the customer. If any personal information is collected indirectly (from some source other than the customer), it is important to justify the reasons for this to your customer and document the necessity for doing so.

It is important to identify any processes by which personal information is linked or matched with other previously collected information. Processes that transfer the information from the point of collection to another point for use and storage should also be identified.

Duration of the Collection of Personal Information

Many collections take place only at one time, but others do not. Some are limited in that there is a start and finish date to the collection, whereas others continue on an ongoing basis. Whenever possible, the collection should either be one time or limited in time because the continuous collection of information poses a threat to privacy. However, to fulfill the application's purpose or to ensure continued accuracy of the information, collection might sometimes have to be continuous.

Accuracy

Personal information must be verified by all appropriate means. Procedures within the application that ensure, as much as possible, the accuracy and timeliness of the personal information are key, not only from a business function perspective, but also to reassure the customer—to provide him or her with the security that actions based on the information will be correct. Where information is gathered and then transferred (collected through the customer completing a handwritten form and then having the data keyed into the computer), how will accuracy be ensured? Also, how do you ensure accuracy when the electronic version of the data is copied, transferred, or used in computations?

Method of Storage

The formats in which the information is to be stored are also important. Some possible options are on the card, in segregated fields on the card, in dispersed databases, or in a centralized database. Safeguards to protect personal information within the application or its associated procedures are again key to the integrity of the data and to the customers' comfort level in allowing the use of their personal information. The level and sophistication of the safeguards should be in keeping with the customer's perception of the sensitivity of the stored information. Not to be forgotten are the original paper forms or entry transactions if they must be retained for record-keeping purposes.

Key Personnel

Certain key personnel associated with the application are crucial to identify. For the individual providing the personal information, these would include the following:

- The overall custodian of the data, who is responsible for the ongoing assurance of privacy protection

- The person responsible for answering questions or resolving customer complaints

- Authorized users of the data along with the levels and types of access authorized for each type of user. [5]

Description of Procedures for Access and Correction

Two components of privacy protection that are extremely important to consider before an application is developed are customer access and correction. Too often customer access is not considered until the situation arises after implementation of the application and often at that point, it is too late. Certain decisions might have been made during the development phase that mean that access is either not possible or prohibitively difficult or expensive.

Procedures for Complaints and Appeals of Denial of Access or Correction

Most important to customers are procedures for addressing these concerns—customer service at its best. These concerns might take the form of complaints about how their personal information is being treated. Individuals might also be concerned about a decision to deny them access to information that they feel is theirs, or to deny a request to change information that they feel is incorrect. Addressing these concerns in a timely fashion not only improves customer satisfaction, but aids in ensuring the integrity of the information obtained—that it is not compromised by upset customers giving incomplete or incorrect information. Providing ways for individuals to opt out of the process or to opt in to only certain parts of the process is also of great benefit in achieving customer satisfaction.

Security

Security issues are not new to anyone in the advanced card technology industry. They form a key component of any application. Adapting previously held notions of security in a privacy context is the challenge because security is only one component of privacy. Access controls and features to prevent unauthorized or unintentional disclosure of information can also be used to enhance privacy. Strong encryption algorithms exist to prevent unauthorized access and extraction of information. The level of security provided by various techniques must be commensurate with the potential harm caused by breaches of access and disclosure restrictions, and ideally, should be under the control of the customer.

Privacy and Your Application

Each time you design a new application or modify an existing one, you should assess the impact of the application on privacy. It should become a natural part of your systems design process and will work well with your existing procedures. It starts by looking at each piece of data and determining who can access it and what they can do with that data element.

During the Design and Development of the Application

You start by identifying each piece of data that will reside on the computer or the card. You will find checklists in Tables 12.3 and 12.4 that you can erase, copy, and use during this phase of your application design. [5] On the check-list, *communicate* refers to transmitting data over a communications port. If your application was to gather frequent flyer points for a loyalty program, your checklist might include the fields shown in Table 12.3.

Table 12.3.   Gathering Frequent Flyer Points for a Loyalty Program

Data Field	Accessed By	Read Only	Add Data	Change	Delete	Copy	Print	Communicate
Card Owner Name	Card owner	Y	N	N	N	N	N	N
	Issuer (Airline)		Y	Y	Y	Y	Y	Y
	Travel agent	Y	N	N	N	N	N	N
Frequent Flyer Number	Card owner	Y	N	N	N	N	N	N
	Issuer (Airline)		Y	Y	Y	Y	Y	Y
	Travel agent	Y	N	N	N	N	N	N

Let's say the application is a health care card. Your fields might include those shown in Table 12.4.

Table 12.4.   Health care card application

Data Field	Accessed By	Read Only	Add Data	Change	Delete	Copy	Print	Communicate
Patient Name	Patient	Y	N	N	N	N	N	N
	Issuer		Y	Y	Y	Y	Y	Y
Drug Allergies	Doctor		Y	N	N	Y	Y	Y
	Nurse	Y	N	N	N	N	N	N

312

It is important to identify each piece of data but it is equally important to identify it by location. That is, if you specify the access rights of the field on the central computer, you must do the same for that data field on the smart, optical, or other advanced card, and also for any backup. Only then can you be assured that you have protected privacy relative to each piece of data.

When you have completed both this checklist and the privacy protection assessment checklist, you will have carefully and systematically planned for the protection of informational privacy for your application, and you will also have documented it! Congratulations—you're way ahead of the game now.

The Process of Implementing Privacy

Most of this part of the chapter deals with the design and development of advanced card applications, but let's take a moment to step back and look at protection of privacy as a corporate strategy.

Protection of Privacy as a Corporate Strategy

A key component of the successful development and implementation of privacy protection is the identification of a person who will be accountable for it within the organization. This designated individual might be your CIO, or you might designate this as the responsibility of another person within your organization. The designated person can also be responsible for the management and coordination of the information resources policies and procedures of the organization. In either case, the person in this position must have sufficient authority to be heard by your executive management and senior staff. This person must have a good general knowledge of the business functions and processes of your organization and knowledge of information management techniques and tools. This person will become the advocate for privacy protection within your organization and for specific applications.

Depending on the size and structure of your organization, the CIO or other designated person can assemble a team of people from across the organization to first develop and then implement privacy protection. It is important that the team not be made up solely of staff with communications, technical, or production responsibilities. Establishing broad policies and procedures requires input from all parts of the organization. Members of the team bring knowledge of the functions and processes of their part of the organization and take back both information about privacy protection and a commitment to making the principles work. Education of other staff and customers will become an important part of their role.

The Corporate Planning Phase

As with any project, the planning phase is extremely important, and it is best to start with what is already known. Before privacy protection principles can be successfully integrated into an organization's policies and procedures, a thorough understanding of those policies and procedures is essential. Any organization that has information gathering, processing, or distribution functions will undoubtedly have information handling policies and procedures, which will likely include some of the components of privacy protection. It is vital at this point to identify the components in place and those that must be introduced. To do this successfully, the team must know and understand privacy protection and particularly how it differs from such concepts as confidentiality and security.

Documenting the Privacy Protection Policies and Procedures Phase

Documentation is the most efficient and effective means of communicating the privacy protection of an organization to customers and staff. It can also provide a clear and concise record of how the process of protecting information is to take place. The documentation should be in a form to make it readily available to those who need it. This might mean brochure format for the customer, whereas the organization's staff is provided with a set of operational guidelines and procedures. To fully maintain the privacy protection phase, you need to do the following:

- To fully benefit from all the work you have done in the previous phases, you need to provide ongoing education for existing staff and training for new staff.

- You also need to periodically reinforce the importance of privacy to staff through such means as memos, internal newsletters, media clipping services, and internal case studies of both well-handled and poorly handled privacy-related issues.

- Periodic reviews and audits of established policies and procedures will give you an opportunity to acknowledge good practices and correct poor ones.

- A periodic review of your policies and procedures will reinforce your corporate strategy.

- Customer satisfaction surveys will show you where you are succeeding and where you are not, providing you with an opportunity to fine-tune your procedures if necessary.

- A periodic report should be made by the individual designated with responsibility for privacy protection.
- A presentation to senior management on the status of the program should include the number of inquiries, the number of complaints, and the outcome of the complaints. [5]

As the Internet is used increasingly as a platform for business transactions, security becomes a primary issue for Internet applications. Some applications are too sensitive for software-only security mechanisms. Higher levels of protection can be achieved with smart-card-based authentication schemes and transaction protocols. This part of the chapter provides examples of typical banking applications implemented with smart cards using symmetrical (DES) and asymmetrical (RSA) cryptography. A pure Java architecture is presented for such applications, which is intended for use on standard Web application servers and client devices enabled for Web browsing and the Java language. It employs applets on the client side to access smart cards via the OpenCard Framework (OCF). The applets communicate with authentication servlets or application servlets on the server side and act as a mediator between the smart card and the application logic on the server.

Using Smart Cards to Secure E-Business Applications

Initially, the Internet was used for academic research and military defense applications. Several years later, the first commercial use was to disseminate information such as company profiles, advertising, product catalogs, and specifications. All business transactions were still performed outside the Internet by means of traditional media—voice, fax, and paper forms. After several more years, interaction with businesses through the Internet became possible. Companies started to allow their customers to order goods or request services via the Internet. Banks introduced home banking and online brokerage applications using basic security functions for the Internet such as server authentication and the SSL. For identification and authentication, the user had to enter an identification string and a password. However, this traditional level of security is not sufficient for such sensitive business transactions on the Internet as payments and legally binding contracts.

As previously discussed, the EU and the United States have passed legislation to establish the conditions for making a digital signature the legally binding identification and authentication mechanism for contracts on the Internet.

The legislation requires that the technology employed not allow secret keys to be copied or used by nonauthorized parties. The consequence of this requirement is the need for a secure secret-key storage, if the digital signature is based on public key cryptography.

Smart cards are an ideal means to provide the required level of security. In recent years, smart card technology has quickly advanced and has now reached a state where smart cards easily integrate into PKIs. Today's smart cards provide memory up to 64 KB to store keys, certificates, and information, and they have cryptographic coprocessors that allow them to generate digital signatures using the RSA (encryption algorithm named for its creators: Rivest, Shamir, and Adleman) or Digital Signature Algorithm (DSA) algorithms with key lengths up to 1,024 bits or 19,844 bits. The Global System for Mobile Communications, derived from the Groupe Spécial Mobile (GSM) standard, uses smart cards as subscriber identification modules (SIMs) for user and service provider identification and authentication. Smart cards are used as an ID card for banking and credit card customers, company employees, or citizens. Standardized access methods such as Personal Computer/Smart Card (PC/SC) for Microsoft Windows and OCF for Java facilitate integration of smart cards in applications.

This part of the chapter first presents examples of smart-card-secured applications. To explain the architecture for such applications, authentication protocols are introduced involving smart cards as cryptographic tokens. Next, a brief discussion ensues about the major smart card types that adhere to these protocols and about the OCF. Finally, there is a discussion of how pure Java architecture is used for the development of smart-card-secured Web applications that use smart cards for user authentication and how to protect individual transactions.

Examples of New Secure Web Applications

Many of the existing Web applications protect the confidentiality of communication through encryption using the well-established SSL, Transport Layer Security (TLS), or Wireless Transport Layer Security (WTLS) protocols. This protection of confidentiality is efficient and considered adequate.

For user authentication, the currently established method employs a user identifier and password. A password provides only limited security because it can be stolen in many ways. An additional means of authentication, for example, through biometry (what you are) or through additional cryptographic hardware (what you possess), provides additional protection. A smart card used as a mobile personal cryptographic token is optimally suited for this purpose.

To secure an individual transaction, a password by itself is not sufficient. Less common methods have been applied in using passwords so far, (e.g., one-time passwords, as provided by the SecurID token from RSA, or transaction authorization numbers, both of which have to be manually fetched and entered by the user). To secure individual transactions and to achieve non-repudiation, a smart card is an attractive option.

Now, let's look at two examples of sensitive Web applications in which individual transactions are protected through digital signatures generated on a smart card and in which the users are authenticated using the same smart card. Obviously, Trojan horse attacks are a threat in both scenarios, especially when smart cards are used on PCs, which allow uncontrolled installation of software by users. However, the use of smart cards decreases the likelihood of successful fraud significantly. A Trojan horse might be able to obtain a PIN for a smart card, but it can only use that PIN in the presence of the smart card. Two common approaches to deal with the Trojan horse threat are the use of trusted devices to display and sign data and appropriate risk management.

Trusted devices used to display and sign data can entirely eliminate the risk of successful Trojan horse attacks. Such devices are usually tamper-evident, have their own display and PIN pad, and do not allow software updates at all, or at least not by unauthorized parties. To generate a signature, the trusted device receives the transaction to be signed (from a PC) and displays the relevant part of the data to the user. It prompts the user to enter the PIN, passes the PIN to the smart card, and lets the smart card generate the signature. The trusted device ensures that the PIN is never visible to the external world and that the user signs what he or she sees.

To avoid the higher cost for trusted devices, the provider of the system can decide to manage a higher risk instead. After identifying the threats and assessing the likelihood of fraud, he or she can calculate the amount of money at risk and reserve that amount to cover the risk. Because use of smart cards typically decreases the likelihood of fraud significantly, less risk has to be covered. Another option is to set up contracts so that the users of the system have to take the risk; that is, require users to control any software installed on their clients and make them responsible for any fraud that might happen if they fail.

Our solution examples were developed together with the Deutsche Bank AG, a member of the Identrus LLC global e-commerce trust organization. The PKI solutions have been based on the guidelines published by Identrus. This allows digital certificates and digitally signed documents created by these solutions to be exchanged with all Identrus member financial institutions.

The db-markets eTrade Project

The db-markets eTrade Project that an IBM Global Services team implemented recently is a typical example of a Web application for highly secure transactions for the money market. It provides the function of an electronic currency market and addresses the following requirements.

All currency brokers worldwide must be enabled to participate in a worldwide network using a standard Internet browser on their personal Windows-based systems. For accessing the central trading application, the broker must be identified by a highly secure authentication scheme. All data transfer must be encrypted using the secure variant of HTTP. In initiating an order, for example, to trade 458000.00 euros for 412965.32 U.S. dollars, all details of the transaction must be digitally signed by the broker together with the correct date and time. The eTrade application must send the data and the associated digital signature to the central bank trading site. At the central trading site, the order has to be validated and an acknowledgment sent to the broker within 10 seconds. Thus, both trading partners can be sure that the trade has been successfully processed. The client-side software for the application must be installable from a central server at the bank. The required hardware must be easy to deploy.

The required highly secure authentication scheme and digital signature call for the use of a cryptographic token. The eTrade system uses the IBM Digital Signature for the Internet (DSI) solution with the IBM MFC (Multi-Function Card) 4.22 smart card. DSI provides smart-card-based generation and verification of digital signatures supporting the two predominant Internet browsers, Netscape Communicator and Microsoft Internet Explorer. The application logic executed on the client side is a Java applet that uses the Java Native Interface to access the smart card through PC/SC and Windows-specific functions.

To initiate an eTrade transaction, a broker inserts his or her personal smart card into a smart card reader. Then the broker opens an Internet browser of choice and selects the db-markets eTrade Web page (*www.db-markets.de>*). If a client certificate is found on the smart card, this information is transmitted to the server and the login process begins. The server uses this certificate for client authentication as described later in the chapter. After successful client authentication, the broker receives an input mask, or screen, for a currency trade, which he or she has to complete (see Figure 12.1). [2]

Figure 12.1 An eTrade client application window.

When the broker has filled in the data for a trade order, the applet creates a message digest of the data and digitally signs this message digest on the smart card using the signing private key. The order data and the signature are transferred via the encrypted communication channel to the server, where the signature is verified. If it is correct, the business transaction is completed and an acknowledgment is sent back to the broker. For each transaction, a record together with the signature is filed in a database at the server. The record, including the validation and display of the digital signature, can be viewed by the bank and the broker.

Both trading parties benefit from the following advantages when using an e-business solution with digital signatures and certificates: A currency trade is settled within 10 seconds. All details are stored on the server in signed format. Both sides accept the basic terms of the trade and cannot repudiate them later.

Trojan horse attacks are possible, although quite complex to mount. Appropriate risk management must consider this risk.

The e-Safe Project

The e-Safe Project that an IBM Global Services team implemented for Deutsche Bank (Hannover, Germany) as a prototype, is another typical example of a Web application that requires use of smart cards. The purpose of the project was to prototype a secure Internet payment system relying on a trusted third party who is responsible for accepting payments on behalf of shops on the Internet. Because the e-Safe system handles all payment-related tasks, there is no need to provide the payment information to the shops. The address information of a consumer can be provided to the shops on a need-to-know basis.

Figure 12.2 shows how the e-Safe system works. [2] Before a consumer can use the e-Safe payment system, he or she has to be registered. Registration is usually done at the banks that also provide the e-Safe smart cards to consumers.

Once a consumer has been registered and has obtained a smart card, he or she can make e-Safe payments via the Internet. The consumer navigates to a shop site and selects the goods that he or she wants to buy. After filling the "shopping cart," he or she presses a button to start the payment process and is redirected to the payment page of the e-Safe Web site. The payment page summarizes the goods being purchased and shows a payment applet that asks the consumer to enter a PIN to approve the payment. The payment applet then sends the PIN to the smart card to activate the capability of the smart card to generate a digital signature. In the next step, the payment applet

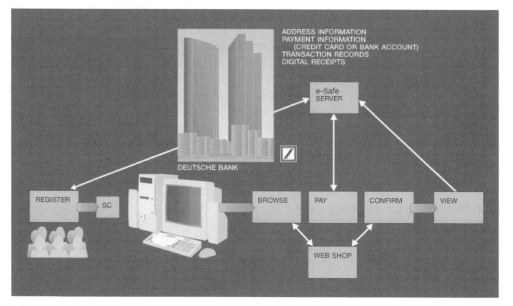

Figure 12.2 The e-Safe system.

requests a challenge from the server, provides it to the card, and lets the card generate a digital signature over the payment transaction record and the challenge. Finally, the payment applet sends the payment record and the digital signature back to the e-Safe server. The server verifies the signature, submits the payment transaction record for clearing, and generates and stores a digital receipt. In addition, it generates a payment confirmation for the shop and redirects the consumer's browser back to the shop site on the Web. The shop receives the payment confirmation and can initiate delivery of the goods.

The consumer can review and check his or her previous payment transactions and digital receipts at any time. To do this, the consumer logs in to the e-Safe server using the smart card. The login page contains an authentication applet that uses a protocol similar to the one described in the next part of the chapter. After successful authentication, the consumer has access to payment transaction statements and digital receipts.

Trojan horse attacks against this system are theoretically possible, but because the result of a transaction is always a transfer from a customer's bank account to a merchant's bank account, only registered merchants would be able to obtain money through fraudulent transactions. Because the concept is based on money transfers that can be canceled, customers could reject fraudulent transactions as soon as they realize inconsistencies exist on their bank account statements. In such a case of fraud, the merchant(s) who obtained money deceitfully could easily be identified. Optionally, trusted devices could be used to display and sign transactions to technically prevent Trojan horse attacks.

Smart-Card-Based Security

As you have seen in the preceding examples, the smart card provides two types of security services in both cases: user authentication and digital signature generation. Being essentially a tamper-resistant cryptographic token, the smart card is specifically designed to perform these services with a high level of security.

Authentication

Authentication of users means proving that users are who they say they are. There are various ways to implement authentication using a smart card, two of them are described in more detail here.

Authentication Using Smart Cards Without Public Key Cryptography. Although the use of public key cryptography allows a more straightforward authentication scheme, smart cards without public key cryptography capability are widely used. These simpler cards have considerably lower prices because they do not require the cryptographic coprocessor needed for executing public key cryptographic operations with reasonable speed.

The server gives a random challenge to the smart card and requests a message authentication code (MAC, a kind of signature) generated over the card ID and the challenge. Often, a password provided by the user has to be given to the smart card before the card generates the MAC. This procedure ensures that a thief or finder of a card cannot use it without knowledge of the password.

The smart card uses a key to generate the MAC over the card ID and the challenge obtained from the server. It sends both the ID and the MAC back to the server. The server uses the card ID to derive the card key from a master key and uses that card key to verify the MAC sent from the card. Figure 12.3 depicts this protocol. [2]

Authentication Using Public Key Smart Cards. With smart cards capable of public key cryptography, authentication can be performed as follows: The server sends a random challenge to the smart card. The smart card uses its private key to generate a digital signature over the challenge. The digital signature and the certificate associated with the private key of the smart card are sent to the server. The server verifies the certificate and then uses the public key contained in the certificate to verify the signature (see Figure 12.4). [2]

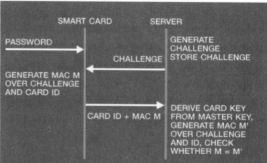

Figure 12.3
Authentication protocol for Smart Cards without public key cryptography.

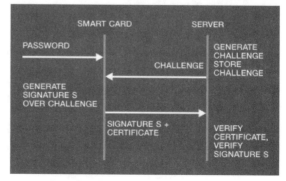

Figure 12.4
Authentication protocol for Public Key Smart Cards

Digital Signature Using Smart Cards

As you have seen from the two application examples, the eTrade transactions in the money market and the e-Safe transactions of the consumers are digitally signed to protect those transactions against modification and repudiation. Any change to the transaction data would cause the verification of the signature to fail. The person who initiated the transaction cannot reasonably repudiate his or her action, because only the person holding the smart card and knowing the password to unlock the signature generation capability of the card can initiate the transaction.

A smart-card-based digital signature requires public key cryptography to be installed on the smart card. For any data to be digitally signed, a cryptographic one-way function, (e.g., Secure Hash Algorithm-1 [SHA-1]) is used to create a hash that is signed by the card using the private signature key stored inside the card. Only the cardholder can sign an order or a statement, but everyone can check the signature using the corresponding public key.

To guarantee nonrepudiation and message integrity, the private key must be stored securely so that only the rightful user can access it. If any other person could obtain a copy of the private key, he or she could impersonate the rightful user's signature.

The most secure place to store such a private key is within a cryptographic hardware unit. A smart card is the most convenient and most portable cryptographic hardware unit. Public key smart cards are able to perform the signing operation inside the card. At the same time, it is not possible to obtain the private signature key without a prohibitively difficult technical effort. Usually, smart-card-based systems are designed so that obtaining a private signature key would be so expensive that fraud does not pay. To ensure that the private key never exists outside the smart card, legislation in some countries requires that it must be generated inside the smart card.

The emerging legislation for digital signatures has significant regional differences. Several countries require that the device used for the signature be tamper-resistant or at least tamper-evident. This requirement not only includes the storage of the private key, but also the hardware and software that displays the content to be signed and prompts the cardholder to initiate the signing by entering the signature PIN.

Common Smart Card Types

In recent years, many brands and types of smart cards have come to market. Several major categories can be identified: simple file-system-oriented smart cards without public key capability, advanced file system smart cards with

Chapter 12 • Digital Signatures

public key capability, Java Cards, Windows-powered smart cards, and multi application operating system (MULTOS) cards.

Simple File System Smart Card. File system smart cards provide a file system where reading and writing of files can be protected by various access conditions. These cards support only symmetric cryptographic algorithms such as Data Encryption Standard (DES) or Triple DES, for example.

To use such a simple file system smart card for authentication, a file containing the card ID can be created on the card with special access conditions. These access conditions must allow that file to be read so that the result is returned together with a MAC of the result combined with a random challenge passed to the card. This allows running a protocol as explained earlier and shown in Figure 12.3. Examples of simple file system smart cards are the IBM MFC 4.1 and the German GeldKarte. Cards of this category are available from every major smart card manufacturer.

File System Card With Public Key Cryptography. File-system cards with public key cryptography capability can store private keys and associated certificates. Key pairs are usually created in the card, and the private key never leaves the card. It is only used internally for generating digital signatures or decrypting session keys or small amounts of data.

To use file system cards with public key cryptography capability for authentication, a private key and an associated certificate must be present in the card. This allows use of a protocol as explained earlier and shown in Figure 12.4. Examples of file system smart cards with public key capability are the IBM MFC 4.22, IBM MFC 4.3, Gemplus GPK4000, Gemplus GPK8000, and others from Schlumberger, Giesecke & Devrient, and so forth.

Java Card. A Java Card allows the creation of custom commands on the card. The programs implementing the custom commands are card applets that are implemented using a subset of the Java programming language, relying on Java libraries tailored for use in smart cards.

A Java Card can host several applets. Off-card applications can select an applet on the card by specifying the application ID of the applet. After that, the off-card applications communicate directly with the selected applet.

To use a Java Card for authentication, the card must contain an applet that exposes an appropriate interface to the external world (a command that can be parameterized with a challenge), returning a digital signature over the challenge and a command to obtain certificates stored in the card. This functionality allows the kind of protocol explained earlier and shown in Figure 12.4.

An example of a Java Card is the Gemplus GemXPresso card. A contactless Java Card has recently been developed in the IBM Zurich Research Laboratory.

Windows for Smart Card. Smart cards with the Windows for Smart Card operating system allow the implementation of custom commands. It is possible to implement commands that use functions from the internal cryptographic library of the card to provide a function for generating digital signatures, storing, and reading certificates. This functionality also allows for PKI authentication protocols as explained earlier and shown in Figure 12.4. Windows for Smart Card was developed by Microsoft; cards implementing this operating system are available from Schlumberger and several other providers.

MULTOS Smart Card. A MULTOS smart card provides a file system interface and, in addition, an execution environment for custom applications. Application developers can create these custom applications using a new language called MULTOS Executable Language (MEL). Assembler language can be used with MEL; for C and the Java language, a translator to MEL is provided. The MULTOS specification is licensed and controlled by the MAOSCO Consortium.

The OCF

An important base for the pure Java architecture presented earlier is the OCF, which has become the standard interface for smart card applications written in Java. IBM developed the first prototype of the framework in 1997. Also in 1997, IBM, Sun Microsystems, Netscape Communications Corporation, and others founded the OpenCard Consortium to establish the OCF as a de facto standard for accessing smart cards from Java. In 2000, the consortium released OCF Version 1.2 and OpenCard for Embedded Devices 1.2. With version 1.2, OCF has reached comprehensive functionality and stability.

OCF permits smart card applications to be implemented in Java. It makes these applications independent from the details of whatever smart card is used and of the device that is used to access the smart card (usually referred to as a smart card terminal, smart card reader, smart card acceptance device, or interface device). To achieve this independence, OCF encapsulates the details of diverse smart cards with equivalent function in the abstraction CardService and details of diverse access devices (physical card terminals) in the abstraction CardTerminal (see Figure 12.5). [2]

Every OCF CardTerminal provides the functions required when accessing a smart card; for example, resetting the card, obtaining the answer to reset, sending data packets to the card, and obtaining the response. There are OpenCard CardTerminal drivers for virtually all PC smart card readers on the market. For several smart card readers, there is a pure-Java card terminal implementation available. All readers that can be used on Windows32-bit platforms through PC/SC15 can be used from OCF via a generic PC/SC CardTerminal for OpenCard that provides a bridge to the PC/SC card terminal interface.

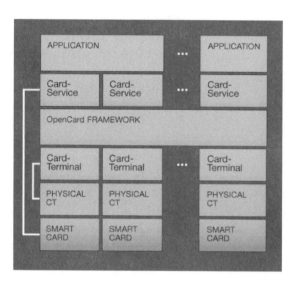

Figure 12.5
The OpenCard framework.

To achieve independence from the specifications of particular card manufacturers, CardServices are used. Card service interfaces can be defined for particular sets of smart card functions. Two interfaces that are defined in the OCF itself are the File Access Interface and the Signature Interface; the first allows files to be accessed on a smart card and the latter allows digital signatures to be generated. Once a card service interface has been defined, various card service implementations that implement this interface can be developed for different makes of cards.

The main purpose of the OCF is for use on the client side of Web applications, running in a Java applet. The most advantageous way to deploy the OCF in such an application is to install the OCF and the required card terminal classes locally on the client by adding the OpenCard Java archive (JAR) files and executables to the paths of the browser. The card services to be used are usually packaged with the applet JAR file that is deployed on the application server.

 **Tip**

The OCF is available at www.opencard.org.

Application Architecture

Earlier in this chapter, two examples of Web applications were introduced that achieve a high level of security through the use of a smart card on the client side, eTrade and e-Safe. Both applications use smart-card-based authentication and digital signatures. Both applications use Java applets on the client side.

The architecture of both applications differs in several respects, however. The eTrade application does not require portability of the client part to operating systems other than Windows. Consequently it uses an architecture that exploits components that are found in Windows operating systems, most notably the smart card access layers provided by PC/SC.15 The eTrade application uses the IBM Digital Signature for the Internet (DSI) solution, which internally uses the PC/SC application programming interfaces (APIs). Toward the calling applications, DSI provides the Public-Key Cryptography Standard #11 (PKCS #11) API, a C-language interface that is used by Netscape Communicator and Netscape Messenger. The PKCS #11 interface is also available to applets through Java wrappers. For the Microsoft Internet Explorer browser, DSI offers the Microsoft CryptoAPI.

The e-Safe application only uses the Java language and does not impose any restrictions on the platform for the clients and for the servers. Therefore, the e-Safe application can easily be offered on such diverse Java-powered devices as, for example, Internet appliances, communicating PDAs, or network computers. Because an HTTP-based protocol is used for communication between client and server, the use of Java on either side does not require using Java on the other side. These decisions are also independent of using a Java Card or any other smart card.

Now, let's focus on this pure Java architecture, which is applicable for Web applications based on the servlet and JavaServer Pages (JSP) technologies. Such applications use the following pattern: The browser sends a request for an HTML document and displays it to the user. In the document, there might be links or forms that refer to servlets. When the user clicks on such a link or submits such a form, the browser sends a request to the appropriate servlet. The servlet processes the request and invokes a single JSP to display the result to the user. The HTML page generated by the JSP is displayed in the browser; it might contain further links or forms. Clicking on these links or submitting these forms starts a new cycle. A page generated by a JSP can contain applets, which in turn can initiate communication with the server from which they originate.

Figure 12.6 shows a component overview with respect to the smart-card-based authentication. [2] A user who wants to use a smart card for authentication to Web applications must have a smart card reader connected to his or her client device. The client device can be a personal computer or an Internet appliance, for example. The Web browser of the device must be enabled for smart card access. For the Java-based architecture discussed here, the Web browser needs to support Java applets and to enable the applets to access the smart card. The OCF or OpenCard for Embedded Devices provides this access for applets.

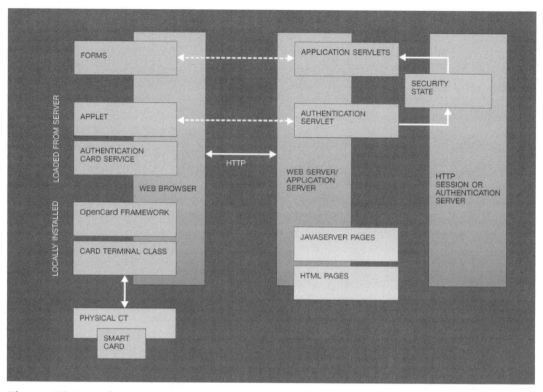

Figure 12.6 Architecture overview.

It can be part of the preinstalled software stack of the device, provisioned via the service management framework of the device (as, e.g., specified by the Open Services Gateway Initiative [OSGI]), or user installed. In addition, the device must have appropriate driver software installed to make the card reader available to applications. This software will in most cases be the associated pure Java CardTerminal. For PCs running one of the Windows32-bit operating systems, alternatively PC/SC plus a PC/SC interface device can be installed.

Card services that encapsulate the application protocol of the smart card are packaged in a JAR file, together with the applets that use them. This JAR file is deployed on the Web application server and will be downloaded on demand.

On the server side, in addition to the application servlets, HTML pages, and JSP, an authentication servlet must be deployed. This servlet implements the server-side authentication protocol logic and provides a security state on successful authentication of a user, for example, by putting it into the HTTP session. Security-aware application servlets can then access the security state before performing sensitive functions. Figure 12.7 shows the mechanism that is executed. [2]

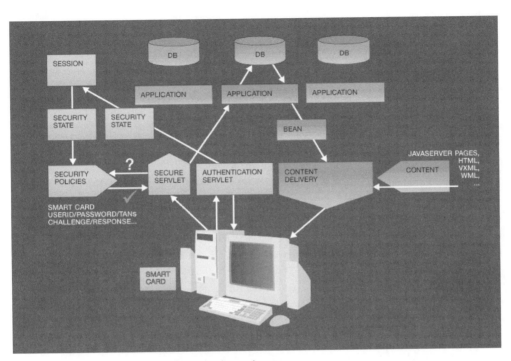

Figure 12.7 Secure access for a Web application.

When the user logs in, a page with the authentication applet is displayed in his or her browser. If the smart card requires a password, the authentication applet prompts the user to enter the password and provides it to the card before starting the actual authentication protocol. The authentication protocol is executed between the smart card and the Authentication Servlet, mediated by the authentication applet. If the user has been successfully authenticated, the authentication servlet adds a security state to the session to indicate that the user has been authenticated.

When the user navigates to a page that invokes a security-aware servlet, the servlet checks whether the security state stored in the session is sufficient to perform the operation. If it is, the servlet invokes the appropriate application logic. Figure 12.8 shows an example where several application servlets access the security state in a session once the authentication servlet has established it. [2]

IBM's WebSphere Application Server allows for single sign-on using custom authentication methods. A servlet that implements custom authentication can call the appropriate API function to perform a single sign-on login. Thus, a slight change in the authentication servlet allows taking advantage of the WebSphere single sign-on and clustering features. Instead of accessing the security state in the session, the authentication servlet would have to use the

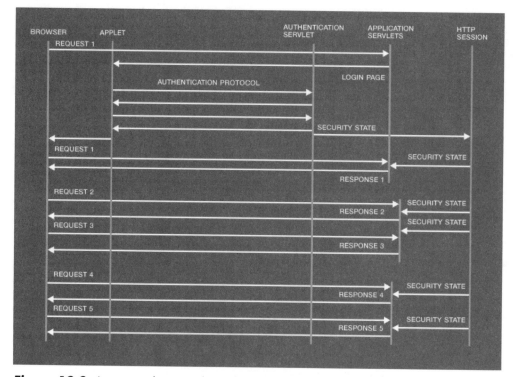

Figure 12.8 Interaction between the authentication servlet and application servlets via the session.

single sign-on API to call on the WebSphere Lightweight Third Party Authentication mechanism.

Nowadays, many systems need a portable media to store some sensible data, such as smart cards. The information can be protected by the user with his or her PIN, or through biometrics. Unfortunately, there is not a smart card today that can verify the biometric template inside it, performing this task in the terminal. This next part of the chapter discusses algorithms and data structures that are needed to solve this problem. Therefore, a smart card with user biometric authentication is presented here, based on an Open Platform smart card (in this case, a Java Card). To achieve these results, different biometric techniques have been studied: speaker verification, hand geometry, and iris recognition. Experimental results are given here to show the viability of the prototype developed.

Using Biometrics in Smart Card Information and Operations

When an IT system needs to store some information in a distributable way, one of the possibilities is to give each user an identification token that stores his or her personal information, as well as any other information requested by the system designed. Some of that information, such as financial data, health care records, and so on, should be protected by the user who owns the card (the cardholder). This protection is usually made with card holder verification keys, which are closely related to the user's PIN. In a smart card, security with this kind of key can involve allowing or denying not only access to some information, but also the possibility of performing some operations, such as a debit from an electronic purse. However, this protection is better because a smart card has the ability to block access for life if a determined number of wrong presentations of the PIN has been reached.

Unfortunately, PINs as passwords can be copied by inspecting the cardholder movements as he or she enters his or her number in, for example, an ATM. The only way to perform a real user authentication is through biometrics. However, biometric verification is just starting to be found in commercial smart cards—it's not quite there yet. The only efforts being applied in this line are to store the user's template inside a smart card, protected with administrative keys, and extracted from the card by the terminal to perform the verification.

This part of the chapter presents works being carried on by researchers to achieve a new authentication system in which the user's template is stored inside a smart card, with the same level of protection as any other key. Then, when the user wants to authenticate himself or herself to the card, he or she asks for such an operation, giving one biometric sample, which is verified inside the card. If the verification is positive, the card allows the access to the biometrically protected information and operations.

To develop the prototype, let's look at different biometric techniques first. Then, the results obtained with those techniques are compared to obtain restrictions to its integration inside a smart card. After that, the way the integration has been performed is explained, giving the results obtained with three different Open Operating System smart cards.

Biometric Techniques Attempted

As previously explained in Chapter 11, "Biometrics," biometrics refers to identifying a human being through biological and behavioral parameters. Therefore, a lot of biometric techniques now exist, such as fingerprint, hand geometry, voice, iris, retinal scanning, written signature, and so on.

It is not really useful to consider one technique much better than any other, because each technique has its own characteristics that make it suitable for specific environments. Nevertheless, several biometric techniques have been studied and many commercial systems available have been tested by the German BKA Office. In these results, iris recognition was proven to achieve the best accuracy, although the cost of any of the commercial systems available makes it unviable for most situations.

Now, to obtain general conclusions about the possibility of integrating biometric authentication inside a smart card, several techniques must be looked at first. Of these, three are examined here: speaker recognition, hand geometry, and iris identification. This part of the chapter is intended to give an overall introduction to each of these three techniques.

Speaker Recognition

In this technique, the user's voice is captured with a microphone, then preprocessed and passed through a block that is in charge of extracting the spectrum coefficients. From all the verification methods being applied to the human voice for speaker recognition, researchers are using the Gaussian Mixture Model (GMM), due to its lower memory requirements and better results.

To obtain the user's template, 60 seconds of continuous speech from the user should be taken to train the GMM. Once trained, only three seconds of the user's speech are needed to perform the biometric verification.

The user's template is 175 bytes long, whereas the sampling utterance that is passed to the verification algorithm (the GMM), is 3,600 bytes long. Considering the computation time spent, the enrollment phase (when the user's template is extracted) lasts for about 1,100 seconds, and the time needed for the verification is 16 seconds. Unfortunately, the error rates obtained for a one-time verification process (if the first verification fails, the user is rejected) are above 10%, obtaining an equal error rate of 20.3%.

Hand Geometry

The hand geometry technique is based on taking a photograph of the user's hand. The hand is placed on a platform painted in blue to increase contrast with all kinds of skin. Six tops are placed on the platform to guide the hand in front of the medium-resolution digital camera. The contour of the hand is obtained using edge-extraction algorithms. Thanks to a mirror located on the right of the platform, the lateral view of the hand is also obtained and its contour extracted.

Several measurements are performed on both contours, obtaining a feature vector of 25 bytes. With five photographs from his or her hand, the user's template is computed, depending on the verification method used. The methods tested have been (a) the Euclidean distance, (b) the Hamming distance, and (c) GMM. The results obtained can be seen in Table 12.5. [3]

Table 12.5. Speaker Recognition Test Results

	Template Size	Sample Size	Enrollment Time	Verification Time	Equal Error Rate (in %)
Euclidean Distance	25 B	25 B	37 s	7.5 ms	16.4
Hamming Distance	50 B		37.1 s	10 ms	8.3
GMM	510 B		37.5 s	30 ms	6.5

Human Iris

Of all the biometric techniques known today, the most promising is iris identification due to its low error rates (nearly null FAR) and because it is not invasive. A high-resolution photograph of the user's eye is taken and preprocessed to extract the inner and outer boundaries of the iris. After that, Gabor filters are used to extract the feature vector, which is 233 bytes long.

The user's template is obtained from a single sample, and the Hamming distance is used to verify the samples with the template stored. Both the template and the sample size are 233 bytes. The enrollment time is determined by the preprocessing and feature extraction blocks, which can be optimized from the results obtained in the prototype that's been developed (142 seconds). The verification lasts 9 ms. The FRR for one-time verification is 3.51% with a null FAR.

 Tip

The results given about these three techniques, especially those referring to the time spent in the algorithms, have been obtained with the execution of the

*algorithms in a PC through the programs developed in a mathematical develop-
ment software called MATLAB. Unfortunately, this development system,
although having many advantages, does not obtain a good performance in computation time, and those results can be easily bettered by coding those algorithms in C or C++.*

Comparison Among Results

From the results achieved with the preceding techniques, several conclusions
can be obtained focusing on the possibility of integrating biometric authentication into a smart card:

- Due to the sample vector size and verification times, speaker recognition
  is not considered a viable technique for the purposes stated in this book.
  Also, the error rates achieved should be improved.

- Error rates obtained with the Euclidean distance in the hand geometry
  technique are not good enough to consider it for a medium- or high-security system. However, due to its simple verification algorithm, it could be
  interesting to integrate this technique in a three-time retry authentication
  method, therefore improving the error rates.

- Hand geometry and iris identification, both with Hamming distances,
  seem to fit perfectly with the purposes of this part of the chapter.

- Hand geometry with GMMs achieve really good results. However, its
  computation cost and the need to use floating-point operations eliminate
  the possibility of integrating it inside a smart card. Further work should
  be applied to enable this possibility. [3]

Integration Inside a Smart Card

To perform the integration, two possibilities exist: building a whole new mask,
which is a very expensive process, but is able to achieve the best results; or
using an Open Operating System smart card, such as a Java Card, which is a
less expensive process, but has certain constraints based on the platform used.
The second way is being used here to implement the biometric authentication
inside a smart card, using three different products from two different manufacturers.

The main difference between one of the cards from one manufacturer and
the other two cards used is the processor architecture. Whereas the other two

use a 16-bit CISC processor, the other one uses a 32-bit RISC processor. The prototypes implemented were built with the following elements:

- Some environmental variables that indicate blocking, successful verification, number of maximum and remaining tries, possibility of unblocking, and so on, of the biometric template.
- CREATE-TEMPLATE-FILE function which creates the file where the user's template is going to be stored, giving some parameters, such as the algorithm that applies to perform the verification.
- WRITE-TEMPLATE-FILE function that writes the data corresponding to the user's template, including the maximum number of erroneous verifications allowed. This function is based on the UPDATE-BINARY standard function.
- PERSONAL-AUTHENTICATION function. This function was coded as the standard function accepted by the industry.
- TEMPLATE -UNBLOCK function, which can be executed only if the template file is defined as having the possibility of being unblocked. This will depend on the level of security needed by the application where the card is going to be used.
- Several testing commands to verify the proper functioning of the prototype. [3]

All these elements have been developed following the available standards, such as ISO 7816. The results obtained with the three cards mentioned in the preceding (sorted in two categories according to the architecture of the processor) can be seen in Table 12.6. [3]

Table 12.6. Test Results of the Three Cards

	RISC	CISC	
Size of the prototype code	2,121	1,511	B
Authentication time (hand geometry, Euclidean distance)	5.11	121	ms
Authentication time (hand geometry, Hamming distance)	30.1	127	ms
Authentication time (iris identification)	7.11	1,230	ms

Three main considerations should be made from these results. The first one is that hand geometry with GMMs has not been covered. This has been impossible because Java Card specifications do not accept floating-point operations. The second consideration is that times obtained with the RISC processor are much lower than the ones obtained with the CISC processor, enabling sophisticated verification methods in the near future. Unfortunately, the high cost of RISC processor manufacturing precludes this version of the card from usage. The last consideration is that verification time obtained with the CISC processor, which is higher than an acceptable time of half a second, can be easily lowered by optimizing the binary functions in the Java Card platform.

Now, let's look at how optical memory cards provide secure identification. In other words, robust and secure optical cards using lithographic and laser technology have found wide application in personal identification.

Optical Memory Cards

Optical discs are familiar objects, but optical cards are much less well-known. Optical cards offer many of the recording capabilities of the disc format plus several significant and unique features. The shape and flexibility of the cards are similar to that of credit cards (see Figure 12.9). [4] Optical cards offer a durable platform, which, unlike an optical disc, can be conveniently carried in a wallet and can carry secure, unalterable digital data that can include images as well as text. Unlike the spinning disc, the optical card uses a rectilinear format in which the tracks are arrayed something like the lines on a ruled sheet of paper with each track being numbered (see Figure 12.10). [4]

Figure 12.9
Exploded view of the optical head shows the laser path between the reader and a typical optical card.

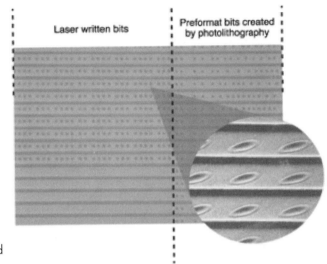

Laser written bits

Preformat bits created by photolithography

Figure 12.10
Track guides and numbers are preformatted by photolithography, and the variable data is written by laser.

To read data from the card, a shuttle moves the card along the track direction at a rate of 1 m/s in a bidirectional fashion. The format permits true random access. Track-to-track translations are achieved by movement of the optical head in the cross-track direction with seek times as fast as 2 ms.

Optical cards find use in many portable data storage applications, with the largest usage being in secure personal identification cards—for example, the U.S. Permanent Resident Card ("green card") and the Italian national ID card. Conforming to ISO standards for identification cards, optical memory cards offer a user data capacity of 2.9 MB, which is much higher than that available on magnetic stripe cards (270 bytes) or smart cards (up to 16 KB). To remain compatible with existing infrastructures and for increased versatility in many applications, the optical card can also include a magnetic stripe or integrated circuit chip.

Optical Memory Card Media

The recording media used in the optical card is based on silver halide photographic film. Formatting of the media is achieved by photographic processes prior to the encapsulation of the media into cards. The photographic formatting process also allows for the creation of other visible high-resolution (12,000 dpi) images in the media, which cannot be replicated by printing processes. The finished optical media is of the write-once, read-many type (see Figure 12.11). [4]

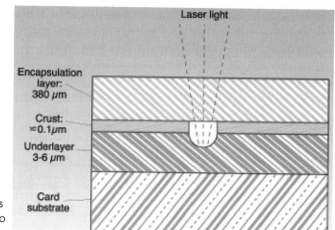

Figure 12.11
The impinging laser beam records bits through the crust of the media and into the underlayer.

On top of the card substrate there are three layers: an encapsulation layer, a crust, and an underlayer. The encapsulation layer is a 380-μm laminated polycarbonate film. The crust consists of silver grains of filamentary and spherical shapes dispersed in an organic colloid. The underlayer consists of the same organic colloid, but it is essentially devoid of silver particles. The underlayer thermally insulates the reflective crust and increases the laser recording sensitivity. Data bits are recorded with a 780-nm semiconductor laser that causes agglomeration of the silver particles, reducing their covering power and hence the reflectivity of the media. Secondarily, thermal deformation of the colloidal binder results in the formation of a pit.

The laser-recorded pits are 2.5 μm in diameter. Although this is large compared to bit sizes used on optical discs, the card is intended to withstand rugged use, such as being carried in a wallet for a period of years. In such applications, the larger bit size and the 12-μm track-pitch confer a degree of robustness that could not be achieved with the geometries normally used on optical discs. To further enhance reliability, a pulse-position modulation (PPM) recording scheme is utilized rather than the pulse-width modulation (PWM) scheme often used on optical discs. Because optical cards can be carried in a wide range of environmental conditions, the PPM recording scheme renders the card less vulnerable to media sensitivity changes or changes in laser output brought about by exposure of the card or read/write drive to environmental extremes.

The Optical Card Drive

The drive is supplied as a peripheral to a personal computer, connected via a Small Computer System Interface (SCSI) card (see Figure 12.12). [4] To the user, the use of the optical card drive is no different from that of a CD-R drive.

Once again, the optical card drive design differs from a typical optical disc system in that the card is designed for maximum durability when carried by the holder. To this end, the drive incorporates a more powerful error-correction code than the Reed–Solomon codes normally used for optical discs. The burst error for satellite transmission code used on optical cards requires a significant overhead, so that the 4.1 MB raw data capacity of the card is reduced to 2.9 MB user data capacity. This enables data to be read from cards that have been damaged from extended use.

The fact that each track on the card is numbered opens up possibilities for novel security measures. For added security in a given application, a unique track numbering scheme different from that specified in the ISO standard can be created. The firmware of the drive is then modified to allow access to the nonstandard tracks for writing to and reading from the card. Thus, the card and drive combination can be specific to the application. The card-issuing authority controls the drives used in its particular application. A forger cannot use a standard drive to make fraudulent cards.

This control measure is inexpensive, requiring only the creation of a master tool for the unique track numbering of the card and a custom firmware chip for the drive. As an added safety measure, the custom firmware chip can be locked by a serial number to a given drive. If the chip is removed from a drive and substituted into a different drive, it will not operate. Most government applications use some version of the unique track numbering scheme to fore-

DRIVE CHARACTERISTICS		LASER CHARACTERISTICS		CARD CHARACTERISTICS	
Data capacities	2.86 Mbytes (4.11 Mbytes without EDAC)	Laser wavelength	830 nm	Track guide pitch	12.0 μm
		Laser power	40 mW	Track guide width	2.5 μm
Card format standard	ISO/IEC 11693 and 11694 Parts 1–4	Nominal read power	200 μW	Outer track beam spacing Cross track dimension	9.5 μm
		Nominal write power	13 mW	Along track dimension	126 μm
Read speed	8.9 kbytes/sec			Bit diameter	2.5 μm
Write speed	4.2 kbytes/sec	Nominal write pulse width	2 μW	Baseline reflectivity	45%
Access time	250 msec (overall width)			Contrast ratio	< 40%
	3 msec (track to track)	Focused beam size	1.8 x 2.25 μm I/e^{-2}	Card polycarbonate cover layer thickness	380 μm
Corrected error rate	less than 10^{-12}				

Figure 12.12 Optical drive and card specifications.

339

stall attempts to make fraudulent cards, as well as to prevent unauthorized access to the data on a genuine card.

Drives can be built as read only or read/write to meet the requirements of the application. For example, applications can use drives capable of writing at a card-issuing location, whereas the drives in use for card verification in the field are read-only.

Optical Card Applications

Optical cards are used in a wide range of portable data storage applications, but the largest usage is for secure identification. This application makes full use of the ability to create visible high-resolution images and watermarks in the optical media at resolutions up to 12,000 dpi, thereby preventing fraudulent duplication of the card by printing or copying techniques. The large data storage capacity of an optical card, compared to other card technologies, allows for recording of multiple identification features such as photographs, fingerprints, and signatures.

In addition, it is possible to create a laser-etched, visibly recognizable graphic in the media itself, irreversibly marking the memory with the identity card holder—a unique security feature (see Figure 12.13). [4] Such images are recorded using the laser card drive. The diffraction pattern created by the recorded pits results in a highly visible image on the optical media. This image cannot be altered because the medium is not erasable, and the permanent laser etching can be compared to the more readily changeable colored photographic image that can also be printed on the card. The visibility of the laser

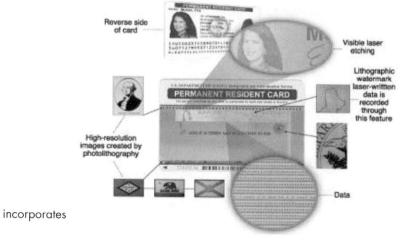

Figure 12.13
The optical memory card incorporates many security features.

etching can be further enhanced by the use of a viewer, which relies on a simple light source and diffraction effects.

Future Developments

Current optical card hardware is intended for use at home, in offices, or in vehicles. Future developments will include battery-powered, hand-held readers. For example, authorities could use such portable readers to authenticate optical cards in the field. These smaller readers would be made possible by the availability of small-scale optics and integrated packages.

Finally, let's take a look at whether there really is a need for a national ID card to prevent and protect individuals and corporations from identity theft. Will this type of card just make matters worse? In other words, the debate over a national identification card has repeatedly, and unfortunately, been cast as Big Brother vs. civil liberties.

The National ID Card: Is Big Brother Watching?

The fact is the United States already has a de facto national ID card, and it is called the driver's license. Americans also have a de facto national ID number, and it is called the Social Security number. The problem, however, is that neither the license nor the Social Security card was designed to act as such. The information systems used to issue the licenses and to store and process personal information related to licenses, were not developed with the idea that the cards would be used as an ID card. It's time they are.

There should be an end to the national ID card debate; states, with input from the federal government to ensure compatibility across borders, should recognize that a driver's license is used to verify an individual's identity and design a secure card using biometrics and tamper-proof technology. The public most likely would not oppose such a move. First, Americans are accustomed to using their licenses as ID cards. Second, a majority are in favor of some national ID card. Just days after the September 11, 2001 terrorist attacks, a Pew Research Center survey found that 70% of Americans favored a national ID card. Much of the support could be attributed to the initial fear generated by the attacks. A later survey by Fabrizio, McLaughlin and Associates Inc., found that 51% of Americans favor a national ID card.

Some members of Congress, civil libertarians, and academics have argued that the card would have done little to deter terrorists or prevent terrorism. That might be true. Applying biometrics and other technologies to licenses, however, would make it more difficult to fraudulently copy licenses, which gives the license the type of security it needs.

The Social Security Administration and Congress also should acknowledge that the Social Security card is used as identification and is easily forged. The same technology used to secure driver's licenses should be applied to these cards. By conceding that these cards are used to verify someone's identity, Congress and state governments would take a big step toward, if not deterring criminals, at least making it harder for them to hide their identities.

True Colors or True Lies?

Ten days after terrorists transformed passenger jets into bombs in attacks on the World Trade Center and the Pentagon, Oracle Corporation CEO Larry Ellison touched off a technological and political furor by suggesting that airline travel could never again be safe until everyone in the United States (citizen and guest alike) was required to present a national ID card to board a plane. The consensus was, and still is, that there is a need for a national ID card with a photograph and thumbprint digitized and embedded in the ID card.

Immediate reactions to Ellison's proposal tended to focus on the political issues of privacy and civil liberties. Almost instantly, it seemed, an ad hoc alliance of strange bedfellows (archconservatives, libertarians, and civil libertarians) spontaneously formed in opposition to the idea of the government issuing a national ID. Although U.S. Attorney General John Ashcroft initially suggested the government might entertain the idea, only days later, the White House announced that President Bush was "not considering it at this time."

However, many others were considering it. Among them was a Harvard Law School professor, Alan Dershowitz, a leading civil libertarian. Dershowitz startled many fellow liberals when he published an op-ed piece in the October 13, 2001 issue of *The New York Times*, asking "Why Fear National ID Cards?" Dershowitz argued for an optional national identity card on the merits of a social trade-off: a little less anonymity for a lot more security. He indicated that a national ID could be an effective tool for preventing terrorism, reducing the need for other law enforcement mechanisms (especially racial and ethnic profiling) that pose even greater dangers to civil liberties.

A sense of national emergency has confounded traditional political ideologies and kept the idea alive. However, as the social debate plays itself out, the focus has quietly shifted to an IT reality check: What kind of card, if any, tied to what kind of database or network might be feasible in terms of technology and cost?

Not surprisingly, the news media focused on Ellison's offer to supply Oracle database software for a national ID system at no charge—an offer that was made to avoid any appearance of profiteering from the war on terrorism. Sun Microsystems, Inc. CEO Scott McNealy quickly backed the notion of a national ID—but one built on distributed smart devices using Java to execute authentication algorithms.

It's not clear if the government could legally take Ellison up on his offer (or if Oracle's software would even be the right solution) but as technologists and government bureaucrats got down to the business of investigating what it would take to implement a national ID card, it quickly became apparent that database software and network architecture were the least of their worries. The real challenge is getting all the various vendors and contractors to agree on interoperability issues—not to mention finding a way to ensure that the data you put in the card is credible in the first place. Neither of those is as simple as it might seem.

The General Services Administration is overseeing a $2.6 billion project to issue 4 million digital IDs to the U.S. military by the end of 2004. The experience gained from that initiative (and, just as important, the standards that result from it) is widely expected to determine the future of global identification systems.

In many ways, instituting a national ID would amount to a typical IT initiative riddled with frustratingly mundane issues: card durability and data capacity; cost and availability of readers; ubiquitous connectivity to an array of government and private-sector databases; and, of course, the ever-present bogeyman in any network architecture, the security of the technology itself. Of all these potential stumbling blocks, the card itself is the most important, because it determines the kind of reader that will go with it. Alas, there's no unanimity yet on the best type of card.

Asking which is the best kind of card is kind of like asking what's the best religion. For example, the typical magnetic stripe encoding used on credit cards can hold only about 275 bytes of information; and, as millions of frustrated consumers can attest, magnetic stripes often lose data, typically at the most inconvenient times, and have to be shipped back to the bank for data recovery. On the other hand, the cards are inexpensive to produce, and readers are inexpensive and ubiquitous among retailers and service providers throughout the world.

One alternative, the two-dimensional barcode card, can hold as much as 2 KB of data, enough to encrypt a thumbprint, plus other identifying information. It is also cheap to issue and rarely becomes unreadable. However, unlike linear barcodes that have become familiar on consumer products, two-dimensional barcodes require readers that are relatively expensive and not widely available.

As previously explained, the technology that many expect will eventually win out as a form of secure identification is the smart card, which incorporates an embedded chip that can hold up to 64 KB of data, although most in use today offer only 4 KB to 16 KB. Smart cards will eventually store many times more than 64 KB.

Smart cards are expensive to produce, and in the United States, readers are costly and rare. However, those drawbacks are likely to be overcome soon because Europe is quickly standardizing on the smart card, and American Express is making a strong push domestically with its Blue smart card.

High-volume production is likely to push costs down for both smart cards and readers if, as expected, the technology is rapidly embraced for applications in telecommunications, financial services, retail, transportation, health care, and perhaps even state governments for driver's licenses and welfare program IDs.

In 2001, the last year for which data is available, the total number of smart cards manufactured for use in the United States and Canada grew 38%, to 39.5 million, according to a report issued by KPMG's Information Risk Management practice. The cost of a technology cannot be measured without weighing its relative value compared with other technologies. When things such as security, privacy, and storage capacity are balanced against the rapidly dropping prices of cards and readers, the smart card is clearly superior. In fact, would Ellison's Oracle database software be needed at all for a national ID, as the essential data would be embedded in the card?

However, it's not quite that simple because the interaction between the card and the network can involve highly complex architectures. For the most part, all data relevant to identification can (and for security reasons should) be encoded in the card itself.

However, identification isn't the same as authorization. For authorization under a variety of situations (e.g., to vote or to board a plane), it would be in the nation's best interest for the ID card to interact with continuously updated databases linked to the ID network.

To a large extent, political questions about a national ID will dictate technology solutions—not exactly a recipe for best practices, especially when the division of responsibilities between states and the federal government is factored in. Airline travel offers a prime example of this, a paradox resulting from the historical reluctance of the federal government to issue a national ID.

During the Gulf War, the Federal Aviation Administration (FAA) made it official policy that airlines had to require passengers to show a form of "government-issued identification" in the form of a photo ID to board a flight. In effect, that meant passengers had to present either a passport or a driver's license. However, no attempt was made to standardize state-issued driver's licenses, by far the most common boarding ID. Because the FAA does not require that ticket-counter personnel receive training in how to spot phony or doctored driver's licenses, almost none do.

It's easy to point fingers at past and present deficiencies, but the path to the future is anything but clear. Should a national ID simply be established by Congressional mandate? If so, should it be required, like a Social Security number, or should it be a voluntary, but official government identification like a passport or driver's license? Should it incorporate the functions and embed the data of all those IDs in a single digital device that adds biometric information, such as fingerprints or iris scans, and encodes it all in a securely encrypted form? Would it be more socially and politically acceptable to encourage a public and private-sector collaboration? For example, sundry identification and database technologies, combined in a single personal smart card, could replace multiple bank cards and serve as secure identification for myriad retail transactions that now require a driver's license (e.g., renting a car or truck, boarding a plane).

Whether a national card is produced by the federal government or some confederation of interested public and private parties, there would almost certainly be greater efficiency than there is in the present creaky system. A national card would be uniform and difficult to forge or alter. It would reduce the likelihood that someone could, intentionally or not, get lost in the cracks of multiple bureaucracies.

The problem is that many Americans cherish the ability (or at least the illusion of the ability) to lose themselves in the cracks. For many, in fact, being able to remain lost until they want to be found is the very definition of privacy. The tension between that widely cherished right and the need for social order and security will probably never be fully resolved. At best, one can hope to find a compass rather than a map and a moving equilibrium rather than a fixed point.

ID Card System Hurdles

If the U.S. government were to seek to establish a national identity card, it would confront a rat's nest of technical problems, despite recent advances. The three immediate technical issues are authentication, verification, and encryption. The good news is that biometrics-based authentication systems based on fingerprint scanning or visual face recognition are now relatively cheap and simple to deploy. In addition, digital signature systems based on PKI infrastructure technology are now mature, providing ways to check the source of information and to ensure data has not been modified since issued.

Furthermore, strong encryption technology (as typified by the new federal Advanced Encryption Standard released December 4, 2001) provides adequate safeguards for transmission of sensitive data. However, even with more resources available to system builders, it has proved very difficult to make large-scale, distributed database systems such as this work.

If officials want to use a centralized database for real-time checks on data, such as for passengers at an airport, the system has to be highly scalable. U.S. airlines carried 777 million passengers in 2001, according to the Air Transport Association of America, Inc. That's about 2.1 million passengers a day, or about 1,945 passengers a minute, assuming an 18-hour airport day. However, performance itself isn't an issue. According to Winter Corp.'s year 2000 large-database-systems survey, the U.S. Customs Service operates the world's fastest online transaction processing database system, one that processes 37,766 transactions a second (or 2.3 million transactions a minute).

Availability is a more difficult technical issue, especially with a widely distributed system dependent on many point-to-point communication links. Communication failures happen; backup links or a fallback to a subset of data stored locally at airports would be needed.

To avoid this issue, the Immigration and Naturalization Service's INSPASS border-crossing program uses scanners that verify handprint data against data stored securely on a smart card carried by frequent U.S. travelers instead of querying a central database. However, even if the technology does its job perfectly and without security compromise, the system is only as strong as its weakest links—human operators, flawed administrative policies, and data quality problems.

As previously mentioned, Oracle CEO Larry Ellison, who is publicly calling for a national ID card system, muted his comments in an October 8, 2001 *Wall Street Journal* article to indicate the real problem was not ID cards, but a lack of database integration among federal agencies that store data about those who live in or visit the United States. Are more databases needed? No, just the opposite: The biggest problem today is that we have too many. Ellison's comments point to an entirely separate problem from the issue of identifying users with an ID card system.

Certainly, consolidating large amounts of data into a single database system would make it easier for federal agencies to share information with one another (and generate considerable revenue for the vendors providing the database system). A master database (or any widely held source of trust) also magnifies the harm of unintentional errors and benefit to those who successfully submit fraudulent entries.

As many have discovered before, the main problem with integration isn't just loading the data into one system; it's correctly correlating records that weren't entered with consistent formats. Matching up name, address, and birth date data is a very expensive process, given formatting and data entry differences. Because of the serious consequence of errors in the system, such as not being able to board a plane or being detained by police, the database must be very carefully cleaned before being put to use.

 Tip

Credit reporting agencies that do such database merging have found the process problematic.

Creating a national ID database from the Social Security number database would also be difficult. It's not a very secure piece of personal data, and it doesn't contain a check digit, so data entry errors are hard to detect.

National IDs Are Coming!

Finally, the time has come for a reasoned, national dialogue on the merits and dangers of a national ID. What is at stake is not just an improvement, however slight, in domestic security, but vastly increased convenience in an ever more digital culture.

Unfortunately, the debate is currently dominated by a din of paranoia and knee-jerk ideology—often from people who do not understand the technology in question. They come from both the right and left fringes of the political spectrum, from folks who sport National Rifle Association bumper stickers and from folks who write off annual contributions to the American Civil Liberties Union. The only thing they share, for the most part, is a fear of government and the unknown.

Clearly, a national ID and the database infrastructure that would be needed to support it pose dangers to civil liberties. Every initiative involving your rights requires a delicate balancing of social values—in this case, a little less anonymity for a lot more security.

At the same time, many opponents of the idea also lack objectivity. Did anyone really think that the American Civil Liberties Union, the Privacy Institute, or the Electronic Privacy Information Center would give a national ID reasoned consideration? These advocacy groups are crucially important to the debate, but cannot be allowed to frame it because they represent only one side of the social trade-off. Likewise, politicians from the far right will smell big government and socialist conspiracy in any identification effort, just as they have since 1935 with the Social Security number.

However, not every attempt by a government to identify you is Big Brother tyranny, and there is a clear difference between identification and authorization technologies and surveillance. The fact is, a voluntary national ID will eventually be a reality. Americans, exhausted by long lines at airports, bridges, and tunnels, and frustrated with having to carry myriad forms of identification, from credit cards to passports, will eventually demand it. The time has come to stop tabulating all the things that are scary about a national ID and start determining how to get it right the first time.

Endnotes

[1]   VeriSign Worldwide Headquarters, 487 East Middlefield Road, Mountain View, CA 94043, USA, 2002.

[2]   E.-M. Hamann, H. Henn, T. Schäck, and F. Seliger, "Securing E-Business Applications Using Smart Cards," IBM Corporation, 1133 Westchester Avenue, White Plains, NY 10604, USA, 2002.

[3]   Raul Sanchez-Reillo, "Smart Card Information and Operations Using Biometrics," *IEEE Aerospace and Electronic Systems Magazine*, (© 2002 IEEE), 445 Hoes Lane, Piscataway, NJ 08855, USA, 2002.

[4]   Christopher J. Dyball and Terri Lichtenstein, "Optical Memory Cards Provide Secure Identification," Drexler Technology Corp., 2644 Bayshore Parkway, Mountain View, CA 94043, and LaserCard Systems Corp., 2751 Marine Way, Mountain View, CA 94043, Laser Focus World, (Copyright © PennWell 2002) 98 Spit Brook Rd, Nashua, NH 03062, USA, 2002.

[5]   "Smart, Optical and Other Advanced Cards: How to Do a Privacy Assessment," Information and Privacy Commissioner/Ontario, 80 Bloor Street West, Suite 1700, Toronto, Ontario, M5S 2V1, 2001.

Chapter 13

ENCRYPTION

Does it really matter who reads your emails? If the answer is no, then email encryption could be a potentially cumbersome luxury. However, if you want to protect your identity and you email sensitive, personal, or business information, encryption is likely a necessity.

☞ **Tip**

Encryption is the translation of data into a secret code. Encryption is the most effective way to achieve data security. To read an encrypted file, you must have access to a secret key or password that enables you to decrypt it. Unencrypted data is called plain text; *encrypted data is referred to as* cipher text. *There are two main types of encryption: asymmetric encryption (also called public key encryption) and symmetric encryption.*

Unless you have been a meditating hermit for the last few years, the media has bombarded you with the woes of sending unencrypted email. Still, 99% of all email traffic travels over the Internet unsecured.

An unencrypted email can bounce from Toronto to Brussels to New York, or anywhere for that matter. It all depends on the state of Internet "traffic" that day. An email message can pass through numerous different computer systems en route to its final destination. Meanwhile, on some computers through which that email is relayed, there may be *sniffers* or other malicious software tools waiting to copy, alter, or tamper with that email in some way. Some are looking for key words or names. Other sniffers are watching for credit card numbers or login passwords.

Those people who use some form of encryption system relax comfortably at their keyboards. Nonetheless, they feel a cold chill each time someone reports a new security hole. Some holes are found in the encryption tools. More often though, the application that uses the encryption tool has bugs. Internet browser applications are prone to this due to their large size and complexity. Although the cryptographic component might remain secure, back-door bugs to the application can nullify the value of the email encryption.

Users of Netscape Communicator and Microsoft Internet Explorer have felt a few cold chills since both browsers were email encryption enabled. Communicator 6.0 had a bug that allowed Web sites access to information from the hard disks of visitors. More recently, Explorer 6 had flaws that allowed Web hackers to access files on a user's system.

What Is Email Encryption and How Does It Work?

It seems that every day, a new email encryption product hits the market. Each claims to have the strongest encryption algorithms and guarantees attack-proof security. Before an individual or organization decides to purchase or use a product, some fact-finding and analysis is necessary. This chapter is not a substitute for that fact-finding, but it does point toward some next steps.

There are more than 1,100 encryption programs currently available with varying levels of quality. Some are secure (those that third parties have tested and could not break). Others are weak (those that can be broken in a few seconds by someone in the business). Finally, there are the dangerous products (the untested ones).

Symmetric Key Encryption

At the heart of symmetric encryption programs are cryptographic keys. The key is nothing more than a binary string of ones and zeros (e.g., 1100101011010100011100101010101). The author creates a pass phrase. The encryption program in turn creates the key based on the pass phrase. The key is used to both encrypt and decrypt the email in a symmetric key cryptography program (see Figure 13.1). [1] That means the intended receiver (and no one else) needs to receive a copy of the pass phrase by other secure means. The encryption program uses that key to scramble or encrypt the email's contents. The number of symmetric encryption programs is legion. A few include PKZIP, BLOWFISH, AES, and IDEA.

Tip

Symmetric encryption is a type of encryption where the same key is used to encrypt and decrypt the message. This differs from asymmetric (or public key) encryption, which uses one key to encrypt a message and another to decrypt it.

Of course, if the author never changes the key for all ensuing emails, there could be problems. The author could make those problems worse if the pass phrase is little more than a word or string of words. A few seconds with a dictionary-based hacking tool will crack that system. That is why authorities urge authors to create long, complex pass phrases with uppercase and lowercase letters, numbers, and keyboard characters. Nevertheless, how does the author of the email get that pass phrase to the intended audience securely?

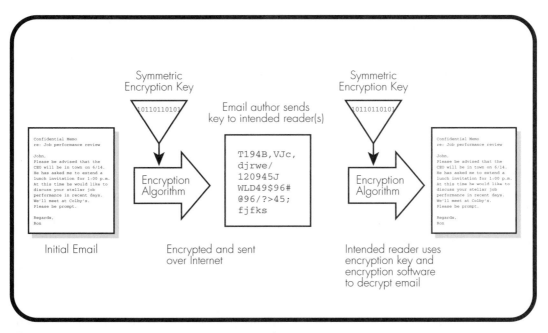

Figure 13.1 Symmetric Encryption: How it works.

Asymmetric Encryption

In 1976, Whitfield Diffie teamed with Stanford professor Martin Hellman. Together they devised what experts greeted as the most important development in cryptography in modern times. They produced a system that allowed people to communicate with total privacy. A year later, a group at MIT used the Diffie–Hellman theory and launched RSA (named after Ron Rivest, Adi Shamir, and Leonard Adleman), which brought asymmetric cryptography to the public.

 Tip

> *Asymmetric or public key encryption is a cryptographic system that uses two keys—a public key known to everyone and a private or secret key known only to the recipient of the message. When John wants to send a secure message to Jane, he uses Jane's public key to encrypt the message. Jane then uses her private key to decrypt it. An important element to the public key system is that the public and private keys are related in such a way that only the public key can be used to encrypt messages and only the corresponding private key can be used to decrypt them. Moreover, it is virtually impossible to deduce the private key if you know the public key. Public key systems, such as Pretty Good Privacy (PGP), are becoming popular for transmitting information via the Internet. They are extremely secure and relatively simple to use. The only difficulty with public key systems is that you need to know the recipient's public key to encrypt a message for him or her. What's needed, therefore, is a global registry of public keys, which is one of the promises of the new Lightweight Directory Access Protocol technology. Public key cryptography was invented in 1976 by Whitfield Diffie and Martin Hellman. For this reason, it is sometime called Diffie–Hellman encryption. It is also called asymmetric encryption because it uses two keys instead of one key (symmetric encryption).*

RSA software can generate a pair of keys that could be used to either encrypt or decrypt a message. Each key is a large integer, and the two integers are mathematically related in a special way. Either key can be used by the encryption software to encrypt a message. The other key is used later to decrypt the message.

 Tip

> *The British intelligence community had invented asymmetric cryptography years before, but had not shared it publicly.*

The reader can share one key, called the public key, with intended authors. The reader's private key remains just that: private. Once an author receives the reader's public key, the author can use the public key to encrypt information. The author can then send the encrypted email. The reader then decrypts the author's email with his or her own private key. In other words, the author encrypts information using the intended reader's public key. The reader then decrypts the information using his or her private key. This concept always makes people blink at first (see Figure 13.2). [1]

Asymmetric encryption overcomes the problem of having to share the same key, whereas symmetric key encryption requires it. Asymmetric encryption made a breakthrough. However, it is a labor-intensive encryption process for computers. Using it to encrypt and decrypt all of a person's email traffic would bring the average PC into submission.

Common practice in most encryption applications today is to use asymmetric encryption to wrap or encrypt only a symmetric key. The key is chosen at random, and the program generates a new one for each message. Remember that the symmetric key is used to encrypt the email. The intended reader of the author's encrypted email can then decrypt the symmetric key using the reader's

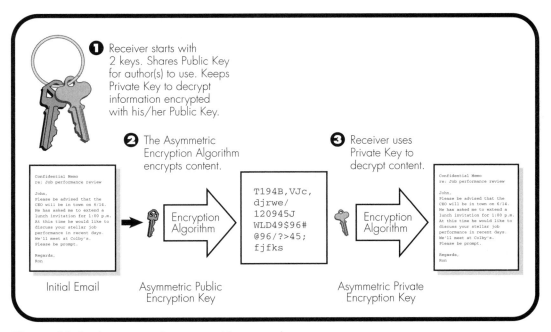

Figure 13.2 Asymmetric Encryption: How it works.

own private key. Now, the symmetric key decrypts the email. Thankfully, the encryption program does all this in the background, so you do not need to remember 300-digit prime numbers or work with long binary sequences.

Digital Signatures

Most email encryption tools have another element. On top of the encryption algorithms, they add a digital signature, which assures the email's reader that no one tampered with the message and that it did in fact come from the author.

To do this, a digital signature combines two pieces of information: a hash and the author's private key. First, let's talk about the hash (see Figure 13.3). [1] The software creates the *hash*, which is a sequence of numbers (ones and zeros) unique to the author's message. The software does this by first scrambling the message. Think of it as making scrambled eggs and hash browns, mixed up together in the frying pan. Then, the software crunches the scrambled mess down digitally. Now think of scrunching the scrambled eggs and hash browns into a small egg cup. That's the hash: the stuff that made it into the small egg cup.

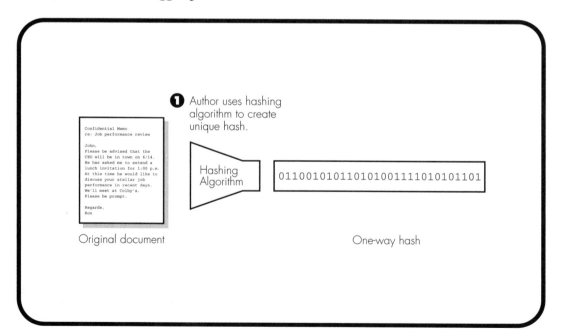

Figure 13.3 Creating a Hash: How it works.

The encryption software can only create one possible hash from an original message. However, there could be other messages that end up creating the same hash. Still, finding those other messages is virtually impossible. Although improbable, a person could find a different message that creates the same hash, but that other message would most likely be gibberish.

This hash cannot be reverse engineered (that is why they call it a one-way hash). The digital hash is just like the scrunched-up hash in the egg cup: There is no way to go backward. The hash cannot go back to the eggs in their shells and the unpeeled potato. Therefore, no one can use the digital hash to find out what the message is, nor can it be used to create a different message, resulting in the same hash. The common length of the hash is 160 bits.

The second step is to encrypt the hash. The author encrypts the hash using his and her private key, and you have a digital signature. The reader can decrypt the encrypted hash using the author's public key. The intended reader's encryption software checks to see if the author's message creates the same hash, ensuring that no one has altered the message.

The digital signatures work the opposite way to ordinary messages. The author encrypts the outgoing hash with his or her private key (see Figure 13.4). [1] Then the author sends out his or her public key to allow readers to verify the hash is right. The reader would also know that only the author could have initially encrypted and sent the email. Only the author has the private key that will make that system work. The weak link is in the complexity of the keys that a user creates. A safe bet is to have keys with a minimum of 230 digits.

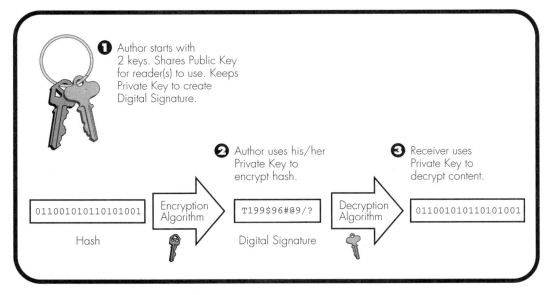

Figure 13.4   Digital Signature: How it works.

Increasingly, email encryption is becoming part of a suite of services that are transparent to the user. These products target private- and public-sector organizations rather than individual users. To use these systems, users don't need to know anything about security. Most important, they need not remember those 230 digit keys.

However, an organization's decision makers do need to know a few things. For a start, they need to remember that encrypted traffic cannot be scanned for viruses at the firewall or the anti virus application level. That applies to encrypted email that is entering or leaving the organization. One option is to stop the encrypted email at the firewall and decrypt it there. Another is to decrypt at the server or individual PC and scan there for potential viruses.

Types of Email Encryption Products

Most email encryption products include all of the features just discussed. However, they fall into two main standards or protocols. The two de facto, ad hoc standards are: S/MIME version 3 and Open PGP. In the tradition of competing ad hoc standards, they are incompatible. This incompatibility will most likely continue. S/MIME version 3 recently became an approved standard by the Internet Engineering Task Force (IETF). The IETF also created an Open PGP standard (see the sidebar, "Advanced Encryption Standard"). Having two incompatible standards is not a problem for a company that decides to use one protocol to communicate internally. However, it does create a challenge for communicating securely with a host of external organizations or individuals that have opted to use incompatible products.

Advanced Encryption Standard

The federal government has a new standard for encrypting electronic documents and messages, a code so secure that federal officials predict its encoded material will remain uncrackable for 20 to 30 years. The Advanced Encryption Standard (AES) received formal approval from the U.S. Department of Commerce on December 4, 2001. It replaces the DES, which was adopted in 1977 and can be deciphered with modern computers. The National Institute of Standards and Technology of the U.S. Department of Commerce selected the algorithm, called Rijndael (pronounced *Rhine Dahl* or *Rain Doll*), out of a group of five algorithms under consideration, including one called MARS from a large research team at IBM.

Now, that the federal government has adopted the standard, it is expected to provide a boost to e-government. In the short term, the use of the new encryption standard is likely to go unnoticed by most people.

Although encryption is already used extensively by the financial industry for such things as online banking and ATM transactions, the encryption is invisible to banking customers, and most users are probably unaware that it is occurring. In the longer term, however, more sophisticated encryption is expected to make more e-government functions possible.

Strong encryption is essential to ensure the security and authenticity of the online transactions envisioned in e-government, such as digitally signing contracts and completing financial, legal, and other transactions. At the heart of encryption technology is a complex mathematical formula known as an algorithm. AES uses a 128-bit encryption algorithm compared with DES' 56-bit one. It's actually capable of up to 256 bits (by design). [2]

Apart from choosing which protocol to use, the consumer has to choose a product. That is where it gets complicated. The following list is just a small sample of the various products available:

- Web-based encryption services
- PC-based applications
- PKI
- Hybrid applications
- Encryption tools [1]

Web-Based Encryption Services

Web-based encryption services give the user an email account on a Web site and provide encryption software at that Web site. The Web site acts as a traffic controller for the user's email.

Using Web-based systems is easy: Simply follow their instructions. Be aware that some Web-based email encryption systems require both the author and reader to register to the Web site to encrypt and decrypt email.

PC-Based Applications

PC-based applications install on a user's PC or network. Application-based tools vary in degrees of usability and strength. A good bet is to look for those computer magazines have tested and given the coveted editors' choice awards. Most of the current products have made encrypting email a one- or two-click process once the program has been set up. This is a major improvement from just several years ago. These PC-based products are independent of the ISP and can be installed with a few mouse clicks.

PKIs

PKIs incorporate end-to-end security for organizations: These solutions add a host of other services to basic email encryption ranging from securing Web sites to managing authentication. This includes handling all the digital certificates (where a third party guarantees your identity) needed by an organization to move information securely. These products are virtually transparent to the user.

Hybrid Applications

Hybrid applications have email encryption plus other features such as anonymizers or pseudonymizers to break the connection between the user and any electronic flotsam that he or she leaves behind on the Internet. The promising software Freedom by ZeroKnowledge was just released. According to the company, it manages all of your digital identities, watches all outbound traffic for personal information, automatically encrypts and routes traffic through their Freedom network, transparently decrypts all incoming traffic, manages cookies, and filters spam.

For example, Proxymate's services (*www.proxymate.com/*) do not include email encryption, but provide aliases. The service is easy to install and use. This proxy-based service gives users anonymity while they surf the Internet. Once registered (the software has an automatic setup option), the only added steps involve entering a user name and password when you start your Web browser. Proxymate provides aliases to Web sites asking for a user's name and email address. Essentially a privacy screen, the service is transparent to the user.

Encryption Tools

Encryption tools in Netscape Communicator and Microsoft Internet Explorer involve purchasing a digital certificate (60-day free trial period) from a third party such as VeriSign. Vendors have simplified and fully integrated the process for installation and use in the browsers. However, expect to pay $13 to $23 per year for your digital ID. Corporate rates are available as well.

Next Steps

Once the user or organization has done some fact finding and is in the market for an email encryption product, keep the following things in mind:

1. Has the encryption code been tested?
2. Is it a mature encryption software?
3. Does it meet the needs of your organization or personal preferences?
4. What is the learning curve and ease of use of the product? [1]

Testing Encryption Code

The testing of encryption code assumes that the code is available for testing. Untested code is dangerous, as Netscape can attest to with Communicator 6. Netscape has published its Communicator 6+ code for testing, but not all companies do this. Third parties tied to academic cryptography bodies do the best testing. For example, the Centre for Applied Cryptography at the University of Waterloo (*www.cacr.math.uwaterloo.ca*) is a fine example.

☞ **Tip**

Never underestimate the time, expense, and effort someone will expend to break a code.

Mature Encryption Software

Mature in this context means the software has been in use for at least three years, has undergone testing and review, and continues to be used. Recently several email encryption systems were reviewed. Two months later, some of these products and their companies were impossible to find, or in the worst case, no longer existed.

Meeting the Needs of Your Organization or Personal Preferences

The user needs to assess whether the product can support the volume of emails generated. He or she needs to decide whether the product provides the required protection.

On the other hand, if the email content is of limited value to others, use a product like PKZIP a commonly used utility to zip or compress files through symmetric encryption. A complex password might be sufficient. Just change the password often and avoid filenames that are too descriptive of the content, because that's another possible clue for snoopers.

Learning Curve and Ease of Use of the Product

Finally, the learning curve and ease of use of the product often come down to the number of keystrokes it takes to encrypt and decrypt email. It also comes down to the steps and time needed to acquire digital certificates (a way to avoid the need to remember and manage multiple passwords).

Endnotes

[1] "Email Encryption Made Simple," Information and Privacy Commissioner/Ontario, 80 Bloor Street West, Suite 1700, Toronto, Ontario, M5S 2V1, 2001.

[2] William Matthews, "Encryption Standard Strengthened," Federal Computer Week Media Group, 3141 Fairview Park Drive, Suite 77, Falls Church, VA 22042, USA, 2002.

Chapter 14

E-Commerce Security

The lack of perceived privacy in electronic transactions is a barrier to the growth of online commerce. Commercial transactions between individuals and businesses using the Internet raise a variety of issues about the adequacy of the medium for this purpose, particularly with respect to how capable this medium is in protecting personal information. At this relatively early stage in the development of electronic commerce, the following problem areas have been identified: the vulnerability of the open network to interceptions and faulty technological design, as well as the question of what laws and procedures can be applied to the Internet to regulate how personal information will be collected, used, and disclosed.

The Vulnerability of Open Networks

The construction of the Internet as an open communications system, although making it interoperable, has also made it vulnerable to certain risks, including surreptitious intrusions such as hacking, as well as human error. Three overlapping types of risk have been identified:

- Bugs and misconfiguration problems in the Web server that allow unauthorized remote users to steal documents, gain information about the Web server's host machine, and in turn break into the system.

- Browser-side risks that could result in the misuse of personal information knowingly or unknowingly provided by the end user.

- Interception of network data sent from the browser to the server or vice versa, via network eavesdropping. [1]

These vulnerabilities have been exploited by criminals and others. Some recent incidents include a man who hacked into company databases doing business over the Internet and stole thousands of credit card numbers. When caught, he had an encrypted CD-ROM containing roughly 200,000 stolen credit card numbers. A recent survey published in the United States indicated that there were 80 serious security attacks a month against high-visibility electronic commerce Web sites. The U.S. Department of Defense reported that 85% of its sites had been penetrated. In 2001 alone, there had been 1,250,000 hacker attacks on Department of Defense computers.

This discussion of the security risks of transmitting personal information over the Internet should not lead to the conclusion that once the Internet is made secure, all privacy problems will disappear. Although making the internet as secure as possible is necessary for privacy, it is not sufficient in and of itself. Security is not synonymous with privacy.

Privacy, as it relates to information, deals with the broader questions of the legitimate collection, use, and disclosure of personal information, and the degree to which individuals are able to exercise control over the uses of their information. Businesses have an incentive to collect as much personal information as possible, to create value-added features through data matching techniques, and to sell that personal information to third parties. This raises issues about the adequacy of existing privacy protection policies on the Internet and what technological solutions can be devised to protect personal information as it is exchanged in electronic commercial transactions.

Inadequate Privacy Laws, Policies, and Technologies

Initially, before the Web portion of the Internet was fully developed, privacy issues had not been much of a concern. However, as the Web grew and matured to the point where it was increasingly viewed as a revolutionary form of communication, privacy issues began to occupy a more prominent role in its further development. The publicity surrounding the vulnerability of the technology to intrusions, criminal activities, and surreptitious collection of personal information has made the public more aware of the pitfalls of this technology. There is now a growing awareness of the need to create a climate of trust and confidence in the use of this technology, particularly as it relates to commercial transactions.

A number of problems have been identified, among them inadequate or nonexistent laws and policies about how those conducting commercial transactions will treat the personal information they collect. In North America (unlike Europe), privacy or data protection legislation does not apply to the private sector except for the Province of Quebec. Canada is committed federally, however, to introducing such legislation. Until then, Canada has encouraged self-regulation in the private sector. The Canadian Standards Association (CSA) has produced a model privacy code that various industries, particularly banking and direct marketing, have adopted and tailored to their respective industries, producing their own sectorial codes.

Debate on whether industry self-regulation or government legislation is the best approach has divided the United States and the EU—the former seeking to rely on self-regulation, the latter favoring government legislation. The Europeans already have in place their data protection directive, as previously noted, which will apply indirectly to countries that import personal information from the EU. In addition, individual EU countries such as Germany have adopted laws limiting the collection of personal information over the Internet. The United States, on the other hand, has resisted calls to introduce private-sector privacy legislation and has lobbied strongly in favor of self-regulation.

Although it is not clear how this debate will ultimately end, the early indicators suggest that there is consensus that neither the United States nor the Europeans will quickly pass legislation to govern the internet. Self-regulation will first be given an opportunity to work (or not) before any final decisions will be made concerning government regulation.

An indication that some type of regulation might be needed is revealed in an Office of Management and Budget Watch survey of U.S. government Web sites. The vast majority of the sites surveyed did not have explicit privacy policies posted on their home pages. Similar results were obtained with respect to the top 100 Web sites in the United States, with only 28 having explicit privacy policies. That this has also been a problem in the private sector is borne out by a recent announcement by the U.S. Information Technology Industry Council, which reported that it had prepared a voluntary code to protect privacy for those who visit its members' Web sites. In Canada, the Canadian Information Processing Society has adopted a code of fair information practices based on the CSA model code as a way to encourage its members to deal with this issue.

363

The issue of online consumer privacy has also been taken on by the U.S. FTC. Over the past several years, the FTC has held hearings and produced several reports on such issues as privacy and databases, children's privacy, and the privacy practices of look-up services (locator services that can identify an individual's whereabouts as well as other personal information). The FTC also took a snapshot of assorted Web sites only to discover that very few had posted their privacy policies (if they existed to begin with). A more thorough sweep of Web sites will be launched in 2003.

As of this writing, solutions concerning how to ensure privacy protection with respect to electronic commerce have focused largely on industry self-regulation. Governments have indicated that they will wait for the private sector to formulate appropriate solutions, and then will step in only if market failure takes place. As discussed previously, Canadian and American industry sectors (those most involved directly or indirectly in electronic commerce) have begun to respond to the public outcry over privacy issues on the Internet. It is expected that in 2003, there will be greater activity at the policy and procedural levels, with more and more businesses placing privacy statements and policies on their Web sites.

Although there appears to be considerable flux in the development of privacy laws and policies, more aggressive efforts to solve the privacy problems associated with electronic commerce have been undertaken on the technology front. If IT has created some of the privacy problems, many believe IT can also be deployed to solve those problems. The next part of the chapter discusses these efforts.

Privacy Solutions

The profiling of individuals by both public- and private-sector organizations, made possible by the accumulation of such personal data, could constitute a new threat to individual privacy, which might inhibit many potential users of the global information infrastructure from participating fully in the information revolution. One way to deal with the problem is to avoid the collection of identifiable personal data in the first place, by allowing anonymous access to the network and anonymous consumption of the services available. This, of course, is not always desirable or possible. Additionally, innovative privacy-enhancing, user-empowering technologies are being developed. These aim at allowing users to make informed decisions about the collection, use, and disclosure of personal information during interactions on the Internet.

Systems analysts and software designers are increasingly seeking new or existing technology solutions to solve the privacy issues raised by the Internet. A number of private-sector IT companies and nonprofit organizations have come together to explore various approaches to dealing with the issue of privacy as it applies to transactions on the Internet. These efforts can be subsumed under the term *privacy-enhancing technologies*. These technologies seek to eliminate the use of personal data from transactions or give direct control for the disclosure of personal information to the individual concerned.

Privacy advocates have generally taken fair information practices as their starting point for any discussion about personal information and data protection. The key principles, in their strict reading, are that personal data should not be collected except for specific purposes and should be obtained by lawful and fair means, preferably with the knowledge or consent of the data subject. The purpose of the collection should be specified to the individual and the data should be used only for that purpose. Except when authorized by law or for clearly compatible purposes, the data should not be disclosed to third parties unless the individual has consented. Personal data should be accurate, complete, and up-to-date. Personal data should be protected by reasonable security safeguards against such risks as loss or unauthorized access, destruction, use, modification, or disclosure of the data. There should be a general policy of openness about an organization's practices and policies with respect to personal data. Means should be readily available for establishing the existence and nature of the data, identifying the main purpose of its use, and contacting those controlling the data. An individual should have the right to access his or her own personal data and correct any errors. Those controlling the personal data should be accountable for complying with measures created to give effect to these principles.

In the context of electronic commerce conducted over the Internet, the principles that bear most directly on the protection of personal data are those dealing with collection, use, and disclosure. Ideally, it is preferable that personal data not be collected in identifiable form, but if data is to be collected in that manner, fair information practices would require that only the minimum be obtained, consistent with the purpose of the collection. Individuals should be made aware that their personal information is being collected, and their consent to the collection should be sought. The objective of these principles is to give individuals as much control over their personal data as possible. This is particularly critical when use and disclosure are considered. It is a breach of fair information practices to use personal data in ways that are not transparent to the individual, and without his or her consent. Similarly, disclosing personal data to third parties cannot be sanctioned unless the individual has consented. Although leeway in interpreting these principles is permitted in appropriate circumstances, the principles should be adhered to as closely as possible. This is manageable when the aim is to regulate organizational behavior, but such adherence poses a real challenge when one tries to embed the principles in the IT itself. What is needed are the design correlates of fair information practices.

Personal Data as a Unit of Exchange

It was argued earlier that the collection of personal data on the Internet through such things as the monitoring of clickstream information and the use of cookies made personal data a unit of exchange. When personal data is collected by these means and then sold to third parties without the knowledge or consent of the individual, a number of fair information practices are breached. The practice of registration on accessing a Web site, although perhaps following the collection principle by asking individuals to volunteer their personal data, might breach other principles such as using the data in ways that were not expected, or having the data sold without first seeking the consent of the individual. If these uses and disclosures remain unknown to the individual, the principle of openness and transparency is also breached.

A number of initiatives are now being developed that seek to give the individual greater control over his or her personal data in the context of the Internet. It should be noted, however, that these applications are not necessarily intended to replace clickstream monitoring, cookies, or other similar techniques.

Labeling and Licensing Technologies

Labeling technologies license the use of symbols called *trustmarks* to online merchants through an ongoing program of certification and auditing. Auditing conducted by well-respected firms will ensure the integrity of the trustmarks and strengthen consumer confidence. It seeks to promote full disclosure of how a merchant's Web site will use and disseminate personal data, thereby promoting consumer choice. Participating Web sites are given a license to post a trustmark on their home page, or on individual pages that confirm that the Web site is committed to disclosing its online personal data collection and dissemination practices. By clicking on the trustmark, the individual can read the Web site's privacy statement. At a minimum, the site should reveal what type of information it collects, how the site uses that data, with whom the site shares that information, whether the individual can opt out of having the data used by that site or a third party, whether the data can be changed or updated by the individual, and whether one can delete or deactivate oneself from the

Web site database. TRUSTe is the most widely known and respected of these technologies.

Another example of such a labeling technology is WebTrust. The result of the combined efforts of the American Institute of Certified Public Accountants and the Canadian Institute of Chartered Accountants, WebTrust involves the awarding of a seal of assurance to Web sites that comply with WebTrust's Criteria and Principles. These include a requirement that a Web site maintain effective controls to ensure that private customer information is protected from uses not related to its business. Audits are conducted to ensure that a Web site's statements are accurate.

The objective of these technologies is to provide a system of recognizing Web sites that are privacy compliant. Beyond labeling and licensing, however, an individual has no ability to negotiate or set limits on the disclosure of his or her personal data to the Web site, nor to control what that Web site does with the data. For that, one must turn elsewhere (discussed later in this chapter).

Blocking Technologies

A technology known as the Platform for Internet Content Selection (PICS), developed by MIT's World Wide Web Consortium (W3C), will attach labels to describe any document on the Internet or any Web site. In browsing the Web, an individual will not be able to enter those sites that he or she has set as being undesirable (e.g., pornographic sites). In addition to labeling offensive material, the technology can also describe a Web site's information practices, such as what personal information it collects and whether that information is reused or resold. PICS will not only allow the blocking of undesirable material, but also the selection of desirable material, such as Web sites that have a clearly posted privacy code. From a privacy perspective, this technology can ensure that personal data will not be released without an individual's consent; however, it has some practical drawbacks. For example, individuals must continuously reset their privacy preferences, depending on how a particular Web site's privacy practices have been labeled.

Data Exchange Technologies

One example of this type of technology is the Open Profiling Standard, (OPS), which permits users to control the release of information about themselves. Individuals enter their personal information once on their computer's hard drive, then a set of rules is established as to how and when that information can be transmitted to online services. However, there are no rules in the standard about how a site can use that information. Essentially what is secured is the electronic transmission of the information. The standard relies on several technologies including digital signatures and public key encryption. The profile of the individual will bear a certificate verifying one's identity. Its main drawback is that it fails to identify the privacy practices of the online service or Web site.

Another project, developed by the W3C is called P3P. P3P seeks to incorporate basic privacy principles accepted in North America, Europe, and elsewhere to make this technology acceptable to as many countries as possible.

Once implemented, P3P would permit Web sites to state their privacy practices, based on a specified set of statements about how they would use, transfer, disclose, and allow access to personal data collected by them, either from clickstream data or data provided by the user in response to a request from a Web site. The user would also create a set of privacy preferences, based on a parallel set of privacy statements about how the user's personal data can be used, transferred, disclosed, and accessed. If the Web site's practices and the user's preferences matched, there would be seamless access to that Web site. However, if a match could not be achieved, the user could negotiate with the Web site (although the possibility exists that a user could be denied entry if not enough personal data was volunteered to the site). These negotiations would not be conducted directly by the user, but through a computer agent, such as a search engine. So that the user would not to have to repeatedly provide personal data to each Web site manually, one's personal data, organized into data elements, would reside in a central depository, maintained perhaps by the service provider. Missing from this technology is the ability to ensure a secure transfer of the personal data from the depository to the Web site, although consideration is being given to the use of OPS technology.

The objection made by privacy advocates to the type of initiatives previously described is that they require individuals to disclose their privacy preferences as a condition of a commercial transaction. There is a certain apprehension that individuals will bargain away more of their privacy than might be necessary, if they think they might obtain a benefit or service in return. One must remember, however, that privacy revolves around choice—the freedom to choose the level of privacy that one wishes and the ability to maintain control over the uses of one's personal information. Such decisions must remain in the hands of the individual.

Anonymous Profiling

An alternative approach to collecting personal data over the Internet is anonymous profiling. Although demographic information would still be released under this scheme, personally identifying data would not. In other words, the data would not be linked to a person or associated with a particular name.

Although this approach has not received wide support in North America, it has gained greater acceptance in Europe, where Germany has specifically introduced this concept in its telecommunications legislation, which also happens to cover the Internet. Service providers are required to offer customers the option of anonymous use and payment, or use and payment under a pseudonym. Moreover, individuals are protected from third parties attempting to access their personal data.

Electronic Payment Systems

Over the last few years, various electronic payment systems have been devised in an effort to create confidence in buyers and sellers using the Internet as a platform for commercial transactions. The lack of trust arises from the accurate public perception that providing sensitive personal and financial information over the Internet could pose serious risks, especially in light of the vulnerabilities of the Internet identified earlier.

From a privacy perspective, sending credit card information over the Internet entails a risk that the information might be intercepted and used by someone other than the individual for whom the information was intended. Quite apart from unauthorized access to the information and loss of confidentiality, this could give rise to various forms of identity theft, wherein individuals not only lose control over their personal information, but also their identities.

To resolve this problem and create trust and confidence in Internet-based transactions, a variety of technologies have been devised. In the first instance, they seek to overcome the security vulnerabilities of an open network. In so doing, they also, to varying degrees, provide confidentiality in the transmitted information. They might also enhance privacy to the degree that they give individuals greater control over how their personal information is collected, transmitted, and used.

Encryption

Although many of these technologies and applications are still in the developmental stage, what can be said with some assurance is that there is a growing consensus that digital signatures and encryption will form the basic tools for electronic transactions. Encryption is needed to ensure security, including authentication, confidentiality, data integrity, and nonrepudiation. Several forms of electronic encryption exist, with public key encryption being strongly favored, often in conjunction with the use of single-key systems.

Digital Signatures

Digital signatures are needed to authenticate the parties to an online transaction, just as handwritten signatures affixed to paper documents authenticate the identity of the individuals involved. A word of caution, however, on relying too heavily on digital signatures as the sole means of authentication: In the absence of proper risk management techniques, the deployment of this technology creates new risks that must be managed to gain possible benefits. Unlike handwritten signatures, digital signatures are transferable, and that transferability needs to be managed and contained.

A digital signature resembles a pseudonym more closely than a real name because it is a secret piece of information that one possesses, which is then linked to an individual's name. This leads to two central risks associated with its use: initial impersonation at the time of certification of the digital signature (the risk of false attestation), and the secret information, namely the digital signature, being duplicated outside of the control of the bona fide individual (the risk of theft, misuse, or loss). In addition, for fraudulent purposes, one could have multiple digital signatures registered by different certification authorities. To address these concerns, a number of measures (including the creation of certification replication lists, revoking certificates issued earlier or elsewhere), and technical standards and controls will become essential to the use and risk management of digital signatures.

In the search for iron-clad methods of authentication for online transactions, there are also proposals, not surprisingly, to use biometric information to authenticate parties to a transaction. A biometric is a unique physiological or behavioral measure that can be associated only with the individual who generated it (e.g., fingerprints, voiceprints, retinal scans, iris scans, hand geometry, facial thermograms, etc.). The advantage of biometrics is its unique ability to unquestionably verify the identity of the individual involved. However, to ensure privacy, the biometrics must, at an absolute minimum, be encrypted; its uses must be stringently controlled; and the biometrics must be rendered incapable of functioning as a unique identifier. Which technology will ultimately be accepted by the marketplace is difficult to predict at this time.

Turning to security, there are essentially three models for secure electronic transactions:

- Those that seek merely to provide secure transportation of transaction information from purchaser to merchant.
- Those that attempt to facilitate the actual funds authorization and transaction settlement process.
- Those that aim to reproduce the essential features of money in digital form. [1]

Secure Transmission

Secure transportation of transaction information from purchaser to merchant applications means the secure transfer of information between a browser and a server through the use of encryption. Two competing standards exist: Secure HTTP and SSL. The drawback to these technologies is that they allow the Web site to deencrypt the transmitted information, opening the door to the possibility of fraudulent use.

Authorization and Transaction Settlement

Using public key cryptographic techniques and digital signatures, Secure Electronic Transactions protocol mimics the current credit card processing system. Its advantage is that it does not permit the online merchant to read the credit card information, thereby providing the individual user with greater security.

Electronic Cash or Virtual Money

Electronic money or e-cash is predicated on a different strategy to be used over an open network. The strategy is to avoid sending personal data, as is the case with credit card information, but rather to send electronic cash or tokens, where an individual provides no identifiable personal data over the Internet. In one form of this technology, the individual remains completely anonymous. From a privacy perspective, the individual can use electronic cash just as he or she would use real cash, without having to reveal his or her identity or have any transactional data captured or linked to one's purchase. Objections have been leveled, however, from auditing and law enforcement circles against this type of anonymizing technology.

Under consideration here are two systems: hardware-based stored-value cards or smart cards, and software-based stored-value or prepaid payment systems for executing payments over open networks. The former are hardware or card-based systems that permit individuals to use plastic cards with a magnetic strip or a smart card embedded with a computer chip. The latter are software- or network-based systems that work with installed software through a personal computer connected to a network.

There are two basic ways to represent the value of the funds stored: *balance based*, in which a single balance is stored and updated with each transaction, and *note based*, in which electronic notes, each with a fixed value and serial number (comparable, to a one-dollar bill, five-dollar bill, etc.), are transferred from one device to another. These values are encrypted when transmitted to ensure confidentiality and data integrity. In one instance, a note-based technology developed by DigiCash uses a blind signature where the process ensures that no identifying information can be traced back to the individual.

From a privacy perspective, electronic cash is the most privacy-protective payment scheme because this technology permits the individual to withhold personal data from being associated with transactions, thereby eliminating the creation of transaction-generated information. In turn, the need to address privacy issues relating to the collection, use, and disclosure of personal data is avoided.

Nevertheless, by all accounts, the online business-to-consumer (B2C) market is growing at a healthy pace, but along with the increase in revenue comes a rise in the number of fraudulent transactions. Although Visa introduced Cardholder Information Security Processing (CISP) in 2000 and MasterCard followed with its Site Data Protection Service (SDPS) in 2001, fraud rates continue to hover 10% higher on the Internet as compared with the brick-and-mortar world, according to industry researcher the Gartner Group. With that in mind, let's briefly look at some ongoing detection solutions that are being implemented to bring these increased fraud rates down.

E-Commerce Fraud Detection Solutions

Although CISP and SDPS focus on network security (from the transport layer to physical security policies), these practices do not address payment for products and services via stolen or generated credit card numbers, which constitute the majority of fraudulent B2C transactions. A thief need only generate or purchase a valid credit card number to steal online.

From a financial perspective, the merchant pays the most for these types of theft. By law U.S. cardholders are responsible for only the first $50 of a fraudulent transaction, and MasterCard and Visa recently waived that requirement for online commerce. However, not only is the merchant responsible for the entire transaction, it also can be charged a fee from the credit card issuer. Visa recently launched its "Verified by Visa" program, which can relieve the merchant from some liability for fraudulent transactions, but the program doesn't work if it isn't used.

Of course, a merchant can prosecute a criminal to recover the transaction, but this rarely happens. Less than 10% of the cases are prosecuted to the point where a merchant receives restitution. A higher percentage are prosecuted, and conviction of the perpetrator might even occur, but unless the merchant receives restitution, it isn't really considered successful.

Typically, the merchant should set the criteria to determine which fraudulent orders will be researched and processed. Some criteria for prosecuting fraud include dollar amount of loss, frequency of the attack, and how much reliable information is available on the attempt. Hard data is difficult to obtain from merchants, but the National Fraud Information Center (NFIC), which tabulates data on all types of fraud, attributed losses of $5.5 million in 2001 to Internet fraud, with 12% of that total in the general merchandise category. Within that category, 42% of the losses were via credit card fraud.

Credit card thieves use the stolen plastic to purchase merchandise, online subscriptions, and even Internet access. Some thieves ship the merchandise to an address other than the billing address; others have the merchandise shipped to the billing address, then somehow pick up the goods. As for service theft, the NFIC reported that in 2001, 4% of the losses to fraud were due to payment for Internet access service.

Of course, you cannot ensure that all fraudulent purchases are caught, but you can reduce your company's risk to an acceptable level. All merchants should determine a dollar amount of acceptable loss as a cost of doing business. This number ranges on average from 0.36% to 2.6% of a merchant's total budget, depending on the type of business and the resources assigned to investigate and prevent fraudulent orders. The industry average is about 2.2%, according to the Gartner Group.

Get the Data You Need

One of the first steps toward reducing your risk is getting as much information as you can about the credit card and the cardholder. At a minimum, you should get the following information from customers:

- Cardholder's name exactly as it appears on the card
- Card account number
- Card expiration date
- Card billing address
- Cardholder's home number, business telephone number, or both
- Cardholder's email address
- Name of the package recipient
- Shipping address
- Phone number at the shipping destination

The name, account number, and address can be used for rudimentary identity verification. The card issuer can determine if the address and name submitted match the information on file for the account number. Once this information is ascertained, the merchant takes over determining if the transaction is fraudulent.

The email address also is important. A recent FBI study of online fraud found that 98.4% of fraudulent orders submitted email addresses originating from a free email service. Some companies reject orders with such addresses outright, deeming the risk too high; others perform additional or manual verification to determine the validity of the order.

For instance, you can do simple comparisons of the addresses within your code to check for possible fraud attempts. Such examinations generally involve comparing the billing address and the shipping address. A billing address that is different from the shipping address should be considered suspicious, especially if the shipping address is an international one. Although you don't want to reject the transaction based on this information alone, you might want to set it to the side for manual verification, perhaps calling the customer and checking the purchase.

In addition, you might also want to determine the customer's location from his or her IP address (easily retrieved via the REMOTE_ADDR HTTP header) and cross-check this against his or her billing address. Note, however, that this technique is not foolproof; for example, most America Online customers will appear to be in Virginia. Also, use of a public proxy will invalidate this check. However, it can be an indication that manual verification is called for, especially for expensive purchases.

Ensure that your site is configured to log as much information as possible about the customer, including his or her IP address, the date and time of the order, and the length of time the customer spends on your site, if possible. Also watch for repeated order attempts coming from the same IP address with different credit card numbers. That customer could very well be someone using a credit card number generator to find a valid number.

Remember, though, that the discovery of some inconsistencies does not mean you've uncovered a criminal. You should use the additional information requested, such as email address or telephone number, to verify the purchase with the customer. You do not want to reject a valid transaction. Unless you are 100% positive your system can determine a fraudulent transaction, you'll want to review questionable transactions rather than reject them outright.

If you're using a third-party software solution for fraud detection, work closely with the vendor to customize your implementation as much as possible. The idea is to reduce the number of transactions flagged for review and ensure that staff is available to check the transactions in a timely manner. As you become more comfortable with the system and its ability to determine what is and is not fraudulent activity, you can allow the system more latitude in its ability to make absolute decisions regarding each transaction.

Products and Tools

Finally, a number of products let you perform more in-depth inspections of online transactions for fraudulent activity. These tools use some of the techniques previously discussed and add an additional layer of transaction risk assessment.

An AVS often is a key weapon in an online merchant's fraud protection plan. This service is generally provided free by credit card processors as part of the credit card verification process.

An AVS cross-checks the billing address submitted by the customer with the address on record with the card issuer and returns a code indicating the validity of the address. AVS is available in the United Kingdom, the United States, Germany, Austria, Switzerland, and a few other countries.

Although AVS systems can be beneficial in stopping some fraudulent activity, it won't catch them all: More often than not, the credit card thief has both the card number and the billing address.

Rules-based systems compare each credit card transaction with a set of rules before the charge can be approved. Based on the rules, the system can send a response ranging from approving the charge to denying the charge to forcing a manual review of the transaction. Rules can be as simple as: "If the credit card number is in the bad list, deny the transaction." They can also be complicated business logic rules that determine the risk associated with the transaction based on the order, such as if the order contains more than three of an item with a cost of more than $600, then review the transaction.

A rules-based system is essentially an expert system. This type of system can be coded manually, although updates and additions will grow increasingly difficult over time and possibly become cost prohibitive. Of course, the system is only as good as the rules it is programmed to use. The merchant must determine what constitutes fraud and configure the system to recognize those situations.

Neural networks are more sophisticated. A neural network can compare and search for patterns in a transaction against a database containing profiles and patterns of known fraudulent activity. These systems are also called predictive statistical modelers, fraud scorers, or screeners. They are extremely accurate because they depend on historical, accurate data to provide a base against which to judge current transactions. The data available is dependent on the system you purchase. Some systems can access a central database con-

375

taining millions of transactions; others depend entirely on the data you have on hand.

The limitations of such a system depend almost entirely on the data used. Data should be updated on a regular basis (every six months or so) and based on as large a sample of sales as possible.

Customization is also necessary to reduce the number of transactions that are flagged for manual review. An off-the-shelf neural network might flag up to 10% of all transactions as possible risks, even though only a few of those might be true attempts at fraudulent transactions.

ClearCommerce Corp. (*www.hoovers.com/co/capsule/4/0,2163,59764,00 .html?referrer=eLuminator*) and HNC Software (*www.hnc.com/*) offer neural-network-based fraud detection systems. CyberSource (*hoovers-asap.com/ info/com.hoovers_capsules_7_0_2163_43287_00_html.html?se=ink*) uses a hybrid model that combines an expert system with a neural network to examine millions of transactions to increase its statistic modeling and reduce the number of false rejections.

Another option is to use a third-party service, such as Equifax Secure's eIDverifier, which can provide identity verification services. This service is integrated into your system. During the checkout process, the user is redirected to a site where the provider attempts to verify the identity of the customer by requiring answers to both "wallet" questions (information that can typically be found in your wallet) and "private" questions (information not found in your wallet but easily answerable if you are who you say you are).

An assessment score and reason codes based on the answers provided by the customer and other industry data sources is returned to the merchant, who can then decide whether to continue processing the transaction as valid, process the transaction as invalid but attempt to garner information from the perpetrator to assist in prosecution, or simply end the transaction.

Endnote

[1]   Ann Cavoukian, "Privacy: The Key to Electronic Commerce," Information and Privacy Commissioner/Ontario, 80 Bloor Street West, Suite 1700, Toronto, Ontario, M5S 2V1, 2001.

Chapter 15

DATA MINING

Globally, issues about informational privacy in the marketplace have emerged in tandem with the dramatic and escalating increase in information stored in electronic formats. Improvements and innovations in computer processing power, disk storage, and networks have been close to explosive. Expansive databases with transactional information about every aspect of business are now measured in gigabytes and terabytes. Fueled daily by massive amounts of data, the volume is so overwhelming that it has been estimated that businesses can only use 12% of the data collected.

Much of this large mass of data is donated by the consumer in the course of conducting his or her daily personal business: withdrawing cash from ATMs, paying with debit or credit cards, borrowing money, writing checks, renting a car or a video, making a telephone call or an insurance claim, and, increasingly, sending or receiving email and surfing the Internet. Because virtually all of these transactions or activities involve some form of electronic identification, each transaction captures some personal information about you and stores it in electronic form.

Speed, convenience, easy access, discounts, bonuses, awards, and frequent flyer points have all encouraged or eased the transition from social interaction to electronic interaction. Often, there is no longer a choice to be made, and if there is a choice, it will rarely match the speed, convenience, or—in a way— the sense of control one gains through electronic interaction.

The sharpening of the competitive edge to improve products and services now demands that businesses make sense of complex and voluminous data. This enables businesses to design effective sales campaigns, precision-targeted marketing plans, and products to increase sales and profitability. In this context, a technology called *data mining* can be a valuable tool for business because it provides for the efficient discovery of valuable, nonobvious information from a large collection of data. Although data mining can be extremely valuable for businesses, it can also, in the absence of adequate safeguards, jeopardize informational privacy.

Tip

Data mining is a hot buzzword for a class of database applications that look for hidden patterns in a group of data. For example, data mining software can help retail companies find customers with common interests. The term is commonly misused to describe software that presents data in new ways. True data mining software doesn't just change the presentation, but actually discovers previously unknown relationships among the data.

This chapter is aimed primarily at consumers and businesses. It covers what data mining is and provides examples. It then reviews the implications of data mining in the context of fair information practices and looks at the choices available to consumers and businesses. The fair information practices discussed refer to the basic principles of data protection.

Generally speaking, responsible data management in private-sector businesses must be firmly based on fair information practices. The protection of personal information can be enhanced if consumers choose to voice and act on their expectations about the privacy of their personal information to the businesses with which they are transacting, and if businesses choose to adopt a culture of privacy through tangible everyday practices and through the use of privacy-enhancing technologies. It comes down to a matter of choice for both consumers and businesses.

Ultimately, however, there is a need for government, businesses, and consumers to share responsibility in the management of the collection, use, retention, and disclosure of personal information held by private-sector businesses. There needs to be a shared responsibility approach that is codified through government enactment of data protection legislation for private-sector businesses, sustained by the business community adopting a culture of privacy, and strengthened by consumers taking greater control of their own personal information and voicing their privacy expectations to the business community.

Information Storage

The transformation of information storage from paper-based records to electronic formats has contributed to the mounting attention and concern about informational privacy in the marketplace. It is true that the information age now upon us is bringing with it recurrent horror stories about loss of privacy and dataveillance, the exploits of hackers and breaches of security, and identity theft. Certainly the Internet and electronic commerce have heightened concerns over privacy and security issues that were unheard of previously.

As all of us move toward a more fully digital world, the cost of manipulating information approaches zero, and the hazards therein multiply. Even our privacy is in peril. The clickstream data pouring into Web merchants, the information that you provide with clicks of your mouse, what music you listen to, and where you like to eat lets those merchants personalize their marketing. However, it might be more information than you want to share widely. What's more, some Web entrepreneurs collect this information and sell it. Supermarket cards might be more convenient than coupons, but they, too, put a price on privacy. The activities in these examples are perfectly legal, of course, but they increase the potential for electronic malfeasance.

It has been estimated that the amount of information in the world doubles every 16 months, and the size and number of databases are increasing even faster. Thus, it is with some sense of urgency that data mining—an entrenched culture of privacy in the business world—will only come to light if consumers speak up and convey their privacy expectations to businesses, and if businesses truly believe that privacy protection makes good business sense.

What really is data mining? Let's take a look.

What Is Data Mining?

Data mining is a set of automated techniques used to extract buried or previously unknown pieces of information from large databases. Successful data mining makes it possible to unearth patterns and relationships, and then use this "new" information to make proactive knowledge-driven business decisions. Data mining then, centers on the automated discovery of new facts and relationships in data. The raw material is the business data, and the data mining algorithm is the excavator, sifting through the vast quantities of raw data looking for the valuable nuggets of business information. Data mining is usually used for four main purposes:

1. To improve customer acquisition and retention

2. To reduce fraud

3. To identify internal inefficiencies and then revamp operations

4. To map the unexplored terrain of the Internet. [1]

Tip

The primary types of tools used in data mining are neural networks, decision trees, rule induction, and data visualization.

Although not an essential prerequisite, data mining potential can be enhanced if the appropriate data have been collected and stored in a data warehouse—a system for storing and delivering massive quantities of data. Data warehousing is the process of extracting and transforming operational data into informational data and loading it into a central data store or warehouse. The promise of data warehousing is that data from disparate databases can be consolidated and managed from one single database.

The link between data mining and data warehousing is explained as follows: Data warehousing is the strategy of ensuring that the data used in an organization is available in a consistent and accurate form wherever it is needed. Often this involves replication of the contents of departmental computers in a centralized site, where it can be ensured that common data definitions are in the departmental computers in a centralized site, and these definitions are in use. Data warehousing is closely connected with data mining because when data about the organization's processes becomes readily available, it becomes easy and therefore economical to mine it for new and profitable relationships.

Thus, data warehousing introduces greater efficiencies to the data mining exercise. Without the pool of validated and scrubbed data that a data warehouse provides, the data mining process requires considerable additional effort to preprocess the data. It is also possible for companies to obtain data from other sources via the Internet, mine the data, and then convey the findings and new relationships internally within the company via an intranet. There are four stages in the data warehousing process:

1. The first stage is the acquisition of data from multiple internal and external sources and platforms.

2. The second stage is the management of the acquired data in a central, integrated repository.

3. The third stage is the provision of flexible access, reporting, and analysis tools to interpret selected data.

4. Finally, the fourth stage is the production of timely and accurate corporate reports to support managerial and decision-making processes. [1]

Although the term *data mining* is relatively new, the technology is not. Many of the techniques used in data mining originated in the artificial intelligence research of the 1980s and 1990s. Only more recently have these tools been applied to large databases. Why then are data mining and data warehousing mushrooming now? IBM has identified six factors that have brought data mining to the attention of the business world:

1. A general recognition that there is untapped value in large databases

2. A consolidation of database records tending toward a single customer view

3. A consolidation of databases, including the concept of an information warehouse

4. A reduction in the cost of data storage and processing, providing for the ability to collect and accumulate data

5. Intense competition for a customer's attention in an increasingly saturated marketplace

6. The movement toward the demassification of business practices. [1]

Tip

With reference to item 6, demassification refers to the shift from mass manufacturing, mass advertising, and mass marketing that began during the industrial revolution to customized manufacturing, advertising, and marketing targeted to small segments of the population.

There are three basic steps in data mining:

1. The first processing step is data preparation, often referred to as "scrubbing the data." Data is selected, cleansed, and preprocessed under the guidance and knowledge of a domain expert.

2. Second, a data mining algorithm is used to process the prepared data, compressing and transforming it to make it easy to identify any latent valuable nuggets of information.

3. The third phase is the data analysis phase where the data mining output is evaluated to see if additional domain knowledge was discovered and to determine the relative importance of the facts generated by the mining algorithms. [1]

Data mining differs from other analytical tools in the approach used in exploring the data relationships. Traditional database queries can answer questions like "What were my sales in Kenora in 2001?" Other analyses, often called *multidimensional* or *online analytical processing*, allow users to do more complex queries, such as comparing sales relative to plan by quarter and region for the prior two years. In both cases, however, the results are simply figures extracted from the data or an aggregate of existing data. The relationship among the data is already known to the user, who, by framing the proper question, obtains the desired answer.

Data mining however, uses discovery-based approaches in which pattern matching and other algorithms are used to discover key relationships in the data, previously unknown to the user. The discovery model is different because the system automatically discovers information hidden in the data—the data is sifted in search of frequently occurring patterns, trends, and generalizations about the data without intervention or guidance from the user. An example of such a model is a bank database that is mined to discover the many groups of customers to target for a mailing campaign. The data is searched with no hypothesis in mind other than for the system to group the customers according to the common characteristic found.

Data mining usually yields five types of information: associations, sequences, classifications, clusters, and forecasting. Associations happen when occurrences are linked in a single event. For example, a study of supermarket baskets might reveal that when corn chips are purchased, 69% of the time cola is also purchased, unless there is a promotion, in which case cola is purchased 89% of the time.

In sequences, events are linked over time. For example, if a house is bought, then 49% of the time a new oven will be bought within one month and 64% of the time a new refrigerator will be bought within three weeks.

Classification is probably the most common data mining activity today. Classification can help you discover the characteristics of customers who are likely to leave and provides a model that can be used to predict who they are. It can also help you determine which kinds of promotions have been effective in keeping which types of customers, so that you spend only as much money as necessary to retain a customer.

Using clustering, the data mining tool discovers different groupings with the data. This can be applied to problems as diverse as detecting defects in manufacturing or finding affinity groups for bank cards.

Finally, all of these applications might involve predictions, such as whether a customer will renew a subscription. Forecasting is a different form of prediction. It estimates the future value of continuous variables (e.g., sales figures) based on patterns within the data. Generally then, applications of data mining can generate outputs such as these:

- Buying patterns of customers, associations among customer demographic characteristics, and predictions on which customers will respond to which mailings

- Patterns of fraudulent credit card usage, identities of "loyal" customers, credit card spending by customer groups, predictions of customers who are likely to change their credit card affiliation

- Predictions on which customers will buy new insurance policies, patterns of risky behavior, customers' expectations of fraudulent behavior

- Characterizations of patient behavior to predict frequency of office visits [1]

As indicated in the preceding, data mining applications can be used in a variety of sectors: retail, finance, manufacturing, health, insurance, and utilities. Therefore, across all sectors—if a business has data about its customers, suppliers, products, or sales—it can benefit from data mining. It is expected that data mining will be one of the greatest tools to be used by the business community in this century as its ability to capitalize on the use of an already existing resource (information) becomes widely recognized, and the cost of data mining software goes down. With regard to customers, the types of data that are needed to perform data mining applications are:

1. Demographics, such as age, gender, and marital status
2. Economic status, such as salary, profession, and household income
3. Geographic details, such as city, street, province, rural or urban [1]

All of these data types can be used to delineate particular sets or segments of customers who share similar interests and have common product requirements.

Examples of Data Mining

It has been estimated that the data mining market will reach more than $1.3 billion by the year 2003. The Gartner Group predicted that by the end of 2003, approximately 85% of the Global 2000 (the world's largest 2,000 companies) will have or will be planning a data warehouse strategy that will likely incorporate data mining.

By the year 2003, at least 54% of the Fortune 1000 companies worldwide will be using data mining. This is not surprising, when you think of the potential benefits to the businesses using various applications. Take, for example, the ability to scour data from multiple databases to predict future trends and behaviors: Blockbuster Entertainment uses it to recommend video rentals to individual customers and American Express uses it to suggest products to its cardholders based on an analysis of their monthly spending patterns.

MasterCard International uses it to extract statistics about its millions of daily cardholder transactions. Furthermore, MasterCard plans to sell a data warehouse of those transactions to its 70,000 business partners—banks and other companies (e.g., Shell Oil) that offer credit card services.

The Internet is also becoming an emerging frontier for data mining. Some technology companies provide "virtual" data mining services via the Internet. With access to an Internet server, it is possible to use File Transfer Protocol (FTP) to obtain the data from the client's server and then conduct various data mining activities.

 Tip

Alternately, if the client does not have access to an Internet server or if the data are too sensitive or voluminous, the data mining services can occur when the client provides a computer tape.

Web sites can be a further source of data for companies that want to know more about visitors to their own Web sites. For example, the Chicago Tribune Company publishes a variety of services on the Web and on America Online, many of which are focused on classified marketing. The Chicago Tribune uses data mining to analyze customer behavior as they move through its various sites.

WalMart is often described as a pioneering leader in data mining and data management. WalMart captures point-of-sale transactions from more than 3,400 stores in 11 countries and continuously transmits this data to its massive 13.5-terabyte data warehouse. WalMart allows more than 4,000 suppliers to access data on their products and perform data analysis. Suppliers use this data to identify customer buying patterns at the store display level. They use this information to manage local store inventory and identify new merchandising opportunities.

Other companies supplement their customers' transactional information with external data such as postal codes to do a market basket analysis. Practically every retailer now records all the details of each point-of-sale transaction for stock keeping purposes. Sometimes these are supplemented by customer information. Home Depot, for example, supplements the data with zip code or postal code of the purchaser. Sometimes the cashier might also enter the sex and appropriate age of the customer into the cash register. Affinity cards and credit card numbers can be used to track repeat customers. Market basket analysis is the analysis of the data that this generates with a view toward improving the performance of the retail outlet.

Another example of what data mining can do involves the directed targeting of customers for new products at a fraction of the cost. A credit card company can leverage its vast warehouse of customer transaction data to identify customers most likely to be interested in a new credit product. Using a small test mailing, the attributes of customers with an affinity for the product can be identified. Recent projects have indicated more than a 70-fold decrease in costs for targeted mailing campaigns over conventional approaches.

In the health care field, data mining applications are growing quickly. Applications can be used to directly assist practitioners in improving the care of patients by determining optimal treatments for a range of health conditions. Data mining is used to help caregivers distinguish patients who are statistically at risk for certain health problems so that those patients can be treated before their conditions worsen. Data mining can also be used to detect possible fraudulent behaviors of health providers as well as health service claimants. For example, patterns of care indicating that a particular practitioner is ordering too many diagnostic tests or conducting tests that are inappropriate can be identified through data mining; similarly, patterns, associations, and overpayments for claims made by patients can be discovered through this process.

However, data mining is not a magic bullet or a simple process. It also presents challenges that go well beyond the technical. Many data management challenges remain, both technical and societal. Large online databases raise serious societal issues. To cite a few of the societal issues, electronic data interchange and data mining software make it relatively easy for a large organization to track all of your financial transactions. By doing that, someone can build a very detailed profile of your interests, travel, and finances. Is this an invasion of your privacy? Indeed, it is possible to do this for almost everyone in the developed world. What are the implications of that?

The next part of this chapter explores the implications of data mining in the context of a set of principles designed to protect and guide the uses of personal information, commonly referred to as fair information practices.

The Implications of Data Mining in the Context of Fair Information Practices

Around the world, virtually all privacy legislation, and the policies, guidelines, or codes of conduct used by nongovernment organizations, have been derived from the set of principles established in 1980 by the Organization for Economic Cooperation and Development. These principles are often referred to as fair information practices, and they cover nine specific areas of data protection (or informational privacy):

1. Collection limitation
2. Data quality
3. Purpose specification
4. Use limitation
5. Security
6. Safeguards
7. Openness
8. Individual participation
9. Accountability [1]

Essentially, these eight principles of data protection or fair information practices codify how personal data should be protected. At the core of these principles is the concept of personal control—the ability of an individual to maintain some degree of control over the use and dissemination of his or her personal information.

Concerns about informational privacy generally relate to the manner in which personal information is collected, used, and disclosed. When a business collects information without the knowledge or consent of the individual to whom the information relates, or uses that information in ways that are not known to the individual, or discloses the information without the consent of the individual, informational privacy might be violated.

Data mining is a growing business activity, but from the perspective of fair information practices, is privacy in jeopardy? To determine this, let's review data mining from a fair information practices perspective. As discussed next, issues have been identified with five of these principles.

Data Quality Principle

Personal data should be relevant to the purposes for which they are to be used, and, to the extent necessary for those purposes, should be accurate, complete, and up-to-date. Any form of data analysis is only as good as the data itself. Data mining operations involve the use of massive amounts of data from a variety of sources: The data could have originated from old, current, accurate or inaccurate, or internal or external sources. Not only should the data be accurate, but the accuracy of the data is also dependent on the input accuracy (data entry), and the steps taken (if any) to ensure that the data being analyzed is indeed "clean."

This requires a data mining operation to use a good data cleansing process to clean or scrub the data before mining explorations are executed. Otherwise, information will be inaccurate, incomplete, or missing. If data are not properly cleansed, errors, inaccuracies, and omissions will continue to intensify with subsequent applications. Above all else, consumers will not be in a position to request access to the data or make corrections, erasures, or deletions, if, in the first instance, the data mining activities are not known to them.

Purpose Specification Principle

The purposes for which personal data are collected should be specified not later than at the time of data collection, and the subsequent use of personal data is limited to the fulfillment of those purposes. Other personal data that is not incompatible with those purposes should be specified on each occasion of change of purpose.

Use Limitation Principle

Personal data should not be disclosed, made available, or otherwise used for purposes other than those specified in accordance with the purpose specification principle except with the consent of the individual or by the authority of law. Purpose specification means that the type of personal data an organization is permitted to collect is limited by the purpose of the collection. The basic rule is that data collected should be relevant and sufficient, but not excessive for the stated purpose. In other words, restraint should be exercised when personal data are collected. Use limitation means that the purpose specified to the data subject (in this case, the consumer) at the time of the collection restricts the use of the information collected. Hence, the information collected can only be used for the specified purpose unless the individual has provided consent for additional uses.

Data mining techniques allow information collected for one purpose to be used for other, secondary purposes. For example, if the primary purpose of the collection of transactional information is to permit a payment to be made for credit card purposes, then using the information for other purposes, such as data mining, without having identified this purpose before or at the time of the collection is in violation of both of the preceding principles. The primary purpose of the collection must be clearly understood by the consumer and identified at the time of the collection. Data mining, however, is a secondary, future use. As such, it requires the explicit consent of the data subject or consumer.

The use limitation principle is perhaps the most difficult to address in the context of data mining or, indeed, a host of other applications that benefit from the subsequent use of data in ways never contemplated or anticipated at the time of the initial collection. Restricting the secondary uses of information will probably become the thorniest of the fair information practices to administer, for essentially one reason: At the time these principles were first developed (in the late 1970s), the means by which to capitalize on the benefits and efficiencies of multiple uses of data were neither widely available nor inexpensive, thus facilitating the old "silo" approach to the storage and segregated use of information.

With the advent of high-speed computers, LANs, powerful software techniques, massive information storage and analysis capabilities, neural networks, parallel processing, and the explosive use of the Internet, a new world is emerging. Change is now the norm, not the exception, and in the quickly evolving field of IT, information practices must also keep pace or run the risk of facing extinction. Take, for example, the new directions being taken intending to replace the information silos of old with new concepts such as data integration and data clustering. If privacy advocates do not keep pace with these new developments, it will become increasingly difficult to advance options and solutions that can effectively balance privacy interests and new technology applications. Keeping pace will enable you to continue as a player in this important arena, allowing you to engage in a meaningful dialogue on privacy and future information practices.

The challenge facing privacy advocates is to address these changes directly while preserving some semblance of meaningful data protection. For example, in the context of data mining, businesses could easily address this issue by adding the words "data mining" as a primary purpose at the time of data collection, but would this truly constitute meaningful data protection? Take another example: When applying for a new credit card, data mining could be added to the purposes for which the personal information collected on the application form would be used. Would this type of general, catch-all purpose be better than having no purpose at all? Possibly, but only marginally so.

The quandary you face with data mining is what suggestions to offer businesses that could truly serve as a meaningful primary purpose. The reason for this lies in the very fact that, in essence, a "good" data mining program cannot, in advance, delineate what the primary purpose will be. Its job is to sift through all the information available to unearth the unknown. Data mining is predicated on finding the unknown. The discovery model on which it is built has no hypothesis—this is precisely what differentiates it from traditional forms of analysis. With the falling cost of memory, the rising practice of data warehousing, and greatly enhanced processing speeds, the trend toward data mining will only increase.

The data miner does not know and cannot know at the outset, what personal data will be of value or what relationships will emerge. Therefore, identifying a primary purpose at the beginning of the process and then restricting one's use of the data to that purpose are the antithesis of a data mining exercise.

This presents a serious dilemma for privacy advocates, consumers, and businesses grappling with the privacy concerns embodied in an activity such as data mining. To summarize, the challenge lies in attempting to identify as a primary purpose an as yet unknown, secondary use. The following sections provide some suggestions on how to address this issue.

Openness Principle

There should be a general policy of openness about developments, practices, and policies with respect to personal data. Means should be readily available of establishing the existence and nature of personal data, and the main purposes of their use, as well as the identity and usual residence of the data controller.

The principle of openness or transparency refers to the concept that people have the right to know what data about them has been collected, who has access to that data, and how the data being used. Simply put, it means that people must be made aware of the conditions under which their information is being kept and used.

Data mining is not an open and transparent activity. It is invisible. Data mining technology makes it possible to analyze huge amounts of information about individuals—their buying habits, preferences, and whereabouts—at any point in time, without their knowledge or consent. Even consumers with a heightened sense of privacy about the use and circulation of their personal information would have no idea that the information they provided for the rental of a movie or a credit card transaction could be mined and a detailed profile of their preferences developed.

For the process to become open and transparent, consumers need to know that their personal information is being used in data mining activities. It is not reasonable to expect the average consumer to be aware of data mining technologies. If consumers were made aware of data mining applications, then they could inquire about information assembled or compiled about them from the business with which they were transacting. Here information means inferences, profiles, and conclusions drawn or extracted from data mining practices.

Ultimately, openness and transparency engender an environment for consumers to act on their own behalf (should they so choose). Consumers could then make known to the businesses they were transacting with their expectations about the collection, reuse, sale, and resale of their personal information.

Individual Participation Principle

Data mining operations are extremely far removed from the point of transaction or the point of the collection of the personal information. As data mining is not openly apparent to the consumer, the consumer is not aware of the existence of information gained through a data mining application. This prevents any opportunity to request access to the information or challenge the data and request that corrections, additions, or deletions be made. In other words, an individual should have these rights:

- To obtain from a data controller confirmation of whether or not the data controller has data relating to him or her

- To have communicated to him or her any data relating to him or her within a reasonable time, at a charge—if any—that is not excessive, in a reasonable manner, and in a form that is readily intelligible.

- To be given reasons if a request made is denied, and to be able to challenge such denial.

- To challenge data relating to him or her and, if the challenge is successful, to have the data erased, rectified, completed, or amended [1]

Consumers and Businesses: Choices to Consider

In the United States, media coverage of public concerns about informational privacy matters began around the start of 1990, with the uproar that erupted over the Lotus Marketplace: Households. This was an early and perhaps defining demonstration of the public's sensitivity about informational privacy. In 1996, the Lexis-Nexis incident drew massive attention to how people feel about their personal information Lexis-Nexis, an online information service in Dayton, Ohio, was accused of making Social Security numbers and other personal information widely available in its P-TRAK locator service. In 1997, after an electronic firestorm, America Online backed off of its plan to rent out its subscribers' telephone numbers. In each of these cases, businesses quickly responded to a public outcry from their customers and either withdrew their products or changed their policies.

Consumers

For consumers to react (and businesses to respond), consumers must have knowledge and awareness that something they could potentially choose to object to is actually occurring. The invisible nature of data mining eliminates this possibility. For data mining to fall into line with fair information practices, the first step for consumers must be an awareness that any large business they are transacting with could be carrying out data mining activities. For some consumers, this knowledge will make no difference; for others, it will matter a great deal.

Once consumers are equipped with knowledge, it is up to each individual to decide for himself or herself what matters, and based on that, what choices he or she wants to make about assuming control over the uses of this personal information. Concerned consumers can choose to take responsibility by informing businesses of their requirements and expectations regarding privacy. To assist in framing privacy-related questions relating to data mining, consumers might wish to consider the questions shown in Table 15.1.

Table 15.1. Data Mining Privacy-Related Questions Checklist

How to Frame Privacy-Related Questions
Framing Privacy-Related Questions Relating to Data Mining Checklist
Date: _____

It is up to the consumer to decide what course of action, if any, to take. As a consumer (mark all questions with a "Yes" or "No"):

❑ 1. Do you expect to be informed of any additional purposes that your personal information might be used for beyond the primary purpose of the transaction?

❑ 2. Do you expect the option to say "no" to secondary or additional uses of your personal information usually provided in the form of opting out of permitting the use of your personal information for additional secondary uses? Do you expect an opportunity to opt-in to secondary uses?

❑ 3. Do you expect a process to be in place that gives you the right to access any information a business has about you at any point in time?

❑ 4. Do you expect a process that permits you to challenge and if successful correct or amend any information held by a business about you at any point in time?

❑ 5. Do you expect an option to have your personal information anonymized for data mining purposes or an option to conduct your transactions anonymously?

For those consumers who wish to have greater control over the use and circulation of their personal information, the following initiatives are suggested. First, ask to see a business's privacy or confidentiality policy. Assess it against your expectations of how you want your personal information handled. If the policy does not meet your expectations, contact the business and inform it of your expectations. If no policy exists, inform the business that you expect respectful and fair handling of your personal information.

Second, give only the minimum amount of personal information needed to complete a transaction. If you are in doubt about the relevance of any information that is requested, ask questions about why it is needed and ask that all the uses of the requested information be identified.

Businesses

Businesses need a corporate will to adopt a culture of privacy—piecemeal or theoretical approaches will not be effective in responding to consumers' concerns. Ultimately, the impact of various technologies on privacy, including data mining, can only be averted by instilling a culture of privacy within the organization.

Instilling a culture of privacy means that businesses will have to tackle the conflict between the use limitation principle and the secondary uses of personal information arising out of data mining. It might be advisable for businesses to provide a multiple-choice opt-out selection whereby consumers are given three choices: the choice of not having their data mined at all, only having their data mined in-house, or having their data mined externally as well. To assist in instilling a culture of privacy, businesses might wish to consider the questions in Table 15.2.

Tip

Studies have shown that less concern is expressed over the internal secondary uses of one's data by the company collecting the data, but far greater resistance to having data disclosed externally for use by unknown parties.

Table 15.2. Instilling a Culture of Privacy Checklist

How to Instill a Culture of Privacy
Instilling a Culture of Privacy in the Organization Checklist
Date: _____

The impact of various technologies on privacy can only be averted by instilling a culture of privacy within the organization. Is your business willing to (mark all questions with a "Yes" or "No"):

❏ 1. Have a privacy strategy that is based on fair information practices and entrenched through tangible actions, resourced throughout all facets of the organization, and evaluated and assessed so that ongoing adjustments and improvements can be made?

❏ 2. Have an open and transparent relationship with its customers?

❏ 3. Do you inform your customers up front about how all information collected about them will be used and disclosed, and by whom?

❏ 4. Do you have a process that makes it easy for customers to find out what personal information you have about them and a process to challenge any information that might be incorrect, incomplete, inaccurate, or out-of-date?

❏ 5. Do you accept that some consumers do not want their personal information to be mined, and nuggets about their buying patterns extracted?

❏ 6. Do you advise consumers of all uses of their personal information and give them a range of opt-out choices about data mining such as:

    ❏ a. No data mining.

    ❏ b. Data mining internally.

    ❏ c. Data mining internally and externally.

❏ 7. Or, for maximum choice and control, do you provide consumers with positive consent, an opportunity to opt in for specified secondary uses of their personal information?

❏ 8. Use privacy-enhancing technologies that can anonymize information and securely protect privacy?

Endnote

[1] Ann Cavoukian, "Data Mining: Staking a Claim on Your Privacy," Information and Privacy Commissioner/Ontario, 80 Bloor Street West, Suite 1700, Toronto, Ontario, M5S 2V1, 2001.

Chapter 16

SUMMARY, CONCLUSIONS, AND RECOMMENDATIONS

P ersonal information can be gathered from numerous sources. A lost wallet or purse will provide a criminal with more than enough information to start a shopping spree in another individual's name. A Social Security number can be found almost anywhere, ranging from a driver's license to a student ID card. Personal checks are placed in unlocked mailboxes every day, providing a criminal with all the information needed to order more checks in the victim's name, or even worse, wipe out the victim's bank account.

Perhaps more prevalent is the fact that identity thieves are now going straight to the source for personal information. Con artists pose as customers and try to get account numbers by using the victim's personal information. Information that is not properly safeguarded by a financial institution can fall into the hands of a criminal who will use it for illegal gains. Computer-savvy criminals are even setting up spoofing Web sites where customers accidentally visit a bank imposter through a mistyped Web address and enter account information that can be garnered for illegal uses.

Summary

As technology continues to become more prevalent, thieves continue to enjoy an open attack on unsuspecting individuals and institutions. The Internet offers an anonymous portal for criminals to use. They no longer have to fear the tedious information verification and face-to-face encounters of traditional financial institution visits.

Although most criminals realize the risk they are taking by masquerading as another person in public, they know technology has made identity theft much safer in today's society. ATMs only require a card swipe and PIN, and even worse, debit cards can be used as credit cards and swiped by the individual at a self-serve terminal. Even Internet purchases only require the user to supply a credit card number and expiration date, as the verification stage has been extremely simplified.

Not surprisingly, individuals aren't the only ones who find themselves becoming victims of identity theft. In an effort to provide the quickest and friendliest service possible, financial institutions trying to attract new customers and keep old ones sometimes make careless and costly mistakes. These institutions sometimes provide information over the phone to individuals who appear to be real customers. They provide loans over the Internet with very little verification. Sometimes, they even open new accounts for an individual in someone else's name. It is important to remember your customer policies in the midst of offering excellent service in your financial institution. These policies are your primary weapon against identity theft schemes.

Once identity theft occurs, the individual usually suffers most. Financial institutions might have to incur some or all of the losses that occur, but individuals have to fight to regain their lives and their privacy. Making customers aware of how to protect their personal information, and then taking steps to safeguard account information from con artists, will help to keep an institution's losses down and its customers happy.

That's great for U.S. institutions and their customers, but what about the international scene? How is identity theft and fraud handled there? The next part of the this final chapter answers those questions by discussing the problem first, then looking at some statistics on international fraud, and finally, how one can use an IP location to uncover international fraud.

Challenges and Technological Solutions for International Fraud and ID Theft

International fraud and ID theft represents one of the fastest growing problems for Internet merchants. Three main factors have contributed to the rise of online international fraud and identity theft:

1. The unlimited reach of the Internet allows fraudsters, identity thieves, and hackers to reach commerce-enabled sites from any location in the world.

2. Governments in developing countries simply do not have the capacity to investigate and prosecute online fraud and identity theft cases. As a result, organized criminal rings find an ideal haven in these countries to pursue their scams undisturbed.

3. Mainstream cardholder validation tools, such as AVS, are primarily supported for credit cards issued in the United States. Online merchants therefore have a limited ability to validate orders that originate from abroad. [1]

Some online merchants, because of the significant risk associated with international orders, no longer ship products abroad and do not accept cards issued outside of the United States. Such drastic policies greatly reduce opportunities for online merchants, locking out millions of potentially legitimate buyers that could be reached via a global Internet commerce site.

As the following cases testify, even these merchants are not immune to the problem, because international fraudsters devise very complex schemes to circumvent policies for fraud prevention. A very recent (and unfortunately still current) triangulation scheme uses online auctions to perpetrate fraud. The fraudster auctions display popular consumer electronic products at deeply discounted prices on a popular online auction site. When a person, unaware of the scam, places the winning bid, the fraudster orders the goods at the manufacturer's Web site or some other retail site and requests that the package be shipped to the address of the auction winner.

The fraudster pays for the order using a compromised credit card number and receives payment from the auction winner via a person-to-person money transfer service that routes the money to a foreign bank account, often in an Eastern European country. The manufacturer then ships the goods to the winner of the auction, but the credit card transaction will obviously be charged back a few months later. In this case, the fraudster never touches the goods as he or she successfully orchestrates the scam from thousands of miles away.

Another recent case of international fraud and identity theft involved a criminal organization and a popular U.S. Web site. The fraudsters placed dozens of relatively small orders using U.S. credit cards. Each order had a U.S. delivery address (the merchant did not ship internationally).

More specifically, there were three different addresses that corresponded to international freight forwarders based in different U.S. locations. When the scheme was uncovered and the shipment companies were contacted, the merchant discovered that the products had actually been shipped to Nigeria.

International Fraud and ID Theft Statistics

ClearCommerce [2] recently conducted a study to quantify the problem of international online fraud and identity theft, and investigate the use of IP geographic location as a tool for detecting these cases. The analysis leveraged an extensive historical database of Internet transactions and an IP database that maps network addresses to the country to which each IP subnetwork is assigned.

The first staggering result was that, although transactions originating from outside the United States represent only 17% of the sample, they accounted for more than 42% of all fraudulent orders. International fraud and identity theft also represent a growing percentage of all the online fraud and identity theft cases: In the last quarter of 2000, international transactions (based on the IP originating country) represented only 11% of all transactions that resulted in chargebacks. In the last quarter of 2001, international transactions represented nearly 51% of all chargebacks.

International fraud and identity theft are highly localized: The majority of fraudulent international orders originate from a relatively short list of countries. Figure 16.1 shows the top high-risk countries, ranked by the percentage of orders originating in each country that resulted in chargebacks. [1] For comparison, the last bar in the chart shows the fraud rate for orders originating from IP addresses located in the United States.

From the chart shown in Figure 16.1, it is clear that the risk associated with orders originating from certain foreign countries is of a different magnitude than domestic orders. It is also important to notice that the top 10 high-risk countries account for more than 35% of all the international fraud, although less than 5% of all the international orders originate in these countries.

Corroborating the evidence from the two reported cases previously described, the analysis also determined that international fraudsters are often

Fraud Rate by Originating Country

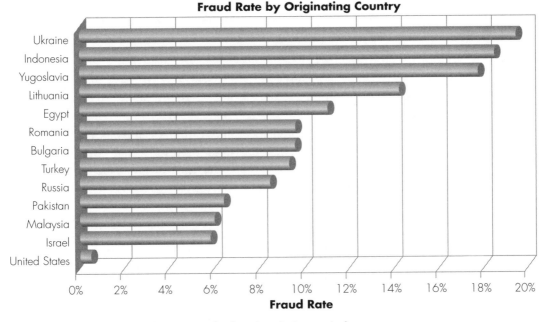

Figure 16.1 Top high-risk countries for fraud and identity theft.

able to mask their transactions as legitimate domestic orders. More than 25% of all fraudulent orders originating outside the United States used credit card numbers issued in the United States. Furthermore, 23% of all the international fraudulent orders had U.S. shipping addresses. The good news is the inconsistency between the billing addresses, shipping addresses, and the geographic location on the IP address can be exploited to detect suspicious orders and therefore prevent international fraud.

Using IP Location to Uncover International Fraud and Identity Theft

The examples of international fraud and identity theft schemes discussed earlier demonstrate the difficulty for Internet merchants in uncovering international fraud schemes. Frequently, the fraudsters and identity thieves have access to compromised credit card numbers issued in the United States or complete billing records that allow them to pass an AVS validation.

International fraud and identity theft schemes often use delivery points in the United States and later forward the goods to a foreign country, or like in the auction scheme, they never even receive the goods. Therefore, in many cases, these fraudulent orders appear just like legitimate domestic orders.

In both of the preceding case studies reported, the only data element that would have uncovered the scheme was the geographic location of the order. For the online auction fraud case, the fraudster connected from various IP addresses located outside of the United States, including Mexico and Eastern Europe. In the second scheme, all orders originated from IP addresses that were located in Nigeria.

Some merchants have been using online resources like the ARIN Web site (*www.arin.net*) to manually research IP addresses associated with suspicious or fraudulent transactions. These databases provide information about the business entity to which each IP address is assigned, like the company name and address.

This back-end investigative process can be useful, but it is also time-intensive because a fraud and identity theft analyst often needs to search multiple databases to obtain useful information about an IP address. In fact, worldwide registration and administration of IP addresses is geographically split between three bureaus: ARIN for the Americas, RIPE (*www.ripe.net*) for Europe and parts of Asia and Africa, and APNIC (*www.apnic.net*) for Asia Pacific.

Recently a few companies have begun offering IP geolocation services and databases that allow online merchants to quickly identify the geographic areas associated with an incoming IP connection. Fraud and identity theft detection are just two of the possible applications of IP geolocation, but the emergence of this technology will help online merchants address international fraud and identity theft. Geolocation products are now available from a few vendors:

- ClearCommerce (*www.clearcommerce.com*), in collaboration with Quova (*www.quova.com*), has recently released a new feature for its fraud detection engine that provides real-time IP-to-country mapping using Quova's GeoPoint[SM] product.

- Digital Envoy (*www.digitalenvoy.com*) also licenses geolocation services with the NetAcuity[TM] product.

- NetGeo (*www.netgeo.com*) provides geolocation with their InfoScope[SM] product. [1]

Most of these services are able to map an IP address not only to the country of origin, but also, with some degree of accuracy, they can determine a metro area or even zip code. This degree of resolution could also be helpful in detecting domestic fraud and identity theft by, for example, spotting geographic inconsistencies between area codes and IP zip codes.

Finally, IP geolocation is yet another defensive weapon that is available to online merchants in the battle against international fraud and identity theft in particular. As for every detection technique in online fraud and identity theft prevention, this technology alone will not be able to detect all fraud and identity theft, and some fraudsters will eventually find ways to circumvent it. Nonetheless, IP geolocation is becoming a best practice in online fraud and identity theft prevention.

Now, continuing with the European fraud and identity theft prevention techniques theme, let's take a look at how smart card security concerns in Europe have migrated to the United States. The smart cards are getting an extra boost from post-September 11 security concerns.

International Smart Card Security

Recently, the American Association of Motor Vehicle Administrators, representing all 50 U.S. states, agreed to develop a common approach and common standards for upgrading driver's licenses. They want to embed biometric information, such as a finger or palm print, iris or facial scans, or even DNA data, into the licenses to turn them into a national ID firmly linked to the holder. The methods of data encoding under consideration include magnetic stripes, barcodes, optical scanning, and smart cards incorporating chips—a technology well-entrenched overseas in banking, health care, and telephony, but with barely a foothold in the United States.

Although Americans like to think they lead the global pack in technology, in the case of smart cards, this country has lagged steadily behind Europe (France especially) and Asia (see Figure 16.2). [3] Until recently, just about the only U.S. application to be invaded by smart cards was the public laundro-

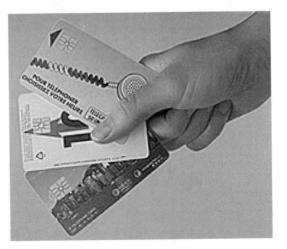

Figure 16.2
Cards for pay telephones, perhaps the first application to incorporate Smart Card technology, caught on fast, first in Europe, then in Asia.

mat, where moisture made magnetic swipe cards unreliable. Now the cards are beginning to make inroads in other areas, notably personal identification, which has loomed larger amid security concerns after the terrorist attacks of September 11, 2001.

Smart cards might still be an unpromising candidate for use in U.S. identification cards, but quite a few other countries have adopted them as national IDs. In Sweden, Finland, and Malaysia, for instance, they do double duty as authentication cards for government services and financial transactions.

Smart cards took off in Europe more than a decade ago, when national telephone companies outfitted their awkward pay-phone systems with them. Previously, special tokens were required in some countries, and in others, the pay phone itself was overly complicated. Plastic smart cards, embedded with microprocessor chips and ample memory, caught on fast, and then invaded other areas, such as national health care.

Europe's Edge

Relatively small markets and government-controlled businesses aided Europe's adoption of smart cards in many sectors. In Europe, you meet with a few ministers, and 80 million health ID cards get ordered; in the United States, you have to navigate local, state, and federal bureaucracies. It's the same situation in banking: European countries are dominated by five or six banks, whereas the United States has 10,000.

In banking, because European data networks were not as reliable as those in the United States for transferring funds, there was a need for a card capable of authorizing payment. Money could also be held in the smart card itself.

Of course, the magnetic stored-value cards of some U.S. transit systems also contain a sum of money or number of units, with money or units subtracted from the card's balance with each use (see Figure 16.3). [3] In this respect they resemble smart cards. However, the latter can hold much more information (up to 64 KB, versus 200 bytes) and can do more elaborate processing. Plus, in certain operating environments, smart cards have a distinct edge.

Nevertheless, as smart card technology has advanced further, and the cards have continued to catch on elsewhere, potential U.S. users are paying them more serious attention. Of special appeal are applications that consolidate functions performed at several locations within a locality or region, involve tougher methods of identification, and offer wireless transmission. Already Royal Dutch/Shell, the U.S. Department of Defense, and others have combined company ID badges and computer passwords into one smart card.

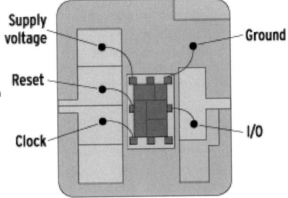

Figure 16.3
The Square on a Smart Card (visible on the pay phone cards in Figure 16.2) consists of contacts with leads going to an integrated circuit buried under the center of the square. The arrangement of contacts varies among applications, but is standard for each individual application.

Computer operating systems such as Microsoft Windows 2000 and Windows XP are now equipped with a built-in smart card reader interface.

Recently, Cubic Transportation Systems, Inc., in San Diego, California, conducted a successful test of a smart card with the Washington, DC, transit system. Participants used a single wireless card that stores a sum of money for paying for local public transportation and parking, plus information for workplace access, speeding up transit times and burdening them with fewer cards.

In another recent demonstration, Netsmart Technologies, Inc., in Islip, New York, is working with California's San Joaquin County to facilitate a county law, in effect since 2001, mandating treatment for nonviolent drug offenders. An offender is issued a card that tracks every class, medical appointment, counseling session, and probation officer meeting, and then deposits the information in a central database. The card is inserted into a computer plug-in and can communicate with several platforms, including many used in the medical industry. Mistakes and treatment overlaps are fewer.

However, the biggest push since September 11, 2001, has been the use of biometric indicators in place of signatures and printed photos on IDs. Fingerprint mapping, eye geometry, voice or facial recognition, and other biological markers are more accurate at identifying people as they try to access buildings, computers, or national borders. The card selects distinctive measurements or pixel patterns of a person's features and compresses and stores them in its embedded computer chip. Then, to grant or deny access, the card compares those patterns to a digital pattern stored in a workplace entry gate, or local or remote database.

Two companies selling this technology are Electronic Data Systems Corp., in Plano, Texas, and Precise Biometrics, in Lund, Sweden. Both make machines that read a person's palm or fingerprint and compare it to information stored on a smart card. The units are already in use at some airports to expedite travel through customs or to block trespassing into secure areas and IT systems.

The debate now is if this type of security could have prevented the events of September 11. This technology has many of the attributes that could have moved the industry toward prevention, but no one security system is without fault. A totally integrated security system using smart cards, databases, biometrics, electronic gating, x-ray, and skilled human intervention would have provided significant security.

Conclusions

Financial institutions work hard to ensure the safety of their customers' personal information, but becoming a victim of identity theft can devastate an individual. In situations such as these, a financial institution needs to do everything it can to help the victim restore his or her life and credit history. After years of being shrugged to the side, identity theft is finally being taken seriously by individuals and institutions alike, but is it too late? The "couldn't happen to me" attitudes displayed by our society in the past are now coming back to haunt us.

Identity theft damages can take on many different forms for individuals, but financial institutions also deal with various aspects. In most cases, a financial institution will incur some or all of the financial losses experienced by their customers. If the institution was at fault, it will more than likely lose the customer's business as well. In some extreme cases, other penalties might be assessed to the institution if it was blatantly careless with the individual's nonpublic information or failed to file an SAR in the event of a questionable transaction.

A joint study between the California Public Interest Research Group and the Privacy Rights Clearinghouse discovered that the average time it takes an identity theft victim to realize something has occurred is about 14 months. In that amount of time, a criminal can easily ruin an individual's credit history by leaving a trail of unpaid debts. It can take a lengthy amount of time for an individual to completely restore his or her life to normal, and the victim will need a lot of assistance from his or her financial institution to do so.

The hardest part of these proceedings is that the victim must prove that he or she didn't commit the fraud. Instead of being innocent until proven guilty, the exact opposite situation prevails. Creditors usually request several pieces of information from the individual, including old documents from the time the fraud was committed to verify signatures and employment information. Not only are some of these documents difficult to find, but the creditors also usually require them to be submitted in a very short amount of time.

In most cases, the individual was the unknowingly careless party in causing the occurrence of identity theft. Financial institutions will play the good neighbor and help to cover the losses experienced by the victim from their account as long as the victim can prove that he or she was in no way directly responsible and do so in a timely manner.

Institutions can play a major role in educating and safeguarding customer information by providing information to their customers on the topic of identity theft prevention. This simple step can prevent hours of additional work and financial losses for both the institution and its customers. It will also boost customer satisfaction and let them know that their financial institution is interested in their financial security and personal well-being.

Recommendations

As previously explained, identity theft is becoming one of society's most feared crimes, yet every day consumers do several little things ever day that put them in danger of becoming the next victim. Falling prey to this crime can be expensive, sometimes costing financial institutions hundreds or even thousands of dollars and the victims several months and a sizable amount of their own money to completely clear their name and credit report. The best way to prevent identity theft on your end is to be as protective of customers' personal information as possible.

It is hard to fathom that some of the most common daily occurrences could cause this much trouble. A financial institution might receive a phone call from someone who sounds legitimate and answer questions regarding a customer's personal information. They might not warn customers of the possibility that someone could gain access to their accounts through illegal measures and how to protect themselves. In some cases, they might even discard an individual's personal information in an unsafe manner where others can view it. Criminals can get all of the information they need to impersonate an individual without even breaking a sweat.

The concern over identity theft is growing so large that Traveler's Insurance recently became the first company to offer an insurance plan covering identity theft. The policy covers the expenses consumers might face while trying to clear their name and their record. Some of the expenses that are covered under this plan are legal expenses, loan reapplication fees, long-distance telephone charges, and even lost wages for the time spent cleaning up the credit mess. In the short amount of time since Traveler's entered into the identity theft protection market, three other insurance companies have followed suit.

Financial institutions that collect and use an individual's personal information are looking into ways to prevent identity theft on their end to keep financial losses down and customer information safe. Fighting high-tech thieves

405

with technology, biometrics uses an individual's unique identifying features (e.g., retina or fingerprint) to ensure that an individual is indeed who he or she claims to be. At the current time, however, this device will only work for in-person transactions, leaving online transactions vulnerable to fraud. The high cost of implementation is another major reason this idea hasn't quickly spread. Digital signatures and smart cards are other ways in which financial institutions are trying to keep customer information and assets secure.

How to Prevent Identity Theft: Business Practices Are the Key

Identity theft can cause business, financial, and personal problems and takes months and sometimes years to clear up completely. Financial institutions can take a more proactive role by educating customers about what they can do to prevent this crime. Tips can include those shown in Table 16.1. [6]

Table 16.1. Preventing Identity Theft Checklist.

Recommendations on How to Prevent Identity Theft
Tips on How to Prevent ID Theft Checklist
Date: _____

Discussions on preventing identity theft often focus on steps consumers can take, such as shredding their trash and restricting access to their Social Security number. Realistically, although such measures can reduce the odds of becoming a victim, there is little consumers can do to actually prevent identity theft. It is recommended therefore, that the key to prevention is for businesses to establish responsible information-handling practices and for the credit industry to adopt stricter application verification procedures, among other strategies (check all tasks completed):

Business Practices

❑ 1. Develop a comprehensive privacy policy that includes responsible information handling practices.

❑ 2. Adhere to responsible information handling practices such as proper document disposal (shredding).

❑ 3. Conduct regular staff training, new employee orientations and spot checks on proper information care.

❑ 4. Put limits on data collection to the minimum information needed. For example, is a Social Security number really required?

Table 16.1. Preventing Identity Theft Checklist. (Continued)

❑ 5. Put limits on data disclosure. For example, must someone's Social Security number be printed on paychecks, parking permits, staff badges, time sheets, training program rosters, lists of who got promoted, monthly account statements, client reports, and so on?

❑ 6. Restrict data access to staff with a legitimate need to know. Implement electronic audit trail procedure. Enforce strict penalties for browsing and illegitimate access.

❑ 7. Conduct employee background checks. Screen cleaning services, temp services, contractors and so on.

❑ 8. Include responsible information handling practices in business school courses, even in elementary schools when children are exposed to computers.

Social Security Numbers:

❑ 1. Take your Social Security number out of circulation. Do not print it on invalid documents unless absolutely necessary. Do not print it on business documents.

❑ 2. Prohibit its use as customer number, as employee ID number, health insurance ID, student ID, or military ID.

❑ 3. Prohibit commercial sale of your Social Security number, available now on information broker Web sites (credit header).

Departments of Motor Vehicles, Public Records

❑ 1. Maintain central clearinghouses in each state for lost and stolen driver's licenses.

❑ 2. Conduct better photo checking and ID checking for new, duplicate, and replacement IDs.

❑ 3. Restrict access to birth certificates in states where they are now public. Redact Social Security numbers and other sensitive information from public records, especially when accessible on the Internet.

Credit Issuers

❑ 1. Conduct better identity verification, especially when address is reported as changed or is different from what is indicated on credit report.

❑ 2. Conduct better identity verification for credit cards obtained via preapproved offers of credit. Don't rely solely on Social Security number, supplement this with utility bills, to confirm address.

❑ 3. Improve identity checking procedures for "instant" credit, favored by identity thieves.

❑ 4. Put photographs on credit cards.

❑ 5. Enable customers to place passwords on credit accounts.

Table 16.1.   Preventing Identity Theft Checklist. (Continued)

❏   6. Truncate digits on account numbers printed on point-of-sale transaction slips.

❏   7. Use account profiling systems to detect unusual activity. Notify consumers of possible fraud.

❏   8. Check if there is an existing account in the applicant's name before operating a credit card..

❏   9. Reduce the number of preapproved credit offers mailed to consumers. Don't mail to anyone under 18. Print an opt-out phone number prominently on all such offers (888-5OPTOUT).

❏   10. Mail convenience checks on opt-in basis only.

Credit Reporting Agencies (CRA)

❏   1. Provide consumers with a free credit report annually on request in all states.

❏   2. Require that when a credit report is obtained by a customer, the subject always gets a copy.

❏   3. Conduct profiling and provide notice to the consumer when unusual activity is detected by CRA.

❏   4. Notify the consumer whenever an inquiry is made, with notice to the original address.

❏   5. Always report a fraud alert to credit issuer including when only the credit score is requested. The credit issuers that grant credit to imposters after a fraud alert has been established should be penalized.

❏   6. Place fraud alerts more prominently on credit reports.

❏   7. Provide the ability for consumers to "freeze" credit files, or at least as in Vermont, require affirmative consent of consumers before any credit reports are issued to customers of credit reporting agencies.

❏   8. Conduct better screening of credit reporting agency customers. Cancel contracts of any customers when consumer credit reports are accessed by staff without legitimate business purpose.

❏   9. Enable consumers to easily obtain fraud alerts, even if they are not fraud victims, with a simple way to deactivate the alert when they need to obtain credit.

❏   10. Credit reporting agencies must make it easier for victims to reach "live" staff. Victims need one-stop shopping so they do not have to replicate their clean-up steps with each agency.

Considering the immense amount of information available on the Internet, it is impossible to completely safeguard your customers. However, with a little care and common sense, you can all help to discourage identity theft from occurring.

Protect Yourself Against Fraud and Identity Theft

It is very important to protect private information about yourself. This includes Social Security numbers, driver's license numbers, PINs, credit card numbers, and deposit account numbers.

Identity thieves might obtain crucial information by stealing from your mailbox, sorting through trash for discarded receipts or statements, using public records, or even spying for your PIN number at ATM machines or a telephone booth. What can you do? You should follow the tips shown in Table 16.2 to avoid becoming a victim of identity theft.

Table 16.2. Protecting Yourself From Identity Theft Checklist

Recommendations on What to Do to Protect Yourself From Identity Theft
Important Tips on How to Protect Yourself From Identity Theft Checklist
Date: _____

It is impossible for you to prevent the distribution of your personal identification and credit information or to exercise control over all of the possible uses of that information. It is recommended nonetheless, that you take the following steps to reduce the risk of theft and misuse of your personal identification and credit information (check all tasks completed):

❑ 1. Do not routinely carry your Social Security card, your birth certificate, your passport, or more than one credit card. When you must carry some or all of these, take special precautions to reduce the risk of loss or theft.

❑ 2. Always take credit card, debit card, and ATM receipts with you. Never throw them in a public trash container. Tear them up or shred them at home when you no longer need them.

❑ 3. Mail all bill payments from the post office or a locked public mailbox rather than having your mail carrier pick them up from your home mailbox.

❑ 4. Consider installing a professionally installed, monitored home security system.

❑ 5. Obtain a post office box if you live in an area where mail theft has occurred.

❑ 6. Tear up or shred unused preapproved credit card solicitations, convenience checks, canceled checks, deposit slips, paycheck or earning statements, and any other documents that contain personal information about you prior to placing it in the trash.

Table 16.2. Protecting Yourself From Identity Theft Checklist (Continued)

❑ 7. Carefully review your credit card statements and utility bills (including cellular telephone bills) for unauthorized use as soon as you receive them. If you suspect unauthorized use, contact the provider's customer service and fraud departments immediately.

❑ 8. Order your credit report each year from each of the three major credit reporting agencies.

❑ 9. Check each credit report carefully for accuracy and for indications of fraud, such as credit accounts that you did not open, applications for credit that you did not authorize, credit inquiries that you did not initiate, charges that you did not incur, and defaults and delinquencies that you did not cause.

❑ 10.Check the identifying information in your credit report to be sure it is accurate (especially your name, address, and Social Security number).

❑ 11. Never give out your credit card, bank account or Social Security number over the telephone unless you placed the call and you have a trusted business relationship with the business or organization.

❑ 12. Guard against overuse of your Social Security number. Release it only when necessary—for example, on tax forms and employment records, or for banking, stock and property transactions.

❑ 13. Do not have your Social Security number printed on your checks. Do not allow a merchant to write your Social Security number on your check.

❑ 14. If a business requests your Social Security number, ask to use an alternate number.

❑ 15. Some businesses have systems to identify their customers that do not use Social Security numbers. If the business does not have such an alternate system, ask to use an alternate identifier that you will remember (for example, a combination of the letters of your last name and numbers). You can lawfully refuse to give a private business your Social Security number, but the business then can refuse to provide you service.

❑ 16. If a government agency asks for your Social Security number, a Privacy Act notice should accompany the request. This notice will explain whether your Social Security number is required or merely requested; what use will be made of your Social Security number; and what will happen if you refuse to provide it.

❑ 17. If you do not receive your credit card statement on time (or if you do not receive a new or renewed credit card when you expect it), it is possible that an identity thief has filed a change of address request in your name with the creditor or the post office. Identity thieves do this to divert their victims' mail to the thief's address.

❑ 18. Call the creditor to see if a change of address request has been filed in your name or if additional or replacement credit cards have been requested on your account. If

Table 16.2.   Protecting Yourself From Identity Theft Checklist (Continued)

either has happened, inform the creditor that you did not make the request and instruct the creditor not to honor it.

❏ 19. Call the post office to see if a change of address request has been filed in your name. If this has happened, immediately notify the Postal Inspector (see the "Postal Service" listing under "United States Government" in the white pages of the telephone directory).

❏ 20. If you shop on the Internet, use a secure browser which encrypts or scrambles purchase information or place your order by telephone or mail.

❏ 21. Check your Social Security Earnings and Benefits statement once each year to make sure that someone else is not using your Social Security number for employment. You can order this statement from the Social Security Administration.

❏ 22. Consider having your name removed from marketing lists.

❏ 23. The three major credit reporting agencies use information from credit reports to develop lists of consumers who meet criteria specified by potential creditors. You can request that your credit information not be used for these purposes. Doing this will limit the number of preapproved credit offers that you receive.

❏ 24. Credit card issuers often compile lists of marketing information about their cardholders based on their purchases.

❏ 25. The Direct Marketing Association (DMA) maintains lists of people who do not want to receive mail and telephone solicitations from national marketers. You can request that your name be added to the DMA's Mail Preference Service and Telephone Preference Service name-removal lists.

❏ 26. Consider not listing your residence telephone number in the telephone book, or consider listing just your name and residence telephone number.

❏ 27. If you decide to list your name and telephone number, consider not listing your professional qualification or affiliation (for example, "Dr.," "Atty.," or "Ph.D.").

❏ 28. Make a list of, or photocopy, all of your credit cards. For each card, include the account number, expiration date, credit limit and the telephone numbers of customer service and fraud departments. Keep this list in a safe place (not your wallet or purse) so that you can contact each creditor quickly if your cards are lost or stolen. Make a similar list for your bank accounts.

❏ 29. Cancel your unused credit cards so that their account numbers will not appear on your credit report. If an identity thief obtains your credit report, the thief may use the account numbers to obtain credit in your name. To help avoid this problem, some credit reporting agencies "truncate" account numbers on credit reports.

Table 16.2. Protecting Yourself From Identity Theft Checklist (Continued)

❏ 30. When creating passwords and PINs (personal identification numbers), do not use any part of your Social Security number, birth date, middle name, wife's name, child's name, pet's name, mother's maiden name, address, consecutive numbers, or anything that a thief could easily deduce or discover.

❏ 31. Memorize all your passwords and PINs; never write them in your wallet, purse or Rolodex.

❏ 32. Shield the keypad when punching in your PIN at an ATM or when placing a calling card call. This helps protect against "shoulder surfers" learning your code.

❏ 33. Install a lock on your mailbox at home, or use a post office box. This will reduce the risk of mail theft.

❏ 34. When you order new checks, pick them up at the bank instead of having them mailed to your home.

❏ 35. When you fill out a loan or credit application, be sure that the business considers the safety of that information by storing them in locked files and by protecting their premises with a monitored security system. These applications often contain all of the information someone needs to assume your credit identity.

❏ 36. Never give your credit card number or other personal information over the phone unless you initiate the call and know you can trust the business.

❏ 37. Tear up papers with your personal information, such as bill statements and mail solicitations for credit cards. Always take ATM and credit card receipts.

❏ 38. When you order checks, consider removing extra information (Social Security number, date of birth, address, middle name) since checks can easily be lost or stolen.

❏ 39. Memorize your Social Security and PIN numbers and passwords. Don't carry extra credit cards, Social Security number, birth certificate, or passport unless essential.

❏ 40. Consider getting an "assigned" driver's license number from the DOT (instead of using your Social Security number). These are available for non-commercial licenses. Assigned numbers work for most purposes that require a driver's license number.

❏ 41. Don't sign up for contests or sweepstakes, unless it's a local one that you trust. Whenever you give information—to contests, subscriptions, charities, manufacturers, or organizations—it may well be sold and reproduced in countless ways.

❏ 42. Consider asking that your personal information be deleted or kept private in public listings such as driver and motor vehicle records, the three major credit reporting bureaus, Direct Marketing Assn. Solicitation lists, and telephone or city directories.

❏ 43. Keep a list of all account numbers in a secure, confidential place in case you experience problems with lost cards or theft of checks.

Table 16.2.   Protecting Yourself From Identity Theft Checklist (Continued)

❑   44. Notify your financial institution immediately if you suspect your accounts have been compromised, or if you have lost any cards or checks.

❑   45. Store extra boxes of checks in a secure place.

❑   46. Do not provide any personal information to a third party unless you are confident of the purpose and feel secure that the information will not be misused.

❑   47. Keep credit cards, ATM cards, debit cards, and check books secure at all times. Do not leave purses or pocketbooks unattended at any time.

❑   48. Place only minimal personal information on the top of your checks.

❑   49. Be sure to carefully review all account statements regularly.

❑   50. Notify your financial institution immediately if there are discrepancies when you balance your accounts.

❑   51. Report any suspicious activity to law enforcement and your financial institution.

❑   52. Do not store or write PIN information on plastic cards or in pocket books or purses.

❑   53. Shred or destroy any documents that contain personal information before putting them in the garbage.

❑   54. Remove mail from your mailbox promptly.

❑   55. Consider mailing payments and checks at the post office instead of leaving them in your mailbox for pickup.

❑   56. Please cooperate fully with merchants or financial institutions that request proper identification. They are doing it to protect your interest.

Victim Recovery From Identity Theft

As stated in earlier chapters, identity fraud is one of the fastest growing white-collar crimes in the nation. The perpetrators consider this a faceless crime, as their targets are financial institutions or retail stores. Little if any thought is ever given to the harm their actions bring to the individuals whose identities they have stolen.

Identity fraud is the criminal misappropriation of another person's identity: identifying data such as name, birth date, Social Security number, mother's maiden name, and other personal information. All such thieves need to perpetrate this crime is a name, Social Security number, and birth date, all easily found on driver's licenses, personal checks, and unsolicited credit card offers.

In addition, identity thieves can search your mail for this information via newly issued credit cards, bank and credit card statements, junk mail, tax information, or bill payments. Sometimes these imposters utilize scams in which they file change of address cards so a victim's mail is sent elsewhere, then they use the mail to obtain the documents needed to impersonate the victim. Thieves also dig through garbage bins, known as dumpster diving, to obtain credit card slips, loan applications, bank statements, and even medical records. Unscrupulous employees who have access to personnel records or other identification information have been known to provide this information to thieves or use this information themselves to perpetrate this fraud.

Recognizing the serious nature of identity fraud and the long-term ramifications for its victims, the Identity Theft and Assumption Deterrence Act of 1998 criminalized fraud in connection with the unlawful theft and misuse of personal identifying information, regardless of whether it appears in or is used in documents. Violation of the provisions of this act can result in imprisonment of up to 15 years, fines, or both. In addition, the Act also provides for the forfeiture of any personal property used in the crime, and it tasked the FTC with creating and maintaining an Identity Theft Consumer Complaint Center to refer complaints to law enforcement as appropriate. By keeping abreast of your personal finances and following the recommendations listed in Table 16.3, you might be able to prevent or minimize losses due to this insidious and destructive crime.

Table 16.3. If You Become a Victim of Identity Theft Checklist

Recommendations on What to Do If You Become a Victim of Identity Theft
Victim Steps on What to Do Checklist
Date: _____

Information gathered by federal agencies tasked with addressing identity fraud reveals that the top five complaints for this type of crime are new credit card openings, existing credit card account usage or change, cellular telephone service obtained, new bank account openings, and newly obtained loans. By being vigilant in all of your financial matters, you become the first line of defense in reducing your chances of becoming a victim. If you believe you have been victimized, you should do the following (check all tasks completed):

❑ 1. Notify your local police and file a complaint. If your loss is $1,000 or greater, you can also contact your local FBI office.

❑ 2. Immediately contact credit reporting agencies and request that a security alert be placed on your account. Follow up with a written letter.

❑ 3. Request and carefully review a copy of your credit report for other false accounts or information.

Table 16.3. If You Become a Victim of Identity Theft Checklist (Continued)

❏ 4. Contact each creditor on your credit report and request that any unusual activity be flagged and verified with you.

❏ 5. Any creditor with fraudulent accounts in your name should be advised that the account is fraudulent.

❏ 6. Request a copy of all documents related to the account and demand that the account be closed immediately.

❏ 7. Follow up each conversation with a letter detailing the exact circumstances and action requested.

❏ 8. Do not pay any bills or charges that result from identity theft.

❏ 9. Contact your financial institution and request new account numbers, ATM cards, and PIN numbers.

❏ 10. Request a new driver's license with an alternate number from the DMV, and ask that your old number be flagged so that any attempted use can be immediately known and reported.

❏ 11. Contact the Social Security Administration and advise them of your situation. Request their assistance by asking them to issue you a new number and flag your old number for fraudulent use.

❏ 12. Contact the post office and telephone company to ensure that no billing changes are made to your account without a written request from you. Request that all changes be verified.

❏ 13. As appropriate, contact an attorney to help ensure that you do not continue to be victimized while attempting to resolve this fraud.

❏ 14. The Federal Trade Commission (FTC) provides additional material which identifies steps you may take to prevent becoming a victim of this fraud or what to do if you become victimized. Reach them at 1-877-FTC-HELP or *www.consumer.gov/idtheft.*

❏ 15. Be persistent and follow up.

In an attempt to make the identity theft victim whole again—emotionally, legally, and financially—the next part of the chapter discusses recommendations that an identity theft victim can make of the court. The problem is that there is usually no one to turn to, to ask about procedures, or to help guide victims through the legal maze.

Recommended ID Theft Victims Court Requests

While the majority of identity theft cases do not result in the arrest and conviction of the imposter, it is important to know your rights in the event that the person is caught. Through your victim impact statement during the sentencing phase of the case, you will need to convey to the courts how this crime has affected you (emotionally, legally and financially) and what it might take to make you whole again. [4]

It is in your best interest to discuss the reasonability of your requests with the district attorney (DA) assigned to the case; or, to the probation officer who is charged with recommending a sentence. If the DA's office has a victim assistance program, this might be another group to speak with prior to finalizing your requests. The following are some items that victims have been granted by the courts. [4]

- Restitution
- Written Letter of Clearance/Declaration of Innocence
- Information retrieval
- Anti-theft counseling
- Regular review hearings/probation [4]

Restitution

Restitution is reimbursement for reasonable and unavoidable expenses. These should be documented with receipts and a journal or log. They may include phone calls, postage, travel, photocopying, fingerprinting, business expenses, notarizing, lost wages, childcare, legal assistance and doctor and therapy bills. For instance, if you work on a production line and need to take time off to make phone calls, that could be considered an unavoidable expense.

Written Letter Of Clearance/Declaration Of Innocence

If the imposter has used your name as an alias while committing a crime you can request a "Letter of Clearance or Declaration of Innocence." It is known by various names, so ask the district attorney or sheriff in your area for the precise title. This letter from the court, will help to establish your true identity should the police stop you and find your name on a criminal database.

Information Retrieval

You should request that the courts either destroy or return to you all documents containing your personal data that are in the possession of the imposter. You may also request that the imposter is never to have your information in their possession for any reason.

Anti-Theft Counseling

You know that identity thieves are often repeat offenders. While there is no proof that this helps, it does send a message.

Regular Review Hearings/Probation

This is one of the most important tools you have. Most often, identity thieves just receive probation. With probation officers handling sometimes 700+ cases, Review Hearings become a way for the courts to make sure the imposter is following all court mandates.

While most victims are only interested in monetary restitution and imprisonment, you should realize any time a person violates probation he or she may be placed in jail. Therefore, terms of probation are an important part of the sentence

Finally, the criminal justice system has been slow in responding to the problem of identity theft and in recognizing the impact of this crime on victims. However, judges are becoming more familiar with this crime and their possible sentencing choices. Your requests will not only help your situation, but also suggest options that the judge has not considered. For updated information on Requests to Make of the Court, go to *www.idtheftcenter.org*, Self Help Guide 17D. [4]

Principles of Privacy Protection

Many of the concerns expressed by consumers about privacy relate to the manner in which personal information is collected, used, and disclosed. When organizations collect information without the knowledge or consent of the individual to whom the information relates, use that information in ways that are unknown to the individual, or disclose the information without the consent of the individual, informational privacy is violated.

Concern about informational privacy in Europe in the early 1970s gave rise to the need for data protection. Data protection focuses on people's personal information and their ability to maintain some degree of control over its use and dissemination. What followed from the concern for data protection was the development of a set of practices commonly referred to as fair information practices, shown in Table 16.4. [5] These are practices that are pertinent to your system as a whole.

Table 16.4.   Set of Fair Information Practices Checklist

Fair Information Practices Recommendations
Fair Information Practices Checklist
Date: _____

There have been several attempts to develop a complete and comprehensive set of fair information practices. The practices that follow reflect these business practices, modified to fit the circumstances relating to advanced card technologies. In regards to each of these principles, it is recommended that those who design applications that use advanced card technologies or those who market them commit to the following (check all tasks completed):

Recognition and Respect for Privacy

❏   1. Recognize that your customers are the owners of their personal information, to be consulted in the development of policies or practices that could potentially impact their privacy.

❏   2. Adopt privacy protection practices and apply them when handling all customer personal information.

❏   3. Assess, prior to implementation, the impact on privacy of any proposed new policy, service, or product.

❏   4. Adopt a policy of redress or restoration so that if any service alters the privacy status quo, you will provide a means to restore that privacy at no cost to the customer.

❏   5. Communicate your privacy protection policies and practices to your customers in a manner that enables them to exercise their rights.

Openness

❏   1. Ensure there is an openness about your policies and practices relating to your customers' personal information, and that the existence of any record-keeping systems containing your customers' personal information are not kept secret from them—they should be transparent.

❏   2. Develop and publicize a process for addressing and responding to any customer inquiry or complaint regarding the handling of their personal information.

Purpose Specification

❏   1. Identify the purposes for which your customers' personal information is to be collected, used, or routinely disclosed before it is collected.

Table 16.4.   Set of Fair Information Practices Checklist (Continued)

❑   2. Do not withdraw access to services or products if your customer subsequently refuses to permit the use of their personal information for a purpose not identified at the time of collection, including the exchange or sale of that information to a third party for marketing purposes.

Collection Limitations:

❑   1. Only collect personal information about your customers that is necessary and relevant for the transaction(s) involved.

❑   2. Collect personal information about your customers directly from the individuals concerned, whenever reasonably possible.

❑   3. Collect customers' personal information with the knowledge and consent of the customers, except in very limited circumstances, and inform the customer of these circumstances at, or prior to, the time of collection.

Notification:

❑   1. Notify your customers at, or before the time of collection, of:

   ❑   a. The purposes for which the personal information is to be used or/and disclosed.

   ❑   b. The source(s) from which the personal information is to be collected, if not directly from the customer.

Use:

❑   1. Only use personal information for the purposes identified to the customer at the time of collection unless the customer explicitly consents to a new use, or the activity is authorized by law.

Right of Access:

❑   1. Establish a right for customers to have access to their personal information, subject to clear and limited exceptions (if such access would constitute an invasion of another person's privacy).

❑   2. Provide customers with access to their personal information in a form understandable to them, without undue delay or expense.

❑   3. If they are denied access, you should inform the customer of the reasons why and provide them with a fair opportunity to challenge the denial.

Right of Correction:

❑   1. Establish a right for customers to challenge the accuracy of their personal information.

❑   2. Amend customer's personal information if it is found to be inaccurate, incomplete, irrelevant or inappropriate.

Table 16.4.   Set of Fair Information Practices Checklist (Continued)

❑   3. Make note in the customer's file of any discrepancies regarding the accuracy or completeness of their personal information.

❑   4. Take all reasonable measures to inform third parties who also use your customers' personal information, of corrections or changes that have been made.

Accuracy:

❑   1. Take all reasonable and appropriate measures to ensure that the personal information you collect, use and disclose, meets the highest possible standard of accuracy, completeness and timeliness.

Disclosure:

❑   1. Obtain customers' consent prior to disclosure of their personal information, except where authorized by law or in exceptional circumstances. These limited, exceptional circumstances should be identified and customer informed of them at, or prior to, the time of collection.

❑   2. Obtain your customers' consent prior to renting, selling, trading or otherwise disclosing their personal information to a third party.

Retention and Disposal:

❑   1. Retain personal information only for as long as it is relevant to the purposes for which it was collected, or as required by law.

❑   2. Dispose of personal information in a consistent and secure manner, or remove all references that would link the data to a specific identifiable person (thereby rendering it anonymous), once it has served its purpose.

Security:

❑   1. Adopt appropriate and comprehensive measures to ensure the security of your customers' personal information against loss or unauthorized access, use, alteration, disclosure, or destruction.

Accountability:

❑   1. Communicate your privacy policies and practices to all staff, and make your staff accountable for adherence to those policies and practices.

❑   2. Conduct periodic reviews of your privacy policies and practices to ensure that they are in keeping with your customers' expectations, as well as international developments.

Contractual Agreements:

❑   1. Stipulate right in your contract:

   ❑   a. The privacy protection measures to be adopted by business partners or third

Table 16.4.   Set of Fair Information Practices Checklist (Continued)

parties using your customers' personal information.

❏   b. The purposes for which your customers' personal information may be used and disclosed by business partners or third parties.

Anonymity and Pseudonymity:

❏   1. Reduce, to the greatest extent possible, the collection and retention of identifiable transactions (transactions in which the data in the record could be readily linked to an identifiable individual). This can be achieved through the use of either:

❏   a. Anonymity: Ideally, there should be no personal identifiers involved in the transaction you have "de-identified."

❏   b. Pseudonymity: Where the functional or administrative needs of the application require some link between transactional data and identity, it is often possible to use pseudonymous techniques. These include such procedures as storage of partial identifiers by two or more organizations, both of whom must provide their portions of the transaction trail in order for the identity of the individual to be constructed; storing of an indirect identifier with the transactional data which serves as a pointer to the personal identifiers; and storing separately a cross-index between the indirect identifier and the individual's true identity.

Final Words

At the end of the day, who should receive an award for the best privacy and identity thief on the face of the planet? The winner is the U.S. government.

Recently, the Bush administration proposed dropping a requirement at the heart of federal rules that protect the privacy of medical records. It said doctors and hospitals should not have to obtain consent from patients before using or disclosing medical information for the purpose of treatment or reimbursement. If you believe the administration's reasoning, I have a piece of swamp land that I'd like to sell you.

The administration's decision smacks of Big Brotherism and medical and insurance profiling. In other words, everyone will have access to your personal and medical data. Based on that information, health insurance companies do not have to insure you and companies do not have to hire you if you are ill. In fact, if you have a serious illness that is hereditary, your future descendants would be profiled as being uninsurable and unhirable. All of this is setting a very dangerous precedent that might never be able to be overturned once set in motion. Our individual rights that are currently protected by the U.S. Constitution could go right out the window.

The proposal, favored by the health care industry, was announced by Tommy G. Thompson, the Secretary of Health and Human Services, who indicated the process of obtaining consent could have "serious unintended consequences" and could impair access to quality health care. The sweeping privacy rules were issued by President Bill Clinton in December 2000. When President Bush allowed them to take effect in April 2001, consumer advocates cheered, but much of the health care industry expressed dismay.

The Bush administration's proposal would repeal a provision widely viewed as the core of the Clinton rules: a requirement that doctors, hospitals, and other health-care providers obtain written consent from patients before using or disclosing medical information for treatment, the payment of claims or any of a long list of health care operations, like setting insurance premiums and measuring the competence of doctors. The proposal was published in the Federal Register, with 30 days for public comment. The government will consider the comments and then issue a final ruling in late 2002 with the force of law.

Secretary Thompson indicated he wanted to remove the consent requirements because he believed they could delay care. Pharmacists and hospitals had expressed the same concern. Drugstores indicated they could not fill prescriptions phoned in by a doctor for pick-up by a patient's relative or neighbor. Hospitals indicated they could not schedule medical procedures until the patient had read a privacy notice and signed a consent form. It's amazing how they have been able to do all of that prior to the proposal.

Hospitals and insurance companies praised the proposal as a victory for common sense, but consumer advocates and Democratic members of Congress denounced it as a threat to privacy. Janlori Goldman, coordinator of the Consumer Coalition for Health Privacy, an alliance of more than 100 groups favoring patients' rights, indicated the administration was proposing "a destructive change."

Representative Edward J. Markey, a Democrat from Massachusetts, indicated that by stripping the consent requirement from the health privacy rule, the Bush administration would be stripping patients of the fundamental right to give their consent before their health information is used or disclosed. The administration's proposal throws the baby away with the bath water. Senator Edward M. Kennedy, Democrat from Massachusetts, indicated that he was very concerned because he believed that an individual should have to give permission before medical information is disclosed.

The Bush administration denied that it was eviscerating privacy protections. The president believes strongly in the need for federal protections to ensure patient privacy. Wasn't that type of misinformation known as "double-talk" in George Orwell's book *1984*?

Under the rules, doctors and other health-care providers would still have to notify patients of their rights and the providers' disclosure policies. Patients would be asked to acknowledge in writing that they had received such notice, but could receive care without the acknowledgment.

Goldman, the director of the Health Privacy Project at Georgetown University, indicated that it's absurd to suggest that a notice serves the same purpose as consent. Signing the consent makes it more likely that people will understand their rights.

Some parts of the Clinton rules would survive the changes proposed by the Bush administration. Patients would, for example, have a federal right to inspect and copy their records and could propose corrections.

Congress could try to set privacy standards by law, overriding decisions by the Bush administration, but that appears unlikely. Under a 1996 law, Congress instructed the Secretary of Health and Human Services to issue rules on medical privacy in the absence of action by Congress, and lawmakers have never been able to agree on standards.

In its proposal, the Bush administration tried to ensure that parents have appropriate access to medical records of their children, including information about mental health, abortion, and treatment for drug and alcohol abuse. The Clinton rules might have unintentionally limited parents' access to their child's medical records. The proposal makes clear that state law governs disclosures to parents.

The Bush proposal would also relax some consent requirements that medical researchers saw as particularly onerous. The rules, the first comprehensive federal standards for medical privacy, affect virtually every doctor, patient, hospital, pharmacy, and health plan in the United States.

Health-care providers and insurers must comply by April 14, 2003. Anyone who violates the rules after that date will be subject to civil and criminal penalties, including a $250,000 fine and 10 years in prison for the most serious violations. Our founding fathers are probably rolling in their graves right about now. What price can you put on privacy?

When Clinton issued the rules in December 2000, he described them as the most sweeping privacy protections ever written. President Bush took political credit for accepting those rules in April 2001. White House officials indicate President Bush would back a wide range of privacy protections for consumers, even if he had to defy his usual business allies. Is this an episode of *The X-Files*? It sure is starting to feel like one.

The White House wanted to avoid the political embarrassment President Bush suffered when he altered Clinton policies on arsenic levels in drinking water, global warming, ergonomic rules, and the contamination of school lunchmeat. However, after studying the medical privacy rules and listening to the concerns of companies in the health-care industry, the administration concluded that major provisions of the Clinton rules were unworkable. I guess they're a glutton for political punishment.

At the end of the day; trust no one. The truth is out there.

Endnotes

[1] Daniele Micci-Barreca, "International Fraud: Challenges and Technological Solutions," ClearCommerce Corporation, 11500 Metric Blvd., Suite 300, Austin, TX 78758, USA, 2001.

[2] ClearCommerce Corporation, 11500 Metric Blvd., Suite 300, Austin, TX 78758, USA, 2002.

[3] Susan Karlin, "Smart Cards, Widely Used in Europe, Migrate to United States," © 2000 IEEE, *IEEE Spectrum*, 445 Hoes Lane, Piscataway, NJ 08855, USA, 2002.

[4] Linda Foley, "Reasonable Requests a Victim May Make of the Court," Identity Theft Resource Center, P.O. Box 26833, San Diego, CA 92196, and Privacy Rights Clearinghouse, 3100 5th Ave., Suite B, San Diego, CA 92103, USA, 2002.

[5] "Smart, Optical and Other Advanced Cards: How to Do a Privacy Assessment," Information and Privacy Commissioner/Ontario Canada, 80 Bloor Street West, Suite 1700, Toronto, Ontario, M5S 2V1, 2002.

[6] Beth Givens, "Preventing Identity Theft: Industry Practices Are the Key," [Presented at the National Summit on Identity Theft, Panel on Prevention, U.S. Department of Treasury, March 15–16, 2000, Washington, DC] Identity Theft Resource Center, P.O. Box 26833, San Diego, CA 92196, and Privacy Rights Clearinghouse, 3100 5th Ave., Suite B, San Diego, CA 92103, USA, 2002.

Part V

APPENDICES

Appendix A

IDENTITY THEFT
FEDERAL LAWS LISTING

Identity Theft and Assumption Deterrence Act

In October 1998, Congress passed the Identity Theft and Assumption Deterrence Act of 1998 (Identity Theft Act) to address the problem of identity theft. Specifically, the Act amended 18 U.S.C. § 1028 (*www.ftc.gov/os/statutes/itada/itadact.htm*) to make it a federal crime when anyone knowingly transfers or uses, without lawful authority, a means of identification of another person with the intent to commit, or to aid or abet, any unlawful activity that constitutes a violation of federal law, or that constitutes a felony under any applicable state or local law. Violations of the Act are investigated by federal investigative agencies such as the U.S. Secret Service, the FBI, and the U.S. Postal Inspection Service and are prosecuted by the Department of Justice.

Credit Laws

Fair Credit Reporting Act

The Fair Credit Reporting Act establishes procedures for correcting mistakes on your credit record and requires that your record only be provided for legitimate business needs. Please see the following credit laws links:

- Facts for Consumers: Fair Credit Reporting (*www.ftc.gov/os/statutes/fcrajump.htm*)
- Fair Credit Reporting Act (*www.ftc.gov/os/statutes/fcra.htm*)

Fair Credit Billing Act

The Fair Credit Billing Act establishes procedures for resolving billing errors on your credit card accounts. It also limits a consumer's liability for fraudulent credit card charges. Please see the following credit laws links:

- Facts for Consumers: Fair Credit Billing (*www.ftc.gov/bcp/conline/pubs/credit/fcb.htm*)
- Fair Credit Billing Act [PDF only] (*www.ftc.gov/os/statutes/fcb/fcb.pdf*)

Fair Debt Collection Practices Act

The Fair Debt Collection Practices Act prohibits debt collectors from using unfair or deceptive practices to collect overdue bills that your creditor has forwarded for collection. Please see the following credit laws links:

- Facts for Consumers: Fair Debt Collection (*www.ftc.gov/os/statutes/fdcpajump.htm*)
- Fair Debt Collection Practices Act (*www.ftc.gov/os/statutes/fdcpa/fdcpact.htm*)

Electronic Fund Transfer Act

The Electronic Fund Transfer Act provides consumer protection for all transactions using a debit card or electronic means to debit or credit an account. It also limits a consumer's liability for unauthorized electronic fund transfers. Please see the following credit laws links:

- Facts for Consumers: Electronic Banking (*www.ftc.gov/bcp/conline/pubs/credit/elbank.htm*)
- Electronic Fund Transfer Act (*www4.law.cornell.edu/uscode/15/1693.html*)

Appendix B

IDENTITY THEFT
STATE LAWS LISTING

W hat follows is a list of states that have passed laws related to identity theft; others may be considering such legislation. Where specific identity theft laws do not exist, the practices may be prohibited under other state laws. States marked with ° do not currently have their law available online as shown in Table B.1.

Table B.1. Listing of ID Theft State Laws

State	Law	URL
Alabama°	2001 Al. Pub. Act 312; 2001 A1. SB 144	—
Alaska	Alaska Stat § 11.46.180 (scroll to section 11.46.180)	*http://old-www.legis.state.ak.us/cgi-bin/ folioisa.dll/stattx00/query=iden- tity+theft/doc/{@3787?*
Arizona	Ariz. Rev. Stat. § 13-2008	*www.azleg.state.az.us/ars/13/02008.htm*
Arkansas°	Ark. Code Ann. § 5-37-227	—
California	Cal. Penal Code §§ 530.5- 530.7	*www.leginfo.ca.gov/cgi-bin/display- code?section=pen&group=00001- 01000&file=528-539*

Table B.1. Listing of ID Theft State Laws (Continued)

State	Law	URL
Colorado	Colo. Rev Stat. § 18-5-102 Colo. Rev Stat. § 18-5-113	*http://64.78.178.12/stat01/index.htm?N&srch=18%2d5%2d102%r=10&r=10&s=416&cr=1* *http://64.78.178.12/stat01/index.htm?N&srch=18-5-113&r=10&s=13518&cr=1*
Connecticut	1999 Gen. Stat. § 53(a)-129(a)	*www.cga.state.ct.us/2001/pub/Chap952.htm#sec53a-129a.htm*
Delaware	Del. Code Ann. tit. II, § 854	*http://198.187.128.12/delaware/lpext.dll/Infobase/f2f3/f325/f641/fa68/fbb2?fn=document-*
Florida	Fla. Stat. Ann. § 817.568	*www.leg.state.fl.us/statutes/index.cfm?App_mode=Display_Statute&Search_String=&URL=Ch0817/SEC568.HTM&Title=->2000->Ch0817->Section%20568*
Georgia	Ga. Code Ann. §§ 16-9-121, 16-9-127	*www.ganet.state.ga.us/cgi-bin/pub/ocode/ocgsearch?docname=OCode/G/16/9/121*
Hawaii°	Haw. Rev. Stat. § 708-810z	—
Idaho	Idaho Code § 18-3126	*www3.state.id.us/cgi-bin/newidst?sctid=180310026.K*
Illinois	720 Ill. Comp. Stat. 5/16 G	*www.legis.state.il.us/ilcs/ch720/ch720act5articles/ch720act5Sub22.htm*
Indiana	Ind. Code Ann. § 35-43-5-4 (2000)	*www.state.in.us/legislative/ic/code/title35/ar43/ch5.html*
Iowa	Iowa Code § 715A.8	*www.legis.state.ia.us/IACODE/1999SUPPLEMENT/715A/8.html*
Kansas	Kan. Stat. Ann. § 21-4018	*www.accesskansas.org/legislative/statutes/index.cgi/21-4018.html*
Kentucky	Ky. Rev. Stat. Ann. § 514.160	*http://162.114.4.13/KRS/514-00/160.PDF*
Louisiana	La. Rev. Stat. Ann. § 14:67.16	*www.legis.state.la.us/tsrs/rs/14/rs_14_67_16.htm*

Table B.1. Listing of ID Theft State Laws (Continued)

State	Law	URL
Maine	Me. Rev. Stat. Ann. tit. 17-A, § 354-2A	*http://janus.state.me.us/legis/statutes/17-A/title17-Asec354.html*
Maryland	Md. Code Ann. art. 27 § 231	*http://mlis.state.md.us/cgi-win/web_statutes.exe?g27&231*
Massachusetts	Mass. Gen. Laws ch. 266, § 37E	*www.state.ma.us/legis/laws/seslaw98/sl980397.htm*
Michigan*	Mich. Comp. Laws § 750.285	—
Minnesota	Minn. Stat. Ann. § 609.527	*http://pigseye.revisor.leg.state.mn.us:8181/SEARCH/BASIS/mnstat/public/www/DDW?W%3DTEXT+PH+IS+%27identity+theft%27+ORDER+BY+SORT_KEYAscend%26M%3D1%26K%3D609.527%26R%3DY%26U%3D1*
Mississippi	Miss. Code Ann. § 97-19-85	—
Missouri	Mo. Rev. Stat. § 570.223	*www.moga.state.mo.us/statutes/C500-599/5700223.HTM*
Montana*	H.B. 331, 2001 Leg. (not yet codified)	—
Nevada	Nev. Rev. State. § 205.463-465	*www.leg.state.nv.us/NRS/NRS-205.html*
New Hampshire	N.H. Rev. Stat. Ann. § 638:26	*http://gencourt.state.nh.us/rsa/html/indexes/default.html*
New Jersey	N.J. Stat. Ann. § 2C:21-17	*www.njleg.state.nj.us/cgi-bin/om_isapi.dll?clientID=89511&Depth=4&advquery=21-17&headingswithhits=on&infobase=statutes.nfo&record={1444}&recordswithhits=on&softpage=Doc_Frame_Pg42&wordsaround-hits=10&x=43&y=17&zz=*
New Mexico	H.B. 317, 2001 Leg, 45th Sess.	*http://legis.state.nm.us/Sessions/01%20Regular/FinalVersions/house/hb0317fv.html*

Table B.1. Listing of ID Theft State Laws (Continued)

State	Law	URL
North Carolina	N.C. Gen. Stat. § 14-113.20	—
North Dakota	N.D. Cent. Codes § 12.1-23	*www.state.nd.us/lr/statutes/century-code.html*
Ohio	Ohio Rev. Code Ann. § 2913.49	*http://ohioacts.avv.com/123/sb7/sec-2913.49.htm*
Oklahoma	Okla. Stat. tit. 21, § 1533.1	*http://oklegal.onenet.net/oklegal-cgi/ifetch?Oklahoma_Statutes.99+88971518 4298+F*
Oregon	Or. Rev. Stat. § 165.800	*www.leg.state.or.us/ors/165.html*
Pennsylvania°	18 Pa. Cons. State § 4120	—
Rhode Island	R.I. Gen. Laws § 11-49.1-1	—
South Carolina	S.C. Code Ann. § 16-13-500, 501	*www.leginfo.state.sc.us/sessions/113/text/1133509t_5.html*
South Dakota	S.D. Codified Laws § 22-30A-3.1.	*http://legis.state.sd.us/statutes/index.cfm?FuseAction=DisplayStatute&txtStatute=22-30A-3.1&FindType=Statute*
Tennessee°	Tenn. Code Ann. § 39-14-150	—
Texas	Tex. Penal Code § 32.51	*www.capitol.state.tx.us/cgi-bin/tlo/textframe.cmd?LEG=76&SESS=R&CHAMBER=S&BILLTYPE=B&BILLSUF-FIX=00046&VERSION=5&TYPE=B*
Utah	Utah Code Ann. § 76-6-1101-1104	*www.le.state.ut.us/~code/TITLE76/htm/76_07097.htm*
Virginia	Va. Code Ann. § 18.2-186.3	*http://leg1.state.va.us/cgi-bin/legp504.exe?000+cod+18.2-186.3*
Washington	Wash. Rev. Code § 9.35.020 (click on title 9, then chapter 35)	*www.leg.wa.gov/rcw/*

Table B.1. Listing of ID Theft State Laws (Continued)

State	Law	URL
West Virginia	W. Va. Code § 61-3-54 scroll down to § 61-3-54	—
Wisconsin	Wis. Stat. § 943.201	*http://folio.legis.state.wi.us/cgi-bin/ om_isapi.dll?clientID=87387 &advquery=943.201&headingswith- hits=on&infobase=stats.nfo &record={2AE32}&recordswith- hits=on&zz=*
Wyoming*	Wyo. Stat. Ann. § 6-3-901	—
U.S. Territories		
Guam*	9 Guam Code Ann. § 46.80	—
U.S. Virgin Islands*	14 VI Code Ann. §§ 3003	—

Appendix C

IDENTITY THEFT REPORTS, TESTIMONY, AND COMMENTS LISTING

Reports

- **Analysis of Social Security Misuse Allegations Made to the Social Security Administration's Fraud Hotline.** Social Security Administration, Office of the Inspector General (*www.ssa.gov/oig/auditpdf/99-920~1.PDF*).

- **Identity Fraud: Information on Prevalence, Cost and Internet Impact Is Limited.** General Accounting Office (*frwebgate.access.gpo.gov/cgi-bin/getdoc.cgi?dbname=gao&docid=f:gg98100b.txt*).

- **FTC Identity Theft Data Clearinghouse.** These reports and charts are updated regularly.

- *Reports: Figures and Trends on Identity Theft*
  - *www.ftc.gov/bcp/workshops/idtheft/trends-update.pdf*
  - *www.consumer.gov/idtheft/reports/01-06r.pdf*

- *PowerPoint Charts*
  - *www.ftc.gov/bcp/workshops/idtheft/charts-update.pdf*
  - *www.consumer.gov/idtheft/charts/01-06c.pdf*

Testimony

- **Prepared Statement of the Federal Trade Commission on Identity Theft: The FTC's Response:** Presented by the Bureau of Consumer Protection, before the subcommittee on Technology, Terrorism and Government Information of the Judicary Committee, United States Senate (*www.ftc.gov/os/2002/03/idthefttest.htm*)
    - FTC Press Release: (*www.ftc.gov/opa/2002/03/idtestimony.htm*)
- **Prepared Statement of the Federal Trade Commission on Internet Fraud:** Marketing Practices Bureau of Consumer Protection, FTC, Subcommittee on Commerce, Trade, and Consumer Protection House Committee on Energy and Commerce (*www.ftc.gov/os/2001/05/internetfraudttmy.htm*)
    - FTC Press Release (*www.ftc.gov/opa/2001/05/iftestimony.htm*)
- **Prepared Statement of the Federal Trade Commission on Internet Fraud:** Planning and Information, Bureau of Consumer Protection, FTC, Senate Committee on Finance (*www.ftc.gov/os/2001/04/internetfraud-state.htm*)
    - FTC Press Release (*www.ftc.gov/opa/2001/04/senfinance.htm*)
- **Prepared Statement for Identity Theft:** FTC Washington State Senate Committee on Labor, Commerce and Financial Institution (*www.ftc.gov/be/v010001.htm*)
- **Prepared Statement of the Federal Trade Commission on Identity Theft:** Planning and Information, Bureau of Consumer Protection, FTC, House Committee on Banking and Financial Services (*www.ftc.gov/os/2000/09/idthefttest.htm*)
    - FTC Press Release (*www.ftc.gov/opa/2000/09/idthefttest.htm*)
- **Prepared Statement of the Federal Trade Commission on Identity Theft:** Western Region, FTC, Field Hearing of the Subcommittee Technology, Terrorism and Government Information, Senate Committee on the Judiciary (*www.ftc.gov/os/2000/08/idthefttestimony.htm*)
    - Attachment (*www.ftc.gov/os/2000/08/idtheftdatas.pdf*)
    - FTC Press Release (*www.ftc.gov/opa/2000/08/caidttest.htm*)
- **Identity Theft:** Bureau of Consumer Protection, FTC, Subcommittee on Technology, Terrorism and Government Information, Senate Committee on the Judiciary (With charts/graphs) (*www.ftc.gov/os/2000/07/idtheft.htm*)
    - FTC Press Release (*www.ftc.gov/opa/2000/07/identity.htm*)

- **Identity Theft:** Director Bureau of Consumer Protection, FTC, Sub-committee on Technology, Terrorism and Government Information, Senate Committee on the Judiciary (*www.ftc.gov/os/2000/03/identitytheft.htm*)
  - FTC Press Release (*www.ftc.gov/opa/2000/03/idtest.htm*)
- **Financial Identity Theft:** Bureau of Consumer Protection, FTC, Sub-committee on Telecommunications, Trade and Consumer Protection and Subcommittee on Finance and Hazardous Materials, House Committee on Commerce: (*www.ftc.gov/os/1999/9904/identitythefttestimony.htm*)
- **Identity Theft:** Financial Practices Division, FTC, Subcommittee on Technology, Terrorism and Government Information, Senate Committee on the Judiciary (*www.ftc.gov/os/1998/9805/identhef.htm*)
- **Identity Theft:** Office of Investigation, U.S. Secret Service, Subcommittee on Technology, Terrorism and Government Information, Senate Committee on the Judiciary (*www.consumer.gov/idtheft/testimony.htm*)

Comments

- **Privacy and Bankruptcy:** Comments on Study of Privacy Issues in Bankruptcy Data Federal Trade Commission (*www.ftc.gov/be/v000013.htm*)
  - For more information on this topic see "Financial Privacy in Bankruptcy: A Case Study in Privacy in Public and Judicial Records" (*www.usdoj.gov/ust/privacy/BnkrStdy011601.htm*)

Appendix D

IDENTITY THEFT CASES AND SCAMS LISTING

Cases

Press releases and further information on recent identity theft-related cases are as follows:

U.S. Supreme Court

- *TRW v. Andrews*; Decision upholding time limit on identity theft suits (*www.consumer.gov/idtheft/TRWcase.pdf*)

Attorney General of New York

- State worker charged in massive identity theft scam (*www.oag.state.ny.us/press/2001/jul/jul17a_01.html*)

U.S. Attorney, Florida

- Two plead guilty in $7 million-plus credit card fraud (*www.usdoj.gov/usao/fls/Prouty2.html*)
- Individual charged in seven-count indictment with credit card fraud and false identification fraud (*www.usdoj.gov/usao/fls/Julio%20Arjona.html*)
- Guilty plea in false identification document case (*www.usdoj.gov/usao/fls/Chwojko.html*)
- Two indicted in seven million dollar-plus credit card fraud (*www.usdoj.gov/usao/fls/Prouty.html*)
- Identity theft mastermind indicted (*www.usdoj.gov/usao/fls/Zhukov.html*)

U.S. Attorney, Texas

- Former employees of Social Security Administration sentenced for conspiracy to issue fraudulent Social Security cards: (*www.usdoj.gov/usao/txs/releases/March%202001/010330-woods.html*)
- Man sentenced to 54 months in prison following conviction for credit card fraud (*www.usdoj.gov/usao/txs/releases/March%202001/010322-richard.html*)
- Two Nigerian citizens indicted for identity fraud (*www.usdoj.gov/usao/txs/releases/March%202001/010309-ogbunamiri.html*)

U.S. Attorney, Washington

- Seattle man pleads guilty to bank fraud and identity theft (*www.usdoj.gov/usao/waw/pr2001/apr/vassar.html*)
- Two men plead guilty in Seattle area mail theft and identity theft cases (*www.usdoj.gov/usao/waw/pr2001/mar/trollinger.html*)
- Man sentenced to federal prison for stealing identity to obtain credit cards and an online car loan (*www.usdoj.gov/usao/waw/pr2000/oct/wahl.html*)
- Man pleaded guilty to three felony counts of identity theft (*www.usdoj.gov/usao/waw/pr2000/jul/tomas.html*)
- Man pleaded guilty to one count of identity theft (*www.usdoj.gov/usao/waw/pr2000/apr/cadello.html*)

Federal Trade Commission

- Consumer fraud, identity theft data goes public (*www.ftc.gov/opa/2001/01/sentinel.htm*)

U.S. Attorney, California

- Woman sentenced to federal prison for stealing identities of two illegal immigrants (*www.usdoj.gov/usao/cac/pr/pr2000/010.htm*)
- Man sentenced to federal prison for stealing identities to obtain new credit cards: (*www.consumer.gov/idtheft/cases/case-alaefule.htm*)
- Arizona man becomes sixth defendant in tax fraud ring, used names and Social Security numbers to file fraudulent tax returns (*www.usdoj.gov/usao/cac/pr/pr2000/188.htm*)
- Charges against man who used Internet to perpetrate identity theft and attempt to file fraudulent tax returns (*www.usdoj.gov/usao/cac/pr/pr2000/131.htm*)

U.S. Attorney, Louisiana

- Bank employee indicted for stealing depositors' information to apply over the Internet for loans (*www.consumer.gov/idtheft/cases/case-williams.htm*)

U.S. Attorney, Oregon

- Man sentenced for stealing identity to obtain employment and passport (*www.consumer.gov/idtheft/cases/case-lira.htm*)

Scams

- **Email from bogus FTC investigator sought personal data:** An investigation into a bogus work-at-home scheme became a bit more complicated after a man pretending to be an FTC employee emailed hundreds of the scam's victims seeking personal information to be used as "evidence" in the investigation. The scam-within-a-scam stemmed from an ongoing investigation into Los Angeles, California-based Medicor, which stands accused of defrauding more than 50,000 customers about the amount of money they could make from using a home computer to process medical bills for physicians in their community.

- **Credit card loss protection offers: They're the real steal** (*www.ftc.gov/bcp/conline/pubs/alerts/lossalrt.htm*)

- **ISP account information:** If you receive an email request that appears to be from your ISP stating that your "account information needs to be updated" or that "the credit card you signed up with is invalid or expired and the information needs to be reentered to keep your account active," do not respond without checking with your ISP first. According to information received by the FTC, this may be a scam!

- **Hoax targets elderly African Americans** (*www.ftc.gov/bcp/conline/ pubs/alerts/hoaxalrt.htm*)

Appendix E

IDENTITY THEFT AFFIDAVIT

If you are disputing fraudulent debts and accounts opened by an identity thief, the Identity Theft Affidavit (*www.ftc.gov/bcp/conline/pubs/credit/affidavit.pdf*) now simplifies the process. Instead of completing different forms, you can use this affidavit to alert companies where a new account was opened in your name. The company can then investigate the fraud and decide the outcome of your claim. Here's a list of some of the companies and organizations that accept or endorse the Identity Theft Affidavit:

- ACA International
- Altoona Postal Employees Credit Union
- Amcrin Corporation
- American Bankers Association
- American Contracting Exchange
- America's Community Bankers
- Arkansas Federal Credit Union
- AT&T
- Atlantic Credit Union
- Bank of Alameda
- Bank of America
- Bankers Trust Company, N.A.

- Call for Action
- Capital One
- Chase Manhattan Bank
- Coastal Federal Credit Union
- Computer Sciences Corporation
- Corporate America Family Credit Union
- Council of Better Business Bureaus
- Credit Bureau of East Tennessee Inc.
- Direct Marketing Association
- Equifax
- Experian
- Federal Reserve Board
- Fifth Third Bank
- First National Bank Omaha
- FleetBoston Financial
- GE Capital
- GetThere LP
- Gold Quest Realty, Ltd. Co.
- Identity Theft Resource Center
- Investors Savings Bank
- Iowa Independent Bankers
- Key Federal Credit Union
- Kimberly Clark Credit Union
- Merrill Lynch
- Nexity Bank
- Nissan Motor Acceptance Corporation
- Oregon Telco Community Credit Union
- Privacy Guard
- Privacy Rights Clearinghouse
- Provident Credit Union
- Providian
- SBC Service
- Sears
- The California Office of Privacy Protection
- The Simpson Organization, Inc.
- TransUnion

- Tri-County Debt Management of CWO, Inc.
- U.S. Bank
- U.S. Postal Inspection Service
- VW Credit
- Western Capital
- Western Funding.com
- Yolo Community Bank

Appendix F

GLOSSARY

Active account: An account for which activity has been reported to a credit reporting agency in the last 90 days.

Address verification system (AVS): A system that runs during the credit card authorization process, matching the billing address provided by the customer with the billing address on file for that credit card.

Adjustment: The percentage of a debt that is to be repaid to the creditor in a Chapter 13 bankruptcy.

Advanced card: A card capable of carrying information. Uses technology more advanced than a magnetic stripe.

Affinity card: A credit card that provides benefits based on how much you use it. Examples of benefits include points toward airline tickets, discounts at certain retailers, and contributions to nonprofit organizations.

Alias: A name reported on your credit file that differs from your primary or given name. This commonly occurs if you've applied for credit or loans under different variations of your name—Robert P. Smith and Bob Smith, for example.

Amortization: The reduction of a mortgage loan by regular payments.

Amount due: Generally, the minimum monthly payment you must make, not the total amount you owe.

Annual fee: A fee charged each year by some credit card companies.

Annual percentage rate (APR): The total finance charges associated with a loan or credit card stated as a yearly rate. Often this is the most useful means of directly comparing one loan or credit card to another.

Anonymity: Anonymity in this context refers to the complete absence of identification data in a transaction.

Asset: Anything you own that has value, such as a car, a house, office equipment, stocks, bonds, or jewelry.

Audit trail: A record of all events that have occurred on a system and across a network. Some people use the term *audit log* instead.

Authentication: The act of establishing or verifying the identity of an individual by examining his or her authentication credentials.

Authentication credential: Something that identifies individuals as eligible and permits them to access the service or benefit on a recurring basis. Traditionally, these credentials have been in the form of cards, passwords, or PINs. Now biometrics are being used in this capacity.

Authorization: The act of determining whether an individual is authorized to do something (e.g., accessing a certain part of a Web site).

Authorized user: A person allowed to charge goods and services on a credit card by the primary user of that card. Authorized users—unlike users of a joint account—are not legally responsible for payment.

Automatic: Something that must work by itself, without direct human intervention. For a process to be considered a biometric technology, it must recognize or verify a human characteristic quickly (some biometric systems function in under two seconds) and without a high level of human involvement.

Available credit: On a credit account, the credit limit minus the current balance. To many creditors, your total available credit on all your accounts is an important criterion.

Backup: An alternate or redundant device that replaces a primary device to maintain continued operation in the event of a primary device failure.

Bad address: A location to which a merchant's goods were shipped and lost due to a fraudulent sale.

Balance: The outstanding amount owed to a creditor on a particular account.

Balance transfer: The transfer of one or more credit card balances onto another card, typically to take advantage of a lower annual percentage rate.

Balloon payment: A final payment at the end of a loan term that is considerably larger than the regular periodic payments. Often associated with second mortgages.

Bandwidth: The amount of data that can be sent through an Internet connection, usually measured in bits per second. A full page of English text is about 16,000 bits. A fast modem can move about 15,000 bits in one second.

Bankruptcy: A legal agreement in which a consumer is declared fully or partially unable to repay debts. In return for full or partial release from those debts, the consumer sacrifices some property or agrees to a payment plan. There are two very different types of bankruptcy for consumers: Chapter 7 and Chapter 13.

Biometric: A unique and measurable characteristic of a human being—such as a fingerprint—used to identify an individual.

Biometrics: Techniques that analyze human characteristics to distinguish one person from another—even identical twins. A more formal definition is a unique, measurable characteristic or trait of a human being used for automatically recognizing or verifying identity.

Biometrics Consortium: An organization that serves as the U.S. government's focal point for research, development, testing, evaluation, and application of biometric-based personal identification and verification technology. The Consortium itself is in the midst of debating the definition, but currently holds that biometrics is automatically recognizing a person using distinguishing traits.

Browser: The program that allows you to surf the Web. The most popular browsers are Netscape Navigator and Microsoft Internet Explorer.

Capacitive card: A capacitively coupled memory card, where value can be stored as tokens. For example a value token can represent a bus ride or payment for a video game.

Capacity: An estimate of the amount of debt you can handle, largely based on your income in relation to the amount you already owe.

Capital: A measure of your current assets, including savings, investments, and property. Capital reassures a lender by providing a means of repaying your loan in case you default. It might also provide evidence that you've met financial obligations in the past—a fully paid car, for example, shows that you've successfully paid off an auto loan.

Card: A rectangular paper or plastic medium used to carry information relating to its issuer and user.

Card issuer: An individual or organization that issues identification or credit cards to individual or corporate cardholders.

Cardholder: Generally the person to whom an identification card or credit card is issued. For financial transaction cards, it is usually the customer associated with the primary account number recorded on the card.

Cardmember Identification Number (CID): An additional identification number that appears on a credit card as a security feature. The CID appears only on the plastic of the card. This makes it difficult for a criminal to obtain it without having seen the physical credit card.

Card Verification Value (CVV2): A six-character value that is embossed on a Visa credit card's signature line, following the card number. This value is used to assist in authenticating the physical presence of a card in environments where the cardholder is not present at the time of purchase.

Cash advance: A cash loan taken out on a credit card. Interest for cash advances is usually higher than it is for purchases, a transaction fee might apply, and the grace period may be waived.

Certification: Formal evaluation of a security system to determine whether or not it conforms to a particular set of security standards.

Chapter 7 bankruptcy: The most common form of consumer bankruptcy, Chapter 7 releases a debtor from all liability for the accounts included in a bankruptcy. In exchange, the debtor must forfeit some personal property. A Chapter 7 bankruptcy remains on the debtor's credit report for 10 years.

Chapter 11 bankruptcy: Normally used for corporations, Chapter 11 can be used by consumers in certain rare cases involving extremely large debt. However, Chapter 13 is simpler and provides better protection for most consumers.

Chapter 13 bankruptcy: A type of consumer bankruptcy under which the debtor doesn't forfeit personal property but agrees to a three- to five-year wage-earner plan to repay all or part of the debt. Chapter 13 bankruptcy remains on a credit report for seven years.

Character: In the context of a credit application, character is one of the three Cs, the traditional set of criteria lenders use to evaluate an application. In most cases, character is determined by your credit report and score.

Characteristic: Today, identity is often confirmed by something a person has, such as a card or token (a driver's license), or something a person knows, such as his or her computer password or PIN for the bank machine.

Charge card: A credit card, such as an American Express or Diners Club card, that requires full payment of the balance each month. Such cards nevertheless appear on your credit report, because they do extend credit to you, if only for short periods of time.

Charge-off: An instance in which a consumer is seriously delinquent in paying a bill and the creditor elects to transfer the account to an accounting category such as "charged to loss" or "bad debt." In such cases, the creditor may also turn the account over to a collection agency.

Ciphertext: Data that is encrypted.

Client/server: The relationship between two computer programs in which one program, the client, makes a service request from another program, the server, which fulfills the request. Although programs within a single computer can use the client/server model, it is a more important idea in a network. In a network, the client/server model provides a convenient way to interconnect programs that are distributed efficiently across different locations.

Client-side certificate: A certificate used for client authentication that is usually installed on an HTTP client. For example, when a Web browser attempts to access a secure Web server, it would send its certificate to the server for verification of the client's identity.

Closed account: An account that has been closed by you or your creditor. Such accounts remain on your credit report for seven years from the date of last activity.

Closing: The point at which the buyer signs the mortgage documents, pays closing costs, and becomes the owner of the property. Also called a settlement.

Closing costs: Expenses that buyers incur in the transfer of ownership of a property. Closing costs can include taxes, origination fees, attorney's fees, and other costs.

Collateral: Property you pledge as a guarantee for a secured loan. If you fail to repay the loan, the creditor can take the property. Sometimes used in place of capital as one of the three Cs.

Collection agency: A firm assigned by a creditor to collect overdue amounts. Some creditors have internal collection departments. Like creditors, collection agencies report account information to credit reporting agencies.

Colocated Hosting: Web hosting setup in which a company owns its own servers, but rents physical space from a Web host or ISP. The space is equipped with a high-speed Internet connection.

Common Gateway Interface (CGI): A set of rules that describes how a Web server communicates with another piece of software (called a *CGI program*) on the same machine, and how the other piece of software talks to the Web server.

Common Gateway Interface (CGI) program: A piece of software that handles input and output according to the CGI standard. Usually a CGI program is a small program that takes data from a Web server and does something with it; common uses include putting the content of a form into an email message, or turning the data into a database query. Whenever you see *cgi-bin* in the URL, you know that a CGI program is being used.

Computer crime unit: The police unit that investigates serious computer-related crimes such as hacking and the planting of viruses.

Computer fraud: The deliberate misrepresentation or unauthorized disclosure or alteration of data, usually for monetary gain.

Confirmation number: Number usually required for real-time transactions.

Confirmation of eligibility: A one-time process to confirm that the named individual is eligible for the benefit or service to be accessed by the biometric.

Consolidation loan: A loan obtained to combine multiple debts into one, typically at a lower interest rate.

Consumer: An individual who purchases products and services.

Consumer statement: Under the Fair Credit Reporting Act, you have the right to add a 100-word consumer statement to your credit file to explain disputed information about your accounts.

Cookie: A message sent by a Web server to a browser. The browser stores this message in a text file, and sends it back to the server each time it requests a page from the server. The main purpose of cookies is to identify users and possibly prepare customized Web pages for them.

Cosigner: Someone who agrees to share responsibility with the primary applicant for a loan or credit card. A consumer with poor credit might need a cosigner to get a loan or to qualify for favorable terms. Because cosigners are liable for debts incurred, cosigned accounts appear on the cosigner's credit report.

Credit: A consumer's perceived ability to pay back borrowed money, which directly affects that person's actual ability to borrow it.

Credit balance: The amount owed on a credit card. Do not confuse this with a minimum payment.

Credit card: A card used to make purchases or take out cash loans that requires the user to pay some or all of the outstanding amount each month. Credit cards are differentiated mainly by their terms.

Credit card issuer: A bank or other institution that extends consumers credit through a credit card.

Credit file: The collection of an individual's credit history, identifying information, and other records maintained by a credit reporting agency. Credit file is sometimes used interchangeably with *credit report*, but technically a credit file is the source from which a credit report is generated.

Credit fraud: The deliberate use of another person's credit card (or credit card information) to make purchases, take out cash advances, or receive other benefits.

Credit header: The identifying portion of a credit report that contains your name, aliases, address, current employer, date of birth, and Social Security number.

Credit history: The portion of a credit report that records your history of borrowing and repaying money. This section contains details about the credit and loan accounts you've held in the last seven years.

Credit Insight: A service that gives you unlimited online access to an enhanced, easy-to-understand version of your credit report.

Credit limit: The maximum amount available to you on a credit card account after you've paid your entire balance. Often called *high credit* on credit reports.

Credit rating: A numerical estimation of the likelihood that you'll meet debt obligations. A creditor gets your information from a credit reporting agency and applies a credit scoring model to calculate your credit rating for a particular loan or credit product.

Credit repair company: Companies that promise to fix or erase your credit history. Many such companies advocate illegal methods and charge money to effect changes consumers can accomplish for free.

Credit report: The form in which a credit reporting agency provides information contained in your credit file. Most credit reports contain a summary of your credit history plus identifying information and notations of legal judgments and public records.

Credit reporting agencies: Commonly known as *credit bureaus*, credit reporting agencies are companies that receive, maintain, and provide information about consumers' credit history. Three national agencies—Equifax, Experian, and Trans Union—dominate credit reporting. There are many smaller agencies, but almost all of them get information from one or more of the three major agencies.

Credit risk: An assessment of how likely you are to fulfill the terms of a credit agreement. Most credit ratings are designed to estimate credit risk.

Credit scoring model: The mathematical model a lender applies to a credit report to evaluate a consumer's credit rating. One commonly used model is the one used to determine a FICO score.

Creditor: A company that enables consumers to make purchases on credit or lends consumers money. Sometimes used interchangeably with *lender*.

Creditworthiness: Your ability to pay back borrowed money, as perceived by creditors.

Daily periodic rate: A credit card's annual percentage rate divided by 365 days.

Database: A collection of data that is organized so that a computer program can quickly select desired pieces of data. It is an electronic filing system with contents that can easily be accessed, managed, and updated.

Data server: A hardware platform with a database that supplies data to other platforms.

Debit card: A card that directly deducts money from your checking account to pay for goods or services. Because no debt is normally incurred, debit cards are not normally reported on credit reports.

Debt-to-income ratio: Expressed as a percentage, a debt-to-income ratio helps lenders predict how much money you'll have on hand to pay newly acquired debts. Ratios under 20% are generally considered good; ratios over 36% could limit your credit choices.

Debtor: One who owes a debt.

Decryption: The act of converting encrypted data back into an intelligible format.

Dedicated hosting: Web hosting setup in which a company rents space on a server that is dedicated exclusively to a single Web site.

Default: Failure to make payments on a debt.

Delinquency: An account with an overdue payment—one of the most common negative items on a credit report.

Digital certificate: A data file that contains information specific and unique to the certificate's owner. The certificates are issued by third-party certification authorities. When you receive the digital certificate from a customer, you contact the certification authority to unscramble the file and verify the identity of the sender.

Digital goods: Files that a consumer can buy and download directly from a retailer's Web site. Because there is no shipping involved, the files have no delivery address.

Digital signature: An encrypted mathematical code that is unique to an individual. The digital signature is locked with a private key that only the individual has access to. It can then be unlocked with a public key that everyone has access to, so that the digital signature can be verified by a certification company.

Digital wallet: A tool that stores and encrypts a user's personal information (name, credit card number, and sometimes even shipping information). The digital wallet makes shopping online easier and safer for consumers. They don't have to input their data each time they make a purchase, and their information is encrypted against piracy. The digital wallet also benefits merchants because it protects them against fraud. It is usually stored on the user's PC, but recent versions are placed on the credit card issuer's server instead.

Directory services protocol: A protocol for the distribution of information. Directory services protocols are used for different types of information, but most often for user information such as name and address.

Discharge: To release a debtor from responsibility for a debt, often as a result of bankruptcy.

Dismissed bankruptcy: An instance in which a judge has ruled against a consumer's petition for bankruptcy, sometimes at the consumer's request. Such cases are recorded in the public records section of the consumer's credit report, and the debts covered in the bankruptcy remain outstanding.

Domain name: The Internet address of a Web site that identifies one or more IP addresses. The Internet is actually based on IP addresses. However, because domain names are meaningful and easy to remember, Web sites use them instead of IP addresses. Every time you use a domain name (*www.merchantfraudsquad.com*), a Domain Name System service has to translate it into the corresponding IP addresses (111.222.333.4).

Domain Name System (DNS): An Internet service that translates domain names into IP addresses. The Internet is actually based on IP addresses. However, because domain names are meaningful and easy to remember, Web sites use them instead of IP addresses. Every time you use a domain name (*www.merchantfraudsquad.com*), a DNS service has to translate it into the corresponding IP address (111.222.333.4).

Down payment: The initial amount paid in cash toward the total price of a home or car. A large down payment might help you get a more favorable interest rate and let you avoid buying mortgage insurance.

Electronic Crimes Task Force: A group within the U.S. Secret Service that was formed to protect citizens from criminal abuses of technology.

Encryption: The scrambling of data so that it becomes difficult to interpret without the key that allows you to decrypt it. Encryption is the best way to achieve online data security. It is commonly used to send credit card numbers over the Internet.

Equal Credit Opportunity Act: A federal law that prohibits creditors from discriminating against applicants on the basis of race, color, national origin, religion, gender, marital status, age, or receipt of public assistance.

Equifax: One of the three major national credit reporting agencies. Often abbreviated EFX. For more information, see *credit reporting agencies*.

Equity: The part of your home you actually own, or the home's current market value minus the amount you still owe.

Experian: Formerly TRW, one of the three major national credit reporting agencies.

Fair Credit Billing Act (FCBA): A federal law that regulates credit card error resolution. Among other stipulations, the FCBA limits consumers' responsibility for unauthorized charges to $50.

Fair Credit and Charge Card Disclosure Act: A collection of amendments to the Truth in Lending Act requiring credit and charge card issuers to disclose certain card costs in direct mail, telephone, and other solicitations.

Fair Credit Reporting Act (FCRA): A federal law that regulates the ways in which credit reporting agencies use consumers' information. Among other rights, it defines who can access your credit report and gives you the right to correct erroneous information on your credit report.

Fair Debt Collection Practices Act: A federal law that prohibits abusive and unfair debt collection practices.

Fair, Isaac Company: The developer of the FICO score, a credit scoring model used by many creditors.

FICO score: A credit scoring model created by the Fair, Isaac Company. Fair, Isaac provides the FICO scoring formula to credit reporting agencies; creditors can choose to apply that formula to consumers' credit reports. FICO scores range from the 300s to the 900s, but almost all consumers have a score between 500 and 850.

File Transfer Protocol (FTP): The protocol used for transferring files from one computer to another on the Internet.

Finance charge: The cost of a loan expressed as a dollar amount.

Finance company: A company that mainly lends money to consumers who cannot qualify for credit at a credit union or bank. Finance companies generally charge higher rates than other creditors.

Firewall: A system that can detect and prevent unauthorized access to or from a network. A firewall can be implemented in both hardware and software, or a combination of both. Private or sensitive information is kept "inside" the firewall, which can stop certain messages (like those that contain viruses) from entering and leaving a network if they do not meet certain security standards.

Fixed rate: An interest rate that remains constant, regardless of economic indicators. Compare *variable rate*.

Foreclosure: The legal process by which a creditor can sell mortgaged property to pay a defaulted mortgage.

Fraud alert: If you suspect that you're the victim of identity theft or credit fraud, you can contact the credit reporting agencies and place a fraud alert on your credit file. Such an alert prevents new credit accounts from being opened without your express permission.

Garnishment: A legal proceeding in which money that would normally be paid to you (e.g., your paycheck) is applied directly to the payment of a debt instead.

Grace period: The time between a credit card's billing date and next due date, during which you can avoid interest charges by paying your balance in full.

Gross monthly income: Total income from employment and other sources before taxes.

Hacking: Unauthorized attempts to bypass security mechanisms in an information system or network.

Hard inquiry: An indication on your credit report that a lender has obtained a copy of the report to evaluate a loan or credit application. An excess of hard inquiries within a six-month period could lower your credit rating.

Hit: A single request from a browser for a single item from a Web server. For a Web browser to display a page that contains three graphics, four hits would occur: one for the HTML page and one for each of the three graphics. Hits are often used as a rough measure of load on a server.

Home equity loan: A loan that lets you borrow money against the equity in your home to get a line of credit. As with any mortgage, if you don't repay the amount, your home could be foreclosed to pay it.

Host: (1) A computer system that a user accesses remotely. (2) A computer with a unique IP address that is connected to either a TCP/IP network or the Internet. (3) To provide the infrastructure for a computer service.

Hypertext Markup Language (HTML): The authoring language used to create most Web pages.

Hypertext Transfer Protocol (HTTP): A protocol that tells computers how to communicate with each other. Most Web page locations begin with *http://*.

ID Guard: A service that checks your credit report weekly and alerts you to changes, including potential signs of credit fraud and identity theft.

Identification: A one-time process to establish an individual as a unique, named person.

Identity: The condition of being a specific person or being oneself. It implies a state of being or quality that defines one's self. It is important to distinguish between *identity* and *identification*. Identification is the process of associating or linking specific data with a particular person. In the context of this book, a biometric is considered an identifier; it does not define a person's identity or who they are, rather it links specific data with that person.

Identity theft: An instance in which someone appropriates your name, Social Security number, or other personal information to commit fraud or theft.

Inquiry: An instance in which all or part of your credit file is accessed by a company or individual. There are many different types of inquiries, most of which don't affect your credit rating. Inquiries normally stay on your credit report for two years.

Installment account: An account such as a car loan or home mortgage for which you make regular payments over a specific period of time. Compare *revolving account*.

Integrity: The assurance that data will not be changed or destroyed by either accidents or malicious behavior.

Interest rate: The percentage a lender charges you to borrow money, excluding any fees.

Internet Fraud Complaint Center: A branch of the FBI that researches claims of fraud conducted on the Internet.

Internet Protocol (IP) address: An identifier for a computer on either a TCP/IP network or the Internet. The IP address is a 32-bit numeric address written in dotted decimal notation, with four dot-separated decimal numbers (148.171.33.121). A central authority assigns Internet IP addresses to avoid duplicates.

Internet Protocol (IP) spoofing: An attack in which one system tries to impersonate another by using a false IP address.

Internet service provider (ISP): A company that provides access to the Internet.

Intrusion detection system: A device that notifies you if someone accesses a private file or server. A firewall is an example of an intrusion detection system.

Investigation: The process a credit reporting agency undertakes to verify credit report information disputed by a consumer.

Investigative consumer report: An extensive report executed mainly for security clearances and background checks. Investigative consumer reports include information from credit reports, but they also contain subjective material about an individual's reputation and lifestyle. The subject of such a report must give written consent before it can be run.

Involuntary bankruptcy: A bankruptcy instigated by creditors rather than the debtor.

Joint account: A credit or loan account held by two or more people. All account holders assume legal responsibility for the repayment of the account.

Joint credit report: A combined report used by creditors to assess a married couple's application. Note that the credit files remain separate.

Judgment: A court verdict that requires a person to fulfill an obligation (e.g., to pay a debt). When a judgment has been satisfied, the consumer has fulfilled its requirements and is no longer liable. Information about judgments is recorded in the public records section of a credit report.

Key: A number or password that locks and unlocks encrypted data by scrambling and unscrambling it accordingly.

Late payment: A payment delivered after its due date. Payments that are late by 30 days or more may be reported to credit reporting agencies and added to your credit report.

Lease: A contract that allows you to use or occupy property (e.g., a car or apartment) over a specific length of time, during which you make regular payments and after which you do not own the property.

Lender: A company that lends money to consumers or enables them to make purchases on credit. Sometimes used interchangeably with *creditor.*

Liability: Legal responsibility for the repayment of a debt.

Lien: A creditor's claim to a consumer's property for the satisfaction of a debt. The creditor can keep the property until the debt is repaid, or sell the property to pay the debt.

Loan: An extension of money that is to be repaid.

Loan-to-value ratio (LTV): The ratio of the amount of a home loan to the appraised value of the home. For example, if you borrow $75,000 to buy a $100,000 house, the LTV is 75%. As a general rule, the lower the LTV, the more favorable the terms of the loan will be.

Local area network (LAN): A computer network that occupies a small area. The computers on the network share data through cable or wireless connections.

Mail/Telephone Order Merchandise Rule: A federal law that protects consumers when placing online orders, dictating that unless the company states otherwise, a purchase must be delivered within 30 days, or the company must notify the customer of any delays.

Magnetic stripe card: A card with one or more magnetic stripes.

Measurable: For identification to be reliable, the item being used must be relatively static and easily quantifiable. For example, hairstyle or color are not dependable characteristics for identifying an individual, as both can be easily and frequently changed.

Minimum payment: The smallest payment you can make on a revolving credit account to maintain your account status as being paid on time.

Mortgage: A loan designed to facilitate the purchase of a home, in which the home itself serves as security for the loan. If the borrower doesn't make the required payments, the lender can take ownership of the home. Mortgage can also refer to the legal document detailing the borrower's responsibilities, including the payment schedule and terms.

National Foundation for Credit Counseling: The organization that oversees Neighborhood Financial Care Centers.

Neighborhood Financial Care Centers: A national network of nonprofit credit counseling services overseen by the National Foundation for Credit Counseling. Funded largely by creditors, these counselors are trained to help consumers work out ways to repay debt without resorting to bankruptcy. Many Neighborhood Financial Care Centers operate under the name Consumer Credit Counseling Services.

Net income: Your total income from employment and other sources, minus taxes.

Obsolescence: After seven years, negative information on your credit report is considered obsolete and should automatically be removed from your credit report. The exception is Chapter 7 bankruptcy, which remains for 10 years.

Optical card: Also known as laser card, because a low-intensity laser is used to burn holes of several microns in diameter into a reflective material, exposing a substrata of lower reflectivity. The presence or absence or a burned hole represents bits. The areas of high and low reflectivity are read using a precision light source.

Opt out: To place your name on do-not-contact lists used by direct marketers.

Opt-Out Manager: A free service that helps you avoid direct marketing phone calls, mail, and email.

Origination fee: The fee a lender charges to process a home loan. It could include the costs to check the applicant's credit report, prepare documents, inspect the property, and conduct an appraisal.

Packet switching: The way in which data is broken up into chunks—called *packets*—before it is transmitted on the Internet. Each packet travels individually, often following a different route than the others. Once the packets arrive at their destination, they reassemble themselves into the original message.

Password: A code used to gain access to a locked system. Good passwords are made up of a combination of letters, numbers, and punctuation marks.

Periodic rate: An interest rate expressed in daily or monthly terms, calculated by dividing the annual percentage rate by 365 or by 12.

Permissible purposes: Legally valid reasons for requesting or granting access to a credit report.

Personal identification number (PIN): A numerical password used to gain access to a locked system, used most often in banking.

Personal information: Recorded information about an identifiable individual, which includes, but is not limited to, information relating to an individual's race, color, national or ethnic origin, sex, and age. If a video surveillance system displays these characteristics of an identifiable individual or the activities in which he or she is engaged, its contents will be considered personal information.

PITI: An acronym representing the main components of a monthly mortgage payment: principal, interest, taxes, and insurance.

Plain text: Data that has not been encrypted or scrambled.

Points: Charges levied by a mortgage lender, usually paid at closing. One point equals 1% of the value of the loan.

Preapproved offer: An offer of a credit card based on a list of qualifying consumers the card issuer has obtained from a credit reporting agency. Only after you return the application does the creditor get your credit report (which counts as a hard inquiry) and decide whether to actually offer you credit.

Prepayment penalty: A fee assessed by a lender when you pay off a loan ahead of schedule. The penalty compensates the lender for interest payments it would have received based on the loan's payment schedule.

Pretty Good Privacy (PGP): A popular program used to encrypt and decrypt email over the Internet. It can also be used to send an encrypted digital signature that lets the receiver verify the sender's identity and know that the message was not changed en route.

Primary user: The person under whose name a credit card account is listed. A primary user can authorize other people to use the account, but the primary user is ultimately responsible for repaying all charges.

Prime rate: The interest rate charged by banks on loans to the largest and highest rated customers. This economic indicator often serves as the basis for variable interest rates.

Principal: The amount you borrowed or the amount you still owe, excluding interest and other finance charges.

Promotional inquiry: A type of soft inquiry made to your credit report for the purpose of a preapproved offer. If your credit report matches a creditor's criteria, that creditor gets your name and address only, not your full credit report.

Protocol: A set of rules that lets computers agree on how to communicate over the Internet.

Proxy server: A server that acts as an intermediary between a workstation user and the Internet so that the enterprise can ensure security, administrative control, and caching service.

Pseudonymity: The use of an identifier for a party to a transaction, which is not, in the normal course of events, sufficient to associate the transaction with a particular individual. To explain in more detail, data can be indirectly associated with a person through such procedures as storage of partial identifiers by two or more organizations, both of whom must provide their portions of the transaction trail for the identity of the individual to be constructed; storing of an indirect identifier with the transaction data; and storing separately a cross-index between the indirect identifier and the individual's real identity.

Public key cryptography: An encryption system that uses two keys: one public and one private. Encrypted messages can be sent to a recipient by using that person's public key, but they can only be decrypted by the associated private key.

Public key infrastructure (PKI): The overall system required to provide public key encryption and digital signature services. The purposes of the PKI are to manage keys and certificates and to establish and maintain a trustworthy networking environment.

Public records: A section of your credit report that contains matters of public record including bankruptcies, credit counseling, foreclosures, garnishments, and lawsuits.

Qualifying ratio: The ratio of your monthly expenses to your gross monthly income. Creditors use qualifying ratios to evaluate loan applications.

Reader: Hardware device enabling smart card usage.

Reception equipment: Refers to the equipment or device used to receive or record the personal information collected through a video surveillance system, including a camera or video monitor or any other video, audio, physical, or other mechanical, electronic, or digital device.

Recognition: To identify a person as someone who is known, or to "know again." A person cannot recognize someone who is completely unknown to them. A computer system can be designed to recognize or identify a person based on a biometric characteristic. To do this, it must compare a biometric presented by a live person against all biometric samples stored in a central database. If the presented biometric matches a sample on file, the system then identifies the individual. This is often called a one-to-many match. Essentially, the system is trying to answer the question, who is this person?

Record: Any record of information, however recorded, whether in printed form, on film, by electronic means or otherwise, including a photograph, a film, a microfilm, a videotape, a machine-readable record, and any other record that is capable of being produced from a machine-readable record.

Refinancing: Restructuring a loan to get a lower interest rate or to borrow money from the amount you've already paid on a loan.

Revolving account: An account, such as a credit card, on which you pay all or part of the outstanding balance at regular intervals, usually monthly. Amounts become available again when they are paid. Compare *installment account*.

Risk management: The process of identifying, controlling, and eliminating or minimizing uncertain events that might affect system resources. It includes risk analysis, cost–risk analysis, and overall security review.

Router: A special computer or software package that handles the connection between two or more networks. Routers look at the destination addresses of the packets passing through them and decide which route to send them on.

RSA: An Internet encryption and authentication system developed and owned by RSA Data Security, Inc. RSA uses an algorithm based on the fact that there is no efficient way to factor very large numbers. Deducing an RSA key, therefore, requires an extraordinary amount of computer processing power and time.

Satisfied: A judgment is satisfied when the debtor has fulfilled its requirements (e.g., paid the outstanding amount) and is no longer liable.

Second mortgage: A mortgage taken out on a home that has an existing mortgage. A home equity loan is a type of second mortgage.

Secure Electronic Transaction (SET) Certificate: An industry-standard protocol that defines how electronic commerce can be conducted over insecure networks while maintaining security, privacy, and authentication.

Secure Hypertext Transfer Protocol (S-HTTP): An extension to HTTP that sends individual messages securely. It allows secure access to a Web site.

Secure Sockets Layer (SSL): A protocol designed by Netscape to enable encrypted, authenticated communications across the Internet. SSL is used mostly—but not exclusively—in communications between Web browsers and Web servers. URLs that begin with *https* indicate that an SSL connection will be used.

Secured credit card: A credit card for which you have made a security deposit to guarantee payment of outstanding balances—the credit limit is less than or equal to the amount of the deposit. Secured cards are a good alternative for people who can't get approved for a regular credit card.

Secured loan: A loan for which an item of property has been pledged in case of default. A mortgage is an example of a secured loan.

Security Administrator Tool for Analyzing Networks (SATAN): A software program that investigates vulnerabilities of a remote system.

Server: A computer or device on a network that manages network resources.

Server-side certificate: A certificate used for server authentication that is usually installed on an HTTP client.

Shared hosting: Web hosting setup in which a company rents space on a server that is used by several organizations' Web sites.

Smart card: A plastic card with an embedded microchip that can be loaded with data and used for telephone calling, electronic cash payments, or other applications.

Social Security number: The unique nine-digit number assigned to every legal resident of the United States by the Social Security Administration. Because no two people can have the same number, the Social Security number is usually the main identifying factor in a person's records, including credit reports.

Soft inquiry: An instance in which your credit report is accessed without affecting your credit rating. Soft inquiries include your own requests for your credit report, promotional inquiries by credit card companies, and "checkup" inquiries by your existing creditors. Compare *hard inquiry*.

Spoofing: Pretending to be someone else, for example, forging mail headers so that messages appear to have come from another address.

Storage device: Refers to a videotape, computer disk or drive, CD-ROM, computer chip, or other device used to store the recorded data or visual, audio, or other captured images.

Structured Query Language (SQL): A standard language for getting information from and for updating a database.

Tax lien: The federal, state, or local government's claim to your real or personal property for the payment of unpaid taxes. A tax lien filed against you normally appears in the public records section of your credit report.

Terms: All the agreed-on conditions of a loan or credit account. Examples include interest rate, annual fees, length of payment schedule, and penalties.

Three Cs: Name for the traditional trio of basic criteria lenders consider when deciding whether to approve a loan: character, capacity, and capital (or collateral).

Top-level domain (TLD): The suffix of a domain name of a Web site. TLDs usually refer to the Web site's native country (e.g., jp signifies a Japanese site) or its type of organization (e.g., com signifies a commercial site). There are a limited number of TLDs because they are the highest subdivision of the Internet.

Tradeline: A credit industry term for an account listed on a credit report.

Transmission Control Protocol/Internet Protocol (TCP/IP): A suite of protocols that defines the Internet. Originally designed for the UNIX operating system, TCP/IP software is now available for every major kind of computer operating system. To be truly on the Internet, your computer must have TCP/IP software.

Trans Union: One of the three major national credit reporting agencies.

Tribureau credit report: A credit report that combines data from all three major credit reporting agencies.

Trojan horse: A computer program that has a useful function, but also contains additional, hidden functions that can secretly exploit the legitimate authorizations and breach the system's security.

Truth in Lending Act: Part of the Consumer Protection Act, the Truth in Lending Act requires lenders to disclose the annual percentage rate, the total cost of the loan, and other terms. It also regulates credit advertising.

Uniform resource locator (URL): A Web site address that usually begins with *http*.

Unique: For something to be unique, it has to be the one and only, have no like or equal, and be different from all others. When trying to identify an individual with certainty, finding something that is unique to that person is absolutely essential.

Unsecured loan: A loan based on your promise to repay, not on pledged collateral. Compare *secured loan*.

User: The person who is accessing the Web site or system from a browser.

User name: A unique name by which each user is known to the system. This name is assigned whenever a user registers to use the system. Sometimes referred to as *user ID*.

Vacated: A judgment that has been rendered void or set aside.

Variable rate: An interest rate that changes according to a predefined formula based on an economic indicator such as the prime rate. For example, a credit card's annual percentage rate might be the prime rate plus 5%.

Velocity of purchases: The speed at which purchases are made. The velocity of purchases can indicate whether or not a person is using a stolen card. A high velocity of purchases is considered a warning sign.

Verification: Establishing the truth or correctness of something. To do this in terms of identity, a computer system can be designed to compare a biometric presented by a person against a stored sample previously given by that individual and identified as such. If the two samples match, the system confirms or authenticates the individual as the owner of the biometric on file. This is called a one-to-one match, and the biometric can be stored in a central database or on a card or token. Here the system is trying to answer the question, Is this person who they say they are?

Video surveillance system: Refers to a video, physical, or other mechanical, electronic, or digital surveillance system or device that enables continuous or periodic video recording, observing or monitoring of personal information about individuals in open, public spaces (including streets, highways, and parks). This can include an audio device, thermal imaging technology, or any other component associated with capturing the image of an individual.

Voluntary bankruptcy: A bankruptcy filed at the consumer's request.

Wage-earner plan: The three- to five-year repayment schedule in a Chapter 13 bankruptcy. The consumer must turn over disposable income to a bankruptcy trustee, who in turn repays creditors.

Wallet client: The portion of the digital wallet application residing on the customer's PC that interfaces with the wallet server.

Wallet server: Server that stores the digital wallet application and the wallet itself.

Web host: To provide the infrastructure for a Web server. Many companies provide the hardware, software, and Internet connection required by a Web server, allowing other businesses to control the actual content on the server.

Web server: A computer that delivers requested HTML pages or files. Every Web server has an IP address, and sometimes even a domain name.

Writ of replevin: A court document authorizing repossession of a debtor's property.

INDEX

I

Please remember that this is a library book,
and that it belongs only temporarily to each
person who uses it. Be considerate. Do
not write in this, or any, library book.